Planning Gain

The Royal Institution of Chartered Surveyors is the mark of property professionalism worldwide, promoting best practice, regulation and consumer protection for business and the community. It is the home of property related knowledge and is an impartial advisor to governments and global organisations. It is committed to the promotion of research in support of the efficient and effective operation of land and property markets worldwide.

Real Estate Issues

Series Managing Editors

Clare Eriksson	Head of Research, Royal Institution of Chartered Surveyors
John Henneberry	Department of Town and Regional Planning, University of Sheffield
K.W. Chau	Chair Professor, Department of Real Estate and Construction, The University of Hong Kong
Elaine Worzala	Director of the Carter Real Estate Center, College of Charleston, USA

Real Estate Issues is an international book series presenting the latest thinking into how real estate markets operate. The books have a strong theoretical basis – providing the underpinning for the development of new ideas.

The books are inclusive in nature, drawing both upon established techniques for real-estate market analysis and on those from other academic disciplines as appropriate. The series embraces a comparative approach, allowing theory and practice to be put forward and tested for their applicability and relevance to the understanding of new situations. It does not seek to impose solutions, but rather provides a more effective means by which solutions can be found. It will not make any presumptions as to the importance of real-estate markets but will uncover and present, through the clarity of the thinking, the real significance of the operation of real-estate markets.

Further information on the *Real Estate Issues* series can be found at:
http://eu.wiley.com/WileyCDA/Section/id-380013.html

Books in the series

Planning Gain

Providing Infrastructure and Affordable Housing

Edited by

Tony Crook

Emeritus Professor of Town and Regional Planning
The University of Sheffield

John Henneberry

Professor of Property Development Studies
The University of Sheffield

Christine Whitehead

Emeritus Professor of Housing Economics
The London School of Economics

WILEY Blackwell

This edition first published 2016

Registered office
John Wiley & Sons, Ltd, The Atrium, Southern Gate, Chichester, West Sussex, PO19 8SQ, United Kingdom.

Editorial offices:
9600 Garsington Road, Oxford, OX4 2DQ, United Kingdom.
The Atrium, Southern Gate, Chichester, West Sussex, PO19 8SQ, United Kingdom.

For details of our global editorial offices, for customer services and for information about how to apply for permission to reuse the copyright material in this book please see our website at www.wiley.com/wiley-blackwell.

Library of Congress Cataloging-in-Publication Data

Crook, Tony, 1944- editor.
  Planning gain : providing infrastructure & affordable housing / Tony Crook, John Henneberry, Christine Whitehead.
     pages cm
  Includes bibliographical references and index.
  ISBN 978-1-118-21981-2 (cloth)
  1. Real estate development–Great Britain. 2. Housing development–Great Britain. 3. Land use–Great Britain–Planning. 4. City planning–Great Britain. I. Henneberry, John, editor. II. Whitehead, Christine, editor. III. Title.
  HD596.C765 2016
  711′.40941–dc23   2015021597

A catalogue record for this book is available from the British Library.

Wiley also publishes its books in a variety of electronic formats. Some content that appears in print may not be available in electronic books.

Set in 10/13pt TrumpMediaeval by SPi Global, Chennai, India.
Printed and bound in Malaysia by Vivar Printing Sdn Bhd

1 2016

Table of Contents

Acknowledgements

We have worked together on research and policy development about the issues described and discussed in this book for more than two decades. Over this period, many colleagues have worked with us on 'planning gain' and on related matters. We are especially grateful to those who collaborated with us on a long series of research projects and who readily agreed to contribute chapters to the book. Many thanks are, therefore, due to Dr Gemma Burgess and Sarah Monk from the Cambridge Centre for Housing and Planning Research in the Department of Land Economy at the University of Cambridge, to Dr Steven Rowley from the Business School, Curtin University, Western Australia, and to Richard Dunning, Dr Ed Ferrari and Professor Craig Watkins from the Department of Urban Studies and Planning at the University of Sheffield.

We also wish to record our thanks to the many other colleagues and organisations who worked with us on some of the projects referred to in this book, including Peter Bibby, Professor Heather Campbell, Jennie Currie, Three Dragons consultancy, Dr Hugh Ellis, Caroline Gladwell, Professor Barry Goodchild, The Halcrow Group, Alistair Jackson, Michael Jones, Diane Lister, Dr Roland Lovatt, Fiona Lyall-Grant, Christina Short, Kerry Smith, Dr Robin Smith, Dr Connie Tang and Roger Tym & Partners.

We gratefully acknowledge the support and funding we received on topics discussed in the book from the Department of Communities and Local Government (and its forerunners, the Department of the Environment and the Office of the Deputy Prime Minister), The Countryside Agency, The Homes & Communities Agency (and its forerunner, The Housing Corporation), Inspire East, The Joseph Rowntree Foundation, The Royal Institution of Chartered Surveyors and the Institution's Foundation, The Royal Town Planning Institute, and The Welsh Assembly Government. The views expressed in this book are those of the authors and not necessarily those of the government departments, agencies and other organisations who funded the work.

Many local authorities, house-builders, housing associations and the staff of professional institutes, trade bodies, government departments and government agencies participated in the research through patiently filling in our questionnaires, helping with case studies, guiding us through official statistics, and sitting on focus and advisory groups. Without their unstinting help, we could not have conducted the research we report on in this volume. Thanks are also due to the four anonymous referees who reviewed our proposal for this book in the RICS Real Estate research series and also to the editorial team at Wiley Blackwell for commissioning the book and for their advice and help throughout its preparation. We are also grateful to Dame Kate Barker for agreeing to write the Foreword to the book.

We wish to thank the following for permission to use data and reprint tables in previously published research reports and journal articles: Davis Langdon in relation to Table 5.1; the Department for Business Innovation and Skills in relation to Figure 5.7; the Department for Communities and Local Government for permission in relation to Figures 6.1, 6.3, 6.4, 7.2, 7.3, 8.2 and 8.3, Tables 6.2–6.10 and Tables 7.5, 7.6 and 8.3; Nationwide Building Society in relation to Table 5.1 and Figure 5.7; Prentice Education, Inc. for Figure 5.2; the editors of *People, Place & Policy Online* for Figure 8.1 and for Tables 8.1 and 8.2; and the Valuation Office Agency for Figure 6.2.

We would also like to thank the following publishers for permission to quote significant text from the following government publications, journal articles and research reports: Her Majesty's Stationery Office (and its successor body the Stationery Office) for permission to quote from the 1942 Uthwatt report, from the 2007 Command Paper 7191 'Homes for the Future', from the National Audit Office 2013 report on the New Homes Bonus; and from the Communities & Local Government Select Committee 2014 report on the Operation of the National Planning Policy Framework; the Department of Communities & Local Government (and its forerunners) to quote from Planning Policy Guidance Note 1 of 1988, Circular 5/05 of 2005, from the National Planning Policy Framework, 2012 and from the 2014 Consultation Paper on the Development Benefits pilot; the Royal Institution of Chartered Surveyors to quote from its 2012 publication 'Financial Viability', the Royal Town Planning Institute for permission to quote from its evidence to the 2007 consultation on Planning Gain Supplement; and Thomson Reuters (Professional) UK Ltd. on behalf of Sweet & Maxwell to quote from a 1989 article by Nathaniel Lichfield and from 1992 and 2000 articles by Malcolm Grant, all in the *Journal of Planning and Environment Law*.

Foreword

Planning gain is complex. The history of various attempts at national development taxation followed by a succession of locally negotiated schemes for planning obligations indicates the persistent dissatisfaction, which arises from the impossibility of devising a perfect solution. This book makes a tremendous contribution to the subject by bringing together a rigorous theoretic approach, a clear narrative of developments since 1947 and a good deal of data on the revenue that has been gained for the public purse and on the new affordable homes secured from planning obligations.

In particular, it is welcome to read a very clear account of why the taxation of land can be rather more distorting of land use than is sometimes supposed. It was also salutary for me to be reminded of why my own suggestion of a Planning Gain Supplement ultimately failed to be adopted. The evidence that the burden from planning gain generally seems to fall on the landowner is a nice confirmation of what theory would predict. However, a big question on land prices of what is the 'right price' to use in a viability calculation is also raised, but perhaps unsurprisingly is not resolved.

There is much stress here on how locally based systems have worked better than attempts at national taxation. However, this also leads to inconsistency in practice, and in monitoring of delivery. While it is encouraging to read that the vast bulk of obligations are delivered, it is also dispiriting that some local authorities do not seem able to devote resources to ensuring that what is negotiated gets done.

There are some real nuggets too, for example, it is often argued that it would be better for there to be more certainty in advance about what planning obligations will be on a particular site. But the international evidence suggests that the flexible negotiations we have in England, which are better able to handle the fact that every site is of course different, are also able to yield more planning gain.

For the tidy-minded economist, it is a bit unsatisfactory that planning gain is seeking to do two things: extract the gain from the public decision to grant planning permission and finance consequential infrastructure. But it is clear this works in practice if not in theory. However, the concluding comment about 'requiring developers to contribute to the infrastructure costs they impose on local communities' concerns me a little. The reason we need more infrastructure as a country is because we have more people. Of course, the location of building affects where we need it. But it is important that this is given the right profile as a national issue – not purely a local one.

This is a highly important book. The stress in the conclusion on moving towards public land banking is one I support. It also draws out the truth that government prefers to raise money from charges on development, rather than from property values (which, perhaps more rationally, could also be used to fund infrastructure) because this is not a tax and the effects are more hidden from the public.

Dame Kate Barker

Dame Kate Barker is a non-executive director of several finance and housing companies. She is also a former member of the UK's Monetary Policy Committee and of the board of the Homes & Communities Agency. She undertook independent reviews for the UK government of housing supply and of the planning system in England.

Preface

Whether and how to capture the development value created through spatial and land-use planning decisions has dominated many conceptual, policy and practice planning debates for several decades, not only in Britain but also in many other countries. Since the early days of planning legislation, Britain has made several attempts, especially after World War II, to capture development value through national taxation. None of these succeeded and, although each new attempt learned something from past failures, they generally led to land being withheld from the market whilst attempts to bring development land into public ownership to counter land withholding were also largely ineffective.

These failures have not stopped debates on the arguments for, and methods of capturing development value. Far from it, scholarly and policy debates on the issue continue to be lively. Over the last three decades, a different means of capturing development value has emerged in Britain, one that does not rely on nationally imposed and levied taxation – and initially did not rely on a national policy initiative. It is colloquially referred to as 'Planning Gain'. This is the long-standing system of planning obligations which permits local planning authorities to negotiate financial and 'in-kind' contributions with developers when they are seeking planning permission. Since 1990, the use of this system has spread from a few innovative authorities experimenting with the system of obligations to raise funds so that now most authorities have adopted and use it to some extent. It has raised large amounts of funding at a time when public funds are increasingly scarce. When the costs that developers incur in making these contributions are passed back to landowners in the form of lower land prices, this effectively captures development value to help pay for local infrastructure such as the roads and schools needed for new development and to pay for new community needs, including affordable housing. Although far from a 'first best' means of capturing development value it has been a successful means of doing so, but one which depends heavily for its success on the buoyancy of local property markets and on the policies and professional skills of local planning authorities.

We have written this book describing how the system of 'planning gain' has developed in Britain for two reasons. First, we and our colleagues have been monitoring the system of planning obligations for two decades. We have published extensively on the results of our work in research reports, in evidence to government consultations and to parliamentary select committees' inquiries, in short articles in professional magazines, and in scholarly refereed journal articles. We have also spoken regularly on the topic at many professional and academic conferences and in briefings for members of the policy and practice communities, including those in government, in the legal, property and planning professions, and in the trade bodies and lobby groups of housing organisations in the private and not-for-profit sectors. This has given us a privileged 'seat' at policy and other debates, as we have provided independent evidence on how the system of planning obligations has been working and critically commented on its effectiveness and on the many policy changes regularly proposed (and implemented) throughout the period under study. So, the first reason for this book is to pull together this evidence so that the 'story' of how planning obligations have emerged as an effective means of capturing development value in England and for charging developers for infrastructure is readily accessible to researchers and policy analysts in this country. Our intention is that the book will form a useful basis for informed policy and scholarly discussion.

Our second reason for writing the book is to ensure that this planning gain 'story' is equally accessible to policy analysts and researchers in other countries. We know from our own experience that many of those working in the research and policy communities in other countries often look to our experience to find lessons about what works in England to use in their own countries. Yet we know that there are limits to what can be transferred. In particular, account needs to be taken both of the specific contexts within which planning gain developed in England and of the often quite different contexts in other countries before any assessment of the legitimacy and likely impact of policy transfer can be made. We also know that the experience in England is all too easily misunderstood and yet there are messages which can be of value in many different circumstances. So our second reason for this book is to try to tell our story with sufficient clarity and detail that it is of value to those in other countries who are looking to fund infrastructure and housing through their planning regimes. This is why we have devoted one chapter out looking at the experience in four other countries to help point to the similarities and differences between those countries and England.

Although the empirical evidence we present throughout this book comes largely from our own recent work on planning obligations, we also draw on the work of others who have researched and written on the topic. We hope this ensures that the book is a comprehensive coverage of the academic and policy debates and of the evidence about the workings and effectiveness of planning obligations policies and practices. The drafting of this book drew to an end in December 2014 and it is from that time we look back and tell the story of planning obligations in England, conscious that the details will inevitably change after publication of this volume. Because we in the United

Kingdom now live in a state which has handed over much domestic policy to devolved governments in Northern Ireland, Scotland, and Wales we have dealt very largely with the experience of England.

Tony Crook, John Henneberry and Christine Whitehead
Sheffield and London, January 2015

Notes on Contributors

Dr Gemma Burgess is a Senior Research Associate at the Cambridge Centre for Housing and Planning Research, Department of Land Economy, University of Cambridge. Her research focuses on land supply and the delivery of housing through the planning system; in particular, she has conducted extensive research on planning obligations, the Community Infrastructure Levy and affordable housing. She recently led research for the House of Commons Communities and Local Government Select Committee on the nature of planning constraints. Her research also encompasses housing options for older people.

Professor Tony Crook is a chartered town planner, Emeritus Professor of Town & Regional Planning and former Pro Vice Chancellor, University of Sheffield. His current research focuses on planning obligations and affordable housing and on the supply side of the private rented housing sector. His co-authored book with Professor Peter A Kemp, *Transforming Private Landlords*, was published by Wiley Blackwell in 2011. He is also actively engaged in policy and practice. He is the Chair Emeritus of the Shelter Trustee Board, Deputy Chair of the Orbit Housing Group, a non-executive director of a regional house-builder, a Trustee of the Coalfields Regeneration Trust, a council member of the Academy of Social Sciences, and a member of the Royal Town Planning Institute Trustee Board. He is a Fellow of the Academy of Social Sciences and was appointed CBE in 2014 for his services to housing and the governance of charities.

Richard Dunning is a Research Associate in the Department of Urban Studies and Planning, University of Sheffield. He completed his MA in Commercial Property in the department and worked as an Industrial Agent for GVA Grimley, returning to the department in 2009 to work on a number of research projects and subsequently to do his PhD in housing economics. His principal research interest is in applying behavioural analysis approaches to issues related to infrastructure, housing and real-estate markets. Richard has recently undertaken research projects for the EU, RICS, the Department for Communities and Local Government, the French Government, the Joseph Rowntree Foundation and local governments.

Dr Ed Ferrari is a Senior Lecturer in the Department of Urban Studies and Planning, University of Sheffield. Having completed his BA and PhD in the department, he left Sheffield to take up a post as GIS Officer for Birmingham City Council and then as a Research Fellow and Lecturer at the Centre for Urban and Regional Studies, University of Birmingham. He returned to Sheffield in 2006. His main research interests are in the analysis of housing markets, mobility in the social rented sector, application of GIS to housing research, and use of secondary datasets for policy research and evaluation. His work involves a wide range of local and central government clients aimed at developing evidence bases for spatial strategy and housing investment purposes. He was closely involved in the development of the evidence base for the government's Housing Market Renewal programme (2002–2010) and was a lead member of the consortium undertaking the national evaluation of the HMR Pathfinders for the Department of Communities and Local Government. He is also a former Chair of the Housing Studies Association, the learned society of all housing researchers in the UK.

Professor John Henneberry is a charted town planner, a chartered surveyor and Professor of Property Development Studies, Department of Urban Studies and Planning, University of Sheffield. His research focuses on the structure and behaviour of the property market and its relation to the wider economy and state regulatory systems. He has particular interests in property development and investment and their contribution to urban and regional development. He has developed a distinctive 'old' institutional approach to property research that focuses on the impact of social, cultural and behavioural influences on market actors, structures, processes and outcomes. He is a Fellow of the Academy of Social Sciences.

Sarah Monk is an applied economist and currently a Departmental Fellow in the Department of Land Economy, University of Cambridge. She was the Deputy Director of the Cambridge Centre for Housing and Planning Research (CCHPR) from 1999 until her retirement in 2014. She remains a Senior Associate of the Centre. Her research interests have focused on the delivery of affordable housing through the planning system and she has published widely on this topic. She has jointly edited two books with Christine Whitehead, the founding Director of CCHPR: *Restructuring Housing Systems: From Social to Affordable Housing* in 2000 and *Making Housing More Affordable: The Role of Intermediate Tenures* published by Wiley Blackwell in 2010. She is a Fellow of the Academy of Social Sciences.

Dr Steven Rowley is an Associate Professor and Head of the Department of Economics and Property at Curtin University, Perth, Western Australia. He is also Director of the Australian Housing and Urban Research Institute's Curtin Research Centre. Prior to joining Curtin, he worked as a Research Fellow in the Department of Urban Studies and Planning, University of Sheffield for nine years, focusing mainly on research, particularly UK Government funded research projects on planning and affordable housing, including being part of the team that calculated the incidence and value of planning obligations in both England and Wales. He also worked on commercial property markets and the impact of environmental improvements on land values. He also consulted for Fordham Planning Consultants in London, specialising in the development viability of residential and commercial development projects with a particular focus on the impact of planning obligations and affordable housing.

Professor Craig Watkins is an applied economist and Professor of Planning and Housing in the Department of Urban Studies & Planning, University of Sheffield. He is also Director of Research and Innovation in the Faculty of Social Science and Director of the Sheffield Urban Institute, a research centre that spans Social Science and Engineering departments and seeks to develop socio-technical solutions to urban problems. His research focuses on understanding the structure and operation of property markets, particularly local housing systems, and on exploring the interaction between planning, public policy and property market behaviour.

Professor Christine Whitehead is Emeritus Professor of Housing Economics at the London School of Economics and was for 20 years the Director of the Cambridge Centre of Housing and Planning Research, University of Cambridge. She is an internationally respected applied economist working mainly in the fields of housing economics, finance and policy. Major themes in her recent research have included analysis of the relationship between planning and housing; the role of private renting in European housing systems; financing social housing in the UK and Europe; and more broadly the application of economic concepts and techniques to questions of public resource allocation with respect to housing, education, policing and urban regeneration. Her latest book, with Kath Scanlon and Melissa Fernandez, *Social Housing in Europe,* was published by Wiley Blackwell in July 2014. She is a Fellow of the Academy of Social Sciences and was appointed OBE in 1991 for services to housing.

1

Introduction

Tony Crook[1], John Henneberry[1] and Christine Whitehead[2]

[1]*Department of Urban Studies & Planning, The University of Sheffield, UK*

[2]*LSE London, the London School of Economics, UK*

Purpose of the book

'Planning gain' raises fundamental issues around the role of the state and the optimal creation and distribution of land values. Such gain may, in part, be the product of better decisions about the use of land as a result of government intervention. But it can also arise because planning constraints affect markets in ways that do not offset market failures. The extraction and allocation of all or part of increases in land values, through government policies to capture planning gain, is a core policy and practice issue in many countries. This is significant because it provides a source of public finance and the potential for resource redistribution.

This book considers how mechanisms to create and extract planning gain have developed in England since the middle of the twentieth century. In the 1940s and 1950s, following the nationalisation of development rights, such mechanisms were a core element of national government policies and finances. Thereafter, there were many changes in the instruments used and in powers of implementation, although the principle of government control over development has remained unchanged. The main contribution of the text is to examine how the system for extracting land development value has operated since the 1990s based on a national legislative provision (currently defined in S106 of the principal planning statute – the 1990 Town and Country Planning Act) and implemented by local decision makers. In this period, planning gain has been in the forefront of policy development

Planning Gain: Providing Infrastructure and Affordable Housing, First Edition.
Edited by Tony Crook, John Henneberry and Christine Whitehead.
© 2016 John Wiley & Sons, Inc. Published 2016 by John Wiley & Sons, Inc.

to enable local authorities to fund the physical infrastructure needed to support new development and meet wider community needs such as additional affordable housing.

The development process and the creation of development value

Our starting point must be the property development process and the way that development is driven by potential returns based on the value of outputs from that development (Brown and Matysiak, 2000; Reed and Sims, 2008). Development is the investment of capital in real property to produce a return. Usually – but not always or entirely – the return is measured in financial terms. Development is viable when its value upon completion exceeds its costs by an amount sufficient to compensate the developer for the risk that is borne and the effort that is expended on the project. These costs include the price paid for the required land, which in turn reflects its value in the best alternative use.

Development can take many forms. It may involve the identification and acquisition of a suitable site, the provision of off-site infrastructure to support the future use (i.e. the servicing of a site), the construction of buildings and other structures on the site and the disposal of the completed scheme to owners and/or occupiers. Developers may perform all of these tasks or only some of them. For example, there are those who specialise in assembling fragmented ownerships and selling on the resulting large site to realise the 'marriage' value. Others, including the original owner, may focus on obtaining outline planning permission and servicing land before selling it to a developer, who then completes the scheme. Developers themselves may retain and manage the resultant asset.

Development is not restricted to undeveloped, un-serviced land. Developers may purchase existing, serviced land and buildings for brownfield development. They may demolish the building and replace it with a larger or more functionally efficient building or one given over to a different use. Alternatively, the existing building may be renovated, refurbished or extended. The common requirement for the development to go ahead, whichever types or stages of development are involved, is that the value of the investment exceeds the cost by enough to provide a competitive return.

We now consider development demand and value. Land values are underpinned by the demand for land generated by the activities of society as a whole and their evolution. Land values are highest when the land is employed in its highest valued use and will, in a well operating market system, be allocated to that use by preparedness to pay and therefore price. Allowing for land productivity, agricultural values depend upon the demand for food and other farm products and the ability of consumers and users to pay for these products. Retail land values depend upon the demand for consumer goods and the way in which they are distributed and so on. As society develops, so gross domestic product (GDP), productivity and personal incomes grow. This inherently increases the average value of scarce land but it also implies that the most appropriate means of production, distribution and consumption are likely to change. The nature and pattern of physical development must in turn change in the face of these trends. The relative values of different types of property and land will wax and wane as a result.

The level and distribution of the value generated by changes in demand are affected by a range of other factors. A key influence is the availability, quality and cost of off-site infrastructure. It is no good building houses on a site that does not have access to the road network, sewers or mains water. In a regulated market, the state, through the land-use planning system, will contribute to the general change in land values by, for example, reducing negative externalities and increasing positive ones. It may also control landowners and/or developers' ability to respond to changes in demand and to achieve that value by permitting or prohibiting any kind of development or restricting land use to specific types of development.

The most dramatic increases in land values occur when a change from a lower to a higher order land use is combined with the physical development necessary to meet the requirements of the new use. One example is the transfer of agricultural land for residential use. The price at which the highest valued completed development may be sold determines the value of the land required to achieve that development. In other words, once development costs (building costs, finance, professional fees and the minimum developer's profit) are covered, any residual establishes the maximum market value of the land. The difference between the market value and the existing use value of the land is termed the 'development value'. Another generally used term for this difference between market value and existing use value is 'betterment' (Cullingworth, 1980; Hall, 1965), reflecting the extent to which property development enables additional benefits to be achieved such as the benefits of public investment in transport that improves the accessibility of a site given planning permission.

The price at which land will be offered and traded in the market will depend upon a combination of the character and motivation of the landowner, the development potential of the land and the nature of the extant planning system (Goodchild and Munton, 1985). Landowners will usually require a significant financial incentive to sell land. They will seek to maximize the proportion of the development value of the land that they obtain in the land price and will calibrate that objective against prevailing market experience. This is the mechanism that brings land forward for development. If the state reduces or removes the landowner's sale premium the supply of land will be reduced or halted unless an alternative means (such as compulsory purchase) is found to bring land forward for development.

The taxation of development value

Attempts by government to capture development values through the planning system have a long history in the UK (Cullingworth, 1980). This was initially seen as a matter of equity (Cullingworth, ibid; Hall, 1965; see also Fainstein, 2012, for international views). It was argued that increases in land values as a consequence of development should not be kept by landowners who had done little or nothing to generate this value but should be shared with the state as the representative of the wider society whose actions, in large part, created them. In line with these principles, national taxation of land development value was introduced, the income from which was used for general public expenditures.

Latterly, much more emphasis has been put on the more pragmatic rationale that development value taxation can be used to finance infrastructure and services both to increase economic growth and benefit communities (see, e.g. Bill, 2004; Campbell *et al.*, 2000; Crook and Monk, 2011; Lichfield, 1989). This, in turn, has shifted the emphasis towards approaches that are both locally based and generate hypothecated revenues.

State intervention in the creation and extraction of development value is by no means confined to the UK (Ingram and Hong, 2012; Monk *et al.*, 2013; Oxley *et al.*, 2009), although England, in particular, has been at the forefront of the development of policy and practice in this field over the last three decades. In all systems, local or national governments regulate and manage land uses in ways that influence the generation of development values which in turn may be taxed in one way or another. Each country has its own legal and institutional framework that helps to determine what types of instrument are feasible and desirable. Even so there has been considerable commonality in the increasing emphasis given to introducing instruments that enable local communities to benefit through improved local infrastructure and services, often through the provision of affordable housing.

Consequently, the book places the English experience in an international context. It looks at these issues in three distinct ways: by setting out the principles involved in generating and reallocating development values; by considering the types of policy instrument that can achieve these goals and the necessary conditions for such instruments to be implemented effectively; and by examining empirical evidence on how the instruments used in England and some other countries have worked.

In this context, 'planning gain' has become a colloquial term to describe the development value that arises as a consequence of the granting of planning permission or of re-zoning in most other countries (Ingram and Hong, 2012). This rise in value reflects all the benefits which are released as a result of changed opportunities that receiving planning permission makes possible. Some of these will arise from the quality of the planning process; some from reductions in constraint and some from the more effective use of existing infrastructure and the expectation of further infrastructure investment. In other words, it is not restricted to the gains in value arising from planning itself.

The proportion of planning gain which is captured depends on the effectiveness of the tax and its implementation. In the UK, this is strongly associated with the increasing use made by local planning authorities of planning obligations. Such obligations result from negotiations with applicants for planning permission for contributions (either in cash or in kind) towards infrastructure and wider community needs, including affordable housing. They are covered by S106 of the 1990 Act in England (and equivalent parts of legislation in the rest of Britain) and by the recently implemented Community Infrastructure Levy – or CIL (Crook and Monk, 2011). The obligations thus address objectives both of efficiency (in the sense that by securing developer contributions towards the off-site infrastructure costs of their new developments, additional investment which has positive net value to the community is enabled) and equity, by securing more funding from private developers for services, including in particular housing for low-income households, in cash or in kind (Crook and Whitehead, 2002). The recent introduction of CIL in 2008 creates a distinction between, on the one hand, those contributions which are negotiated through S106 agreements for site-specific infrastructure and mitigations and affordable housing and, on the other hand, those sub-regional and regional infrastructure costs for which local planning authorities may (but are not obliged to) impose a charge (related to the size of development) on all developers implementing a planning permission.

Planning obligations were once a rarely used mechanism within British planning legislation (Jowell, 1977). They enabled local planning authorities to regulate aspects of development not directly related to land use and to ensure that developers mitigated some of the side effects of development. They have now become a frequently used method of obtaining substantial funding for wider infrastructure requirements and for meeting affordable housing and other community needs.

What is especially interesting about the British experience of using instruments to extract planning gain is that the once separate means of capturing land development value and of applying the resultant funds have now come together at the local level. For some significant period after 1947, increases in development values were taxed on a *de jure* basis at the national level. Importantly, because government owned the development rights there was never a need to compensate those who were restricted in the use of their land – the focus was purely on the taxation of what were seen as unearned gains. Quite separate national systems of allocating public expenditure provided the means for funding off-site infrastructure and community provision.

Now these once separate systems for taxing development values and for funding infrastructure have come together at the local level. Local planning authorities are charging fees or negotiating contributions from developers to meet some of the costs of off-site infrastructure and community needs. Significant sums have been raised in this way. As we shall see in Chapter 6, the scale of these contributions has grown very considerably in England in the last two decades, with a large proportion of permissions for major housing and commercial developments now covered by planning agreements (Crook *et al.*, 2010). The growth of these agreements has arisen in part because of the financial pressures on the public sector, the traditional funder of capital for infrastructure and affordable housing. Faced with these contributions, developers have reduced the prices they are prepared to pay for land. The result is a *de facto* extraction of development value which is, at least in principle, paid by the landowner and is hypothecated for local use.

In telling the story of how systems for extracting planning gain have evolved and of their impact on development, we focus on England rather than the rest of the UK. Although the systems in Scotland and Wales are not dissimilar to those in England,[1] the advent of devolved administrations means that there are increasing differences between the nations of Britain in the ways these issues are being handled.

Factors affecting effective development value capture

Planning as a state activity has been conceived in several ways: as substituting administrative for market allocations to favour the state's objectives rather than those of individual actors; as regulating, shaping, and stimulating markets to operate more effectively; and as pro-actively developing the capacities of market participants often by the provision of infrastructure (which itself may be paid for by the captured development value). We need to bear this in mind when examining planning gain from different perspectives. Each highlights a specific way of looking at the system. No one perspective offers a full understanding of planning gain or of how it works within any country's system of land ownership, governance, spatial planning, public finance and property markets. It is therefore necessary briefly to consider

---

[1] Policy and practice in Northern Ireland are distinctive.

the fundamental drivers that affect planning gain capture to ensure that our presentation of the English system is clearly located within a framework that allows comparison with the systems in other countries.

Property rights and ownership

Whether land and/or development rights are in public or private ownership makes a big difference to how development values can be secured for public benefit and to the consequences for the supply of development land. Ownership is best understood as a set of property rights. One is the right to the benefits of development and another is the right to choose how to develop. The form and arrangement of these rights range from outright private ownership through to outright public ownership with a variety in between, for example, involving joint ventures of private and public bodies.

Where land is in public ownership the benefits are, at least in principle, directly available to be used for public benefit. The need for value capture arises where there is private ownership or a mix. Moreover, what may appear to be a simple allocation of ownership is often far more complex because these rights may involve restrictive or positive covenants that limit what the owner can do or place obligations on the owner. Property rights over the same plot of land may be split among several owners. In the UK, as we have already noted, the right to develop has been nationalised (for details, see Chapter 3). Hence, a parcel of land may only be developed by the owner if the state exercises *its own* development rights. Formally, this is done through the granting of planning permission.

Other public–private relational complexities may arise. For example, the state may bring land into temporary public ownership with a view to selling it on to the private market, following aggregation into appropriate lot sizes and the provision of key infrastructure. This approach – state acquisition of land perhaps at existing use value or somewhat above (compulsorily if necessary), servicing and sale at its value in its intended future use – may provide a more effective means of extracting gains than either land taxation or development charges. It is an approach which has been successfully employed in Germany and the Netherlands (as we shall see in Chapter 9) but has been used relatively rarely in the UK.

When land remains in private ownership, the main ways of extracting gain are taxing the development value when planning permission is granted, raising infrastructure funds through charging mechanisms and placing restrictions on development that require the developer to provide infrastructure and other services. All these create a possibility that landowners will not bring land to the market because they reduce the uplift in land value consequent upon development and, therefore, reduce the financial incentive to sell. In addition, landowners will make a judgement about the prospects for future legislation or practice affecting taxes or charges in the future.

The public or private nature of ownership is not the only factor affecting the capacity to extract planning gain. Private landowners have many reasons for owning land. They also have different time horizons. Financial motives may include a desire actively to trade land to take advantage of new development opportunities, longer term investment motives or indeed sentiment or family obligation. The complexity of financial rules (including tax and accounting rules) affecting landowners, combined with the fragmented nature of their interests and holdings, means that there can be no one simple determining relationship between land prices and the supply of land for development that actually enters the market. Similarly, public bodies may own land for many reasons including historic circumstance. So, while under current legislation in England, public bodies are expected to own land primarily to carry out their obligations (e.g. owning the land on which schools are built), they may also own unused stocks of vacant land to meet future requirements or to achieve other objectives.

The need for finance

The need to raise funds for infrastructure and other local facilities and services through negotiated or prescribed charges and *de facto* taxes on development value depends to an extent on the role that the state plays in financing these requirements. Where the state funds most of these from national taxes on income, capital gains and transactions (plus local taxation on property and sales), local charges and *de facto* taxes on development values lose some of their appeal – at least on financial grounds. This is one reason why taxation and expenditure were seen as separate in the early post-war years, when most infrastructure provision was by the state. It is also one reason why they are now far more central as a result of privatisation. In many jurisdictions developers are generally responsible for providing on-site infrastructure, including service roads, water, sewerage and energy supplies. These are part of the developer's costs. Off-site infrastructure is another matter and may include a wide range of costs that have to be incurred to support new development.

Where the state is not the direct provider of development and its supporting infrastructure, any changes to market incentives created by introducing charges and taxes on development value may be crucial to the supply and price of development land. A high charge or tax rate may work, but only if it does not keep land off the market – or if the state is empowered, funded and prepared to step in and replace the land market with compulsory acquisition of land and its subsequent disposal. In many jurisdictions utilities (water, sewerage, gas, electricity and so on) are now provided by private companies rather than by national and local states. In such circumstances arrangements are made for developers to negotiate directly with utility companies for the provision of off-site infrastructure (as well as paying for the on-site components). All of the developers' commitments affect the price of the land and therefore the extent of additional value available for extraction.

The ownership of development rights

Where land is in public ownership, development rights sit alongside the state's (or municipality's) ownership. They will still normally be subject to any limitations imposed by the land-use planning system and broader legislation constraining how the state may use these rights. However, where land is privately owned matters are different – often development rights are reallocated by government intervention of one sort or another. Systems vary between countries. In many ways, the British system is unusual because, as we have already noted, development rights have been nationalised (without compensation) and thus can only be allocated to landowners and developers by the state granting permission. Separate policy and legislation is needed to extract any of the resultant value for public purposes. In other countries, development rights remain in private ownership with their use constrained by zoning systems and covenants that enable the state to intervene in private decisions for reasons of public interest and potentially to gain some of the benefits arising from development and infrastructure provision.

Taxing value or raising charges

The policies and instruments discussed in the book cover two conceptually different objectives. On the one hand, there are instruments designed to tax development value that are applied through the planning system. On the other hand, there are instruments designed to raise funds from developers to help pay for the infrastructure needed, on the one hand, to allow their development to go ahead or to mitigate its impact and, on the other hand, simply to pay for future infrastructure requirements. What developers are asked to pay is then often related to the costs of the infrastructure and not (at least in principle) to the development values created. As we shall see, the current arrangements in England are a hybrid of these approaches.

Rules versus discretion?

As we shall see in Chapter 9, some planning systems in developed countries are much more 'rule bound' than those in the UK. Many are 'zoning systems' in which a physical plan specifies the allowed future development of the relevant area and determines the permits needed for development to take place. The differences between zoning and more discretionary approaches to planning such as the British planning permission system can be more apparent than real. Zoning rules can be changed and decisions in discretionary systems are bound to consider relevant policies. Nonetheless, discretion gives spatial plans in the UK system more inherent flexibility (and equally more uncertainty) in their implementation than zoning plans in other systems. Crucially, discretion provides the possibility of enabling planning authorities to negotiate planning obligations. It is this that has allowed planning authorities simultaneously to obtain contributions to infrastructure and community needs and – formally completely separately – to decide whether or not to grant planning permission.

However, the exercise of discretion by different local planning authorities (LPAs) may result in significant differences both in the extent of betterment created and in the policy and practice across administrative boundaries (and indeed over time) in extracting some of this. In part, these variations relate to market factors. The spatial pattern of demand for, and the value and cost of development, determine the amount of development value that may be extracted. However, variations in policy and practice also matter. Political and professional attitudes to extracting development value and practical competence in designing and implementing policies and in pursuing negotiations are important in this regard. There is also the possibility of perverse outcomes. These may include attempts to tighten restrictions on land supply to boost development values or to permit development in areas where development values have increased significantly but where there are other external costs to the development.

Fixed taxes, tariffs and negotiated contributions

When seeking to tax betterment or to raise contributions for infrastructure and other needs, policy makers have a choice of instruments that depends on the legal and institutional context and on political realities. At one end of the scale is a nationally imposed levy or charge covering a defined percentage of the uplift in development value, the latter spelt out formulaically in legislation, whilst at the other end, local authorities (or regional bodies) can be given powers to set and collect levies. They may have the right to determine whether the charge is made as a percentage of the uplift in value, as a fixed tariff or as a negotiated contribution. There is the possibility of mixing tariffs and negotiated contributions to collect funds for different purposes (as we shall see, this is the latest approach in England with planning obligations and CIL). Where sub-national bodies are given powers (or duties) important matters arise regarding the extent of their discretion and how this is limited. The latter may be affected by the imposition of rules – such as a requirement to maintain the viability of development – and by the extent to which developers can appeal to a higher authority against requirements.

Local discretion also gives rise to important consequences. In particular, it allows levies or charges to reflect local variations in underlying development costs and prices. However, variations in practice may mean that developers face differences in the costs within areas with otherwise similar market conditions. This may affect decisions about where to develop.

Hypothecation and contract

Part of the appeal of infrastructure charges and of locally negotiated contributions lies in the ability of the jurisdictions receiving them to devote the finances accrued to the funding of specific local investments. Conventionally, national systems of taxation do not permit such hypothecation so there can usually be no guarantee that funds raised from a locality through nationally defined taxes on development value will find their way back to the locality to meet its needs. This is precisely what local charging and contributions permit. They enable planning authorities to raise the funds (in cash and in kind) needed to support development. From the developers' perspective, whilst liability for nationally defined and levied taxes provides an element of certainty when scoping a project, locally negotiated contributions can give them contractual certainty that the local authority, having received the funds, will provide the agreed infrastructure required to support that development. Conversely, if the agreement specifies an 'in kind' contribution from a developer then, having granted consent with the related agreement, the LPA has the certainty that the developer will deliver that contribution.

Key factors behind the development of planning gain policy in England

The factors set out mentioned above are crucial to understanding the choices that can be made about extracting development value. In England, a fundamental difference from most other systems, which has been constant since 1947, is that development rights (but not land ownership) are nationalised so the state owns the power to determine how land is used. How that power has been used and with it how instruments to tax the outcome of its use have developed has depended on three factors (or 'drivers'). These are as follows:

1. changes to the political economy of the UK;
2. the nature of the UK planning system and how it has adapted to these changes; and
3. the nature of local discretion, especially in England.

Political economy

Whilst the UK is now often characterised as having a liberal market economy (Hall and Soskice, 2001), this has not always been the case. Moreover, there continues to be a strong state role in the provision of many services, especially education and health. In the immediate post-war period, following the election of a Labour Government in 1945, there was a strong ideological drive to ensure state control of the commanding heights of the economy and also to harness the state to address welfare provision. In our context this involved setting up a comprehensive system of land-use planning and becoming the main provider of infrastructure. It also acquired development land and, through local authorities, built new homes for social renting. Inner cities were to be comprehensively redeveloped with the overspill population accommodated in New Towns or other public sector developments.

Fairly rapidly state planning in its extreme form was replaced by a more mixed economy. This was undoubtedly the case in housing where there was an increased private sector role building for owner occupation from the early 1950s. Housing output from then to the end of the 1970s was split roughly 50:50 between the public and private sectors.

From the 1980s onwards, Britain became more of a liberal market economy than a mixed economy. There was substantial deregulation of key sectors. Some public services and most nationalised industries were privatised. Crucially for the subject matter of this book, many utilities were privatised; a proportion of social rented housing was sold to its tenants at discounts under a right to buy policy; and local authorities were no longer seen as providers of new homes but as facilitators of supply by other agencies. Public expenditure (especially on capital) was reined in, whilst local authorities' freedoms and ability to raise their own funds through both local taxes and borrowing were increasingly restricted.

The planning system

The planning system in the UK had to adapt to this changing political economy. One of the enduring achievements of the first post-war Labour government was the establishment of a comprehensive system of land-use planning, following much debate and discussion by reconstruction committees sitting during the war time (Cullingworth, 1975). In 1947, all development rights were nationalised whilst leaving the ownership of land and other property rights unchanged (for descriptions of the planning system see Cullingworth *et al.*, 2014; Rydin, 2003).

Those wishing to develop land had to apply for planning permission from the LPA. Government policy created a presumption in favour of development so that applicants for permission did not have to prove the need for it;

rather LPAs have to give good reasons for refusing permission. In deciding whether or not to grant permission LPAs have always been obliged to have regard to the provisions of their development plan and to any other material considerations.

All LPAs are thus required to draw up a development plan for their area, having regard to national policy guidance and to keep it under review. The exact form of what is required of a plan has changed in detail over the years but the fundamentals of the planning system have not.

Unlike the zoning plans of many other jurisdictions (see Chapter 9) development plans in Britain do not, of themselves, grant permission. Instead LPAs must have regard both to the provisions of the plan and to other considerations so far as they are material. Thus, the British planning system is a system for decision making where there is a balance between rules (plans and policies) and discretion (taking other material circumstances into account). Getting this balance between certainty and flexibility right was a key matter facing the designers of the post-war planning legislation and the relevant 1944 White Paper emphasised that plans would not confer the right to develop but instead provide a policy background for the taking of decisions on planning applications (Cullingworth, 1975). The obligation to take other material considerations into account means that LPAs may grant permission for something that does not accord with their plan whilst also refusing something that does, provided good reasons can be given. Those whose planning applications are refused have the right to appeal to central government.

This brief sketch of the planning system in Britain identifies two key matters relevant to our book. First, central government plays a key role in the planning process. Ministers have both a policy role and an appellate role. Second, the planning system is a discretionary decision-making system that has the flexibility needed to accommodate policy, demographic, economic, social and other change but also generates uncertainty about decisions. These two matters (the role of central government in determining policy and the inherent discretion in the system at the local level) have enabled the planning system to adapt to changes in the political economy of Britain, whilst leaving the fundamentals of the system unchanged. Development rights have remained nationalised, development continues to need consent and LPAs are required to have regard to national policy, their adopted plans and other material consideration when making decisions. As the political economy changed, so too did planning practice with more emphasis on a collaborative style of planning (see Healey *et al.*, 1988; Healey, 1997) to enable development to proceed and to negotiate acceptable outcomes.

Central–local relations: Local discretion, innovation and adoption

The third factor behind the growth of planning obligations as the means of capturing planning gain is the significance of local discretion. The development of a more negotiative and participatory style of plan making and development management has been fundamental to the success of planning obligations in delivering funding for infrastructure and affordable housing.

Chapter 3 shows how attempts to extract development value through measures of national taxation foundered. This was partly because landowners kept land off the market because the high rates of tax made them indifferent to development and also because of expectations of political change. Measures introduced to enable land banking by the public sector to address such land withholding foundered on inadequate borrowing approvals from central government and insufficient eligible development land allocated in LPAs' development plans.

From the 1980s onwards, public spending cuts and the privatisation and marketisation of services arising from the emergence of a liberal market economy all made it problematic for LPAs to secure either infrastructure needed for development or community requirements. At the same time, central government used national planning policy statements to make it difficult for LPAs to use their development plans as vehicles for pursuing wider social and economic objectives and restricted the role of planning to the shaping of physical developments.

These centrally imposed constraints led several LPAs to find other ways of securing the funding they needed and using the planning system to pursue wider objectives. The legal framework of planning has always allowed LPAs to negotiate agreements with developers to contribute funding or in-kind facilities in connection with their proposed developments. Such agreements make it possible for LPAs to give consent to acceptable developments that they would otherwise have to refuse because of the lack of supporting infrastructure.

Once innovating LPAs had demonstrated the possibility of successfully using planning obligations to secure funding, other early adopters followed and eventually the practice became widespread. The more negotiative style of decision making in planning that emerged from the growth of a liberal market economy in Britain thus made it possible for LPAs to pursue this approach. As a result, planning obligations are consistent with the tenets of a liberal market economy in the sense that private (development value) funding has (partially) replaced public funding of infrastructure and of affordable housing. This reflects the wider changes in the relationships between state and market and the private and the public.

This use of planning obligations was not uncontroversial. Inevitably, questions were asked not only about the legality of obligations practice but also about the ethical challenges for planning practitioners in terms of the conduct of negotiations and the temptation to use planning policy to shape financial outcomes. These challenges by property and other interests and the wider questions these raised about the ethics of professional practice ultimately led central government to establish a clearer policy framework in the 1990s. This did not limit the use of obligations. Instead it endorsed as government policy what had essentially been a local initiative. Consequently, the use of obligations for these purposes was legitimised and legalised, whilst at the same time greater transparency (policies to be included in plans) and accountability (openness about the content of agreements) were introduced into the process.

Definitions

A wide variety of terms have been used to describe the phenomenon discussed in the book. Confusingly in the literature, the same terms have often been used to describe different phenomena and a specific phenomenon has sometimes been discussed using different terms. Thus, the term 'planning gain' is sometimes used to describe the contributions developers make through planning agreements but it is also sometimes used to discuss the increase in market value of land arising from planning permission from which such 'planning gain' can be extracted. The focus of this book is the variety of ways, including taxation and negotiated planning agreements, used to capture some of the development value created through the granting of planning permission and we have tried to use the term 'development value' consistently throughout the book to describe the increase in the market value of land arising when planning permission is granted and to use the phrase 'capturing (or extracting) development value' when discussing methods to tax or negotiate some or all of it.

Box 1.1 lists and defines the principal terms used throughout the book. Although the three definitions of betterment are conceptually separate, it has proved difficult to capture them through mechanisms specifically related to each of the three types identified in Box 1.1 mentioned above. Although the mechanisms we describe and discuss in this book are in practice related to capturing development value at the time when planning consent is granted, the increase that is captured can arise not just because the state allows new uses or new physical development on the parcel but may also reflect a land parcel's improved accessibility arising from transport investment by the state and from the general uplift in values arising from greater prosperity. It is the granting of planning permissions that provide that state with the opportunity to secure some 'betterment'.

Box 1.1   Definitions of terms used in the book.

Terms	Definition
Betterment	Increases in the value of a parcel land that arise from many factors including:
	(a) the impact of public investment, such as transport, which increases accessibility, thus raising demand for that parcel and hence its market value
	(b) the impact of granting planning permission for development, including change of use, which in itself increases market value by allocating development rights
	(c) the impact of overall economic performance of the nation and of specific locations which is reflected in higher land values
Betterment Levy	The levy on development value introduced in 1967
Community Infrastructure Levy	A levy that local planning authorities may charge developers for contributions to infrastructure introduced in 2008
Development Charge	The tax on development value introduced in 1947
Development Land Tax	The tax on development value introduced in 1974
Development Value	The difference between the market value of a parcel in its existing use and that in a proposed new use
Market value	The value of a parcel of land, including any buildings erected on it, when it is traded in the market or acquired compulsorily when compensation is paid at market value
Planning agreements	The legal agreements between developers and local planning authorities setting out the obligations that have been agreed. Known as S106 agreements after the clause in the principal planning legislation
Planning Gain	The gain in market value created by granting planning permission (i.e. also definition (b) under 'Betterment' above), some or all of which may be extracted through taxation of contributions via planning obligations. It is a term that has also been used colloquially to describe planning obligations *per se* as well as the overall increase in market value of the land
Planning obligations	The contributions developers agree to provide in terms of infrastructure and community facilities – in cash and in kind – following negotiations with local planning authorities about planning permission

The structure of the book

This book on England's experience of planning gain is timely for three reasons. First, there is much interest in the ways that we tax betterment and capture planning gain. However, because this experience is peculiar to England, there is a risk of inappropriate policy transfer and application in quite different contexts. This book tries to ensure that both the context and the operation of planning gain in England are made clear. Second, following the global financial crisis, fiscal austerity has dominated the economies of many of the world's developed countries, making it necessary to find new ways of financing infrastructure and community needs, especially from the private sector. This places an imperative on understanding the potential for designing planning and taxation systems for achieving new sources of funding. Third, the conceptual and empirical literature on planning gain is scattered across many learned journals and a range of research reports commissioned by government and related agencies. The aim is therefore to bring this source material into one place and to critically examine experience. The editors and the other collaborating authors have undertaken much of this earlier work, but each chapter has been specifically written for this volume, informed by our experience and knowledge.

This book describes and analyses the ways the planning system in England addresses three related challenges.

1. First, it clarifies how the land-use planning system may contribute to the generation of development values.
2. Second, it considers whether these increases in development values may be taxed without adversely affecting the efficient allocation of land and, if so, how.
3. Third, it demonstrates how these gains can help to fund the infrastructure and other community needs, including affordable housing, required to implement agreed development and land-use plans.

To address these questions, in the chapters of the book that follow this introductory chapter, we set out the conceptual and policy frameworks for looking at development values and the funding of infrastructure; second, we examine the specific experience of English policy and practice in the last two decades; and third, we look at the experience of selected countries as well as more general international evidence to see how others have addressed these issues. Finally, we seek to draw lessons both for England and elsewhere on how planning systems can deal with significant growth and development pressures in the face of continuing austerity.

Thus, in Chapter 2 we use the perspectives of economic theory and relevant empirical evidence to examine the price and supply of development land, to show how planning and the capture of planning gain impact on these and to examine the potential costs and benefits of implementing such policies. In Chapters 3 and 4, we look at how policy to 'capture' development value evolved. Chapter 3 looks back at the four attempts to tax development value through explicit national taxes and levies and shows how and why these failed to achieve their objectives. Chapter 4 then explains how planning obligations policy has evolved to become a *de facto* means of capturing development values at the local level to help fund infrastructure and affordable housing. In Chapter 5, we draw on financial economics and institutional theory to examine development costs, values and funding, how development projects are appraised, how outcomes vary spatially and temporally and how planning gain policies (both charges and taxes) affect the viability of developments.

The following three chapters look at empirical evidence on the operation of the planning gain system in England. They make use of a variety of perspectives to examine the extent of planning gain, how it is distributed across the country and how its extraction is achieved. In Chapter 6, we assess the evidence on the incidence and value of planning gain secured, using valuation principles based on economic theory to measure the value of planning gain contributions. In Chapter 7, we look at the significant variations in planning gain across England, using statistical analysis and insights from policy, subsidiarity and discretion to understand the differential impact of the market and the state on planning gain. The distinct contributions of tariffs and negotiated contributions to the capture of planning gain are also considered. Chapter 8 looks at what has been delivered in terms of affordable housing and infrastructure, in particular showing how far negotiations following initial agreements have maintained or indeed increased what is delivered as well as maintaining viability for developers. It also reveals how recent policy changes (described in Chapter 4) that mix fixed charges with negotiated contributions are affecting delivery in a changed economic environment.

In Chapter 9, we examine the planning gain capture systems in four other developed countries and use our framework to compare the range of approaches. Finally, in Chapter 10 we draw conclusions about the achievements and failures of the planning gain systems in England and other countries and identify lessons for the future that can be drawn from this evidence.

Conscious that some readers may 'dip into' the book and read specific chapters before reading the book as a whole, we have deliberately repeated or summarised some limited relevant material from previous chapters so that the context for the detailed analysis or findings of the selected chapter are clear.

References

Bill, P. (ed) (2004) *Building Sustainable Communities: Capturing Land Development Value for the Public Realm*, The Smith Institute, London.

Brown, G.R. and Matysiak, R. (2000) *Real Estate Investment: A Capital Market Approach*, Pearson Education, Edinburgh Gate, Harlow.

Campbell, H., Ellis, H., Gladwell, C., and Henneberry, J. (2000) Planning obligations, planning practice and land-use outcomes. *Environment and Planning B* **27**, 759–775.

Crook, A.D.H., Dunning, R., Ferrari, E.T., Henneberry, J.M., Rowley, S., Watkins, C.A., Burgess, G., Lyall-Grant, F., Monk, S., and Whitehead, C.M.E. (2010) *The Incidence, Value and*

Delivery of Planning Obligations in England in 2007–08, Department of Communities and Local Government, London.

Crook, A.D.H. and Monk, S. (2011) Planning Gains, Providing Homes. *Housing Studies* **26**, 997–1018.

Crook, A.D.H. and Whitehead, C.M.E. (2002) Social housing and planning gain: is this an appropriate way of providing affordable housing? *Environment and Planning A* **34**, 1259–1279.

Cullingworth, J.B. (1975) *Environmental Planning 1939–1969. Volume 1: Reconstruction and Land Use Planning, 1939–1947 [Peacetime History]*, Her Majesty's Stationery Office, London.

Cullingworth, J.B. (1980) Environmental Planning 1939–1969. *Volume 4: Land Values, Compensation and Betterment [Peacetime History]*, Her Majesty's Stationery Office, London.

Cullingworth, J.B., Nadin, V., Hart, T., Davoudi, S., Pendlebury, J., Vigar, G., Webb, D., and Townshend, T. (2014) *Town and Country Planning in the UK*, Routledge, London.

Fainstein, S.S. (2012) Land value capture and justice. In: Ingram, G.K. and Hong, Y-H. (eds) *Value Capture and Land Policies*, Lincoln Institute of Land Policy, Cambridge.

Goodchild, R. and Munton, R. (1985) *Development and the Landowner: An Analysis of the British Experience*, Taylor & Francis, Abingdon, Oxford.

Hall, P. (1965) *Land Values*, Sweet & Maxwell, London.

Hall, P.A. and Soskice, D. (2001) *Varieties of Capitalism, the Institutional Foundations of Comparative Advantage*, Oxford University Press, Oxford.

Healey, P. (1997) *Collaborative Planning*, Macmillan, Houndmills, Basingstoke.

Healey, P., McNamara, P., Elson, M., and Doak, A. (1988) *Land Use Planning and the Mediation of Urban Change*, Cambridge University Press, Cambridge, MA.

Ingram, G.K. and Hong, Y-H. (2012) *Value Capture and Land Policies*, Lincoln Institute of Land Policy, Cambridge.

Jowell, J. (1977) Bargaining in development control. *Journal of Planning Law* 414–433.

Lichfield, N. (1989) From planning gain to community benefit. *Journal of Planning and Environment Law*, Feb, 68–81.

Monk, S., Whitehead, C., Burgess, G., and Tang, C. (2013) *International Review of Land Supply and Planning Systems*, Joseph Rowntree Foundation, New Earswick, York.

Oxley, M., Brown, T., Nadin, V., Qu, L., and Tummers, L. (2009) *Review of European Planning Systems*, National Housing and Planning Advice Unit, Titchfield, Fareham.

Reed, R. and Sims, R. (2008) *Property Development*, Routledge, Abingdon, Oxford.

Rydin, Y. (2003) *Urban and Environmental Planning in the UK*, Macmillan, Basingstoke.

2

The Economics of Development Value and Planning Gain

Christine Whitehead[1]

LSE London, the London School of Economics, UK

Introduction

The immediate objective of this chapter is to clarify the sources of planning gain and its distribution in order to better understand the relationship between planning systems and market responses. This in turn should provide some clarification of the factors which enable planning gain to be captured for the public good and the possible costs and benefits of such an approach.

The starting point must be the reasons why land is special and so allows the possibility of intervention to capture value without adversely affecting the allocation of land to its highest and best use. In order to clarify how and when this may occur we then look at how the market would allocate land in the absence of government intervention; clarify how intervention modifies the uses of land and can increase development values resulting in planning gain; and identify the extent to which this might occur without adversely affecting the efficient use of scarce land resources; and, thus, whether its capture by government for re-distributional purposes carries with it any trade-off in terms of that efficiency. The final section evaluates the results of this analysis with respect to the different approaches to generating and capturing

---

[1]Much of this chapter develops the approach first presented in Whitehead and Monk (2004). The author wishes to thank Sarah Monk for her continued involvement on this topic over many years.

---

planning gain and their overall impacts on land allocation and the distribution of wealth.

Why is land and its value special?

Land is one of the three identified factors of production – land, labour and capital – which are brought together to produce goods and services. Land plays a necessary part in all economic activities and like other factors is valued in terms of derived demand – that is, the value to the investor in the best possible use. In the land-use planning context land will normally be combined with capital and the necessary labour to produce property where production takes place and people live.

Land is also a consumption good in that people obtain direct value from its use and attributes – for example, we value gardens, both our own and other people's; the location of our home and also the availability of green space for its benefits to ourselves and others. How much we are prepared to pay for these attributes determines, as compared to other uses, the price of land in a free market.

Land is seen as a particularly complex and important factor of production for at least five main reasons:

1. The total quantity of land is almost completely fixed (except to the extent that small amounts fall into the sea and some is reclaimed). This is true at global, national and even local level to the extent that administrative boundaries are relevant to decision making.
2. Land is also physically fixed – it cannot be shifted to a more appropriate location, as is possible with labour or capital.
3. On the other hand, the attributes of specific plots of land can be modified by past and future investment in that land and by the impact of past uses on its attributes.
4. The use to which land is put and the investment that occurs in that land will often impact on the potential use of land in the surrounding area, generating both external costs and benefits.
5. Most importantly, all productive and consumption processes need land, although the amount varies greatly between products. On the production side, its use is most obvious in agriculture where the land directly generates the output; it is a core element in manufacturing, providing the location for both factories and distribution; it is the location of the vast majority of services because it helps to determine the size of the market and even web-based and intangible services need small amounts of land to enable provision. On the consumption side, land enters most obviously into housing choices but also impacts on the costs and accessibility of goods and services. Finally, the relationship between locations, notably

between residential and job locations, helps to determine both incomes and productivity.

The potential to tax increasing land values without generating inefficiency

In general, taxation (and subsidy) modifies market decisions – taxation reduces returns and shifts resources away from the production of taxed activities. This is undesirable in efficiency terms if the market was working well before the tax was imposed as the resources shift to a lower valued product. However, where the market is imperfect taxation can be used positively to address these failures and so incentivise a more efficient outcome.

Land is seen as different because we cannot create land (*pace* the odd bit of land reclamation) unlike additional capital or indeed labour of a given quality. To the extent that land is in fixed supply, land values are ultimately demand determined. As opportunities expand demand will also increase, leading to higher land prices. Because raw land cannot be lost or increased, suppliers simply accept the highest price they are offered and are seen as doing nothing to generate this value (Figure 2.1a). Equally if the government imposes a tax on the resultant value there is nothing the owner can do to avoid the tax. The highest and best use will remain the same and there are therefore no efficiency costs (Figure 2.1a). This is the basis of the Henry George School of Thought which remains an important element in thinking around taxation policy in many contexts, notably in the Marxist literature (Brown, 1997). George argued that the total revenue from land holding was 'economic rent' – that is, not necessary to keep it in that use so could at the limit all be taxed. This conceptualisation also lies behind much of the early thinking on planning gain, where it was argued that if the change of use and

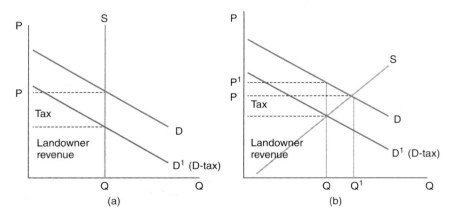

Figure 2.1   The impact of land taxation. (a) Land in fixed supply, (b) Land supply in a particular use.

therefore higher value use is fixed administratively then that value can be taxed without adversely affecting decisions around land use.

This model is highly simplistic: it assumes that all participants are fully informed and that there is certainty about all elements of decisions. Most importantly the assumption is that the model is addressing the *total* supply and demand of land and that all land is homogenous and all taxed equally (Evans, 2004).

None of these assumptions are realistic. In particular, land is not homogenous and there are costs to transferring land between uses. Demand for land for any particular use therefore depends on the whole range of attributes listed above, some of which are inherent and some of which are the result of investment and past use. This means that different physical attributes – quality of the soil, climate, accessibility, the ease by which attributes can be changed and so on – lead to the possibility of land being transferred between uses to achieve higher value. Suppliers can therefore vary their supply to different uses based on the costs and revenues/utility involved. The market will then in principle ensure that land is allocated to its highest valued use by matching land attributes through the productivity of the land in that particular use to the profitability (value in that particular use less costs of production) or net utility (value) perceived by the highest bidder. Thus, values depend on the quality and accessibility of each plot of land in relation to its potential uses. Possible uses will be affected by past investment in land and transport and by past uses which may have caused degradation or indeed improvement. Figure 2.1b therefore shows that for any particular use of land there will be an upward supply curve reflecting the capacity to shift land between uses as well as a demand curve which reflects other opportunities to achieve similar outcomes (so, for instance, there are different technologies using different amounts of land to achieve similar outcomes and which is chosen will depend on relative profitability – itself affected by the market price of suitable land). Any taxation or regulation which affects these choices impacts on the allocation of land resources. So if different uses are taxed at different rates (as is normally the case between rural and urban land or between different administrative areas) this will modify the mix of land uses and result in inefficiencies. So, for instance, the total land in the City of London is fixed but there are opportunities to move uses elsewhere meaning that a tax, subsidy or regulation on that land will change the uses and value of the land in the City as well as in the area to which the activity gets transferred – and land will be less productive.

Thus, only if all land is taxed at the same flat rate (i.e. no difference between areas – at the limit globally, between uses or between users – all of which are normal elements in practical land taxation) will there be no distortion in land use. Moreover, because in practice land values cannot be separated from the investment made in land, for example, by improving accessibility, and investment is often differentially taxed there are further distortionary possibilities.

Even in these circumstances, there are issues around vacant land which implies that there is no use with positive value. In simple models with homogeneous land there is no possibility of land vacancy but in reality there are many reasons why land may be vacant while other land has significant positive value. In urban areas, this tends to be about the degradation of land by past uses or possibly about the expectation of higher valued future uses, while in less accessible areas it may be because of the lack of transportation. But in all cases, differential taxation or regulation will lead to different proportions of vacant land as well as different uses for that land which has a net value.

The Alonso model of the allocation of land to urban uses and the resultant development value of that land provides one example of how land uses and values may be changed by taxation or regulation and so impact on the resource allocation (Alonso, 1964). Urban uses that are prepared to pay a price above the alternative use value – here assumed to be a homogenous agricultural value – determines the quantity of land that will transfer from agriculture to urban use. If urban opportunities increase (e.g. because of higher incomes, a larger population or higher productivity) demand for urban land will grow and the size of the urban area will also increase at the expense of agricultural land. Taxation or regulation which affects that transfer price will lead to a different allocation. If the market was otherwise working well this would result in too little urban land and too much agricultural land reducing overall societal incomes. The same applies if there are restrictions on allocating land between uses within the urban area. Of course, there may well be good reasons for modifying market decisions but the basis for that intervention needs to be clearly identified.

This leads us to another important issue: that of external costs and benefits which arise because one land use interacts with others in the surrounding area or sometimes locations quite far away. These external costs and benefits will not be taken into account by market decision makers but are relevant if land allocation is to be optimal. Indeed bringing together activities that benefit each other and separating those that do harm is a core reason for land-use regulation (Harrison, 1977).

The existence of externalities, the need for land-based public goods and infrastructure as well as other more general failures associated with inadequate information and uncertainties about the future generate the need for government intervention in the allocation of land if efficiency is to be achieved. However, it is important to note that each form of government intervention has different implications for land values and thus for distribution. Taxation of land reduces the net benefits to the owner; subsidy increases them but in particular the costs and benefits of regulatory intervention 'lie where they fall'. For example, if a given productive activity generates external costs then the amount of land given to that use will be reduced and the price of the land that is allocated will increase leading to higher economic rent while that which is not allocated declines leading to lower prices. As such, the change in value is borne by the owner, unless there is further intervention through taxation or subsidy which intentionally transfers resources, for example, through the capture of the resultant economic rent.

Thus, the idea of taxation without adversely affecting the efficient choice of land uses is firmly based on market economics. While the assumptions are unrealistic it clearly suggests that there is the potential for land value taxation to improve distributional outcomes without generating inefficiency. But it also makes the case for taxing all land values rather than concentrating on the taxation of betterment or planning gain. So why the emphasis on 'capturing' particular increases in land values, rather than the land values more generally through property taxation?

The impact of planning on development values – the creation of planning gain

Planning gain is defined as the increase in value which occurs at the time that planning permission is granted. Land-use planning provides a regulatory framework by which changes in land use are determined and standards are set through building, energy and sustainable environment regulations. It thus substitutes administrative for market decisions. By giving planning permission the authority opens up opportunities which have higher net revenues than those available before the permission. These are capitalised into a higher land price. The difference in price reflects the market estimation of the increased net revenues discounted at the market interest rate to determine the net present value of the change in use and is defined as planning gain.

How are these values achieved?

In terms of economic principles the objectives of the land-use planning system are first to improve the allocation of resources by organising the location of economic activities in such a way as to increase value and to modify the allocation of land in order to ensure a better distribution of resources among different groups of users. The first, if successful, must increase the value of land because, as we have already noted, land itself is in short supply and good planning increases the value of the activities undertaken on that land. As a result, demand for land increases and so does price. The second may actually reduce the market value because it reallocates the available land resources to those with less purchasing power (e.g. in the form of affordable housing) or less direct productive capacity (e.g. a public park). Even so, such regulation may increase social welfare by helping to achieve equity goals – but will be reflected in lower prices because the market does not recognise this social value. The core practical issue is that the granting of planning permission crystallises the net return from land-use change and provides a specific opportunity of capturing that increased value.

The examples mentioned above reflect situations when the planning system is working well. However, the system may also introduce administrative failures because of the lack of good information; inadequate responses to market power among potential land users; political pressures to constrain the use of land or to favour a particular use or many other factors that affect the authorities' decisions. Undesirable constraints, for instance, may already be in place before the planning permission is requested. Granting a permission to use the land for a purpose where the land is in short supply will result in higher increases in land prices than under a better operating system. An example of this occurring is when a local authority allows a site for residential use where overall the amount coming forward is less than optimal. So the price of the site may rise from £10 000 a hectare in current (say agricultural use) to maybe a million or even 10 million if a high-density residential site is allowed.

In all these examples, there is planning gain arising from the higher valued use of the land – but importantly that gain provides a market valuation of moving from one administrative decision to another. That decision may be the best that the developer and the market thinks is achievable given the way the law is determined and the authorities implement their powers – but it is a choice constrained by the land-use planning system for good or ill.

In order to better understand the implications of this process of generating planning gain it is important to clarify the different ways that planning impacts on land use and on prices in more detail (Bramley, 1994; Monk and Whitehead, 1999). We therefore now examine how planning works on supply, demand, densities and other aspects of development to modify decisions and outcomes and therefore prices, value and the potential to realise planning gain. In the discussion below we assume the change of use is to housing.

Planning affects land supply

Planning directly affects the supply of land by restricting the range of choices open to landowners. Where this restriction bites, the supply of land made available for development in that use will be less than would be expected without planning and the price of that land will be higher. This leaves land in its existing use which by definition has lower market value – but as there is now less available in that use that price may also rise depending on the scale of overall supply. The only obvious circumstances where this might not be the case would be if the planning system was totally ineffective.

Planning reduces the choices available to landowners in at least four ways:

1. it restricts the total quantity of housing land available for development;
2. it restricts the location of the land that is made available;
3. it restricts the way in which the land is developed; and
4. it alters the timing of the development.

All these impacts affect the profitability of development and thus whether development takes place and in what form. Equally importantly past planning decisions directly impact on what is currently profitable and desirable – it is not a static situation (Bramley, 2003).

In principle, it would be possible for planning to impose a binding constraint that fixes the total quantity of housing land, in which case the price of housing land would be entirely demand determined. But in practice, even under stringent planning conditions, the supply made available is responsive to demand to some degree. Therefore, the total supply under planning, while less than in a free market, will increase or decrease in response to changes in demand. When a new permission is given the supply curve shifts to the right. The price of housing land overall goes down – usually by an unobservable amount because the effect on total supply is tiny – but the price of the land with permission increases by the difference in value between the old and new use.

Importantly, different plots of land and types of houses are not complete substitutes for one other (Whitehead and Monk, 2004). Therefore, a constraint in one location cannot be fully offset by increased land availability elsewhere. The same is true for the form of development allowed and the timing of the investment. In the housing market for instance, more high-rise blocks of apartments on brownfield land may be given permission in order to achieve density objectives, while less greenfield land is released for single family homes. The total number of units achieved might be the same. However, because location and house types are only *partial* substitutes for each other, the effect of a given planning constraint is twofold: housing land prices increase in *all* locations and house types where permission is granted as there is overall constraint and some substitutability; but to the extent that substitutability is not complete, relative prices will increase more for the constrained locations (in this case the greenfield sites) and house types (low-density single family homes) than elsewhere.

Planning affects demand

Planning also affects the demand for land. Again using housing as an example, the planning system can, by improving design and environment, positively affect the price that consumers are prepared to pay for that housing. It can also affect their expectations of future house prices and therefore the value of housing as an investment good by their general stance of making land available.

Planning can affect demand negatively by limiting development and dwelling types, so that consumers cannot get what they want and so demand less. Similarly, planning may increase the costs of transforming land into housing, for example, by requiring particular attributes and limiting supplier options and by imposing a cost associated with obtaining planning permission. It can also reduce these costs by the better organisation of land between developments and by more effective infrastructure provision.

Because different locations and house types are not complete substitutes and because the costs of transforming land into housing vary, development profits also vary between sites. Therefore, the price developers will be prepared to pay for land will differ between and even within areas. Moreover, and importantly, the effect on profitability of development may affect whether builders are prepared to develop at all, even on land with planning permission.

Planning affects density of construction and use

If land prices rise relative to other factors of production, developers will try to reduce their use of land and increase densities – substituting capital for land. The extent of substitution is limited by technology, by the effect on the final house price as the product becomes less desirable, and directly by the planning system. As demand for better quality housing rises with increasing affluence, demand for plot size, dwelling size and quality will increase. But if planning causes the relative price of land to go up, substitution away from land towards dwelling size and quality would still result in larger plot sizes over time but to a lesser extent than size and quality. However, a direct planning constraint on plot size may increase both the density of development and the relative price of better quality existing units – and thus the incentive to provide new units at different densities.

New units may be required further down market to meet increasing demand from lower income households. In a free market, such households would demand small plots at high densities, but the planning system may restrict densities to maintain environmental standards and the nature of the local neighbourhood and so frustrate this demand. This is seen to be the situation in many better-off neighbourhoods in the USA where planning legislation is seen as a way of excluding lower income households (Gyourko, 1991 in the context of impact fees).

Finally, where planning restrictions help to determine what is provided, the actual use of the properties may be very different from that projected by planners as markets respond to these constraints. Thus, dwellings intended for families when planning permission is granted may be purchased by richer, single person or couple households who want more space than provided in the smaller dwellings or households may choose to have two homes in order to obtain the attributes they want. Thus, constraints can further increase the demand for additional units.

Planning affects prices and quantities

Through restricting the total quantity of land available and the type and location of development, planning will reduce the total quantity of new housing units produced. For a given demand for housing, average house prices will therefore be higher. The quantity of land cannot be adjusted as easily as other inputs, so as house prices rise, the proportion of the price attributed to land will also increase. Because the extent of planning constraints varies between areas, that proportion will also vary.

In the short run, house prices are demand determined because the total quantity of housing cannot be varied significantly and rapidly. Prices vary between house types and locations because of different demands for their relative attributes. These prices affect the residual value that builders are prepared to pay for housing land and therefore modify the quantity of land made available, the total quantity of house building and the location and types of dwellings produced.

In the long run, the price of housing is determined by its marginal cost of production, which includes the marginal cost of land. In a market system the marginal cost of land is its opportunity cost, that is, the cost in its next best use, and in the long run land will be brought on to the market into its highest valued use. In a planned system, transfer only occurs if the decision makers are prepared to agree. It may be that the decision is based correctly on relative net social values of different uses. But equally it may reflect quite other objectives, information or indeed decision-making capacity.

Bringing together the possibilities

Thus, land-use planning can, in principle, increase both demand and price; it can reduce market demand and thus reduce price and value; it can limit supply and therefore increase price; or it can increase supply and reduce price; or, most likely, it can do all of these together at the same time and in different parts of the market. In the context of residential land it is usually argued that land-use planning restricts the availability of land overall; it modifies the mix of land available – restricting supply and increasing prices in some areas and maybe expanding supply/reducing prices in others; it increases prices where the benefits of good planning are reflected in

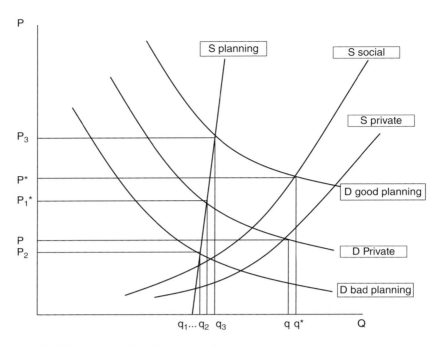

Figure 2.2   The impact of land-use planning; some scenarios.

higher demand and reduces demand in other areas where the process is less successful (Whitehead and Monk, 2004).

Figure 2.2, which sets out the possible impacts of land-use regulation, gives some idea of how complicated it can be to measure value and evaluate the impacts of planning decisions, even in a static world where we assume there is a single land market. In Figure 2.2, the market outcome (the baseline) is given by pq, and p_1q_1 reflects a constrained planning system where there is no impact on demand as a result of the constraints. However, at the worst the effect could be say p_2q_2 (lower price and quantity) because the quality of planning decisions adversely affects value; or p_3q_3 (higher prices and quantity) because the constraint is partially offset by higher demand reflecting the high quality of planning decisions which increase value for everyone. Finally, where would we ideally want to be? – perhaps at p^*q^* which reflects both the social costs of development and the value of high-quality planning decisions – but without unnecessary constraints?

It is an objective of planning to increase external benefits and reduce external costs. That is, planning has goals such as preventing urban sprawl and loss of countryside, unsustainable commuting, congestion and pollution, incompatible neighbouring land uses, and encouraging compatible land uses, sustainable development, mixed communities (because these are perceived as providing greater sustainability especially in terms of crime and low demand) and an enhanced environment. A related objective is to not only encourage the rehabilitation of depressed and dilapidated areas, including city and town centres, but also individual housing estates, so that these become attractive places to live and to visit. All of these, where successful, will add value to the uses of land that are permitted. So will the provision of infrastructure, including roads, schools, community facilities, green spaces and recreational spaces such as play parks and swimming pools. This increased value will be reflected in land and house prices. These will be higher than they would have been without the actions of land-use planning. This enhanced value is often known as 'betterment' in the planning literature.

The planning system does not aim to generate negative impacts. However, examples of negative impacts include the fact that there is now a very large gap between the value of land in agricultural use and its value in housing use. This is the result of planning constraint, in particular locations, notably in much of the South East where over 80% of the region's non-urban land is subject to one or more policy designations or constraints (ODPM 2001, p. 5). Of course, because planning reduces choice of what to build and where, it could be argued that all of England is subject to planning constraint – sometimes reflecting necessary adjustments for external costs and benefits but sometimes having no welfare reasons. Constraints have a cost because they push up house prices, making it increasingly difficult for new entrants to the housing market to be able to purchase a house. Thus, they suffer, while landowners gain in terms of the increased value of their asset.

Whatever the reason for the increased constraint, the result is that there is a difference in value between the existing uses for that land and in its new use. So taxing at the time of planning permission has four main benefits:

1. the permission itself is a well-defined point in time when the increased value can be captured in some way – by taxation, ownership or negotiation;
2. it allows the benefits of infrastructure investment which may not have been fully realised under existing land allocations better to achieve its potential;
3. because the new land value reflects expected future economic growth it enables these longer term benefits to be included in the capture base; and
4. it has the potential to provide funds for further infrastructure and other investment in the economy – although of course the 'tax' revenue could be used for more general purposes.

There are however costs, especially if the system involves the developer providing upfront finance before the actual development is generating revenue. In a perfect market, of course, this is readily addressed but in reality it can be a major issue.

Instruments available to capture planning gain

In principle, different instruments can generate similar revenues without impacting on efficiency. In practice, what works will be an outcome of legal systems, past experience, administrative capacity and many other factors (Mirrlees, 2010; 2011, Chapter 16). As Chapters 3 and 4 will clarify, the UK's experience of capturing increases in land values includes national taxation of all planning gain; some purchase of land at existing use value which then allows the provision of infrastructure and appropriate change of use and local planning obligations which allow negotiations to provide affordable housing and other local infrastructure.

National taxation apparently provides the simplest means of appropriating increases in land values arising from change of use. It can be set as a proportion of the increase in value and collected through the established tax system. As such, it will generate large-scale revenues in areas with economic growth potential and ensure that areas with relatively limited opportunities do not suffer. The revenues can go either to the national coffers or can be hypothecated to particular uses.

In practice, however, national taxation has proved to be extremely difficult in the UK context. The most immediate problems were associated with the tax rate of 100%. This reflected the most simplistic understanding of Henry George – that the enhanced value could all be taxed without adversely affecting the optimal use. However, this formalised model took no account of the fact that there is equally no incentive to change to the higher valued use – so at its simplest why bother? At least it was assumed that there were no transactions costs involved. The result was very little development took place except on public land.

There was a rather different but equally important problem with the use of public land – which continued into the 1980s – it was that land was not valued in public accounts let alone in relation to its economic value. As a result, the value of land was often taken to be zero which meant it was allocated to purposes which bore no relation to its most efficient use (Cheshire and Sheppard, 2005; Prest, 1981).

Many of the problems were associated with the uncertainties around valuation which resulted in a bonanza for lawyers and consultants and limited the revenues achieved. Political and other uncertainties also put off the development – and these continued even when tax rates were reduced to levels closer to more general capital gains rates. Perhaps most importantly, the funds went into the general national pot and local government felt disadvantaged by the lack of hypothecated funding for local infrastructure. A related issue was that national taxation adversely impacted on the incentives for local decision makers to make the most efficient use of the land – both because of the local external costs of much development (for which there was no offset) and because local interests played a significant role in determining decisions (Prest,1981). Thus, although economics would say that national taxation proportional to the enhanced values arising from planning permission might be expected to be the easiest approach to capturing planning gain, it actually proved highly ineffective.

The second approach is the one which is used in a number of European and other industrialised countries – that of purchasing land at existing use value, putting in the infrastructure and selling back into the market in its higher use (see Chapter 9 of this volume). Historically, in the UK, it has been applied mainly with respect to new town development corporations. It is now re-emerging in somewhat different guises in the context of revolving funds, joint ventures between local authorities and developers and the possibilities around garden cities (Chapter 4 of this volume; TCPA, 2014; Monk *et al.*, 2013). The process is simple – the local authority identifies where they wish to enable urbanisation and purchase that land at or near existing use value. They then put in the necessary infrastructure to make the value as high as possible in its desired use given social objectives and sell the land on to the market. In particular, they may decide to keep the land in public ownership at least until the potential market benefits of development are clear-cut (this may be of particular importance where regeneration is involved). One benefit is that no taxation is involved – at least until the development is in place and is generating revenues, at which point the property is subject to general local property taxation.

The model has worked well in countries with strong interventionist local governments as well as for very large-scale, long-term diverse investments where the sum is far more than the parts but realisation of benefits may take decades (Chapter 9 of this text; Monk *et al.*, 2013). However, it also brings with it the potential costs of administrative failure and wasted resources where the decision makers are not in a position to ensure development occurs in the identified locations or simply make the wrong choices. But most importantly, it requires upfront commitment, both political and financial, from the relevant government. In the UK it has worked well mainly in the context of national policy with respect to new and expanded towns and to a lesser degree Canary Wharf in London's Docklands. It has not been seen as relevant to more mainstream development opportunities.

It is in this context that the use of planning obligations has become the accepted approach to capturing planning gain. The approach was codified into something of its current form in the 1990 Town and Country Planning Act and now forms part of the National Planning Policy Framework (DCLG, 2014). It lies at the opposite extreme to a national tax with a country-wide tax rate being a set of requirements, including the provision of affordable housing, which is negotiated between the local planning authority and the developer. In principle, under conditions of certainty – that is where both sides know the details of the requirements – developers will take the net cost of these requirements into account (including any benefits to the development as a result of the negotiated infrastructure investments) and will reduce the price that they are prepared to pay for the land by that amount. Thus, the landowner pays for the obligations through a lower sales price; the developer puts forward the most profitable development for permission and the most valuable development takes place. More importantly, what is possible under this arrangement is determined by negotiation and so must fall within the available planning gain. Land valuations are not required (except as evidence on feasibility) and the extent of the obligation may vary not just by authority but also by site taking account of varying economic circumstances. Most importantly, the planning gain is used for the benefit of the local community whether in the form of site-specific or local infrastructure or affordable housing.

In practice, the model suffers from many of the same difficulties faced by other instruments aiming to extract planning gain for the public good. It is often unclear what the cost of the obligations will be; there are difficulties associated with the relative power of developers and local authorities; authorities may use their powers to generate inefficient investments; there are significant transactions costs and delays; the economic cycle impacts on both feasibility and the amount that can be captured; the environment for negotiation is anything but certain. Thus, the system may well generate considerable inefficiencies and, in particular, may raise considerably less than is in principle available.

There are two main forms of local planning obligations – a local tariff (which may in practice be set at a different level of government as with the transport precept) and a full site by site negotiated agreement. The first is clearly the more certain and the simpler to implement. However, it brings with it the usual average cost problem – the tariff cannot both maximise capture and stop some less profitable developments. It therefore may be set 'too low' in order to ensure development or 'too high' to gain the community benefits from higher valued development but at the cost of less development activity. The fully negotiated agreement in principle can avoid these problems but brings with it much greater uncertainty and transactions costs.

Including affordable housing within the remit of planning obligations adds an additional complication to their use on residential development the details of which are discussed in Chapter 4. It provides a particularly good case study of how planning obligations work and the economic costs and benefits of the approach as compared to other means of achieving similar aims (Crook and Whitehead, 2002; Whitehead, 2007; Austin *et al.*, 2014)

Overview

The economics of planning gain are apparently straightforward and as such have, like many other simple economic theories, appealed to politicians without the nuances being adequately understood. The simplest models of planning gain do suggest that it is possible to capture these gains without interfering with the efficiency of development. The reality is that there will always be trade-offs and deadweight losses associated with the reallocation of value away from landowners to the community – whether national or local.

Even so, the evidence suggests that land *is* different and the generation of large-scale increases in land values when change of use occurs presents the opportunity for taxation or other approaches to enable gains to be captured for the common good. What is also clear is that the legal and institutional environment as well as the history of taxation helps to determine what is feasible and has the best chance of generating incentives to ensure reasonable efficiency. The UK, as we have already noted in Chapter 1, is atypical in using individual site by site planning permissions. This, in turn, has helped to determine the relative success of particular approaches to capturing planning gain in the UK as compared to other countries. What is also true is that the UK system has been the subject of many changes over the decades. However, the economic principles remain the same.

References

Alonso, W. (1964) *Location and Land Use*, Harvard University Press, Cambridge, MA.

Austin, P., Gurran, N., and Whitehead, C. (2014) Planning and affordable housing in Australia, New Zealand and England: Common culture, different mechanisms. *Journal of Housing and the Built Environment* **29** (3), 455–479.

Bramley, G. (1994) The impact of land use planning and tax subsidies on the supply and price of housing in Britain. *Urban Studies* **30** (1), 5–30.

Bramley, G. (2003) Planning regulation and land supply in a market system. In: O'Sullivan, T. and Gibb, K (eds) *Housing Economics and Public Policy*, Blackwell, Oxford.

Brown, J.H. (ed) (1997) *Land Use and Taxation: Applying the Insights of Henry George*, Lincoln Institute Centre, Cambridge, MA.

Cheshire, P.C. and Sheppard, S.C. (2005) The introduction of price signals into land use planning decision-making: A proposal. *Urban Studies* **42** (4), 647–663.

Crook, A.D.H. and Whitehead, C.M.E. (2002) Social housing and planning gain: is this an appropriate way of providing affordable housing? *Environment and Planning A* **34** (7), 1259–1279.

Department of Communities and Local Government (DCLG) (2014) *National Planning Policy Framework, Planning Practice Guidance: Planning Obligations*, Available: http://planningguidance.planningportal.gov.uk/blog/guidance/planning-obligations/planning-obligations-guidance/

Evans, A.W. (2004) *Economics and Land Use Planning*. Blackwell, Oxford.

Gyourko, J. (1991) Impact fees, exclusionary zoning, and the density of new development. *Journal of Urban Economics* **30** (2), 242–256.

Harrison, A.J. (1977) *Economics and Land Use Planning*, Croom Helm, London.

Mirrlees, J. (2010 and 2011) *Reforming the Tax System in the 21st Century: The Mirrlees Review*, Oxford University Press, Oxford.

Monk, S. and Whitehead, C.M.E (1999) Evaluating the economic impact of planning controls in the United Kingdom: some implications for housing. *Land Economics* **75** (1), 74–93.

Monk, S., Whitehead, C.M.E, Burgess, G., and Tang, C. (2013) *International Review of Land Supply and Planning Systems*, Joseph Rowntree Foundation, York.

Office of the Deputy Prime Minister (ODPM) (2001) *Regional Planning Guidance 9*, ODPM, London.

Prest, A.R. (1981) *The Taxation of Urban Land*, Manchester University Press, Manchester.

Town and Country Planning Association (TCPA) (2014) *New Towns and Garden Cities – Lessons for Tomorrow. Stage 1: An Introduction to the UK's New Towns and Garden Cities*, TCPA, London.

Whitehead, C.M.E. (2007) Planning policies and affordable housing: England as a successful case study? *Housing Studies* **22**, 25–44.

Whitehead, C.M.E and Monk, S. (2004) *Does Spatial Planning Increase Value and Walfare?* Royal Town Planning Institute, London.

3

Capturing Development Value Through *de jure* National Taxation: The English Experience

Tony Crook

Department of Urban Studies and Planning, The University of Sheffield, UK

Introduction

This chapter describes the history of the four post-war attempts to tax development value through systems of nationally imposed taxes and levies. It describes the legislation, examines their impacts and explains why the four attempts were largely unsuccessful in collecting development value and the lessons that can be learned from them.

These attempts sought not only to collect development value through taxation measures but also tried, by bringing development land into public ownership, to deal with potential land withholding by owners liable to the taxes and who anticipated repeal of the legislation by a successor government. Although bringing development land into public ownership was as unsuccessful as were the attempts to collect development value taxes, the rationale was not solely to combat land withholding but also to ensure there was an adequate flow of development land to meet the needs identified in development plans. Bringing development land into public ownership through land banking was additionally seen as a means of collecting development value, by allowing public land banking agencies to buy development land at a price net of owners' development tax liability and then selling on serviced

Planning Gain: Providing Infrastructure and Affordable Housing, First Edition.
Edited by Tony Crook, John Henneberry and Christine Whitehead.
© 2016 John Wiley & Sons, Inc. Published 2016 by John Wiley & Sons, Inc.

land at the market value in its intended use after development, thus collecting some of the development value in the difference between the prices at which land was bought and later sold (net of holding and servicing costs).

The four attempts were the 1947 Development Charge, the 1967 Betterment Levy, the short lived 1974 Development Gains Tax and the combined 1975 Community Land Scheme (CLS) and 1976 Development Land Tax. The national agencies responsible for these (and for any associated land acquisition) were, in 1947 the Central Land Board, in 1967 the Land Commission and in 1974 and 1976 the central government department responsible for collecting taxes, but, in the case of the 1975 legislation, local planning authorities (hereinafter LPAs) played the role of acquiring development land, net of owners' of tax liabilities. No special land acquisition powers were created by the 1974 development gains taxes legislation.

These attempts mostly originated in left wing and Labour party policy discussions when in opposition and were later enacted, usually with major changes, in subsequent Labour government legislation. Each can be seen to have built on the lessons of earlier taxation schemes. Thus, for example, the 1947 legislation learned from the inter-war attempts to tax betterment (and from the 1942 Uthwatt report on the issues which had been commissioned by the wartime coalition government); the 1967 betterment levy was pitched at a lower rate than the 1947 development charge to reduce land withholding and also set up a central agency to buy development land; and the 1975 CLS similarly set an initial low levy rate but placed the land banking role in the hands of LPAs. Each of the attempts was, however, short lived. The 1947 legislation on both development value tax and compensation was scrapped in a series of steps in the mid- to late-1950s; the 1967 legislation was repealed in 1970; the 1974 legislation was replaced by the 1976 Development Land Tax, the CLS legislation ran from only 1975 to 1980, although the Development Land Tax was kept until 1985.

Although these attempts at collecting development value through nationally imposed taxes and levies and through nationally designed land banking schemes were short lived, this does not mean that the periods in between these attempts were ones where the issues were not salient because in each of the intervening periods (and also since the abolition of the Development Land Tax in 1985) governments were much concerned about rising land prices, shortages of development land with planning consent and about the problems of funding infrastructure to support development. Governments that abolished the four national schemes that could, *prima facie*, have addressed some of these concerns have constantly looked for other solutions which, as we shall see, included exhorting LPAs to make more land available with planning consent for development, finding ways of ensuring such land had adequate infrastructure in place, with initiatives such as land hoarding charges and local authority land banking schemes being regularly on the policy agendas.

Significantly for the theme of this book, the intervening periods between the later national schemes also included attempts to use planning obligations to get developers to fund infrastructure to ensure that planning permission was not refused because of the lack of supporting infrastructure. As we shall see, to the extent that the cost to developers of providing this infrastructure through planning obligations was passed on to landowners in the form of lower land prices, this became a *de facto* method of 'taxing' the development value enjoyed by landowners as a result of planning permission being granted for their land.

But the planning obligations 'story' is told in the next chapter. The purpose of this chapter is to examine the post-war attempts to collect development value through *de jure* taxation authorised by Parliament. This chapter has four further sections. The first section covers definitions of 'betterment' and how aspects of it might be subject to taxation. Second a review of the 'compensation and betterment' debates in the years leading up to the 1947 Town and Country Planning Act. The third, and the largest section, contains a description of the policies to tax development value through national taxation over the years 1947 to 1985 and the evidence about tax collected and their side effects on land supply. The fourth and the final section concludes with an assessment of the effectiveness of these measures and the lessons we can learn from them.

Betterment and development value defined

As we pointed out in Chapter 1, discussions of the issues analysed in this book have taken place within a set of terms that, because they overlap, can be confusing. The literature (including policy papers) refers variously to 'development value', 'planning gain' and 'betterment' sometimes as if they were the same thing. As we show in this section 'betterment' is a term used to define at least three types of increases in land value: that arising from infrastructure improvements, development value arising as a result of planning consent and all other increase in land values caused, for example, by increases in national income and the like. Here we are specifically interested in 'development value' – the increase in land value arising from the development of a parcel of land, including changes in its use as a result of planning consent.

In this chapter, we discuss how specific national land taxation measures have addressed the taxation of development value, that is, the increase in land value arising from the granting of planning consent. Land value can be defined as the economic rent arising from the carrying out of economic activity on a parcel of land and is the difference between all of the income arising from that activity on a distinct parcel of land and all the costs of winning that income (including the 'normal' profits expected from that activity). The difference between all of the income and all the costs (plus normal profit) is usually referred to as the residual land value and for any potential user this is the maximum amount that is worth paying to buy (or rent) that land. Competition for the land means it is likely that the actual land value will be the maximum residual value that can be extracted from that parcel and hence this will determine the land use, subject to any planning, other regulatory or private legal (e.g. restrictive covenants) constraints. Development value arises when development (which can include just a change of use as well as physical development) takes place, thereby increasing the income by more than any extra costs so that the residual value rises. Development value is the difference between the value of the land in its current use and its value after development, most often in the public imagination conceptualised as the difference between the value of land in farming use and its value following housing development. This is not to suggest, of course, that, subject to planning decisions, it is changes in land value alone that determine the use and other development of land. As we saw in Chapter 1, there are many other factors that determine whether land is bought and sold and how it is used and developed, including owners' sentiment and family and family trust obligations (e.g. especially in the case of aristocratic and other landed estates).

In countries with planning regimes development will generally only arise after the granting of planning consent (including by virtue of a zoning ordinance) and so the realisation of any development value is contingent on achieving planning consent (or complying with zoning ordinances) for the proposed development, including changes of use. Part of the argument for taxing the development value arising from permitted developments and changes of use has been that owners of parcels of land can often receive this without any effort on their part (an 'unearned increment') when developers buy their land and undertake new development on it. Moreover, where owners themselves carry out the development the residual value of their land will rise giving them both normal profits from the new activity on the parcel and the development value of that parcel.

Many have doubted whether it is possible to truly identify this unearned increment arising from (the alleged) 'no effort' on the part of landowners which justifies taxing all or part of it. Increases in land values arise from many factors and it may be difficult to identify that which is development value from all other factors affecting betterment. As Grant (1992) has pointed out (and we follow his argument closely in the remaining paragraphs of this section) there is no single authoritative definition of 'betterment' but the term can be used:

in a broad sense, as referring to any increase in the value of a parcel of land that can be attributed to factors other than the effort or investment of the owner or occupier (Grant, 1992).[1]

Grant argues that it arises in one of three ways, first, because the public sector undertakes physical improvements; second, because regulation (and in particular planning control) makes development possible, affecting the demand and the supply of parcels of land and third, because of a wide range of other factors, including private improvement of neighbouring parcels of land; fluctuations in the national economy and all other such factors affecting changing demands for land.

Grant then places the claims of the state or others to share in these three classes of 'betterment' into four main categories. First, it can stay in hands of those who receive it without any liability to tax. Second, betterment should be subject to capital gains tax, noting developers' claims that land is indistinguishable from other assets and that imposing differential land tax on developers constitutes a special tax on their trading profits rather than on windfall profits. Grant, however, argues that the windfall element may be far more significant to landowners and developers than to commercial enterprises. The third category has betterment being paid, wholly or partly, to the local or central state, through a differential system of taxation, treating land differently from other capital assets, treating accruals and real-isations under any of the three betterment classes mentioned above. They may be un-hypothecated taxes or applied specifically to some land-related policy such as infrastructure provision. Fourth, recoupment of betterment can be instruments of land policy designed, for example, to encourage land to be brought forward for development.

Grant shows that the most common mechanism for recouping better-ment is capital taxation. It was the basic method chosen in each of the four post-war schemes to tax development value. Other mechanisms involve public acquisition of the land at lower than market value in a proposed use, including in designated new towns and urban development corporations, where compensation for land purchase ignores any uplift in land values attributable to the statutory designation. Other methods in England include planning obligations (see Chapter 4), including the cross subsidisation of affordable housing by market housing on the same site (also Chapter 4). The nationalisation of land has also been mooted, and, as we shall see further in this chapter the basis for temporary public ownership of development land was made possible in the Land Commission Act of 1967 and the Community Land Act 1975, but this has not been a significant technique for capturing development value. Grant argues that each mechanism needs

---

[1] Quotation reproduced by permission of Thomson Reuters (Professional) UK Limited on behalf of Sweet & Maxwell Ltd.

to be assessed in terms of its incidence (to see who actually bears the cost); equity (as between different classes of affected agents), efficiency (past techniques have never scored particularly well under this heading) and land policy effects.

Although the arguments for capturing betterment vary according to Grant's three categories, all are to some extent based on the idea that the 'unearned increment' is wholly due to external factors and can be recouped through tax without unfairness to the owner and to the benefit of the state. It has also been regularly argued that such taxation has no impact on economic efficiency and on the allocation of resources. The cost of the tax is borne by the landowner and has no other impact, an argument which has been strongly refuted (see, e.g. Prest, 1981; this volume, Chapter 2).

In the case of local improvements (Grant's first class), the arguments for taxation are, according to Grant, the simplest (and there have in fact been attempts to do this going back over many centuries in Britain – see Prest, 1981). Where an off-site improvement is carried out by a public agency exclusively for the benefit of a particular parcel of land the cost should rest with the landowner rather than with taxpayers at large. But the answer is less clear where there is not exclusive benefit and consent. Collective benefit must imply collective charging, and the broader the area of betterment the greater the practical difficulty in apportioning the cost amongst all benefited landowners, so there comes a point where arguments of both equity and practicability require a shift to general taxation (if a practical method for taxing only those benefiting cannot be found).

As Grant argued the impact of planning controls provides a wholly different basis for betterment arguments. The pattern of land value distribution in an unplanned town is distorted by the introduction of planning. Some sites are favoured for development; others are not, and many development expectations are unrealisable. There is a significant change in the distribution of land values, as demand switches to sites allocated for higher value uses. The case for taxing betterment in the form of development value here rests on the argument that the owners of benefited properties have received an unearned increment and should be taxed on it. However, it is also accompanied by the proposition that owners of the other properties not obtaining permission have suffered 'worsement' and accordingly should be compensated for these losses. The wartime coalition government set up the Uthwatt committee to examine these intertwined issues and we review its arguments (and its critics) in the next section.

Grant's third category comes about partly by default, but has not been undertaken much in practice partly through the seeming impracticability of separating out the contributing factors in land value enhancement. Although to the classical political economists, it was a more obvious base point for land taxation, not related simply to betterment arguments, but to the monopolistic position of landowners, it has received much less attention in practice than in theory compared with Grant's first two classes (Prest, 1981, summarises the views of Adam Smith and JS Mill on this). And, in practice, it has been the arguments about taxing the unearned increment arising from the grant of planning permission that have received the most attention, both in political debate and in practice.

Compensation and betterment: the Uthwatt principles

Having defined how we are using terms, we now turn to a key government report on compensation and betterment commissioned during the Second World War. Although the report used the term 'betterment', it mainly, but not exclusively, addressed the specific problem of taxing development value.

Land values can increase, as we have seen in the previous section of this chapter, for several reasons including that of public action, for example, when new transport infrastructure, funded by general taxation, improves accessibility and increases development opportunities which are then reflected in higher land values, raising the question of whether the beneficiaries, that is the landowners, should be taxed on all or some of the increase. These questions relate to both allocative efficiency (the effect on the allocation of resources) and distributional equity (the fairness of whom in society receives this increased value). Pre-war debates mostly concerned the equity issues arising from the introduction of a comprehensive system of land-use planning. It was assumed that taxing the development value which would be created when planning permission was granted would have no effect on the allocation of resources and output and that it was only fair to tax these 'unearned increments'.

When a parcel of land is allocated for development in a formal statutory development plan, greater certainty is created about its future use, especially when planning permission is granted for new development on allocated (and on any unallocated or 'windfall' sites) sites. Such prior allocations and the later granting of planning consents can create significant development value. The ethical argument for taxing this increased value is based on the proposition that the landowner has not created the value of a particular parcel, but that the 'community' has done so in agreeing a development plan for an area. Of course, this does not negate the initiative and enterprise of the developer (who may also be the landowner) in undertaking the development but argues that development value is economic rent which can be taxed with no impact on efficiency, whereas the developer will be rewarded by taking normal profits from the proposed scheme. Hence, the development value should be taxed.

The debate in the immediate pre-war years hinged fundamentally on this equity issue which those wanting to introduce a comprehensive system of land-use planning in England had to address (for reviews and analysis, see: Bill, 2004; Cullingworth, 1975, 1980; Hall, 1965; Lichfield and Connellan, 2000; Parker, 1987; Prest, 1981). The principal issues they faced, analysed in detail in the report of the Expert Committee on Compensation and Betterment chaired by Lord Uthwatt (Ministry of Works and Planning, 1942), were whether those benefiting from planning consent through a rise in development value should be taxed on all or some of this and whether those whose land was not allocated for development who did not get consent should in some way be compensated for a loss of putative development value. As Uthwatt noted, this problem would not arise if land was in public ownership but, although land nationalisation was a 'logical' solution, there was not likely, given the political controversy about land nationalisation, to be a change from the private nature of ownership in Britain (except at the margin as a result of compulsory or other acquisition for various 'public' uses including defence, health, education and social rented, housing). Thus, the issues of compensation and betterment had to be addressed.

The 'compensation' issue was a particularly critical one because when a comprehensive planning system is introduced, *de novo*, all existing landowners can have a claim that their land would have been selected by a developer, at least at some time in the future. Hence, it would be inequitable if those whose land was given consent benefited from development values, whilst they whose land was not selected for development through the planning system did not get any compensation. However, this posed a difficult challenge because, whilst it was simply unfeasible that all land would eventually be selected for development, the landowners of every parcel of land would have some argument that theirs ultimately would have been. Uthwatt identified this as 'floating value', recognising that receipts in a tax on development values (which the report called 'betterment') would not be enough to fund compensation for the loss of 'floating values'. This had been a crucial problem in the 'compensation and betterment' schemes set up in pre-war years in 1909 and 1932 which worked on an 'as you go' principle, run by local authorities with tax on development value ('betterment') being collected (50% under 1909 legislation and 75% in 1932) when development took place and compensation paid out when consent was denied. However, 'betterment' was hard to collect whilst compensation was difficult to avoid, and made worse when the collecting authority was different from the compensating authority. To avoid this problem, planning authorities allocated enough land for a population of 290 million people (although this was also the result of optimism by all planning authorities about the prospects for development in their individual areas). Between 1909 and 1939, only three cases of betterment were ever collected under planning legislation. Although this idea of 'floating value' has since been much criticised (see, e.g. Prest, 1981) it was very influential in the Uthwatt's committee's thinking, as we shall see below.

The Uthwatt committee's other central proposition was about 'shifting values' which is that planning shifts land values but does not increase them. To quote the report:

> the public control of the use of land, whether it is operated by means of the existing planning legislation or by other means, necessarily has the effect of shifting land values: in other words, it increases the value of some land and decreases the value of other land, but it does not destroy land values. Neither the total demand for development, nor its average annual rate is materially affected, if at all, by planning ordinances. If, for instance, part of the land on the fringe of a town is taken out of the market for building purposes by the prohibition of development upon it, the potential building value is merely shifted to other land and aggregate values are not substantially affected, if at all. (Ministry of Works, 1942)

This has since been much criticised, owing to its unrealistic assumptions of being based on a static, rather than dynamic understanding of land prices. For planning in practice does not simply shift values but also affects the profitability of the uses from which the demand for land is derived. So if planning produces greater certainty and also a more efficient arrangement of land uses, overcoming negative externalities and providing public goods it will increase utilities and profitability and lead to higher land values. Likewise poor planning policy can lead to lower land values. Although values will shift under planning, it is clearly not a 'zero sum' operation. The impact of regulation may be to suppress demand, to cause it to be met by other supplies of land (e.g. redevelopment of existing sites), to force some actors out of the market altogether or simply to move to another location (Adams and Watkins, 2014; Chapter 2, this volume; Prest, 1981).

The Committee proposed to deal with these two challenges of 'floating' and 'shifting' value by not only recommending the nationalisation of all development rights on undeveloped land but also recognising the need to provide incentives for landowners to bring land forward for development. Development rights were to be vested in the State with compensation paid to all owners from a fixed sum defined as the fair value to the State of the development rights taken as a whole and divided amongst all claimants in proportion to the 1939 estimated development value of their holdings. When development took place the land involved would be acquired compulsorily by the state. When the State needed to acquire the land for itself it would pay pre-war prices, other development land would be bought at post-war (but existing use) prices and leased back to developers with a 75% levy on future increases in site value, thus securing a share in future increase in land values for the whole community, irrespective of the source of the 'betterment' (and hence covering all Grant's classes of betterment: see aforementioned), and dead ripe land (needed for immediate development with schemes in existence) would be bought at full value.

But after much discussion and debate (Cullingworth, 1980; Prest, 1981) the legislation that finally emerged in 1947 was different.

Taxing development value: post-war national schemes

The subsequent history of taxing development values through national levies is complex, but the key lessons of the four post-war attempts to formally do so are pertinent to the subsequent use of planning obligations as a local and *de facto* alternative means of securing a share in development value with proceeds hypothecated to fund local infrastructure and affordable housing. Table 3.1 summarises the key attributes of these four attempts. In general, much less tax was raised by each of the measures than was expected by protagonists and by Ministers as the legislation went through Parliament. We have quoted the sums raised in tax both at the nominal prices at the time of collection and we have also calculated their yield at 2007–2008 prices, using the GDP deflator. We use 2007–2008 as the year for this latter calculation as it is one of the years for which we can compare the yield from national taxes with that raised by LPAs from planning obligations (see Chapter 6).

As Cox (1984) has remarked, this post-war history represents a series of policy changes, alternating between approaches which were neither dramatically different nor radical, that is, between fiscal-regulatory (Conservative) and fiscal-interventionist (Labour) approaches. More radical approaches were constrained by many interests including landed (whose interests are not solely economic), property (with economic power, despite not being accepted as 'respectable' in the way landed interests were), productive (willing to accept limited state interventions), professional (rejecting *laissez-faire* approaches), financial (interests that were increasingly tied up with land), pressure groups (from the middle classes and social democratic traditions) and state agencies (which did not support a dominant role for the state). Cox argued that fiscal regulatory approaches were the only realistic ways of getting compromises between most of these interests, especially the state, productive, landed and financial interests, whereas fiscal interventionist approaches (enabling public land assembly and development) were at the boundary of what radical approaches could achieve. Although the latter were feasible in the UK, they were difficult to implement because of reluctant local authorities and the difficulties of persuading landowners and developers of the advantages of this for them.

Cullingworth (1980, p. 414) also noted that 'looking back' on the debates on these oscillating policies as government changed hands 'one cannot but be

Table 3.1 The four national attempts to tax development value.

Dates	Tax	Agency collecting tax	Tax/Levy rate on development value	Total gross tax/Levy raised per annum (nominal prices)	Total tax/Levy raised per annum (2007–2008 prices)	Agency acquiring land	Land acquired
1947–1952	Development Charge	Central Land Board	100%	£8m in 1952	£172m	Central Land Board	35 Compulsory purchase orders
1967–1970	Betterment Levy	Land Commission	40% initially, due to rise to 80%	£32m in 1969–1970	£356m	Land Commission	2800 acres
1974–1976	Development Gains Tax	Inland Revenue	82% (individuals) and 52% (companies)	Estimated at £80m pa at time of legislation	Na	Na	Na
1975–1986	Community Land Scheme and Development Land Tax	Inland Revenue but with local authorities buying net of tax	66–80% depending on amount to be taxed; reduced to 60% in 1980	£68m in 1983–1984	£147m	Local Planning Authorities (Land Agency in Wales)	2357 acres between 1967/77 and 1977/78

Source: Taken from the text in this chapter.

struck by the extraordinary amount of heat engendered by arguments over a relatively narrow field of disagreement' for throughout the period there was consensus over the need for planning control, for the recovery of some development value and the payment of some compensation.

Prest (1981) thought some of this apparent consensus arose from the pressure to ensure that local authorities could acquire land cheaply for redevelopment and for rented housing. He also noted that debates about the impact of planning on land prices were shaped by a discourse about the role of the 'community' in contrast to that of the 'landowners', with proponents of taxation arguing that, as it was 'the community' and not 'landowners' who had created these higher values, the 'community' too should share all (or some) of them. In contrast to this discourse he noted the lack of adequate economic analyses of development tax proposals compared with those carried out on other public policies. Thus, earlier 'classical' ideas about economic rent being special to land were constantly perpetuated in order to justify treating gains in the development value of land differently from, say, other capital gains, even when repudiated (he argued) by later economic thinking.

1947: The development charge and the central land tribunal

The 1945 post-war Labour government did not proceed with the full Uthwatt recommendations. Instead in 1947 all rights to development were nationalised (henceforward all development has needed permission and planning authorities have been required to prepare development plans as one of the bases for deciding whether or not to permit development). The development values associated with these development rights (but not the land itself, save on compulsory purchase for necessary development) were also nationalised. The Labour government decided to tax the development value realised by the grant of planning permission at the rate of 100% (the development charge) to be paid to a newly created Central Land Board by the purchaser or developer before the permitted development was carried out. Thus, landowners received (at least in principle) only the existing use value.

Since the totality of development value was to be taxed there was no need to compensate those whose land did not receive permission. Similarly, those whose land was acquired compulsorily would receive only the value in its existing, not intended, use in compensation. However, to compensate for the nationalisation of development rights, and to overcome the problem of floating value in doing this, the government set up a 'once and for all' *ex gratia* compensation fund of £300m against which all who considered their land had some expectation of future development and hence some 'floating value' in 1947 could claim. Once these claims had been examined and, if eligible, paid 'once and for all' there would be no merit in charging less than 100% on development value when permission was granted and no merit in paying any compensation when permission was withheld or land was compulsorily acquired. The plan was to pay out on all admitted claims on the *ex gratia* fund in 1951. It was assumed that land would henceforward change hands only at the value in its existing use. Under these 1947 arrangements future increases in land value were not, as had been proposed by Uthwatt, to be taxed.

The operation of these arrangements was given to a Central Land Board whose duties were to assess and levy development charges on new developments and to administer the *ex gratia* compensation payments out of central funds. The board was also empowered, with ministerial approval, to acquire land by agreement or compulsory purchase and to dispose of it for development.

The design of the 1947 system had assumed that the majority of development would be undertaken by the public sector and that much development would take place in publicly funded and organised New Towns. But when both of these assumptions proved unfounded and there was a move towards a greater mix of private and public development, the 100% charge on development value acted as an inhibitor to private land coming forward for development. This was at a time when the state had inadequate funds to acquire it and transfer the land to private developers. There was also doubt about the legal authority for the Central Land Board or local authorities to compulsory purchase for 'land banking' in this way and thus to overcome land withholding or the trading in land above existing use value (Cullingworth, 1980; National Archives, 2013).

As a result, land for private development changed hands at more than existing use value adding to development costs. At the time building materials were rationed and licences were required in order to obtain them. Those gaining the limited number of licences were keen to acquire land. As a result, discussions (but no decisions) took place about reducing the charge to 80%. The development charge had in any case proved difficult to estimate, little had been collected (£13.4m between July 1948 and December 1951), although there was evidence that total charges were increasing by 1952 and were running at a rate of £8m per year (House of Commons Hansard, 1952), equivalent to £172m at 2007–2008 prices. And there were also worries about the inflationary effect of paying out the £300m fund. The Board had made only 35 compulsory purchase orders by the time it was wound up in 1952. As Cox (1984) remarked in his own conclusions on the 1947 Act, it took profit and incentives out of the market, but without ending the operation of the market.

To restore incentives to ensure that private landowners and developers came forward with building projects, the subsequent Conservative government (elected on a manifesto to greatly increase house building) dropped the development charge and suspended compensation payments in 1953 but restored the latter in 1954 on a much more limited basis so that until 1959 a dual market was established, distinguishing the market prices that landowners received for land for private development from the existing use prices they only received if their land was subject to public acquisition (Cullingworth,1980).

Whilst the position with respect to the nationalisation of development rights has remained unchanged since 1947, the state has, over time (but with the exception of the later national 1967 and other schemes), returned all the associated development values to developers. However, giving compensation to those refused planning consent would have made land-use planning impossibly expensive and ensured that planning decisions were strongly influenced by financial consideration in limiting compensation payments (as had happened in pre-war years). But there were perceived problems in creating what would be in effect a dual market: full development values realised when (mainly private) development took place but only claims on the *ex gratia* fund for those whose land did not get planning consent and who had an admitted claim, or claims plus existing use value for those whose land was requisitioned by compulsory purchase. In the view of the then Minister of Housing, Harold Macmillan (whose Ministry included responsibilities for planning), this 'rough justice' was acceptable to ensure development proceeded whilst also ensuring planning decisions were based on sound planning principles, not financial considerations. Macmillan's counterpart in the Treasury, 'Rab' Butler, disagreed and thought that a surge of compensation claims would be impossible to prevent and that paying out at more than 1947 values could not be resisted for long. Because there was no longer to be a development charge to help fund these claims the Treasury would argue for fewer planning restrictions.

The Macmillan view prevailed. The Development Charge was abolished, claims on the 'once and for all' fund were not paid out (unless owners could prove there was no reasonably economic use possible and permission had been refused) and compensation for compulsory purchase was restricted to existing use value and admitted claims. Some have argued (e.g. Merrett, 1979) that this limitation was also needed because paying market prices to buy land for social rented housing built by local authorities would have made construction costs and subsidies for council housing prohibitively expensive. But the 'odium' of this dual market became hard to defend (there was a suicide of someone whose land had been compulsorily acquired) and as a result, from 1959 onwards, compensation for compulsory acquisition was subsequently based on market value (based on a certificate of alternative use) but with two important exceptions, compulsory acquisition of land for New Towns and for the comprehensive redevelopment of city centres in declared and confirmed Comprehensive Development Areas (CDAs) where the price paid took no account of the impact of the proposed development on market values. Without these two exceptions, funding for the land needed in New Towns and in CDAs would have become impossibly expensive.

1967: Betterment levy and land commission

However, controversy over rising land values in the 1960s drew government back into these matters in order to deal as much with development land shortages as to ensure equity about development values (Parker, 1987). The Conservative government argued in the early 1960s that rising values reflected growing prosperity and the answer was not to tax land values (although a speculative capital gains tax was introduced in 1962) but to ensure that LPAs provided an adequate supply of development land with planning consents. Although policy proposals made towards the end of the government's life (in 1964) included programmes of advance purchase of development land by the public sector followed by disposals to private developers (thus also enabling some development value to be collected), especially in the context of implementing the South East Study (which was drawn up to examine how increasing development pressures should be handled), these more interventionist proposals were thwarted by landed and property interests (Cox, 1984).

But after the 1964 election of a Labour government, legislation created a new central body in 1967, the Land Commission, whose duty it was to collect a 'betterment levy' to be fixed at 40% of development value. The levy was to be collected on all transactions where development value was realised. It was to be paid by the recipient of the development value when a chargeable event such as the commencement of development occurred (and not on the grant of planning permission as in the 1947 legislation), including if there were any further increases in development value. The levy was calculated as the market value less a base case. The latter was set at more than the existing use value used by the Central Land Board under the 1947 arrangements and was 110% of current use or the acquisition price to provide incentives (Cullingworth, 1980; Hall *et al.*, 1970).

Initially the incoming Labour Government, having been persuaded to move away from outright land nationalisation as it would disrupt the market too much, had wanted the Land Commission to be a body that would assemble all development land, put in the infrastructure required, and then sell it on to developers, thereby gaining some of the development value created. Thus, the dual aims were not only to collect development value (similar to 1947) but also to ensure land was available when and where needed by giving the Commission stronger powers of land acquisition than had been afforded the Central Land Board in 1947 (including compulsory purchase and quick conveyancing). But as the detail was worked up (and as officials worried that the market would be disrupted) it became clear that it would take time for the Commission to build up the necessary expertise and capacity. During this period, a levy would be needed to collect development value, but set at a low rate (i.e. 40%) that would not encourage land withholding. When the Commission was a major land acquiring body (and then buying at existing use value) the levy would rise, perhaps to 60 or even to 80%. The Commission would be able to sell land at concessionary prices to not-for-profit housing associations (who provided social rented homes) and local authorities, but reserving the right to any future increases. Meantime it would buy land net of the levy.

But the Commission had a short lived life and did not proceed to a significant fiscal interventionist role that some (but not all) Minsters had wanted. It acquired very little land, first because it had to acquire it within a framework of approved (but badly out of date) statutory development plans drawn up by LPAs. This restriction aimed to ensure the Commission's land buying did not stray into areas where development had not been identified in approved plans. Second, its budget for buying land was inadequate. In the course of its short life there was discussion about allowing the Commission to buy 'white land', that is, land not allocated in development plans in order to build up a larger land bank. Although it was intended that it acquired a quarter of all house building land it had, at the time of its winding up, acquired only 2800 acres between 1967 and 1971, mainly in the north of England and in areas of slack housing demand (Hall *et al.*, 1973), and had spent only £6m of the initial £45m provided to it for land acquisition (Cullingworth, 1980, p. 366).

It also collected little betterment levy, partly because developers were able to avoid the levy by establishing that works had begun before the levy had been imposed. It collected only £54m out of the £81m it had assessed and at a cost of 12.5% of the betterment levy collected (Cullingworth, 1980, p. 392), running at the end of its life at a rate of £32m a year in 1969–1970 (£28m net of collection costs), the gross amount being worth £356m at 2007–2008 prices.

Although abolition was announced in 1970 when the Conservatives returned to power (the Conservative-dominated shire counties in England had felt threatened by the Land Commission) the Commission had by then lost a lot of its credibility (and the previous Labour government had even itself discussed its abolition). It was formally abolished in 1971. Many argued that the Commission was responsible itself for rising land prices because the levy was passed on by sellers, land was kept off the market because of the levy and by the opposition's promise to repeal the legislation. As a result, developers had to pay high prices to get the land they needed (Hall *et al.*, 1973). However, its inability to acquire land was also the result of the lack of up-to-date statutory development plans because the Land Commission was unable to acquire other land for its land-banking role and was in any case hampered by the lack of borrowing to undertake this task. Any land withholding was as much due to the expectation of early repeal by a new government as it was to the impact of the betterment levy as such, showing that owners' and developers' expectation about continuity in legislation is as important as the impact of the detail of the legislation (e.g. levy rates) itself.

Abolition paradoxically removed the one body that could have addressed the intransigence of LPAs to the release of adequate development land, the continuing lack of which troubled all post-war governments with resulting concerns about high house as well as land prices (because the shortage of development land constrained the output of new homes), especially its impact on the costs of building social rented homes, the way rising prices encouraged land hoarding and also, it was argued by some, by the way it sucked finance into land speculation rather than other enterprises (a problem exacerbated by lax monetary policy in the early 1970s).

To address this problem, the incoming 1970 Conservative administration did not attempt to collect development value via an explicit levy but instead taxed gains as part of general capital gains taxation. But whilst it mainly focused on exhorting planning authorities to improve the availability of developable land in development plans and granting enough planning permissions for 5 years' worth of needed development, it also allowed local authorities to borrow funds to buy land, service it and then sell it on to developers in areas where comprehensive development was needed but where there was also evidence of land withholding. Some of these initiatives included joint ventures with house builders, involving equity sharing arrangements. It additionally encouraged planning authorities to use planning agreements (now known as planning obligations) to secure developer contributions to infrastructure in circumstances where permission would otherwise be refused for want of public funds to build the infrastructure required (see, e.g. Heald, 1974; see also DoE, 1972). In addition, policies were mooted (but dropped) to set up a land hoarding charge on land held by those with unimplemented planning permissions, with the charge rate being dependent on the length of time over which planning consent on a site went unimplemented, but starting at 30% if left for 4 years (DoE, 1973). A higher rate of capital gains tax from disposals (including through leases) of land with development potential was briefly introduced through the proposed 1973 Development Gains Tax legislation (82% for individuals and 52% for companies). This was to be charged on 'substantial' capital gains arising from the disposal of land or buildings with actual or potential development value; and also, a capital tax to be charged on the occasion in which a building (other than housing) was first let following material development (Lichfield and Connellan, 2000). The government estimated the tax would yield £80m a year (House of Commons Hansard, 1973).

To sum up, having abolished the Land Commission, rising land prices continued to haunt the government and amongst its initiatives were in effect a series of 'mini land commissions' involving local authorities in joint ventures with developers which traded in land in ways which enabled the *de facto* collection of some development value.

1974, 1975 and 1976: Development Gains Tax, the Community Land Scheme and Development Land Tax

During their years in Opposition the Labour Party and others on the political left had regularly attacked 'the immense capital gains made by ... wicked land speculators' (Crossman, 1973) and the 'vulgar and offensive profits of land speculators' (Crosland, 1972) and had indicated that they would seek to nationalise all development land if returned to office, arguing the case for bringing development land into public ownership, including setting up regional land and development corporations to do this (see, e.g. Lipsey, 1973). Some went further and campaigned for the outright nationalisation of all freehold land, not just development land, arguing that the previous attempts to collect development value were half-way houses that had failed to work (Brocklebank, *et al.*, 1973; Massey *et al.*, 1973). Many of these ideas were based on proposals put forward in the early 1960s whereby all freehold land would be taken over by regional bodies, leased back to occupiers initially rent free (with subsequent reviews for the life of the buildings) and with new leases at market rents granted upon change of use, upon development or upon the expiry of the lease (see, e.g. Socialist Commentary Group, 1961). But the Labour party was not the only organisation advocating land banking by public bodies such as county councils, acquiring development land at existing use value and selling on at current use value after servicing it, cementing a key link between planning authorities and the bodies buying and selling development land. Strong arguments in favour of this approach were made by professional and lobby groups in planning (see, e.g. RTPI, 1974; TCPA, 1973).

Rising land prices also provided part of the backcloth to the election of the 1974 Labour government which introduced the third and fourth attempts to collect development value through a nationally determined scheme (the third being the temporary 1974 enactment of the 1973 Development Gains Tax proposals of the previous Conservative government until its own new scheme was launched). The new scheme, the CLS as it was known, was different from both its 1947 and 1967 predecessors (Crosland, 1974; DoE, 1974, 1975).

Although it again involved a nationally determined tax (the Development Land Tax, or DLT) to collect development value (including on deemed disposals as well as actual sales) at a rate of 80% of the development value realised (66.6% if it was less than £150 000), it also gave a pivotal role to local authorities, not a national body, to acquire, service and dispose of development land to private and public developers. Because local authorities were permitted to buy land, net of the liability of landowners to DLT, they were able, in effect, also to collect development value through subsequent sales of serviced land at market prices. Thus, the scheme had twin aims: to collect development value and to ensure adequate land was available for the development needed, with the aims being achieved through a local land banking exercise. This would enable local authorities to act much more positively and proactively to achieve their development plan objectives.

The scheme ran from 1976 to 1980 (with the DLT continuing until 1985) with two linked but separate statutes: the 1975 Community Land Act and the 1976 Development Land Tax Act. The CLS was complex and involved a lengthy transitional stage (which would possibly have run for a decade or more) beginning in April 1976 and giving LPAs[2] the duty to consider the desirability of bringing development land into public ownership and the power (but not duty) of doing so. If they did pursue this power they acquired at a price net of landowners' liability to DLT. Where local authorities did not acquire, owners were liable for any DLT if development took place. Once the scheme was fully operational, LPAs would have been placed under a duty to acquire all relevant development land at existing use value (and DLT would no longer be required). No relevant development would be permitted except that taking place on land acquired by local authorities. The expectation was that the scheme, once in full operation would become self-financing, although in the initial stages it required borrowing to fund land acquisitions. Borrowing for the CLS needed specific central government approval of 5-year rolling programmes of development plan led land acquisition. LPAs would sell land on a freehold basis to owner occupiers but only on a leasehold basis to other users.

However, a complex structure for land acquisitions was set up, including the need to establish Land Acquisition Management Schemes whereby counties and districts (there was a two-tier local authority structure at that time throughout England) agreed on their respective roles under the CLS. They could acquire the relevant development land needed for a decade ahead and in doing so had to have regard to securing the proper planning of their areas (i.e. this placed development plans at the heart of the scheme). Some land was exempted altogether (agriculture, minerals) or excepted (that owned by builders or in receipt of planning consent when the legislation was first announced plus land for small-scale residential and other developments – all meaning that special justification was needed to acquire such excepted land). Purchases were funded by borrowing and surpluses, where made, had to be

---

[2] In Wales a new body, The Land Authority for Wales, was created and it, not local authorities, was given the duties and powers under the CLS.

shared with central government with some of the shared funds being used to help fund local authorities whose land schemes were in deficit. It was estimated that within a decade local authorities would be saving £350m a year on land acquired for their own needs while at the same time the total annual surpluses on land they acquired and sold on to developers would be running at approximately £500m per year. Initially they were able to keep only 30% of their surpluses, with 40% going to the Exchequer general funds and the remaining 30% to a pool for all local authorities to help those in deficit on their CLS accounts, ratios later changed to 30, 50 and 20, respectively. Moreover, there were limitations on the way surpluses could be used, preventing their use to fund off-site infrastructure costs. Interestingly (in the light of the subsequent use of planning obligations to fund affordable housing – see Chapter 4) some lobbyists, including the then National House Building Council, argued that some of the surpluses should be specifically used to help 'lower income families' secure new homes on the grounds that the surpluses from land trading were funded by those households buying new homes (Tait, 1975).

Early commentators on the Act argued that it would be hard to reconcile the two competing objectives set out in the White Paper (DoE, 1975) of local authorities collecting development value and of securing development in accordance with their needs and priorities. This was because the planning base upon which such reconciliation might be founded was weak, given the lack of geographical coverage of approved plans and because opportunity purchases of 'windfall sites', that is, land not identified in land policy statements were likely to be important. It would also be difficult to undertake financial planning because of the unpredictability of the tax base of owners whose land was acquired for relevant development and because the compulsory purchase route to acquisition was complex despite some changes that enabled Ministers to dispense with inquiries where there was an adequate planning basis for the land concerned.

Some not only doubted LPAs' competence to undertake these tasks but also their ability to reconcile conflicts of interest (Raison, 1975). Some argued that to handle such conflicts, local public corporations with the private sector as minority shareholders should be set up to handle the CLS tasks (TCPA, 1973). Grant argued that planning had already moved from a model of planning that was wholly judicial and had by then embraced matters that went far beyond the use and other development of land to wider economic and social policy as well (and was already using taxation of development value through planning obligations to achieve these broader objectives). However, planning generally lacked the accountability and transparent governance structures to openly and 'even-handedly' reconcile the competing financial and planning objectives (Grant, 1976, a, b, c).

Hence, it came as no surprise that, as with the Land Commission, little land was acquired under the CLS. There were inevitably differences in the political appetite of LPAs for the scheme (including those who did not want to work up acquisitions and make surpluses only to find them swept away to fund those in deficit), but the fatal blow was the attitude of the Treasury in central government to the scheme, wanting it to move to overall surplus as quickly as possible. This meant priorities had to be given to acquiring the limited amount of land not covered by exemptions or exceptions in the early stages of the CLS and ready for immediate development. This however was expensive to acquire and made few surpluses (partly because the base case against which tax liability was calculated was more than the existing use value). In contrast, LPAs wanted to take a long-term view, acquire land needed well ahead of development, service it and make it ready for development in the future. This latter approach, whilst bringing surpluses in the long run, required deficit funding for some years ahead. However, soon after the CLS was set up the original intention of government approving rolling capital programmes of funding for acquisition was abandoned in favour of a site-by-site approval exercise (Emms, 1980; Grant, 1980). It was telling that, not only was little land acquired, but that local authority spending on acquisitions was less than half that allocated in government spending plans, despite an increase in public spending allocated to purchases in later years, combined with a relaxation of Whitehall's stringent criteria for approving loans for land. Only 2,357 acres were acquired in total in England for 1976–1977 and 1977–1978 (Milne, 1979), while the initial public expenditure allocations allowed for 5400 acres over these 2 years building up to 12 300 acres in 1978–1979 (Grant, 1976). Commentators argued that this lack of success was due to the overall financial restrictions, the profit sharing rules, the rules on the application of retained surpluses and the inability to fund off-site infrastructure costs through the CLS accounts or of getting developers to pay for it themselves if this resulted in reduced market prices for the land local authorities were trying to sell from their land banks (Grant, 1980; see also Barrett and Boddy, 1978).

Meantime the details of the separate DLT legislation were complex and little tax was collected in relation to the development value being realised as a result of land undergoing private development rather than being acquired, net of DLT, by LPAs under the CLS arrangements. The tax was levied on the development value realised upon the disposal of a material interest in land or upon the commencement of material development. In 1980 the CLS was abolished, the DLT rate dropped to 60% (and exemptions were increased) to ensure owners had no reason for holding back development land. But 5 years later it was abolished. In the year ending March 1978, only £8.2m had been collected in DLT with an additional benefit of £10.6m to local authorities buying land net of DLT (House of Commons Hansard, 1978).

In 1978–1979, local authority land accounts were in deficit to the tune of £33m with only £200 000 having been redistributed to deficit authorities (Cox, 1984). In 1983–1984 (after the abolition of the CLS), £67.9m was collected in DLT (£147m at 2007–2008 prices) (House of Commons Hansard, 1984). It had been expected that DLT would bring in an annual tax income of £600m (Grant, 1986).

In a prescient editorial in 1975, when the draft legislation was first unveiled, the London Times 'thundered' that the legislation was 'predestined to join those noble failures that have preceded it', referring to both the 1947 and 1967 schemes discussed before, despite its sensible twin objectives of collecting development value and making planning more positive. Unfortunately, the editorial argued, the detailed mechanics of the legislation were likely to prove unworkable as local authorities were not up to the job of running a monopoly land banking function, whether in character, financial ability or staffing competencies (Editorial, 1975). And while the Times leader writer proved to be right that the legislation would be 'unworkable' the failures were as much the fault of central as of local government.

Although the Community Land Act was abolished in 1980, the decision by the incoming Conservative government to retain the Development Land Tax Act had been 'widely interpreted as symbolising at least some common ground in land policy between the two main political parties' (Grant, 1986, p. 4). However, the retention was relatively short lived and DLT was abolished in 1985. The arguments for abolition were that DLT was expensive to collect, it restricted the supply of development land and distorted the market, was set at a discriminatory rate compared with other capital taxes and its existence as a special tax on development values was no longer justified as the government had brought inflation under control. As little tax had been collected its abolition had only a small net cost to the Treasury. The tax had a distorting effect on the land market including encouraging phasing of development, the splitting of sites into several parts, and encouraging housebuilders to make contributions to off-site infrastructure through planning obligations because this increased the base value against which DLT was assessed (Grant, 1986).

Following the abolition of DLT, no subsequent national tax on development value has been implemented. Subsequent governments, including Conservative, Labour and Coalition governments, have focused instead on ensuring, through a variety of measures, that adequate land is available for development, including measures to reform the planning system, for example, to speed up decision making. As we shall see in the next chapter, these governments endorsed LPAs' use of planning obligations as a means of ensuring developers contributed to infrastructure funding, rather than installing new national taxes to raise funds, although one proposal to tax development value and to hypothecate the proceeds for LPAs to spend on infrastructure was actively considered as part of the reforms to the planning obligations system, but as we shall see this was not implemented.

Lessons learned

Despite its weaknesses and its ineffectiveness in taxing development value, one commentator on DLT remarked a few years later that

> however impotent that tax had become, its abolition restored in full the remarkable financial imbalance at the heart of theBritish planning system. It is still one of the most dirigiste land planning systems in the world, but its distributional consequences seem to be ignored completely. Losses and gains rest where they fall. The ground rules are that, if planning permission is refused for development of land, no compensation is payable. The losers always lose. Yet if planning permission is granted, no differential tax liability now arises. Gains from increments in land values are treated on a comparable basis to all other capital gains (Grant, 1992).[3]

We can also note a point made by Prest (1981) in his review of part of the period reviewed in this chapter that attempts to tax development value have increasingly had to make more conscious links with the planning system whilst at the same time, compared with the pre-war experience, the locus of decisions on taxation moved from local to central government. The 1975 CLS represented a partial reversal of that trend, especially by allowing LPAs to buy land at existing use value and, as the next chapter on planning obligations shows, the experience after 1986 gave even greater emphasis to the role of local authorities through the pursuit of planning obligations. As Prest remarked in his review, 'planning considerations and power to acquire land on an existing use value basis came to dominate the form of land taxation ... ' (Prest, 1981, p. 106).

But notwithstanding the imbalance that Grant (1992, op cit) referred to, there has since then been no scheme of national taxation to collect development and no centrally determined scheme for land banking. So what are the lessons from the attempts at collecting development charge (1947), betterment levy (1967) and Development Gains and Development Land Tax (1974 and 1976) – and the CLS connected to DLT? First, that nationally determined development value taxes and levies appear to keep land off the market even when the amount of the levy is pitched (as in 1967 and to some extent in 1974) to avoid that consequence. Second, that the arrangements to combat land withholding by state intervention

---

[3] Reproduced by permission of Thomson Reuters (Professional) UK Limited on behalf of Sweet & Maxwell Ltd.

in land banking through national agencies (the Central Land Board and the Land Commission) proved inadequate for the task, partly because of insufficient funding but also because local development plans, to which acquisition was linked, were out of date. Third, that whilst devolving land banking to local authorities in the CLS addressed some of the previous schemes' difficulties this too was beset by inadequate funding, out of date plans and an (understandable) unwillingness of local authorities to share their surpluses with central government and other authorities.

In all cases the key lessons are that little betterment was collected, the administration was complex, tax avoidance was widespread and land was kept off the market in part because parliamentary oppositions promised to repeal the legislation and in part because inadequate funds were made available to enable an offsetting public acquisition to counteract the land withholding, especially in the context of out of date and poor coverage of adopted development plans.

In Chapter 4, we shall see how the evolution of planning obligations after the demise of the CLS enabled local authorities to negotiate (rather than impose through a tax on value) substantial contributions to infrastructure and community needs from developers. Through this mechanism local authorities have collected far more from development value through this *de facto* tax than all the attempts in 1947, 1967, 1974 and 1976. We shall also see how a proposal made in 2004 and taken up by the Labour government in 2005 to introduce a further national tax on development values (Planning Gain Supplement) to fund infrastructure was not finally implemented. This was partly because of widespread opposition to the concept of taxing development value through a nationally imposed and spatially invariant tax instead of continuing to seek contributions from developers based on the costs involved and taking account of the impact of contributions on the viability of development.

References

Adams, D. and Watkins, C. (2014) *Value of Planning*. RTPI Research Report No. 5, Royal Town Planning Institute, London.

Barrett, S. and Boddy, M. (1978) *Implementation of the Community Land Scheme*, University of Bristol School for Advanced Urban Studies, Bristol.

Bill, P. (ed) (2004) *Building Sustainable Communities: Capturing Land Development Value for the Public realm*, The Smith Institute, London.

Brocklebank, K., Kaldor N., Maynard, J., Neild, R., and Stuchtbury, O. (1973) *The Case for Nationalising Land*, Campaign for Nationalising Land, London.

Cox, A. (1984) *Adversary Politics and Land*, Cambridge University Press, Cambridge, MA.

Crosland, A. (1972) Report on the debate on the motion for an address in reply to the Queen's Speech, *The Times*, 3rd November.

Crosland, A. (1974) Socialism, land and equality. *Socialist Commentary*, March, pp. iii–vi.

Crossman, R. (1973) The way to put all landlords under one roof – At a stroke. *The Times*, 19th September, p. 18.

Cullingworth, J.B. (1975) *Environmental Planning 1939–1969. Volume I: Reconstruction and Land Use Planning, 1939–1947*, HMSO, London.

Cullingworth, J.B. (1980) *Environmental Planning 1939–1969. Volume IV: Land Values, Compensation and Betterment*, HMSO, London.

Department of the Environment (DoE) (1972) *Report of Sheaf Committee on Local Authority Private Enterprise Partnership Schemes*, HMSO, London.

Department of the Environment (DoE) (1973) *Widening Choice: The Next Steps in Housing*, Cmnd Paper 5280, HMSO, London.

Department of the Environment (DoE) (1974), *Land*, Cmnd Paper 5730, HMSO, London.

Department of the Environment (DoE) (1975) *Community Land Circular 1. General Introduction and Priorities*. Circular 121/75, DoE, London.

Editorial (1975) Unworkable. *The Times*, first leader, 21st March.

Emms, J.E. (1980) The Community Land Act: a requiem. *Journal of Planning and Environment Law*, February.

Grant, M. (1976a) The Community Land Act: an overview. The Planning Framework. *Journal of Planning Law*, 614–626.

Grant, M. (1976b) The Community Land Act: an overview. Financing the Scheme. *Journal of Planning Law*, 675–690.

Grant, M. (1976c) The Community Land Act: an overview. Planning in the Market. *Journal of Planning Law*, 732–748.

Grant, M. (1980) Community Land? *Journal of Planning Law*, 669–684.

Grant, M. (1986) Planning and land taxation: development land tax and beyond – I and II. *Journal of Planning Law* 4–19 and 92–106.

Grant, M. (1992) The planning balance in the 1990s: Betterment again? *Journal of Planning and Environment Law*, 67–83.

Hall, P. (ed) (1965). *Land Values*, Sweet & Maxwell, London.

Hall, P., Thomas, R., Gracey, H., and Drewett, R. (1973) *The Containment of Urban England*, Allen & Unwin, London.

Heald, T. (1974) Land banking in Hampshire. *Public Finance and Accountancy* **1** (4), 123–126.

House of Commons Hansard (1952) *House of Commons Debates*, 29th January, Volume 495, cols CC18–9W, HMSO, London.

House of Commons Hansard (1973) *House of Commons Debates*, 17th December, Volume 886, col 955, HMSO, London.

House of Commons Hansard (1978) *House of Commons Written Answers*. 3rd May, Volume 949, cols 190–2W, HMSO, London.

House of Commons Hansard (1984), *House of Commons Debates*, 14th June, *1984*, Volume 61, cols 1054–55, HMSO, London.

Lichfield, N. and Connellan, O. (2000) *Land Value and Community Betterment Taxation in Britain: Proposals for Legislation and Practice*. Working Paper WP00NL1, Lincoln Institute of Land Policy, Washington, DC.

Lipsey, D. (1973) *Labour and Land*, Fabian Tract 422, Fabian Society, London.

Massey, D., Barras, R., and Broadbent, A. (1973) Labour must take over land. *Socialist Commentary*, July.

Merrett, S. (1979) *State Housing in Britain*, Routledge and Kegan Paul, London.

Milne, R. (1979) Appraising the Act. *Planning*, 12th January, 10–11.

Ministry of Works and Planning (1942) *Expert Committee on Compensation and Betterment, Final Report*, Cmnd Paper 6386, (Chair Lord Uthwatt), HMSO, London.

National Archives (2013) *Central Land Board*, http://discovery.nationalarchives.gov.uk/SearchUI/details/C583-details (last accessed, 3rd December 2013).

Parker, H.R. (1987) From Uthwatt to DLT – The end of the road? In: Fyson, A. (ed) *Planning in Post War Britain: The JR James Memorial Lectures*, The Royal Town Planning Institute, London.

Prest, A.R. (1981) *The Taxation of Urban Land*, Manchester University Press, Manchester.

Raison, T. (1975) Debate on Clause 2 of Community Land Act. *House of Commons Hansard*, 13th October 1975, Volume 897, cols 915–917, HMSO, London.

Royal Town Planning Institute (RTPI) (1974) *The Land Question*, RTPI, London.

Socialist Commentary Group (1961) The face of Britain. *Socialist Commentary*, September, Special Planning Supplement. pp. i–xxvi.

Tait, A.W. (1975) Land bill: Letter to the editor. *The Times*, 11th April.

Town and Country Planning Associations (TCPA) (1973) Statement by the TCPA on Development Values and Land Assembly. *Town and Country Planning*, May, pp. 268–269.

4

Planning Obligations Policy in England: *de facto* Taxation of Development Value

Tony Crook

Department of Urban Studies and Planning, The University of Sheffield, UK

Introduction

This chapter describes the evolution of planning obligations policy in England[1] over the post-war years. Two separate, but linked, issues have underpinned post-war discussions about development value and the implementation of development plans. First, as we saw in Chapter 3, whether it is fair to allow landowners and developers to benefit from the development value arising when planning permission is granted. Second, how can funding for the necessary infrastructure for permitted development be secured? Planning obligations have brought these two issues together, providing *de facto* taxation of development values with the tax 'take' being locally hypothecated for infrastructure and community needs.

In the last three decades, planning obligations in England have also brought together at the local level the once separate policy instruments for, on the one hand, allocating enough land in plans for the expected development and giving planning consents for it, and, on the other, securing funding for infrastructure and community needs. Local planning authorities (LPAs) can now require developers to contribute to the cost of the infrastructure needed to support new development and to provide community facilities,

[1] The discussion deals with England only because policies in Scotland and Wales have some differences from those in England, especially in Scotland where there has been separate legislation throughout the period under review in this chapter and which pre-dated devolution to the Scottish Government in 1999.

Planning Gain: Providing Infrastructure and Affordable Housing, First Edition.
Edited by Tony Crook, John Henneberry and Christine Whitehead.
© 2016 John Wiley & Sons, Inc. Published 2016 by John Wiley & Sons, Inc.

including some affordable dwellings on sites with new market housing. These obligations run as private contracts alongside planning consents and in effect enable the hypothecation of locally negotiated levies on development value to meet local needs. In the context of increasingly limited sums of public money, planning obligations secure both efficiency objectives, by better aligning private and social costs by requiring developers to pay for their externalities such as new schools and improved roads, and equity objectives, by increasing the output of affordable homes and requiring developers to pay for a share of this out of development value.

These policies and practices have not been uncontroversial, especially the use of planning obligations to fund community needs like affordable housing, a practice which some argue does not fall within the acceptable approach of requiring developers to pay the costs of the impacts of their development. While it has been seen as legitimate to charge developers for the costs of infrastructure (especially where the infrastructure in question is provided for the exclusive benefit of the developments concerned), obligations policies have been criticised, first, in so far as they are seen as taxing development values in ways not authorised by legislation and, second, because helping to provide affordable homes and other community needs cannot be categorised as mitigation of impact as is the case when providing infrastructure. As we shall see, however, governments have increasingly argued in favour of the legitimacy of such approaches to 'taxing' development value and have also endorsed using obligations to support the provision of new affordable homes. In that way planning obligations have become a hybrid kind of tax, partly a charge for infrastructure and partly a tax on development value.

This chapter has four further sections. The first section presents a description of planning obligations legislation and practice and an analysis of how this evolved into a significant means of collecting development value. The second section describes one aspect of planning obligations policy – its use to fund affordable housing. The third section looks at some of the recent policy changes designed to improve certainty, efficiency and transparency in the design and application of planning obligations policy. The final section summarises some of the debates about the legitimacy of using planning obligations to secure infrastructure and community needs, matters we return to in the final chapter after we have examined the detailed evidence about the application and impact of the policy in England (and of similar policies in other countries) in later chapters.

We continue to use the term 'development value' to describe the increased land value that helps pay for planning obligations, but the term 'planning gain' has also been used by other commentators, some of whose work is cited in this chapter, both to describe development value and its 'taxation'. In this chapter, we also use the term 'S106 agreements'. This is the section of the principal planning legislation in England, which permits LPAs to negotiate planning obligations. Once negotiations are concluded, the obligations are then set out in a legal (S106) agreement between the LPA and a developer.

Planning obligations: the key principles

In contrast to the lack of success of national taxation in capturing development value, planning obligations represent *de facto* and, as we shall see in detail in Chapters 6–8, very successful attempts by LPAs to collect locally that which proved very difficult to collect through national taxes and levies. They allow LPAs to negotiate with developers on matters that cannot be addressed through conditions on planning permission, specifically to mitigate the impact of proposed developments, for example, by making contributions to the costs of the required infrastructure. Authority for LPAs to enter into legal agreements to secure such obligations is currently provided for by S106 of the principal planning statute, the 1990 Town and Country Planning Act.

In the early 1990s, Grant, a regular legal commentator on these matters, argued that a 'vacuum in national policy on betterment in this country' was being filled locally by an alternative system of planning obligations. He made the point that in theory, this is not a tax at all, but a

> process under which developers make voluntary contributions to the local planning authority in order to overcome some legitimate planning objection to their proposed development. It is a process of exchange which takes place within a framework of clear Government guidance, and with the safeguard to developers of a right of appeal to the Secretary of State against excessive demands. (Grant, 1992)[2]

Although this practice has been subject to criticism, not the least its past lack of transparency, he argued that planning obligations are a 'substantial and legitimate transfer of off-site infrastructure costs from the public sector to the private sector' (Grant, 1992). He pointed out that the approach to obligations had gradually emerged through practice and by consent, not imposed by Parliament, and wondered whether obligations were 'a model for betterment taxation which could be built upon and improved' (Grant, 1992). We will return to this question at the end of the chapter, but first we must trace how this practice originated and evolved.

Although the detail has changed since the introduction of comprehensive planning legislation and the nationalisation of development rights in the 1947 legislation (which came into effect in July 1948), LPAs are still charged

---

[2] Reproduced by permission of Thomson Reuters (Professional) UK Limited on behalf of Sweet & Maxwell Ltd.

with the duty of deciding planning applications. All 'development' needs permission and those seeking it have to apply to their LPAs for consent. Development covers both physical development, including operations 'in on over or under land' and changes of use, the latter requiring permission even if the change of use does not involve building or other operations. So that LPAs do not have to determine minor and immaterial changes of use, central government makes secondary legislation, passed by Parliament, through Use Classes Orders (UCOs) so that changes within a class are excluded from the definition of development and hence do not need planning permission. Similarly to ensure that very small-scale development involving building operations does not need permission, central government, also through secondary legislation, makes General Permitted Development Orders (GDOs), which grant permission for these sorts of development, such as small-scale housing extensions. What is included in a GDO or UCO changes from time to time, both in terms of administrative tidying up of detail but more particularly as a consequence of policy change if, for example, government wishes to encourage a specific type of development and removes the 'bureaucratic' hurdles associated with undertaking it.

In deciding upon planning applications, LPAs are required to have regard to the provisions of their statutory development plans and to any other material considerations (Duxbury, 2009; Moore and Purdue, 2012). The long-standing national planning policy 'default' (first declared in 1932 and again confirmed in a circular in 1949) is that there is always a presumption in favour of development (Harrison, 1992), now defined as a presumption in favour of 'sustainable development' (DCLG, 2012a). Applicants do not have to prove the need for development (except for inappropriate development in a Green belt). If their proposals are unacceptable to LPAs, then it is up to them to give reasons for refusing planning permission. Since 1991, planning legislation has made development control decisions 'plan led'. In an amendment in 2004, legislation now requires that where a planning decision has to have regard to a development plan (as LPAs must, when determining planning applications), 'the determination *must* be made in accordance with the plan *unless* [emphases added] material considerations indicate otherwise' (Planning and Compensation Act, 2004 S38 [6]). LPAs are obliged to adopt development plans and to keep them under review (although these are often very out of date[3]). In drawing up their development plan policies, LPAs have to take account of national planning policy, currently set out in the National Planning Policy Framework (NPPF) determined by central government ministers (DCLG, 2012a) and to have regard to the resources available for implementing proposals. Until recently, they also had to have regard to regional

---

[3]The current Coalition government has announced its intention of making it mandatory for LPAs to update their plans.

strategic planning policies but the 2010 Coalition government abolished the latter. District (and unitary) councils outside London are now the tier of local government responsible for almost all planning matters and thus their adopted Local Development Frameworks and Development Plan Documents, including their core strategies, are keys to determining planning applications. The exceptions are, first, Greater London where the Mayor and the London Boroughs both have planning powers and, second, where there are two tiers of local government the upper tier county councils retain responsibility for minerals and waste disposal matters (and in most national parks the park authorities, not the local authorities within them, are the LPAs). If a planning application is turned down, applicants have the right to appeal to central government to overturn the decision. The relevant Secretary of State is bound to take account of the same matters as LPAs when reaching decisions on appeals. Most decisions are taken by Planning Inspectors hearing appeals on behalf of the Secretary of State, with only the most important (and controversial) ones reaching government Ministers' desks for decision. Ministers thus have both appellate (deciding on appeals) and policy-making (the NPPF and other advice and guidance) responsibilities.

One of the reasons that LPAs need to take 'other material considerations' as well as the provisions of their adopted plans into account when determining planning applications is that plans take a long time to prepare, adopt and then update, with the inevitable risk that these can be out of date. Indeed the post-war history of planning shows that England has been generally covered only with out-of-date plans. Thus, as circumstances change, adopted plans, whilst still being important, may indicate that a planning application decision consistent with the plan would be inappropriate to the new circumstances. So, for example, inward migration may have increased since a plan was adopted rendering its housing land allocations inadequate. The 'other material consideration' clause in the legislation enables permission to be granted to a site not originally included in a plan.

These provisions thus provide the necessary flexibility for LPAs to have regard to changing circumstances and not to be tied only to what their adopted plans indicate. As we saw in the Introduction, development plans in England are not zoning plans to be followed regardless of circumstances[4] but part of the framework, along with other material considerations, including changing national policy, for deciding on planning applications to develop land. Thus adopted plans sit alongside discretionary decision making by local authorities (Booth, 2003).

---

[4]Although we should note that zoning schemes in other countries do not always provide the certainty that might be expected since the particular circumstances of specific proposals lead with some inevitability to negotiations about proposals, albeit within the context of the zoning arrangements (Booth, 1989).

This discretion and built-in flexibility is also a reason for the success of planning obligations policies and practices because they enable LPAs to negotiate agreements with applicants for planning permission, allowing them to secure planning obligations from developers on matters that cannot be readily achieved through conditions on planning permission. This is because the latter must be restricted to matters strictly related to the development and other use of land and cannot be used to secure broader social and economic objectives (Jowell, 1977) and specifically not to specify tenure nor price of housing whereas agreements can specify occupancy restrictions (Barlow *et al.*, 1994a). So, for example, conditions cannot be used to determine who lives in a new dwelling given planning permission or to require financial contributions to fund the necessary infrastructure. However, S106 planning agreements can do these because they are private contracts running alongside statutory planning permissions and they use private contract law to bind parties to the agreements, especially important where positive obligations are involved (Healey *et al.*, 1993).

Planning agreements thus create enforceable property rights, are registered as local land charges and bind successors in title, not just the original applicants for the planning consent (Duxbury, 2009; Encyclopaedia of Planning Law, 2013; Grant, 1975, 1982; Moore and Purdue, 2012). Agreements can thus be enforced in the courts by either party (although this is rare in England, in contrast to the experience of impact fees and the like in the USA where case law has become important – see Chapter 9). Obligations on developers can be negative or positive and powers to enable LPAs to enforce positive agreements were introduced in 1974. Before that, it was possible to enforce only negative agreements but not positive ones involving financial or in-kind contributions. This weakness led LPAs to secure private Acts of Parliament to enable them to agree and enforce such contracts (Grant, 1975).

They were first introduced in the 1909 planning legislation. In 1932, legislation allowed them to be enforced against successors in title and in 1947 LPAs became obliged to secure Ministerial approval to proposed agreements (not now the case; see below). Obligations are thus special powers conferred on LPAs to regulate land use by agreement and not by control. As Grant remarked, they are an 'unusual provision', supplementing regulation with a flexible power to enter into agreements and to make them property rights enforceable in contract. Their 'consensual character is well suited to a negotiated style of development control' (Grant, 1991).

Obligations ensure that the consequences of new developments can be mitigated by developers so that schemes that are acceptable in planning terms can proceed. Thus, for example, if a proposed housing development meets agreed requirements and fits the planning strategy for an area, but also requires a new extension to a local school which the local council cannot fund, the LPA is entitled to reject the application. Planning obligations overcome these obstacles by allowing LPAs to negotiate contributions from developers towards meeting these infrastructure needs, thus enabling them to grant permission. The obligations can be either in the form of direct payments or 'in-kind' contributions, such as developers doing the work themselves, or in a combination, such as making land available for a school which the local authority then builds itself. Because agreements are enforceable, LPAs can ensure developers deliver their agreed obligations and developers ensure that LPAs provide the infrastructure that they, the developers, have funded (provided this does not restrict the operation of an authority's statutory functions) – and if they do not, developers can secure repayment. Agreements covering obligations towards the costs of improving local roads and improvements to the strategic road network are handled under separate legislation (S278 of the Highways Act) but within the same principle of seeking developers' contributions to the infrastructure required to support their development. Planning obligations are thus designed to regulate development, to require land to be used in specific ways, to require specific operations to be carried out and to require financial or in-kind contributions. They also help secure those aspects of planning that try to achieve broader social and economic objectives (Campbell *et al.*, 2000; Claydon and Smith, 1997; DoE, 1972; Ennis, 1997; Grant, 1975; Jowell, 1977).

Although the obligations tied up in S106 agreements are matters of negotiation between LPAs and developers, this does not mean that the former have unfettered discretion to exact contributions from developers for any purposes. They cannot, for example, use their flexibility simply to permit developments which are inconsistent with their adopted plans just because they can extract obligations from the developers. The 1947 Town and Country Planning Act originally made it necessary for planning authorities to seek Ministerial approval for agreements, but this requirement was removed in 1968 legislation. By the late 1970s, the growing use of what had become by then colloquially (but not statutorily) known as 'planning gain' (through what was then S52 of the principal planning statute) was causing some disquiet, with accusations that it was being used to bargain for benefits that went beyond a legitimate purpose and raised questions about the use of discretion by LPAs. Jowell, for example, argued that the negotiating practice underlying these agreements raised important issues of discretionary judgement, moving planning to a contractual, not judicial mode of decision making (Jowell, 1977; see also Harlow and Rawlings, 1984, Chapter 15).

The Government's Property Advisory Group was asked to clarify matters (DoE, 1981). It was critical of using 'planning gain' to secure benefits that were unrelated to developments for which permission was sought but considered it was acceptable where 'planning gains' were strongly related to proposed developments (such as funding the off-site infrastructure needed). In all other cases where the contributions being requested went beyond this these were not acceptable, in part because these offers, or requests for 'collateral' benefits, would create doubts about the integrity and objectivity of planning decisions. At the time of the report development value was still being taxed (through Development Land Tax as we saw in the last chapter) and the group considered that 'planning gains' were attempts to secure something that was not fairly related to proposed developments and was an additional *ad hoc* local tax unauthorised by Parliament. Instead what was acceptable was 'planning gain' that helped overcome what would otherwise be valid reasons for refusing permission. In other words, the group thought 'planning gain' had evolved to become a tax on developers' profits to pay for what used to be provided by the public sector – and went beyond the 'internalisation' of external costs.

Subsequent advice from government clarified the use of 'planning gain' and set out a three-part test of reasonableness for planning authorities to use when considering whether or not to seek 'gains'. Reasonable gains would be those that were directly related to and would assist development which was acceptable in planning terms to go ahead, including infrastructure contributions, open space, car parking (the latter might be provided off site) and creating an acceptable balance of uses in mixed developments. If the proposed 'gains' were reasonable they also had to be 'fairly and reasonably related in scale and kind to the proposed development' and to also represent a reasonable charge on the developer compared with defraying the costs from national or local taxes or user charges (DoE, 1983). Hence, there must be a 'rational nexus' between the development proposed and the obligations sought (Purdue *et al.*, 1992; Grant, 1982; Healey *et al.*, 1993). The term 'rational nexus' is much used in similar cases in the USA to justify the collection of impact fees, as we shall see in Chapter 9, where court cases have held that the levying of such fees (or exactions or dedications) is justified where the development will cause the need, the contribution required is proportionate to that need and will be used to meet it. This term (although not used as such) also has relevance to the position in England, where obligations must be justified as contributing to proposed developments and not arbitrarily sought as a contribution to LPAs' general funds, although legal commentators in England have argued that a 'reasonable relationship' is more appropriate than the more restrictive 'rational nexus' test applied in courts in the United States, notwithstanding the similarities of the issue (Purdue *et al.*, 1992). But as the government argued in 1988,

> the planning authority is not entitled to use the mechanism and the applicant's need for planning permission as an opportunity to exact a payment for the benefit of ratepayers at large. The obligation of land-owners and users to pay tax on development profits is met through the general arrangements for the taxation of individuals and companies. (DoE, 1988, para 25)

Later advice in 1991 restated the tests of reasonableness and endorsed the inclusion of policies about obligations in statutory development plans, whilst 1991 legislation created the concept of planning obligations rather than of planning agreements (as 'planning gain' was then technically called) because it provided for the possibility of developers offering unilateral undertakings which planning inspectors could then take into account when hearing appeals against refusal of planning permission by LPAs (DoE, 1991a). This 1991 circular was primarily about process and did not deal with the substantive concerns about what might be sought through obligations although it did drop the use of the term 'planning gain' which it thought was by then inappropriate because in the past it had been used to describe both legitimate and potentially unlawful transactions involving the buying and selling of permissions (DoE, 1991a).

These 'policy tests' were further confirmed in 2005 (DCLG, 2005) and the government emphasised the three purposes of obligations: to prescribe the nature of development, to compensate for loss or damage (e.g. open space) caused by the development, and to mitigate impact (e.g. increased traffic on nearby roads). In these examples, compensation for loss and mitigation for adverse impacts might be addressed, for example, by developers including open space within a development and by the local authority improving local roads (with the developer paying for the costs). The five policy tests required obligations to be (i) clearly and necessarily related to proposed developments; (ii) relevant to planning; (iii) necessary to make proposed developments acceptable in planning terms; (iv) directly related to the site and the development proposed and fairly related to the proposals; and (v) reasonable in all other respects. These tests are now incorporated in the latest National Policy Planning Framework emphasising that obligations should only be sought to make development acceptable in planning terms, be directly related to the development, and fairly and reasonably related to the scale of the development (DCLG, 2012a). As we shall see below, this 2012 version of the policy tests was necessary as a result of the introduction of Community Infrastructure Levy, a planning charge that secures strategic infrastructure funding, leading to the scaling back of planning obligations.

Policy on obligations has also been increasingly set out in adopted development plans with two benefits: clarity and transparency. First, clarity creates greater certainty for developers by providing them with a framework about the matters planning authorities are likely to negotiate with them, with the result that authorities doing this agree and collect far more in obligations than those authorities without such clarity of policy (and consistency of practice too) (Gielen and Tasan-Kok, 2010; also Chapters 6 and 7, this volume). It also enables developers to 'lobby' for policies that are in their interests and object to the ones that are not, by getting involved in the consultation and public inquiry processes that precede the formal adoption of development plans.

Second, by fostering this greater transparency and accountability it removes some of the past suspicions surrounding planning obligations that enabled LPAs to 'sell' and developers to 'buy' planning permission. In its report on local government, the Nolan Committee stated that 'planning obligation ... is the most intractable aspect of the planning system with which we have had to deal' (Nolan Committee on Standards in Public Life, 1997, para 302) but it also went on to argue that it was entirely right for developers to be required to contribute to the costs of infrastructure, including social infrastructure like schools. The solution to the allegations that obligations potentially allow planning consent to be bought and sold was to be found in a refined definition in central government policy about what was and was not appropriate and in greater openness about negotiations and agreements (Nolan Committee on Standards in Public Life, 1997, para 320).

The greater formalisation, transparency and accountability of planning obligations policy that has evolved over the last two decades since the Nolan and other reports has meant that there are now far fewer doubts about the legitimacy of policy and the integrity of practice than there were three decades ago (hence the then commissioning of the Property Advisory Group report in 1981 and the subsequent concerns by the Nolan Committee). This chapter returns to these issues in its penultimate section when reviewing proposals for further reform.

Planning obligations address off-site infrastructure. On-site infrastructure is handled separately. Developers provide these themselves including estate roads and water supply and sewerage and then directly requisition (and pay for) access to the mains to connect their developments to the water, gas, electricity, IT and sewerage supplies and pipes. If these services are to be connected in good time for the completion of new development, this requires significant coordination between a wide range of public agencies and private providers, recent evidence suggesting that there were fewer problems in relation to utilities than the provision of roads, water, water treatment and flood prevention measures. There were also risks for developers if one of them ended up paying for a larger share of the facilities in an area of new development than its final share of the development warranted (Barker, 2004, 2006; Calcutt, 2007; NHPAU, 2009). These 'hook up' costs mean that developers also contribute to the costs incurred in flood plain management and building new sewage treatment plants. What planning obligations do is to oblige developers to also pay for some other off-site costs, such as the requirement to pay for extra school classrooms as a result of new housing schemes.

Always used to a very limited extent over the post-war period, their use has grown very significantly since the 1980s, as public funding for infrastructure essential to support new developments declined (Bailey, 1994; Campbell *et al.*, 2000; Ennis, 1997; Healey *et al.*, 1993; Chapter 6, this volume). As a result, the previous balance of responsibilities for on-site (developers) and off-site (public bodies) infrastructure has shifted, with the private sector now taking on more and more responsibility for the latter as well as the former. This shift advanced in the late 1970s and early 1980s when property and land prices were rising rapidly and developers became more willing to contribute to infrastructure costs to enable profitable proposed developments to take place. As we saw in Chapter 1, this increased use of planning obligations also reflects the changes that took place in England from a mixed to a liberal market economy with the market playing a much more important and key role in planning (in this case through permissions and planning obligations) and facilitating development. This point was emphasised by the then government minister responsible for housing and planning in a debate on the planning obligations clauses in the 1991 legislation when he argued that it was right for developers to contribute to meeting wider needs because the private sector would be able to provide more than the public sector could (Young, 1991).

Planners also came under increasing pressure from elsewhere within local authorities to secure funds through planning obligations (Campbell *et al.*, 2000). Thus, notwithstanding previous government advice, the use of obligations in practice evolved with LPAs seeking (and developers offering) contributions towards needs that did not strictly arise from developments being proposed. These included such matters as securing jobs and associated training for local people arising from any construction associated with the permitted development or accepting offers from developers to provide infrastructure that went beyond that necessary to support proposed developments (Healey *et al.*, 1993). Case law determined on planning appeals (e.g. the House of Lords decision on the Tesco case[5]) upheld this use of obligations. The Lords allowed this, provided obligations passed the tests of reasonableness and were not treated as material considerations in ways that would result in permissions being given to otherwise unacceptable proposals (Fordham, 1995; Mole, 1996). The Lords held that if an obligation had nothing to do with a proposed development, it would plainly not be a material consideration but an attempt to buy planning permission but if it had a connection which was not *de minimis*, the LPA was entitled to have regard to it and it would be a matter for the LPA, using its discretion to do so, having regard to its policies. As a result, case law enabled the pursuit of a wider range of planning obligations than did government policy (Cunliffe, 2001).

---

[5] See: *Tesco Stores Ltd. v. Secretary of State* [1995] 1 WLR, 759; 2 All ER 636.

The government then took steps to clarify once again the use of obligations and further established the necessity test, that is, that obligations must be necessary; relevant to planning; directly related to the proposed development; fairly and reasonably related in scale and kind to the proposed development; and reasonable in all other respects. It also emphasised that planning obligations should not be used to secure a betterment levy (DoE, 1997). At the same time many continued to argue, including in government commissioned reports, that obligations should be increasingly used to fund the infrastructure needed to support urban regeneration. For example, the Urban Task Force, chaired by Lord Rogers, argued this, and, whilst recommending the adoption of impact fees as an alternative to planning obligations (because it thought these would make green field sites more expensive to develop and hence encourage more brownfield development), also recommended 'fast track' processes to get speedier resolutions of the legal agreements involved (Urban Task Force, 1999; see also Punter, 1999).

Whilst this general approach to planning obligations has been sustained for three decades, with an increasing use of them to secure contributions to wider community needs, not just off-site infrastructure, there have also been further changes to the policy and to the operation of obligations in the last decade, involving moves to fixed not negotiated contributions, including a proposal (not implemented) to fund these by levies on explicit proportions of development value. But before we review these proposals and changes, we first look at an example of the use of obligations to secure wider community needs – affordable housing.

Using planning obligations to secure land and funding for affordable housing

The overall framework

LPAs have long had the duty of ensuring that adequate development land is made available to meet agreed targets for the number of new homes required in their areas. Locally determined targets in local development plans have to take account of national policy guidance and, until recently, were also obliged to take account of regional spatial strategies.[6] Targets for new homes, including for new affordable homes, are included in locally adopted Local Development Frameworks after lengthy processes of consultation and independent review. The land needed to meet these targets includes specific sites

---

[6]The Coalition government scrapped Regional Spatial Strategies in July 2010 on the basis that the each local planning authority should decide for itself, but taking into account national policy, the number of new homes that are appropriate.

allocated in development plans for new residential development plus pro-vision for some 'windfall' sites', the latter generally being small sites not identified in plans but which landowners and developers subsequently bring forward for planning permission. LPAs are also required to ensure a read-ily available supply of housing land for 5 years ahead, either with existing planning permission or if without consent, sufficiently free of constraints (planning policy, physical and marketing considerations) that it would be granted consent and come forward within the time period. Currently (DCLG, 2012a), LPAs are required to demonstrate that they have a supply of 5 years' worth of specific deliverable sites (rolled forward annually) to deliver their targets plus a buffer of 5–20% to provide choice and competition (the latter figure if the LPA has consistently under-delivered). They also have to iden-tify a supply of specific developable sites for 6–10 years and (where possible) for 11–15 years.

Despite policy requiring LPAs to have targets for affordable housing in their development plans, planning legislation in England does not permit LPAs to distinguish between different forms of housing tenure when allo-cating land and granting planning permission for its development, although they can and do address matters related to types, sizes and densities. The tenure of completed dwellings is thus a matter for developers, not for LPAs. Thus whilst the allocation of land for residential development in a plan sig-nificantly impacts on its development value once permission is granted, it is not possible to shape the pattern of land values through the planning sys-tem by allocating specific sites for, say, social rented housing and others for owner occupation – or a mix of both. This has meant that, historically, those seeking to acquire and develop land for social rented housing for low-income households have had to pay the market price for residential development land, values that have been primarily shaped by the market for homes built for sale to owner occupiers.

In practice, until the latter part of the 1990s, housing associations, now the main providers of new affordable homes, tended not to compete with the private sector for land. Instead they relied on the public sector, including local authorities, to sell land from their land banks, including land that had been acquired under compulsory purchase during slum clearance and other redevelopment programmes. Land also came from the surplus stocks of other public sector bodies, including the National Health Service. Valuation rules do not, however, permit public bodies to sell land below its market value. It has to be sold for the 'best consideration' so that although land for housing association development came from the public sector, it did not come at a discounted price but at the market price for the sites in question. These sources started to dry up from the year 2000 onwards (Monk *et al.*, 2005).

To ensure that housing associations could provide affordable homes whilst paying market prices for the land and for construction contracts, governments have provided them with 'producer subsidies' in the form of grants whilst also providing tenants with help to pay rents. Until 1988, these grants took the form of deficit grants where, subject to housing associations meeting requirements in relation to standards and cost limits, the government paid a grant to cover the land and construction costs that could not be covered by a loan raised on a net rent. At that time all housing association rents were Fair Rents, fixed independently by Rent Officers broadly on the lines used to fix rents in the regulated private rented sector. In effect, the government substantially underwrote development risk by giving grants and also providing loans on the cost of development, net of any grant paid.

This changed significantly in 1988 as a result of attempts to reduce government spending on housing associations by replacing public with private funding. Grants were fixed in advance as a proportion of defined costs (at the time approximately 60% of costs) and housing associations were required to finance the rest by raising private loans, thus transferring development risk from the government to housing associations (and the loans taken out by associations do not count as public expenditure). To give confidence to the capital markets that associations could fix rents that could defray new loans, associations became able to fix their own (assured) rents and the legal basis for tenants' security was changed. As a result of all these changes, new affordable housing was funded by a mix of lower grant and rents. Tenants continued to receive income-related assistance to help pay rents while limits were also imposed on subsequent rent increases (see Hills, 1991; Stephens *et al.*, 2005, for reviews of these changes). Because grant levels per new dwelling have continued to be reduced (typically now only about 20% of costs) associations are now allowed to construct new 'affordable rent' homes where they may charge up to 80% of the local market rents. These changes in grant levels inevitably put pressure on associations to maximise efficiency and minimise costs of production whilst still being required to meet specific design, space and energy standards.

These two separate systems of securing land and funding remained in place for many years. One, the land-use planning system, addressed overall housing requirements and managed a system for allocating and giving permission for enough development land to meet these needs. The other, the housing finance system, allocated public funding to enable housing associations to produce new affordable homes on the sites secured through the planning system. In practice, of course, it was never as simple as this (in particular in terms of the adequacy of land allocated). But now the distinction has broken down with the gradual adoption of the system of planning obligations to help secure some funding as well as the land for new affordable homes.

In the 1980s, LPAs began seeking ways of using the planning system to secure low-cost housing, including using density and dwelling size policies and attempting to restrict occupancy to meet locally arising needs (Bishop and Hooper, 2001; Rogers, 1985). They also began using planning obligations to negotiate contributions from private housing developers towards meeting local affordable housing requirements and in particular to get private developers to provide affordable housing on sites which were not allocated for housing in development plans, including on small rural sites and on much larger schemes for proposed new settlements in South East England. The discretionary nature of decision making in the planning system enabled planning authorities to grant permission on these unallocated sites. This was at a time when many development plans were out of date, despite significant development pressure, allied to rising house and land prices. On such unallocated sites, development values rose sharply when permission was granted, thus providing landowners and developers with very significant 'windfall' profits (see Barlow and Chambers, 1992; Crook, 1996; Jackson *et al.*, 1994).

This 'experimental' use of S106 thus tapped into the development value created to enable developers to fund new affordable homes as well as the infrastructure required for the schemes proposed. The problem with these 'experiments' was that they worked best on 'off-plan' sites because developers who had acquired these sites speculatively secured more development value than when they acquired allocated sites (where landowners' reasonable expectations that permission would be granted was factored into their required selling prices). This approach to getting developers to fund affordable housing thus potentially undermined emerging local planning strategies but subsequent events led to planning obligations being seen as a legitimate tool for securing affordable homes and in a context that accepted a much wider role for spatial planning in achieving broader economic and social objectives (Crook, 1996; Gallent, 2000).

To begin with, in 1989, in the face of rapidly rising house prices (and pressure from MPs concerned about the lack of affordable homes for their constituents – see Jackson *et al.*, 1994; Stephens *et al.*, 2005) the government formally encouraged the use of planning obligations, initially to help provide more rural housing on what became known as 'rural exceptions sites' where permission would be granted exceptionally on small sites in existing villages where there was no plan allocation and thus no 'hope' value attached to these sites (Gallent, 1997; DoE, 1989). Later, and more significantly, in a 1991 circular (DoE, 1991b), the government then endorsed the use of planning obligations to negotiate with developers to provide an element of affordable housing on all larger development sites on the basis that such sites should include a mix of house types and cater for a range of housing needs. The policy circular explicitly stated that a community's need for affordable housing was a material planning consideration which could be properly taken into account in formulating local plan policies. Where there was a demonstrable lack of affordable housing, LPAs could reasonably seek to negotiate with developers to include it within their schemes. The government's endorsement required these negotiations to be conducted within the framework of approved development plans and, if so, these would be backed by the Government and its planning inspectors when dealing with planning appeals, unless a planning authority imposed quotas irrespective of market and site conditions. The need to take account of site viability in negotiations was emphasised in the 1991 circular as was the need to ensure successive occupiers of the affordable housing benefited from its affordability, and that involving housing associations was likely to be a secure way of achieving this. This circular also confirmed the government's earlier endorsement of rural exceptions policies and stated that, to ensure long-term affordability on rural exceptions sites, shared ownership owners would not be permitted to 'staircase' to full ownership. Cross-subsidy from market to such off-plan sites would also not be appropriate.

To use planning obligations in this way, estimates of the need for new affordable homes and policies to meet them must be included in Local Development Frameworks. Targets should be stated (as a percentage of overall housing requirements) and these may also include site-specific targets (but not quotas; see DoE, 1992) and a stated intention to negotiate with developers for those contributions. The definition of 'affordable' now includes intermediate as well as social rented housing and low-cost market homes, provided the latter are sold below market price, this condition being a change on previous policy where low-cost market *per se* housing was acceptable (DCLG, 2006a; Monk and Whitehead, 2010). Although the policy has been stated in terms of larger development sites because they are large enough for a reasonable mix of sizes and types of houses, the thresholds for sites where affordable contributions may be sought have been changed. Initially outside inner London this was a 1.5-ha site – or one with 40 dwellings – later progressively altered (see below) but with planning authorities empowered to adopt lower thresholds, provided these were adopted in their local development plans. Whilst a formal threshold no longer applies (DCLG, 2012a), the Coalition government announced plans to return to a 10-dwelling threshold (HMT, 2013a) as it considered there is a 'disproportionate burden' for developments below this, impacting negatively on viability, including for those building their own homes (and, as we shall see below, consulted on excluding such schemes from any tariff style S106 obligations). It also proposed to exclude buildings being brought back into use from affordable housing contributions, although rural exceptions schemes would be excluded from this restriction (DCLG, 2014a). Following consultations, these proposals are to be implemented and further new measures are proposed to 'speed up' negotiations and to introduce timescales (HMT, 2014, para 15.23).

Finally, given the negotiated nature of contributions, emphasis has been placed on good practice and other advice on the importance, when setting targets and undertaking negotiations, of ensuring that sites remain viable to developers as well as securing the obligations needed. Targets for affordable housing on private development sites have typically varied between 30% and 50%, covering a range of social rented (and now affordable rented), intermediate and below market price homes for sale. Contributions can be made either in cash or more generally through the provision of land and housing at discounts. The principle involves private developers providing market housing and working in partnership with housing associations who buy the discounted land and/or completed dwellings from the developer at a price reflecting the rents they can charge, being typically half to two-thirds of construction costs. The involvement of housing associations ensures that the affordable homes secured are available in the long run, without the need for additional occupancy restrictions as part of the agreement.

The implicit expectation of the 1991 endorsement was that such development plan policies would reduce land prices since developers would know what was expected of them and that these lower prices and any cross-subsidy from the market housing would help fund the affordable element of the mix (Grant, 1991). The policy has been in place ever since, being continually endorsed in all subsequent planning circulars and Planning Policy Guidance Notes and Planning Policy Statements issued by governments since then (Crook *et al.*, 2006; DoE, 1992; DCLG, 2006b, 2012a; Stephens *et al.*, 2005). Indeed in 2000 the government reiterated its 1998 advice (see below) that developers' unwillingness to make a contribution of affordable homes 'would' be, of itself, a good reason for refusing permission – but changed the phrase 'would' to 'should' (DETR, 2000).

Detailed requirements

Whilst the overall policy has remained largely unchanged for many years, the detailed advice and steer from central government to LPAs and others has changed regularly, partly to reflect changing government housing and planning policies, partly to ensure that LPA practice is properly subsumed within the legal framework of planning and partly to reflect and disseminate good practice. The relevant circulars and policy guidance notes deal with a wide range of matters but especially cover the evidence base for policy, the extent to which policy is a 'material interest' for the purposes of making decisions on planning applications, the definitions of what could properly be secured as affordable housing, how to secure affordability in the long term, changes to thresholds for sites being used to secure affordable homes, the significance attached to securing on-site provision and of creating 'mixed communities' on them, the use of commuted payments and (increasingly) the need to examine the impact of policy on-site viability. The following paragraphs attempt to capture these changes in chronological order, picking out the most salient changes.

A 1996 circular (DoE, 1996) advised LPAs on the need to ensure that there was a mix of types and sizes of dwellings to 'encourage the development of mixed communities' (Ibid, para 3) as the government wanted to avoid excessive concentrations of any one tenure. It also dealt with the issue of how to retain affordability once the new affordable homes had been completed and first occupied, which was much more of a concern then than in later years. If housing associations were not to own or manage these, LPAs were advised to show how affordability would be otherwise secured in the long term. There was significant criticism that this circular had left thresholds unchanged (Johnston, 1996; Robinson, 1996) since housing associations were finding it difficult to secure sites by routes other than those secured through planning obligations.

Similarly a 1998 circular (DETR, 1998) re-emphasised that affordable housing need was a material consideration that 'could' be taken into account when formulating plans and deciding planning applications. If a LPA did this, an applicant's refusal to make provision of affordable housing in accordance with policy would itself justify refusing planning permission. It also pointed out that the policy was crucial to delivering the government's mixed communities and brownfield re-development agendas, the former achieved by securing agreed contributions 'on-site', thus mixing affordable rented with private market housing, rather than as a direct payment by developers enabling the affordable rented provision to be made elsewhere. It thus encouraged the use of obligations to create 'mixed and balanced communities to avoid areas of social exclusion' (Ibid, para 1). Commentators have subsequently remarked that the size of a site must be a factor when considering how mixed communities can be created and that the case for creating social mix on small sites was poorly evidenced (e.g. Crook and Whitehead, 1999a; RTPI, 1999). Policy was not permitted to favour a particular tenure as the means of achieving affordability but could include low-cost market as well as subsidised rented housing. The circular also answered the critics of the high thresholds by setting a lower threshold of 25 dwellings or 1 ha outside inner London below which LPAs should not normally pursue negotiations (15 dwellings or 0.5 ha in inner London). The 1992 Housing Policy Guidance Note stressed that preserving affordability was best secured by using housing associations because planning policies could not be used to determine tenure or price, although planning conditions that defined occupancy and density policies could also secure low-cost provision. It also stressed the importance of negotiation and the avoidance of uniform quotas (DoE, 1992).

The revised Planning Policy Guidance (PPG) note on housing in 2000 (DETR, 2000) made an important change when it stated that developers' willingness to agree to provide affordable housing 'should' (i.e. it changed the word from 'could' that had been in the earlier advice) be taken into account when deciding whether or not to grant planning permission, placing much greater emphasis on endorsing LPA's freedom to refuse permission for an entire development when developers would not provide affordable housing as part of it (Ibid, p. 10). LPAs were also challenged to secure a better social mix through planning obligations by 'avoiding the creation of large areas of housing of similar characteristics' (Ibid, p. 7). LPAs were advised to determine affordability on the basis of local incomes and prices. To foster more transparency, obligations about affordable housing should be placed on the statutory planning register.

The 2000 PPG had also placed emphasis on re-using brownfield sites and achieving higher densities and several commentators, including those giving evidence to a House of Commons select committee inquiry into the 1999 draft that had preceded the new guidance doubted whether all the changes made to the affordable housing policy since its inception in 1991 would deliver any more new affordable homes. Although policy was similar to the past, the context had changed so outcomes were likely to be different and in particular the then growing emphasis on prioritising brownfield sites and on higher densities for all housing development could result in less afford-able housing because lower market prices would create less development value to fund the affordable homes and hence more subsidy might be needed (see, e.g. Crook and Whitehead, 1999b).

A subsequent 2003 policy note set out to enhance the effectiveness of the policies by changing the advice on thresholds (ODPM, 2003a). The inner London threshold of 15 dwellings was effectively rolled out to the rest of the country. The government estimated that an additional 12 000 new afford-able homes would have been provided in 2002 had these lower thresholds been in force then. Setting lower thresholds than this needed justification, including demonstrating that there would be no impact on the overall sup-ply of housing. The policy note also removed low-cost market housing from the definition of affordable homes but proposed, in a change of approach, to allow tenure to be specified if there was no other way of protecting long-term affordability. The threshold changes were widely welcomed (e.g. see Crook *et al.*, 2003) but Grant, in his assessment, noted that, whilst the govern-ment's regulatory impact statement said the costs of providing more afford-able housing on smaller sites would fall on landowners, this was not likely to be the case with small urban sites (Grant, 2003a).

Following consultations on a new housing policy statement in 2005 (ODPM, 2005a,b), the government reiterated the need to have a mix of private market and affordable housing, particularly in terms of tenure and price, and to ensure that the supply was responsive to the market (DCLG, 2006b). Adopted plans had to conform to Regional Spatial Strategy policies on housing and establish the affordable housing needed overall with separate intermediate and social rented housing targets, also setting out the size and type of affordable housing required. On large sites policy should specify the proposed mix of market and affordable housing and tenure and price mix. On smaller sites, the mix should contribute to the creation of mixed communities. On-site provision of affordable housing was the presumption, but off-site provision was acceptable provided it secured mixed communities. LPAs were told to take account of viability issues, including looking at what subsidy was available and what could be reasonably expected of developers, balancing need against viability. Minimum thresholds were confirmed as 15 dwellings, but LPAs could justify lower ones in their plans. In the consultations, the government reinforced its view that a mix of tenures and types 'did not make bad neighbours' (ODPM, 2005b, p. 9). If proposed developments did not constitute mixed communities, LPAs would be justified in refusing permission. The partial regulatory impact statement assumed that the costs of providing affordable housing would fall on landowners, because land values would reflect plan requirements (Ibid, p. 37).

In a separate statement on what constituted affordable housing, the government stated that low-cost market housing could no longer be considered part of the affordable mix, although it could be part of the overall housing mix (DCLG, 2006a). Affordable housing was for those whose needs could not be met by the market, related to their incomes and house prices locally. Affordable housing, therefore, included social rented and other affordable including intermediate rented, discounted sale and shared equity ownership. The receipts of any that were subsequently sold had to be recycled into new provision. The statement was very optimistic about what could be achieved, arguing that high house prices everywhere made it possible to negotiate for more contributions of affordable housing and that all LPAs should attempt to match the performance of the best – as performance varied.

Finally, we come to the most recent policy statement, that of the Coalition government in the National Planning Policy Framework (DCLG, 2012a; see also House of Commons, 2014, for a review of evidence about its operation). The NPPF states that LPAs should

> use their evidence base to ensure that their Local Plan meets the full, objectively assessed needs for market and affordable housing in the housing market area, as far as is consistent with the policies set out in this Framework, including identifying key sites which are critical to the delivery of the housing strategy over the plan period. (DCLG, 2012a, para 46)

Where they

> have identified that affordable housing is needed, [*they should*] set policies for meeting this need on-site, unless off-site provision or a financial contribution of broadly equivalent value can be robustly justified (e.g. to

improve or make more effective use of the existing housing stock) and the agreed approach contributes to the objective of creating mixed and balanced communities. Such policies should be sufficiently flexible to take account of changing market conditions over time. (DCLG, 2012a, para 50).

The NPPF changed the definition of affordable housing from that in previous PPGs. The latter defined it as meeting the needs of eligible households at a cost low enough for them to afford, determined with regard to local incomes and house prices. The NPPF instead defines it as 'social rented, affordable rented and intermediate housing, provided to eligible households whose needs are not met by the market' (DCLG, 2012a).

Most recently, as we have noted above, the Coalition was consulting on proposals to re-introduce a minimum threshold of 10 dwellings. Also putting affordable housing contributions at risk was the proposal to allow private rented housing to count towards the proportion of affordable homes that was made in the Montague review of how to attract institutional investment into the private rented housing sector, involving the transfer of part of an obligation to contribute affordable rented towards private rented housing instead (DCLG, 2012b).

But the implications of this evolution of planning obligations as far as affordable housing is clear: it has brought together the two once quite separate state mechanisms for allocating funding and land for new affordable homes. It has thus used planning obligations to extract development value to help pay for some of society's need for new affordable homes. And as we shall see in Chapters 6–8, planning obligations have delivered substantial proportions of all new affordable housing secured. And although these have not all been additional to that which would have otherwise been secured in the absence of obligations, the policy has made a major contribution to securing land for new affordable homes and to creating mixed communities as well as providing some extra funding (see also Crook *et al.*, 2002a; House of Commons, 2003).

Recent policy initiatives

The success of planning obligations in securing and delivering funds for infrastructure and affordable housing in England (which we will see in detail in Chapters 6–8) depended on two specific circumstances. First, until the global financial crisis and credit crunch in 2007 there was buoyant demand, rising house prices and rising values of commercial development producing the high development values that enabled developers to agree and fulfil obligations. In general, developers accepted the principle of contributing to infrastructure costs (Calcutt, 2007). Second, the policy was generally stable, with much dissemination of good practice (on the latter, see Chapter 7). As a result, many LPAs had effective policies and practices in place, providing developers with the certainty they needed and enabling LPAs to achieve negotiated outcomes.

But since 2007, both the economic and policy environments have changed with potentially profound impacts on the feasibility of LPAs using planning obligations to fund infrastructure and other community needs. Moreover, although the pattern of demand and the period of stable policy may have enabled many LPAs to achieve desired outcomes, the pattern across England was very uneven, as Chapter 7 shows. By no means have all LPAs achieved their targets, due to a lack of policy, skills and resources. And the discretionary nature of the policy plus the growing emphasis on 'localism' under the Coalition government allowed local choice to undermine national policy goals, with NIMBYism[7] amongst voters fostering political opposition to development. Without new private development, there can be no planning obligations to help meet needs.

Although this was a period of relative policy stability, there was also a decade of debate about its rationale and effectiveness, including its lack of transparency and accountability (see the Nolan Committee on Standards of Conduct in Public Life, 1997), its partial coverage since it mainly addressed larger sites (see Chapter 6), the uncertainty and costs of negotiations, their slowness (and also their asymmetry with developers being seen to be better informed and resourced to conduct negotiations than LPAs) (see Chapter 7), the growing disconnect from the 'rational nexus' (as the 'Tesco' case had revealed) and the problem of free riders (Barker, 2003). The latter was a particular issue in areas of large-scale development where the first or last developer might run the risk of having to pay for the entire extra infrastructure required whilst others benefited from its contributions so the exclusive benefit justification of requiring contributions to infrastructure could not stand. To an extent, this latter problem was addressed in areas of very substantial development, such as Milton Keynes, with the introduction of a so-called roof tax, in effect an average cost charge per dwelling for all infrastructure (but not contributions to affordable housing or sites for schools, open spaces and other community purposes). The tariff was £18 500 per dwelling and £66 per square metre of commercial floorspace, although covering only the defined areas of expansion and incorporated under the Milton Keynes Partnership's planning powers. The total costs of the obligations (i.e. the roof tax and the affordable housing and other contributions) were between £30 000 and £40 000 per dwelling (House of Commons, 2006, Ev 15, 24; Merrick, 2006), a large proportion of the cost of constructing new homes.

---

[7]NIMBYism refers to the phrase 'Not in My Back Yard', one designed to cover the negative attitudes of local people towards proposed new developments.

As well as 'local' initiatives, like this 'roof tax', and a series of good practice publications (Audit Commission, 2006; DCLG, 2006c), there was also a series of national proposals to introduce alternatives or variants of planning obligations. We now describe each of these in turn.

Tariffs

In 2001, the government proposed to move towards a tariff approach (DTLR, 2001a). As part of a wider package of planning reforms, including the abolition of county council structure plans and the introduction of local development frameworks for all LPAs and regional spatial strategies (DTLR, 2001b), it proposed to replace site-by-site negotiated agreements with a standard fixed tariff for different types of development, including tariffs for affordable housing. The government had considered introducing impact fees on the lines of practice in the USA (see Chapter 9) but rejected this because of the difficulty of setting fees and also of withdrawing the ability of LPAs to negotiate site-specific issues through such arrangements. The proposal was that LPAs would set out the contributions expected and how these would be spent within their new development plan frameworks, thereby enhancing speed, certainty and transparency. The government cited the Nolan Committee's statement that planning obligations were the most intractable aspect of the planning system it had to deal with. It proposed that all S106 agreements would be entered on the planning register (a statutory register kept by all LPAs with details of all planning permissions) and that details of heads of terms of legal agreements would be included in reports going to LPA planning committees. Pooling of contributions from several agreements would also be permitted and there would be standard legal agreements.

But the proposals were abandoned in the face of much criticism, including from independent commentators as well as a Parliamentary Select Committee, the latter after taking evidence from professional bodies, trade associations and others (Crook *et al.*, 2002b; Grant, 2002; House of Commons, 2002). Criticisms centred on four aspects of the tariff concept. First, it would be impossible to fix an average tariff that would reflect all the underlying factors affecting all individual sites: it would be too high for some (destroying viability) and too low for others (reducing possible contributions). Inevitably this would mean that negotiations would have to continue; thus undermining one of the central objectives of the tariff idea.

Second, tariffs as presented by the government started to take on aspects of a tax or levy on development value and not a contribution to infrastructure costs since one of the suggested bases for calculating tariffs was to have regard to such values. Many of those giving evidence to the Select Committee thought tariffs were a way of introducing a betterment levy. Grant (2002) noted that tariffs would not be bound by the necessity test and so would be broader in purpose than simply defraying impacts and that the wider the purpose the more the tariff became a tax, although the more it was explicitly hypothecated the more it stayed a charge.

The third criticism was that tariffs would risk separating financial payments from the provision of land for affordable housing and undermine the mixed communities' agenda. Planning's role would become one of taxing development value rather than negotiating the provision of infrastructure and of land for affordable housing. If on-site provision of the latter declined, it was not clear where the land for affordable housing would come from, or its funding, so there was a real possibility that provision would fall, not increase – unless tariffs included commercial developments generating more overall funding. It was in fact likely that substantial negotiations would still be necessary even if tariffs were introduced, especially with respect to affordable housing given the variations between sites. Fourth, there was legal doubt as to whether tariffs were planning obligations and hence would not be enforceable through contract.

In summary, the select committee thought that tariffs would replace one form of complexity (the existing system) with another one and in its recommendations argued that instead of introducing a tariff system straight away the government should achieve improvements in the existing system of negotiated agreements. Only if these did not speed up the process and create more certainty should the government move to a tariff approach (House of Commons, 2002). In the end, the government decided to abandon the tariff proposal and to streamline the existing system instead (ODPM, 2003a, paras 52 and 53). In doing so, the government did not permit pooling nor require developers of later stages of major projects to contribute to the infrastructure earlier developers had paid for in negotiated obligations, a matter the government was forced to return to within the decade. The government's response to the Nolan committee was to undertake to hold seminars on the issues raised and act only if the issues raised suggested that changes were needed.

Optional planning charge

But the government returned to these issues again when, in 2003, it proposed a variant of tariffs, enabling developers to opt for either a tariff-like optional planning charge, giving them certainty, or if they wished instead they could negotiate planning contributions, affording them flexibility (ODPM, 2003b). The Government's objective was again to introduce more speed, certainty and transparency into the process, but not to enlarge the scope of planning obligations beyond current practice. The proposed optional charge would have included 'in kind' and on-site contributions of affordable housing as well as 'cash payments'. The consultation document suggested that optional charges might work well for small sites with negotiations continuing for larger sites. As one commentator noted, this looked like a 'highly pragmatic measure', proposing the introduction of tariffs whilst also retaining negotiated planning obligations. It also looked as if charges could cover contributions to matters going beyond the necessity test and allow pooling of contributions (Grant, 2003b).

Responses to the consultation were, however, not entirely positive (Bate, 2004; ODPM, 2004a; Winkley, 2004). Respondents recognised the need to deal with delays but also the value of negotiated contributions. Many supported an optional planning charge, unlike mandatory tariffs, but they also wanted more detail and to see a better balance between flexibility and simplicity. Problems would arise from averaging contributions via the charge (i.e. too high on some developments or too low on others in relation to the costs of mitigation). Respondents were also worried that the rational nexus and contractual links would be broken, compared with negotiated obligations, if the optional charge was paid in cash with no guarantees that the income would be spent on addressing the impacts of specific developments. The view that charges and obligations should not be used to extract more development value but only to mitigate impacts was strongly held. Hence there was general support for retaining the five tests (see above). Respondents also thought that the developers of large sites paid a disproportionate amount of infrastructure costs so there was a welcome for the voluntary pooling of obligations.

Despite the criticisms, the government pressed ahead and introduced legislation in 2004 for an optional planning charge, but it was not implemented. This was partly because the government was anticipating the Barker review (see below) and, because of this, stated in Parliament that 'it was in principle acceptable to fund social housing and other measures out of the uplift in land values associated with the planning process'. It did not think that the obligations were the right measure to tax development value but instead of implementing the optional planning charge it further consulted on planning obligations in 2004 (ODPM, 2004b). This proposed some short- to medium-term changes after which might follow the more fundamental changes recommended by Barker (see below). This consultation noted that whilst there was merit in extending what could be addressed via planning obligations, the government's view was that

> S106 is not the right mechanism with which to achieve the successful capture of development gain ... therefore ... S106 should continue to be an impact mitigation or positive planning measure linked to planning necessity and that it should not be used for tax-like purposes such as the capture of land value increases for purposes not directly necessary for development to proceed. (ODPM, 2004b, para 26)

The consultation (paras 29 and 30) also sought to clarify the use of obligations to secure affordable housing given that it was distinct from impact mitigation. Instead it was a positive planning measure to secure mixed communities and a revised circular was to clarify this by separating out affordable housing from impact mitigation measures but still requiring it to fall within the five policy tests. In effect, this statement was designed to legitimise current practice and was also in line with the distinction drawn by Barker in her final report between impact mitigation and affordable housing (see below).

In the circular which followed (ODPM, 2005c), the government endorsed the use of standard charging which it hoped LPAs would adopt as interim measures whilst the government came up with a more long-term approach. Standard charging was especially useful for contributions to infrastructure requiring, for example, fixed amounts per square metre of floorspace or per new house for contributions to education. These charges would be published in LPAs' supplementary planning guidance and, as the circular stressed, were not unlike the unimplemented optional planning charges. The circular clarified policy in relation to planning obligations, stressing the importance of including them in development plan documents showing what and how LPAs would collect obligations to make development acceptable. It stressed that obligations could prescribe the nature of development (e.g. require that some is affordable housing), compensate for loss or damage (e.g. open space) or mitigate impact (e.g. more public transport provision). It re-stated the 'Secretary of State's five policy tests' and stressed that obligations should not be used as a means of securing a 'betterment levy' (para B7) but used only to make developments acceptable in planning terms. To emphasise this, it changed the 'necessary', in the five policy tests to the phrase 'necessary in planning terms'. Standard agreements and the use of third parties in negotiations were also commended.

Planning gain supplement

In the meantime whilst this review of obligations was proceeding, a major report commissioned by the government on housing supply was published. Its author, Kate Barker, was then a member of the government's Monetary Policy Committee. In her interim report, she had noted that previous attempts to tax development gains had all foundered on 'strong opposition, widespread avoidance and the difficulty and complexity of their operation, often aggravated by poor design .... As a result, none have been particularly successful in achieving their aims' (Barker, 2003, p. 118). In her final report, she nonetheless argued that 'The Government should actively pursue measures to share in these windfall gains which accrue to landowners, so that these increases in land values can benefit the community more widely' (Barker, 2004, p. 7).

Having considered the range of options for doing this (including capital gains tax, development gains taxation, changes to VAT and to the operation of the planning obligations regime), she recommended that a planning gain supplement (PGS) should be introduced to fund infrastructure. PGS would be levied on the actual gains in development value realised at the point at which full planning permission was granted, whereas, for example, imposing VAT on newly built homes as an alternative would only have an indirect effect working back to land prices through the effect of VAT on developers' costs. Barker recommended that PGS would be levied nationally (i.e. UK wide) at a low rate on the development value of all developments and the proceeds returned in part to local authorities. She argued that this supplement would fall on the prices landowners received and have little impact on house prices. Although imposing taxes tends to discourage supply, she expected the effect to be small given the interaction of land supply with the planning system and given that PGS was to be part of a wider package of measures to increase the supply of development land (Barker, 2004, p. 69). Allied to PGS would be a scaling back of S106 to deal only with site mitigations and affordable housing (the latter to enable mixed communities to be secured through on-site provision). Hence, one commentator argued, Barker was proposing to mix an explicit (PGS) with implicit (scaled back S106) taxation of economic rent (Oxley, 2006).

Barker thought PGS had 'considerable advantages' compared with previous attempts to tax development value and with the alternative of planning obligations (Barker, in Bill, 2004). It could bring greater certainty for developers about what the combined PGS and S106 costs were likely to be. It could avoid lengthy and complex S106 negotiations. It could also avoid many planners feeling 'they have become reluctant and inefficient, tax collectors'. The tax rate could be varied between greenfield and brownfield sites, and have regional and local flexibility. S106 agreements were unsatisfactory, as the developments yielding the largest amounts of development value in obligations may not have been those that created the biggest mitigation costs to the locality. PGS could be used to provide incentives for housing planning permissions, fund the requisite infrastructure and potentially help high-cost brownfield developments. PGS was also fair and would reduce the windfall gains made from planning permission. The perception that developers and landowners made undeserved gains was, she thought, one of the factors that caused developments to be regarded cynically by those affected.

The then government took forward many of the Barker proposals in the 2005 pre-Budget report (HMT, 2005; HMT and ODPM, 2005; HMT, HMRC and ODPM, 2005). The Government accepted the principle of funding infrastructure and affordable housing out of development values. The latter was not properly captured by capital gains tax as it dealt only with disposals, whereas PGS and S106 were payable on the commencement and subsequent phasing of development. PGS was to be levied as a proportion of the value of a site with full planning permission, less the costs of any obligations under a scaled back S106 agreement, and less the site's current use value as permitted by the planning system. PGS would be paid once development had commenced. It would be charged at a 'modest' rate. It would help finance additional local and strategic infrastructure whilst maintaining development incentives; ensure local communities better shared in the benefits of development; secure a fairer, more efficient and more transparent way of capturing a proportion of development value; and be simple and effective to administer whilst also responding to changing market conditions and not distorting development decisions. The scope of S106 was to be scaled back as Barker had proposed. The alternative of developing planning obligations instead of introducing PGS would not fairly capture some development value for community benefit because planning obligations addressed planning issues at a local level and were less suitable for funding the infrastructure needed to unlock more development land (HMT, 2005). Prior to the introduction of PGS, LPAs were once again encouraged to use standard charging. The government also announced plans to make the planning system more responsive to demand, to ensure more funding was available for infrastructure through a Community Infrastructure Fund and established a number of growth areas and increased the funding for affordable homes.

Some of the initial responses to this consultation (HMT, HMRC and ODPM, 2006), including from those in the development industry, supported the principle of using development value to finance additional infrastructure but argued that tariffs (including the formerly proposed optional planning charge) were better ways of capturing development value for infrastructure funding. But the Government reiterated its support for PGS saying that a 'workable and effective PGS ... represents a fairer and more effective means of releasing land value to help finance infrastructure' (HMT, 2006, p. 69).

There were subsequent consultations on technical matters, including on the valuation and the collection of 'planning gain', the latter indicating it would be collected when development commenced on a self-assessment basis by central government through Her Majesty's Revenue and Customs, with the emphasis on simplicity and on avoiding the complexities which developers had faced in previous attempts to tax development value (HMRC, 2006a,b). There were also consultations on how a scaled-back S106 system would work both by improving the system (reducing negotiations costs and increasing certainty) and by ensuring PGS and S106 could work alongside each other, especially to avoid developers paying twice for the same infrastructure (so-called double dipping by LPAs). Agreed liabilities for scaled-back S106 obligations would reduce the development value of sites and hence reduce developers' liability for PGS payments. The government recognised the importance of ensuring that developers had confidence that the infrastructure to be funded by PGS in the future (and previously by S106) would be delivered on time to enable development to proceed (DCLG, 2006d). Instead of drawing up a list of matters that would fall within scaled-back S106, a criterion-based approach was to be adopted. To help foster negotiations for affordable housing contributions through scaled-back S106, the government proposed to put this requirement on a statutory footing and also to endorse common starting points for such negotiations to help developers understand what was expected from them (for a critical review, see Monk *et al.*, 2008). The government noted that PGS and S106 combined would raise more funds than S106 had done alone because PGS would embrace all but the very minor types of development.

However, whilst many welcomed the objectives behind PGS it was subject to a number of concerns (Blackman, 2005; Dewar, 2005; Henneberry, 2005; Hilditch, 2006; see also Oxley, 2006, for a review of these) including how the rate would be set, how much of the levy would be returned to the LPAs where the development on which levy has been extracted was located, about the lack of a specific contractual link between payments and the infrastructure to be funded, and the potential impact on the supply of affordable housing (Monk *et al.*, 2006). There were also concerns as to whether the levy rate would be adequate enough to secure the infrastructure funding needed whilst also low enough to avoid being a disincentive on development (a rate of about 20–25% was assumed to be necessary to provide the funding by many of those who gave evidence to a parliamentary inquiry on PGS). Many witnesses to this inquiry (House of Commons, 2006) argued that these problems could be avoided by retaining and improving the planning obligations system, given the evidence that good practice was successfully improving its speed, certainty and transparency. The Committee agreed that there were many advantages to PGS as it would give LPAs the opportunity to plan ahead and fund infrastructure in a more 'strategic manner' whilst also reducing incentives to give planning permission solely to secure financial gain through S106 agreements. Developers would also benefit from greater certainty, greater fairness and a less onerous planning regime. But the detailed implementation needed to take account of the many concerns and risks which threatened its potential success. In particular the administration needed to be simple and clear and avoid the pitfalls of complex administration (by limiting any exemptions and discounts) which had undermined all previous attempts to tax development value. It also urged that the majority of funds collected should be returned to the LPAs where the development took place.

The RTPI and Halliwells in their response to the consultations were particularly concerned to find ways of linking PGS to the timely delivery of clearly necessary infrastructure in order to retain the confidence of the property and development sector, stressing the importance of having adequately funded infrastructure plans in place alongside statutory development plans. (RTPI and Halliwells, 2007, p. 7)

They were also worried that valuations would be contentious and time consuming and that PGS payments to HMRC would be slow so that the flow of funds back to local authorities to fund infrastructure would not match the needs and timing of the infrastructure required to support the developments from which PGS would have been levied.

Others argued that a modest fixed standard rate of PGS everywhere, allied to a scaling back of S106, could result in PGS producing far more income for local authorities in the 'low-pressure regions' of England than had been secured through S106 negotiations but far less in the 'high-pressure' areas which would lose funding under the proposals (Rowley and Crook, 2006). It would also reduce the viability of development on small sites which tended not to be subject to S106 agreements. It was also argued that the proposed system would produce perverse outcomes in terms of securing affordable housing (Crook *et al.*, 2007). As PGS would be levied on the development value less the contributions negotiated on scaled-back S106 obligations, developers might try to minimise the latter to (perversely) maximise the net sum available for PGS, given the modest rate likely to be set. Overall they might pay less than under the current arrangements and this could result in less affordable housing being secured. Conversely LPAs might have an equally perverse incentive to minimise affordable housing contributions to maximise the amount that could be secured through PGS. Others argued, and with concern, that PGS might incentivise LPAs to give permission to developments that did not accord with their adopted plans solely to secure a financial benefit (House of Commons, 2006).

In its response to the Committee's report, the Government argued that having looked closely at alternatives it still believed that a workable and effective PGS was the 'right approach to securing a portion of value uplift for public benefit' (DCLG, 2006e, p. 1). It would be fairer than planning obligations, applied to a wider range of developments and, because it would be based on a portion of development value and not the cost of infrastructure, it was less likely to inhibit development. None of the alternatives proposed by consultees to the government's consultations 'have the same potential as PGS' (Ibid, p. 2).

After these consultations and further critical comments (Bowes, 2007; Gallimore, 2007; Papas, 2007; Wilson, 2007), there was a further 2007 consultation on alternatives (DCLG, 2007a; HMT, 2007a). The Government argued that, although it still planned to introduce legislation to adopt PGS to secure the uplift in development values to fund infrastructure, it would be willing to defer the legislation if a better way was identified. It noted that:

> the test of an effective approach to planning gain will be its ability to raise significant additional funds to support the infrastructure needed for development in a fair and non distortionary way, and in a way that preserves incentives to develop .... (DCLG, 2007a)

It also noted that the Barker PGS proposals had been published after the consultations on tariffs (2001) and on optional planning charges (2003) had shown that the development industry had reservations about these. If PGS was introduced, the rate would be 'modest', and the same across the whole of the UK and to provide stability would not change from year to year, there would be no separate rate for brownfield development (since development values would already be lower than on greenfield sites), 70% would be paid directly to the LPA where the development had occurred and the rest retained within the region (and in London allocated to the Mayor) to support strategic infrastructure, especially transport. It would not come into operation until 2009. It stressed the need for LPAs to spend their PGS revenue in the context of adopted development plans including infrastructure plans. In the meantime, the Government sought views on four alternatives: (i) a lower rate of PGS and less S106 scaling back than had been proposed in a 2006 consultation document (DCLG, 2006d); (ii) a PGS for greenfield sites alone; (iii) a charging mechanism based on an expanded S106 regime; and (iv) a statutory planning charge – in effect somewhat like the Milton Keynes tariff, the so-called roof tax.

Community infrastructure levy

Following this further consultation, the PGS was eventually abandoned by the then government and instead tariffs were endorsed, *pro tem* the search for an alternative approach. Then in the Pre-Budget Report for 2007 (HMT, 2007b) the Government announced that, following discussions with key stakeholders it would legislate for a new planning charge in the Planning Bill, to be called the Community Infrastructure Levy (CIL), which LPAs would have the discretion, but not the duty, to introduce. It would be a charge on all but the smallest developments and would help fund the local and sub-regional infrastructure necessary to support the development of an area. It would be more predictable and certain than S106 and (like PGS was to have been) also fairer by ensuring all development was charged, would address better the cumulative impact of small developments, and would allow sub-regional infrastructure to be funded (DCLG, 2008a, b, 2009).

Despite the way PGS would have addressed the 'free rider problem', many of its critics, as we saw above, had been concerned with the way PGS 'delinked' the payment of the levy from the funding of specific items of infrastructure and also the fact that the levy rate would be nationally imposed and related to development value, not a locally chosen one related to infrastructure costs. Whilst the CIL proposal accepted the legitimacy of using value uplift to fund infrastructure, it also addressed these concerns about PGS (Davey, 2007). The government once again argued that it was right for all developments to bear a share of the cost of the infrastructure needed to support it and it was also right for the community to get some benefit from development values. CIL would enable this to be achieved and at the same time give developers certainty (DCLG, 2010a, paras 8 and 9). The government also stressed, in the debates on the passage of the CIL legislation through Parliament, that the CIL charge would be based on the costs of the infrastructure required and would not be a straight 'tax' on development values as would have been the case with PGS, although in ensuring that schemes remained viable under a CIL regime it was important that charging schedules took account of development value (House of Commons Hansard, 2008). The point was also made in other Parliamentary debates that, whereas PGS was to have been a nationally set levy on the assessed development value of each site and collected nationally with some of it redistributed to LPAs, CIL was to be an area-wide locally determined standard charge and not a tax collected on development value and it would be raised and spent locally (Donatantonio, 2008; House of Lords Hansard, 2008, Col. 1249). The government emphasised that the CIL's 'overall purpose is to ensure that development contributes fairly to the mitigation of the impact it creates' and contributions could be made without removing incentives to develop (DCLG, 2008a, para 4). It explained that CIL followed the example of the tariff schemes of some LPAs, would also improve certainty for developers and had the potential to raise 'hundreds of millions of pounds of extra funding for infrastructure' (Ibid, para 24: see also DCLG, 2007b). The government noted that CIL had been broadly welcomed by trade and professional groups (DCLG, 2008a, Box 3). It also emphasised that CIL funding would be additional and that most infrastructure funding would come from core public funding which the government was seeking to co-ordinate better.

CIL was provided for in legislation in 2008 and came into operation in April, 2010 (DCLG, 2010a). The legislation provided for a discretionary levy on all new development specifically to fund sub-regional and local infrastructure, with LPAs as the charging authorities. If a LPA decides to charge CIL, it decides on the charge itself, taking account of its adopted development plan, its infrastructure plan and overall funds required, what is available from other sources and the viability of development in its area. It fixes the

CIL charge by striking an 'appropriate balance' between viability and raising funds. The draft charging schedule is subject to independent review by a planning inspector, similar to reviews of development plan documents (the review tests if CIL rates put the overall development of an area at serious risk, not the viability of every single allocated site). Charges are kept up to date by up-rating using building costs indices. CIL must be spent on infrastructure, including sub-regional infrastructure that crosses LPA boundaries. It can also be used to remedy existing deficiencies provided this is necessary to support new development. Some early evidence on implementation suggested that LPAs found many of the processes for establishing CIL charging schedules challenging, partly because the preparation of infrastructure plans, on which these depended, was not then well developed (Dobson, 2012).

All except very small scale new developments[8] are eligible to pay CIL charges which are averaged and not site-specific, but also not necessarily the same across a whole of a LPA's area. CIL becomes liable when full planning consent has been obtained and the developer notifies the LPA that the development has commenced (CIL also becomes a registered land charge so anyone acquiring land is aware of the liability if the permitted development has started). This timing presents problems for small builders whose constrained cash flow may make it difficult to fund this upfront payment (Office of Fair Trading, 2008). When CIL is introduced, it becomes a compulsory and non-negotiable levy on all development (except minor development and any parts of sites used for charitable purposes or devoted to social rented or shared ownership housing[9]), leaving only the balance of development value available for negotiations to cover affordable housing and site-specific mitigation. CIL exemptions are deliberately limited to comply with European Union state aid rules.

CIL thus runs alongside S106, which has been (as PGS would have been) scaled back to address site mitigation and affordable housing (DCLG, 2010b). Affordable housing has been maintained within scaled-back S106 rather than as part of the funding secured through CIL, because of the importance of on-site provision as a means of securing mixed communities. The five 2005 policy tests for S106 agreements were reduced to three and became mandatory for LPAs to use by being part of the CIL regulations so that any S106 obligations agreed as part of a planning consent must be: (i) necessary to make development acceptable in planning terms, (ii) directly related to the development and (iii) must be fairly and reasonably related to the development. Thus the 'rational nexus' is now an explicit requirement for S106

---

[8]Only less than 100 m^2 gross internal floor-space is exempted; change of use is covered too unless the use change is permitted within the Use Classes Order.
[9]The rented housing must be let on an assured tenancy and the initial tranche of shared ownership acquired must not exceed 75% of the open market value. If the dwellings subsequently cease to be occupied as affordable homes, the CIL charge appropriate at the time of commencement of the site is then levied.

obligations but does not apply to the CIL charge for new development where there is an averaging approach to the charging schedule. Because of this, pooling of S106 contributions is limited to five developments where CIL is introduced and nationally everywhere, even if CIL is not introduced, from 2015 onwards (originally to have been 2014, but postponed for a year). Regulations also specify that S106 obligations cannot be used to fund the types of infrastructure funded through CIL and identified in a LPA's charging schedule. Most recently, as we saw above, the government has proposed changing the threshold to 10 dwellings below which LPAs should not seek to negotiate contributions to affordable housing (DCLG, 2014a).

The CIL provisions thus explicitly accept that gains in development value should be used to fund infrastructure, that a close 'rational nexus' is no longer needed to do this (and it removes the explicit S106 contractual link between contributions raised and the infrastructure provided) and that an averaging approach to charging for infrastructure is desirable (DCLG, 2011a). This represents a considerable break with the S106 system described above. In principle it increases equity, certainty, speed, transparency and accountability in charging development value to fund infrastructure.

A key concern has been whether the new provisions hinder the use of the now scaled-back S106 to negotiate developer contributions for more new affordable homes (Lee, 2008) whilst CIL fixed charges also raises many of the same issues as tariffs by impacting differentially on site viability (Whitehead *et al.*, 2007). In relation to affordable housing provision, CIL reverses the arrangements under PGS. Under the latter, PGS would have been levied on the development value remaining after obligations had been negotiated for affordable housing and site mitigation. Under CIL, the levy is a mandatory first charge and negotiated site mitigation and affordable housing contributions have to come out of what is left over from the development value after the CIL charge. Because it is always more difficult and time consuming for LPAs to negotiate affordable housing than simply to collect standard charges from developers the government actively considered at one stage using CIL proceeds to fund affordable housing (Carpenter, 2011). It did not do so, stressing the importance of securing site-specific contributions to create mixed communities rather than just securing a 'pot' of funds for affordable homes. It has also continually emphasised that, when drawing up CIL charging schedules, LPAs must take account of their formally adopted affordable housing policies so that the costs to developers of affordable housing contributions must be factored into CIL charges, a point reiterated by planning inspectors examining draft charging schedules. The concerns about the potential negative impact of CIL on securing affordable housing by planning obligations was heightened by the decision taken in 2011 by the Homes and Communities Agency (the government agency providing grants to housing associations) to move to a zero grant policy on affordable housing schemes on S106 sites (HCA, 2011), the Housing Corporation having previously indicated that it would need convincing that additional housing was provided beyond that reasonably expected of an obligation before it would allocate grants to an affordable housing development on a S106 site (Housing Corporation, 2007, paras 4.13–4.21).

Changes to CIL and new LPA incentives

It is difficult to predict the long-term impact of the new CIL arrangements on securing development value for infrastructure and for affordable housing, not only because of the changed economic environment but also because there have been changes to CIL and the creation of new fiscal incentives for LPAs to grant planning permissions since the Coalition government took office (see also Chapter 8).

The new Coalition Government decided to keep CIL, unlike the Conservative Party had stated when in opposition (Conservative Party, 2009; Tilley, 2010). The Coalition accepted that CIL was a simpler, fairer and more transparent approach than sole reliance on S106. It also noted that CIL mitigated the pooling failure arising from the fact that the cumulative impact of small developments is not funded adequately through S106 because developers have neither the incentives nor the resources to contribute to this. In the 'best estimate' in its initial impact assessment the Coalition expected CIL to raise just over £1bn a year towards infrastructure funding, assuming housing completions ran at 200 000 a year and that 92% of LPAs charged CIL (DCLG, 2011b).

But in keeping CIL the Coalition government also introduced some procedural changes to it so that what was once conceived as a simple fixed tariff (with some limited variations in types of development and in specific zones of a LPA area) has now become very complex. The regulations were originally poorly drafted in 2010 and since then there have been four amendments in as many years trying to improve matters but also making some key changes. As a result, the collection of CIL funds for infrastructure has now become very complex indeed, although the main principle that CIL charges are not negotiable has remained (Editorial, 2013; Webb, 2013). The changes are as follows: (i) make it a requirement for LPAs to seek an appropriate balance between raising funds through CIL and ensuring charges do not make development unviable (whilst also raising the funding for the infrastructure needed to support developments); (ii) give LPAs more flexibility over payment schedules; (iii) no longer oblige them to fully comply with independent examiners' reports on draft charging schedules; (iv) exempt more development from CIL charging, including self-built homes and empty property brought back into use (unless more floor-space was created); (v) allow developers to comply with CIL charges by making provision in-kind and extend previous provisions which permitted land to be transferred as payments for a CIL charge, giving developers greater confidence in the infrastructure being provided than relying solely on LPAs funding necessary schemes from CIL receipts. The government also committed itself to reviewing CIL in 2015 (DCLG, 2013, 2014b, c).

In addition and importantly to increase incentives for local communities to support new development, the Coalition provided for a proportion of CIL income to be paid over to local neighbourhoods where development takes place (DCLG, 2010c, 2011c). The intention is to reduce resistance to development proposals by ensuring that local communities bearing the brunt of new development have the resources to address these themselves by funding neighbourhood facilities – and thus be less likely to oppose such developments. Following consultation (and provisions in the Localism Act of 2011), the government finally decided in 2013 that 25% of CIL funds raised would be handed over to local groups where development took place provided they had neighbourhood plans in place (if not, the proportion is 15%). It is still too early to say if this has had any impact on reducing local resistance to new developments. Moreover in 2013 as part of the documents released during the Autumn Statement, including an update of the National Infrastructure Plan (HMT, 2013b,c), the Coalition announced a pilot to test a proposal to distribute some CIL directly to households affected by new developments. The pilot is to take place in autumn 2014 and would make payments directly to households who live in proximity to new housing developments

> to reduce the extent to which development is blocked or delayed as a result of active opposition by local residents … in fairness to those who live closest and who bear the greatest burden of development in the short term we may want to do more to ensure they also see the benefits of the development. (DCLG, 2014d)

At the same time, a 'New Homes Bonus' has been introduced to provide LPAs with fiscal incentives to grant more permission for new housing in their areas, with additional incentives when permission is given for new affordable homes (see DCLG, 2010d). The Coalition believes that these incentives will be more effective in ensuring that new housing is given permission than the previous government's 'top-down' targets in regional spatial strategies. The Bonus was introduced in 2011 (DCLG, 2011d) to reward those LPAs that give planning permissions above a benchmark with additional funds. These are provided by central government to those who qualify, drawn from the (now cancelled) housing and planning delivery grant, plus other funds drawn from the existing 'pot' of support grants it provides all local authorities. For each new home (or empty home brought back into use), local authorities are paid an amount equivalent to the national average for that home's council tax band every year for 6 years as a non-ring-fenced grant (so that at the end of the sixth year the enhancement progressively diminishes).

The Coalition estimated that 140 000 extra new homes would be provided as a result of the bonus arrangements. These have subsequently come under criticism from the National Audit Office (NAO, 2013) and the Public Accounts Committee (PAC, 2013) specifically on the grounds that it is unclear whether the incentive works and that the £1.3bn paid up to 2013–2014 was not being adequately monitored, creating a substantial risk to LPAs because of the scheme's redistributive nature. In fact, the scheme was changed after it was launched so that LPAs receiving funds had to pool some of them with other LPAs operating within the same Local Economic Partnership Areas, potentially reducing local incentives, although this has very recently been changed so that LPAs now keep all their bonuses, except in London (HMT, 2013c). The National Audit Office was very unconvinced about the efficacy of the scheme

> It is difficult for local authorities to persuade communities of the benefits of new housing. New housing is often unpopular with residents who may be concerned about pressure on local services, loss of amenities, traffic congestion and disruption during building. Some councillors, local authority officers and stakeholders with whom the NAO spoke suggested these views were often strongly held and difficult to change. (NAO, 2013).

Subsequent research (DCLG, 2014e) found that both staff and elected members of LPAs knew about and understood how the scheme worked, including its financial implications for them, although only small proportions of the fund had been directly used to support new housing development. Although the bonus was seen within LPAs as an incentive for supporting the provision of new homes this was much less true of others in the wider community. More generally, the bonus scheme was one of several factors behind more proactive approaches but was not found to be directly shaping attitudes at the time of the research.

Viability and S106

However at the same time as these incentive schemes were introduced, the Coalition government also became concerned that S106 agreements which had been struck in the more buoyant economic conditions prevailing before the global financial crisis could be rendering developments unviable and stalling them (DCLG, 2012c). It produced evidence showing that in March 2012 there were 1400 housing schemes with over 10 potential new dwellings that were stalled but capable of producing 75 000 new homes, with over half being in weak or very weak markets. It introduced legislation in the 2013

Growth and Infrastructure Act that allowed developers to seek modification from LPAs of the affordable housing content of any agreement (whenever agreed) and allowed appeal to the Planning Inspectorate against LPAs' decisions on the matter. Until this was put in place, developers had to wait for 5 years before they could insist modifications were considered. In assessing requests, LPAs must use viability guidance issued by DCLG. Any resulting changes to affordable housing requirements last only three years and the legislation 'sunsets' automatically in 2016. What this legislation does is to make into a statutory obligation what many LPAs have always been willing to do to enable stalled development to proceed, including deferring payment and re-phasing obligations over time, typically reducing affordable housing requirements by about a third (LGA, 2012). Although this has also highlighted the difficulties of undertaking viability assessments (McAllister *et al.*, 2013; this volume Chapter 5), it has also led to a better understanding that landowners need much more than existing use value if they are to make it available for development. New NPPF guidance on viability introduced in 2014 indicated that policies, CIL and obligations must allow landowners and developers a competitive return, the latter being the price at which a reasonable landowner would willingly sell their land for the development (DCLG, 2014f). Chapter 8 discusses the impact of these changes on the renegotiation and delivery of obligations.

CIL policy: concluding comments

The changes made by the Coalition government mean that what had been designed as a scheme to secure contributions from all development to fund strategic infrastructure has now become a scheme where there are many exemptions and some of the funds are now used to incentivise local communities to accept development. This, together with the revisions to S106 agreements under the reviews of viability, potentially reduces the flow of funds for essential infrastructure and for new affordable homes (Carpenter, 2014; Walker, 2010).

As a result, alternatives are also being pursued by some LPAs, specifically Tax Increment Financing (TIF), which the Coalition government promoted in the 2010 Comprehensive Spending review (Kochan, 2010). TIF allows LPAs to borrow on the basis of projected council tax income, specifically business rates, on schemes (especially commercial ones) which are unable to proceed because LPAs cannot fund their infrastructure needs. The borrowed funds are used to secure this infrastructure and complete the development. The tax proceeds from this help repay the debts taken out through the TIF method. TIF is not without risk, specifically that the rate income does not arise or that the new development (and associated income) might simply be diverted from other schemes. In addition, the Coalition government is keeping under review the possibility of enabling LPAs to auction land (HMT, 2013c), and have provided £675m worth of revolving infrastructure funds to local economic partnerships to help progress stalled projects in the recession (DCLG, 2014g) and have also announced similar funding for a limited number of housing zones to help speed up development on large brownfield sites (DCLG, 2014h).

Conclusions

We have seen how planning obligations policy has been changed and adapted by successive local as well as central governments over the last few decades, moving from negotiations to tariffs and from seeking contributions to costs to implicitly taxing development value. In the past planning obligations policy was based solely on negotiating contributions to infrastructure costs and mitigating impact arising from the development of a specific site, where the 'rational nexus' underpinned legitimacy. LPAs also began to use obligations to collect wider contributions than this and the courts held this was *intra vires*, provided they did not refuse permission for development that accorded with their policy, simply because applicants refused to contribute to these wider needs or permitted it only to secure a financial contribution. In the past, obligations policy was explicitly stated as not taxing development value but getting developers to contribute to demonstrable mitigation costs for specific sites. Now CIL is a policy based on a tariff-like approach whereby developers are required to contribute to the average costs of providing infrastructure across a wide area. It is also now seen as legitimate to collect some of the development value accruing to landowners and developers and to use this to pay for infrastructure and wider community needs including affordable housing. It has also most recently become a means of using development value to finance facilities which may remove local communities' resistance to new housing and other development.

Thus it has evolved from the provision of basic infrastructure (road access, transportation) to wider community benefits (open space, education) and then extended to include affordable housing. The model has thus developed to encompass two different economic objectives, both in the context of increasingly limited public finance. The first is to promote efficiency in the allocation of resources by facing developers with having to pay for more of their externalities (i.e. the costs their developments impose on the rest of us like the need for new schools and improved roads), thus better aligning private with social costs. But commentators have pointed out that obligations are not explicitly designed as price signals to shape the pattern of development (Clinch and O'Neill, 2010a,b; Webster and Lai, 2003).

The second economic objective is to improve equity by increasing the output of new affordable homes and requiring developers to provide land and some funding. Bowers (1992) agreed in part with Keogh (1985) that communities are better off under a system where 'planning gain' is permitted compared to one that is not. He argued that 'planning gain' should not just address compensation for social costs in the form of a Pigouvian tax but should also extract the economic rent as betterment with a LPA 'acting as a discriminating monopolist after first internalising all externalities' (p. 1334).

The legitimacy of requiring developers to pay infrastructure costs and thus mitigate the wider impacts of their schemes has now largely been accepted. As we shall see in later chapters, planning obligations have raised large sums for this – and for affordable housing. Indeed in 2007–2008 total contributions worth £5bn were secured in planning obligations, much of which was subsequently delivered (Chapters 6 and 8). This compares with the very much smaller sums collected under the post-war nationally imposed levies: £172m in 1952, £356m in 1969–1970 and £147m in 1983–1984, all at 2007–2008 prices (Chapter 3, this volume). As Chapter 6 shows, this 2007–2008 funding did not come from all development sites but mainly from the larger ones, making the total sum secured even more impressive, compared with previous national attempts to levy a tax on development value on all sites with planning permission.

But why were planning obligations as *de facto* taxes on development value so successful compared with their predecessor *de jure* charges, levies and taxes? The answer lies in three key facets of planning obligations policy and its implementation. We explore these in more detail in Chapters 6–8, but a brief summary is appropriate now. First, the sums extracted have been raised as a result of site by site negotiations and not national 'imposts', the former set within locally determined policy frameworks that take account of viability issues. Second, the sums agreed are spent locally to help fund the very infrastructure on which the success of developers' schemes depend. Both the local authority needing a new school, for example, and the developer needing to sell new developments have every reason to reach agreement on the developer's contribution to the cost of the school and to ensure it is built. Third, these sums were achieved during an 'upswing' in the development and hence in the development value cycle. Developers were keen to get consents to take advantage of the profits to be made and had the development values to afford the contributions. In the subsequent downturn this was much more difficult – as we shall see.

Lichfield (1989) gave an earlier explanation for this success. Originally conceived as a minor addition to planning control powers, planning obligations expanded considerably during the 1970s for reasons of expediency.

The practice is a common-sense response to the contemporary situation. With the firm abandonment by the current government of the third [*sic*] post-World War II attempt at collecting betterment (in the Community Land and Development Land Tax Acts) landowners/developers/financial institutions can make fortunes out of a planning permit for using development rights which are still nationalised. Concurrently, under the present Administration, local government has restrictions on its financial resources and freedom to spend. Thus, the tax which planning gain [*sic*] imposes on the development industry, which it is generally prepared to accept to obtain the planning permission, offers a way of assisting local government in the financial trammels in which it finds itself, and comforts the taxpaying public in seeking social justice. (Lichfield, 1989)[10]

Likewise a few years later, Grant (1992) argued that planning obligations were 'a phenomenon based on pragmatism, not principle' and that in 'its crudest form, planning gain [*sic*] constitutes simple but effective capital taxation of land'. Even though the authority for this was in doubt, few challenged it or had reasons for doing so since it helped developers to get consent and LPAs to get infrastructure which could not otherwise be secured. Planning obligations had become 'an essential component in the functioning of the British planning system' and the key to its success was negotiating at the point of maximum financial leverage: the granting of planning permission. As Grant later remarked, although it is a policy that resides 'uneasily' in the British planning system, in practice it 'seems to be an effective system' with a 'directness of purpose and a flexibility which is absent from other methods of land taxation' (Grant, 2000). Fordham (1993) also argued that, given the changed role of the state, it was reasonable that developers no longer had a 'free ride on public expenditure' but should be expected to pay a share of the costs they impose.

While Healey and colleagues (1996) also agreed, they did not think that obligations should be the vehicle for taxing development value. Obligations had grown because of the restrictions on public funding and when there was growing public resistance to development. Because high development values had increased developers' willingness to contribute to infrastructure and thereby secure planning permission, the planning system had evolved to include more negotiation, collaboration, partnership and contractual arrangements than had regulatory control in the past. But they thought there were limits to what could be negotiated, especially if obligations were to be used to collect development value. This risked mixing up two different matters: addressing impact and paying tax on development values. They argued that the way forward was to focus 'on alleviating impacts alone and not on using planning gain [*sic*] to tax betterment as this risked ensuring the

---

[10]Reproduced by permission of Thomson Reuters (Professional) UK Ltd. on behalf of Sweet & Maxwell Ltd.

income from it competes with securing adequate mitigation' (Healey *et al.*, 1996). Others noted that obligations practice had the potential to subvert planning policy in favour of securing financial contributions (Campbell *et al.*, 2000). Many professionals involved in obligations practice also agreed with these views (Fordham, 1993; Rose, 1998).

There were also specific criticisms of using obligations to fund affordable housing since this could not be defended as the legitimate internalisation of the external costs of development. Kirkwood and Edwards (1993) argued that it was improper for the public sector to impose an obligation on the private sector to provide goods that were generally the responsibility of the public sector, especially as the need for affordable housing arose irrespective of the developments being proposed – and therefore could not fall within the 'reasonable relationship' test. In their view, obliging developers to provide affordable housing did not serve a 'valid planning purpose' (Ibid, p. 323). The Joseph Rowntree Foundation (1994) argued in similar vein. When obligations required developers to contribute to infrastructure costs, this was legitimate since developments had created the need for extra infrastructure. This was not the case for affordable housing since new private market developments did not in themselves increase the need for more affordable homes. It was the Foundation's 'strongly held view' (Ibid, p. 33) that subsidies for social housing should be provided from general taxation and not by private developers and landowners.

Grant (2000), however, looking specifically at the lawfulness of affordable housing policy, reiterated his view that whilst the policy resided 'uneasily in the British planning system' in practice it was effective. Developers accepted it as a development cost and passed it back into lower land prices and that

> it is a simple cross-subsidy from development value to affordable housing. It has a directness of purpose and a flexibility which is absent from other methods of land taxation. (Grant, 2000, p. 1)[11]

As government circulars had ruled that affordable housing need was a material consideration and because circulars are themselves material considerations, it was lawful for LPAs to regard contributions of affordable housing as material considerations (Ibid). Nonetheless Grant argued that the issue needed further clarification (see also Barlow *et al.*, 1994a, b).

Of course it depends upon who pays for these contributions: the critics of using planning obligations to fund affordable housing assume the costs fall (inappropriately) on landowners. But how much of a financial contribution landowners make, including the provision of land as well as funding, depends in detail on the interplay of a complex range of factors, including

---

[11] Reproduced by permission of Thomson Reuters (Professional) UK Limited on behalf of Sweet & Maxwell Ltd.

the specific planning obligation policies of each planning authority, the relative negotiating strength of developers and planners, the authorities' requirements for other S106 contributions, such as off-site infrastructure, the stance taken by the government agency providing subsidies for housing associations on the extent to which grant will be provided on S106 sites (as we have seen, it no longer does this for all such sites) and the ability of the housing associations themselves to contribute funding from their reserves (see Chapters 6–8 for the evidence).

In fact the cost could fall on any or all of three parties: purchasers of the market homes through higher prices, a squeeze on developers' profits and a reduction in the price paid to landowners. The price elasticity of demand for housing will determine whether costs can be passed on to market buyers and the short- and long-run price elasticities of the supply of development land will determine the extent to which landowners pay. If the development value extracted by obligations has no impact on the supply of land, costs and prices, the policy will simply be a transfer of economic rent (see also Chapter 2, this volume). However, in practice there is likely to be a much wider range of impacts, depending on levels of demand across regions, the cost of using brownfield land and the costs of delays to developers whilst negotiating planning gain. We review the empirical evidence in more detail in Chapter 6, but it shows that where LPA policies are clear and implemented consistently and where large developers acquire land through options agreements, the costs appear to fall on landowners.

Hence given that it may well fall on landowners and developers (in the latter's capacity as landowners), many critics argue not only that it is unfair for landowners and developers to pay for affordable housing, as we have seen, but also inefficient because providing new affordable homes on the same site as market homes could create distortions in the prices of market homes and hence in development values. This may then produce lower financial contributions, compared with a direct cash payment from a site wholly devoted to market housing towards provision elsewhere. If, instead of obligations costs falling on land prices, developers carry the costs, this may act as a deterrent and house-building rates would slow. That this has not happened (in the buoyant market in Britain in the early and mid-2000s) provides partial evidence that landowners have been bearing the costs of planning obligations (again see the detailed evidence in Chapter 6). However, the system evolved during a period of increasing house prices and even if developers paid over the odds for land, the final development value may have been higher than anticipated, protecting their profit and softening the impact of the obligations and of the significant transaction costs developers incur in negotiating contributions with LPAs. Finally, critics argue that the approach is ineffective in securing what is needed because it relies on the discretion of LPAs to pursue the policy and on their ability to negotiate outcomes, with the result that there are large variations in the use of planning gain as we shall see in Chapter 7.

In summary then, the equity objective of obligations policy has proved more controversial than the efficiency one. However, planning obligations can be seen in another light as a way of compensating the poor who disproportionately bear the costs of planning. Planning limits the supply of new homes, especially in tightly constrained areas, but does not limit demand. As incomes rise, demand rises, therefore fuelling house prices. In England the price elasticity of supply is very low so that new supply is slow to respond to rising prices and this works through to higher land prices (Chapter 2, this volume). As a result, not only do homes become less affordable but affordable housing providers find that rising land prices makes it more difficult to produce affordable homes.

In effect, the 'poor' pay for the wider benefits society enjoys from its planning policies, whilst landowners of the limited development land that is released enjoy substantial development value. Planning obligations policies have the effect of taking away some of this value to help fund affordable homes. This may not be a 'first best' outcome since only landowners of above threshold sites whose land receives planning permission for new housing contribute some of their development value. Neither owners of small sites nor those existing owners whose houses increase in value are taxed on these increments. This seems inconsistent with taxation principles: the tax base is narrow, the beneficiaries are limited and the approach breaches the principle of equal sacrifice. The concept of the 'negotiated tax' is also unrelated to ability to pay or benefits received but to the bargaining strengths of the negotiators (Oxley, 2008). Moreover, the higher the costs of negotiating agreements, the less is available to developers for funding contributions (making negotiated levies a burden in comparison with standard charges). The implicit levy on development value is thus a hybrid one, 'taxing' betterment for equitable purposes and getting a better alignment of the private and social costs of development (Crook and Whitehead, 2002).

To sum up, obligations policy has worked successfully to compensate low-income households by requiring some of the beneficiaries of planning policy to help fund housing for them whilst also contributing to the infrastructure required by all new housing and other developments. However, the success of obligations has depended on a buoyant private market. When the market turns down, matters of viability come much more to the fore and it is to this issue that the next chapter turns.

References

Audit Commission (2006) *Securing Community Benefits through the Planning Process*, The Commission, London.

Bailey, S.J. (1994) User charges for urban services. *Urban Studies* **31**, 745–765.

Barker, K. (2003) *Review of Housing Supply: Securing Our Future Needs*. Interim Report – Analysis, HMSO, London.

Barker, K. (2004) *Review of Housing Supply – Final Report*, HMSO, London.

Barker, K. (2006) *Barker Review of Land Use Planning. Interim Report – Analysis*, Her Majesty's Treasury, London.

Barlow, J. and Chambers, D. (1992) *Planning Agreements and Affordable Housing in Britain*, University of Sussex, Centre for Urban and Regional Research, Brighton.

Barlow, J., Cocks, R., and Parker, M. (1994a) *Planning for Affordable Housing*, Department of the Environment, London.

Barlow, J., Cocks, R., and. Parker, M. (1994b) Pitfalls on the path to affordability. Inside Housing, 20th May, pp. 14–15.

Bate, R. (2004) Decisions will be for sale. *Axis* Jan/Feb.

Bill, P. (ed.) (2004) *Building Sustainable Communities: Capturing Land Development Value for the Public Realm*, The Smith Institute, London.

Bishop, K., and Hooper, A. (2001) *Planning for Social Housing: A Report for the National Housing Forum*, Association of District Councils, London.

Blackman, D. (2005) Levy on land values gets industry rap. *Axis*, November/December, pp. 8–9.

Booth, P.A. (1989) How effective is zoning in the control of development? *Environment and Planning B. Planning and Design* **16**, 401–415.

Booth, P.A. (2003) *Planning by Consent: The Origins and Nature of British Development Control*, Routledge, London.

Bowers, J. (1992) The economics of planning gain. *Urban Studies* **29**, 1329–1339.

Bowes, C. (2007) Roof tax offers potential to ward off national levy. *Planning*, 5th October, p. 7.

Burgess, G., Crook, A.D.H., Jones, M., and Monk, S. (2014) The nature of planning constraints. *Written Evidence to the House of Commons Select Committee on Communities and Local Government Inquiry Into the Operation of the National Planning Policy Framework*. Available at http://www.parliament.uk/documents/commons-committees/communities-and-local-government/Report-on-nature-of-planning-constraints-v3-0.pdf, last accessed on 13/10/2014.

Calcutt, J. (2007) *The Calcutt Review of Housebuilding Delivery*, Department of Communities and Local Government, London.

Campbell, H., Ellis, H., Gladwell, C., and Henneberry, J. (2000) Planning obligations, planning practice and land-use outcomes. *Environment and Planning B* **27**, 759–775.

Carpenter, J. (2011) Levy homes switch mooted. *Planning*, 25th February, p. 5.

Carpenter, J. (2014) What the new CIL rules mean for you. *Planning*, 6th June, pp. 17–19.

Claydon, J. and Smith, B. (1997) Negotiating planning gains through the British development control system. *Urban Studies* **34**, 2003–2022.

Clinch, P. and O'Neill, E. (2010a) Assessing the relative merits of development charges and transferable development rights in an uncertain world. *Urban Studies* **47**, 891–911.

Clinch, P. and O'Neill, E. (2010b) Designing development planning charges: settlement patterns, cost recovery and public facilities. *Urban Studies* **47**, 2149–2171.

Committee on Standards in Public Life (Chair Lord Nolan) (1997) *Third Report: Standards of Conduct in Local Government in England, Scotland and Wales*. Cmnd. 3702-I, HMSO, London.

Conservative Party (2009) *Planning: Open Source Document*, Conservative Party Central Office, London.

Crook, A. D. H. (1996) Affordable housing and planning gain, linkage fees and the rational nexus: using the land use planning system in England and the USA to deliver housing subsidies. *International Planning Studies* **1**, 49–71.

Crook, A.D.H., Henneberry, J.M., Rowley, S., and Watkins, C.A. (2007) Levy raises complexity fear. *Planning*, 19th January, p. 16.

Crook, A.D.H., Monk, S., and Whitehead, C.M.E. (2002a) Planning and affordable housing. *Affordable Housing – Report of the House of Commons Select Committee on the Office of the Deputy Prime Minister, 2001–2002. Vol II: Memoranda of Evidence.* House of Commons Paper 1206: II. The Stationery Office, London, pp. 47–50.

Crook, A.D.H., Monk, S., and Whitehead, C.M.E. (2002b) *Reforming Planning Obligations: Will the Proposals Secure More Affordable Housing?* Joseph Rowntree Foundation, York.

Crook, A.D.H., Monk, S., and Whitehead, C.M.E. (2003) *A Response to ODPM Consultation Paper on PPG3: Influencing the Size Type and Affordability of Housing.* University of Cambridge, Cambridge Centre for Housing and Planning Research, Cambridge.

Crook, A.D.H., Rowley, S., Monk, S., and Whitehead, C.M.E. (2006) Planning gain and the supply of affordable housing in England: understanding the numbers. *Town Planning Review* 77, 353–373.

Crook A.D.H. and Whitehead, C.M.E. (1999a) Revision of PPG3: a response, 17th Report of House of Commons Select Committee on Environment, Transport and Regional Affairs, 1998-99. *Housing: PPG3. Volume I: Report and Proceedings, Together with Minutes of Evidence and Appendices.* House of Commons Paper 490-I. The Stationery Office, London, pp. 75–77.

Crook A.D.H. and Whitehead, C.M.E. (1999b) Footing the bill for affordable homes. *Planning*, 28th May, pp. 20–21.

Crook, A.D.H. and Whitehead, C.M.E. (2002) Social housing and planning gain: is this an appropriate way of providing affordable housing? *Environment and Planning A* 34, 1259–1279.

Cunliffe, M. (2001) Planning obligations: Where are we now? *Journal of Planning and Law Occasional Paper* 29, 31–63.

Davey, C. (2007) A positive charge for communities. *Planning*, 2nd November, pp. 16–17.

Department for Communities and Local Government (DCLG) (2005) *Planning Obligations. Circular 05/05.* DCLG, London.

Department of Communities and Local Government (DCLG) (2006a) *Delivering Affordable Housing: Policy Statement*, DCLG, London.

Department of Communities and Local Government (DCLG) (2006b) *Planning Policy Statement No. 3: Housing*, DCLG, London.

Department of Communities and Local Government (DCLG) (2006c) *Planning Obligations: Practice Guidance*, DCLG, London.

Department of Communities and Local Government (DCLG) (2006d) *Changes to Planning Obligations: A Planning Gain Supplement Consultation*, DCLG, London.

Department of Communities and Local Government (DCLG) (2006e) *Government's Response to the Communities and Local Government Committee's Report on Planning Gain Supplement.* Cm 7005, HMSO, London.

Department of Communities and Local Government (DCLG) (2007a) *Homes for the Future: More Affordable, More Sustainable.* Cm Paper 7191, The Stationery Office, London.

Department of Communities and Local Government (DCLG) (2007b) *Community Infrastructure Levy: Initial Impact Assessment*, DCLG, London.

Department of Communities and Local Government (DCLG) (2008a) *Community Infrastructure Levy: Background*, DCLG, London.

Department of Communities and Local Government (DCLG) (2008b) *Community Infrastructure Levy*, DCLG, London.

Department of Communities and Local Government (DCLG) (2009) *Detailed Proposals and Draft Regulations for the Introduction of the Community Infrastructure Levy: Consultation*, DCLG, London.

Department of Communities and Local Government (DCLG) (2010a) *Community Infrastructure Levy: Overview*, DCLG, London.

Department of Communities and Local Government (DCLG) (2010b) *New Policy Document for Planning Obligations: Consultation*, DCLG, London.

Department of Communities and Local Government (DCLG) (2010c) *Communities to Share in the Advantages of Development: Press Notice*, DCLG, London.

Department of Communities and Local Government (DCLG) (2010d) *New Homes Bonus: Consultation*, DCLG, London.

Department of Communities and Local Government (DCLG) (2011a) *Community Infrastructure Levy: An Overview*, DCLG, London.

Department of Communities and Local Government (DCLG) (2011b) *Localism Bill: Community Infrastructure Levy: Impact Assessment*, DCLG, London.

Department of Communities and Local Government (DCLG) (2011c) *Community Infrastructure Levy. Detailed Proposals and Draft Regulations for* Reform: Consultation, DCLG, London.

Department of Communities and Local Government (DCLG) (2011d) *New Homes Bonus: Final Scheme Design*, DCLG, London.

Department of Communities and Local Government (DCLG) (2011e) *Renegotiation of S106 Planning Obligations*, DCLG, London.

Department of Communities and Local Government (DCLG) (2012) *National Planning Policy Framework*, DCLG, London.

Department for Communities and Local Government (DCLG) (2012a) *Review of the Barriers to Institutional Investment in Private Rented Homes, Report of the 'Montague' review*, DCLG, London.

Department for Communities and Local Government (DCLG) (2012b) *Renegotiation of Section 106 Planning Obligations*. Consultation, DCLG, London.

Department for Communities and Local Government (DCLG) (2013) *Community Infrastructure Levy. Consultation on Further Regulatory Reforms: Government Response*, DCLG, London.

Department for Communities and Local Government (DCLG) (2014a) *Planning Performance and Planning Contributions: Consultation*, DCLG, London.

Department for Communities and Local Government (DCLG) (2014b) *The Community Infrastructure Levy (Amendment) Regulations 2014*, DCLG, London.

Department for Communities and Local Government (DCLG) (2014c) *Community Infrastructure Levy Guidance*, DCLG, London.

Department for Communities and Local Government (DCLG) (2014d) *Development Benefits Pilots: Invitation for Expressions of Interest*, DCLG, London.

Department for Communities and Local Government (DCLG) (2014e) *Evaluation of the New Homes Bonus*, DCLG, London.

Department for Communities and Local Government (DCLG) (2014f) *National Planning Practice Guidance*, DCLG, London.

Department for Communities and Local Government (DCLG) (2014g) *Growing Places Fund*, DCLG, London.

Department for Communities and Local Government (DCLG) (2014h) *Housing Zones Prospectus*, DCLG, London.

Department of the Environment (DoE) (1972) *Report of Sheaf Committee on Local Authority Private Enterprise Partnership Schemes*, HMSO, London.

Department of the Environment (DoE) (1981) *Planning Gain. Report by the Property Advisory Group*, HMSO, London.

Department of the Environment (DoE) (1983) *Circular 22/83: Planning Gain*, DoE, London.

Department of the Environment (DoE) (1988) *PPG1: General Policies and Principles*, DoE, London.

Department of the Environment (DoE) (1989) *Planning Policy Guidance Note 3: Housing*, DoE, London.

Department of the Environment (DoE) (1991) *Circular 16/91: Planning and Compensation Act 1991, Planning Obligations*, DoE, London.

Department of the Environment (DoE) (1991) *Circular 7/91: Planning and Affordable Housing*, DoE, London.

Department of the Environment (DoE) (1992) *Planning Policy Guidance Note 3: Housing*, DoE, London.

Department of the Environment (DoE) (1996) *Circular 13/96: Planning and Affordable Housing*, DoE, London.

Department of the Environment (DoE) (1997) *Circular 1/97: Planning and Compensation Act: Planning Obligations*, DoE, London.

Department of the Environment Transport and The Regions (DETR) (1998) *Circular 6/98: Planning and Affordable Housing*, DETR, London.

Department of the Environment Transport and The Regions (DETR) (2000) *Planning Policy Guidance Note 3: Housing*, DETR, London.

Department of Transport, Local Government and the Regions (DTLR) (2001a) *Reforming Planning Obligations: A Consultation*, DTLR, London.

Department of Transport, Local Government and the Regions (DTLR) (2001b) *Delivering a Fundamental Change: The Planning Green Paper*, DTLR, London.

Dewar, D. (2005) Levy faces tough inception. *Planning*, 16th December, p. 8.

Dobson, T. (2012) Community infrastructure levy: Will it deliver? *Journal of Planning and Environment Law*, 13 Supp, 117–138.

Donatantonio, D. (2008) Rethink on levy set to help bill progress. *Planning*, 14th November.

Duxbury, R. (2009) *Planning Law and Procedure*, Oxford University Press, Oxford.

Editorial (2013) Levy proposals may bring back haggling. *Planning*, 19th April, p. 3.

Encyclopaedia of Planning Law Volume 2 (2013) *1990 Town and Country Planning Act: Planning Agreements*, Sweet & Maxwell, London, pp. 2-3418/2–2-3440/2.

Ennis, F. (1997) Infrastructure provision, the negotiating process and the planner's role. *Urban Studies* **34**, 1035–1954.

Fordham, R. (1993) Why planning gain is not a tax on land betterment. *Planning* **1014**, 13.

Fordham, R., (1995) Hoffman weighs balance in tale of planning loss. *Planning* **1127**, 24–25.

Gallent, N. (1997) Planning for affordable rural housing in England and Wales. *Housing Studies* **12**, 145–155.

Gallent, N. (2000) Planning and affordable housing. *Town Planning Review* **71**, 123–147.

Gallimore, M. (2007) Budget fails to lift cloud of uncertainty over levy. *Planning*, 6th April, 11.

Gielen, D.M. and Tasan-Kok, T. (2010) Flexibility in planning and the consequences for public value capturing in UK, Spain and the Netherlands. *European Planning Studies* **18**, 1097–1131.

Grant, M. (1975) Planning by agreement. *Journal of Planning Law* 501–508.

Grant, M. (1982) *Urban Planning Law*, Sweet & Maxwell, London.

Grant, M. (1991) *Encyclopaedia of Planning Law and Practice*. Monthly Bulletin, June, Sweet & Maxwell, London.

Grant, M. (1992) The planning balance in the 1990s: Betterment again? *Journal of Planning and Environment Law*, 67–83.

Grant, M. (2000) Is the government's affordable housing policy lawful? *Encyclopaedia of Planning Law and Practice. Monthly Bulletin*, August. Sweet & Maxwell, London.

Grant, M. (2002) Analysis: Reforming planning obligations. *A consultation paper. Encyclopaedia of Planning Law and Practice*, Monthly Bulletin, January, Sweet & Maxwell, London.

Grant, M. (2003a) Recent developments: Housing and planning. *Encyclopaedia of Planning Law. Monthly Bulletin*, August, Sweet & Maxwell, London.

Grant, M. (2003b) Recent developments: Planning gain, the new consultation paper. *Encyclopaedia of Planning Law*. Monthly Bulletin, November, Sweet & Maxwell, London.

Harlow, C. and Rawlings, R. (1984) *Law and Administration*, Weidenfeld and Nicholson, London.

Harrison, M. (1992) A presumption in favour of planning permission? *Journal of Planning Law* 121–129.

Healey, P., Purdue, M., and Ennis, F. (1993) *Gains from Planning? Dealing with the Impacts of Development*, Joseph Rowntree Foundation, York.

Healey, P., Purdue, M., and Ennis, F. (1996) Negotiating development: Planning gain and mitigating impacts. *Journal of Property Research* **13**, 143–160.

Henneberry, J.M. (2004) Supplement or charge? The fiscal choice posed by the Barker review. *Planning*, 13th August, p. 22.

Her Majesty's Revenue and Customs (HMRC) (2006a) *Valuing Planning Gain*, HMRC, London.

Her Majesty's Revenue and Customs (HMRC) (2006b) *Paying PGS*, HMRC, London.

Her Majesty's Treasury (HMT) (2005) *Pre Budget Report*, HMT, London.

Her Majesty's Treasury (HMT) (2006) *Pre Budget Report*, HMT, London.

Her Majesty's Treasury (HMT) (2007a) *Meeting the Aspirations of the British People*. Command Paper Cm 7227, The Stationery Office, London.

Her Majesty's Treasury (HMT) (2007b) *Building Britain's Long-term Future. Prosperity and Fairness for Families: The 2007 Budget Report*, HMT, London.

Her Majesty's Treasury (HMT) (2013a) *Autumn Statement*, Cm 874. The Stationery Office, London.

Her Majesty's Treasury (HMT) (2013b) *National Infrastructure Plan 2013*, The Stationery Office, London.

Her Majesty's Treasury (HMT) (2013c) *Budget 2013*. House of Commons Paper HC 1033. The Stationery Office, London.

Her Majesty's Treasury (HMT) (2014) *National Infrastructure Plan 2014*, The Stationery Office, London.

Her Majesty's Treasury, Her Majesty's Revenue and Customs and Office of the Deputy Prime Minister (HMT, HMRC, ODPM) (2005) *Planning Gain Supplement: A Consultation*, HMT, HMRC and ODPM, London.

Her Majesty's Treasury, Her Majesty's Revenue and Customs and Office of the Deputy Prime Minister (HMT, HMRC, ODPM) (2006) *Planning Gain Supplement: Summary of Consultation Response*. HMT, HMRC and ODPM, London.

Her Majesty's Treasury and the Office of the Deputy Prime Minister (HMT and ODPM) (2005) *The Government's Response to Kate Barker's Review of Housing Supply*, HMSO, London.

Hilditch, M. (2006) All aboard? *Inside Housing*, 24th February, pp. 16–17.

Hills, J. (1991) *Unravelling Housing Finance*, Clarendon Press, Oxford.

Homes and Communities Agency (HCA) (2011) *2011–2015 Affordable Homes Programme – Framework*. HCA, London.

House of Commons (1999) *Housing: PPG3. 17th Report from the Environment, Transport and Regional Affairs Committee*. House of Commons Paper HC 490-I. The Stationery Office, London.

House of Commons (2002) *Thirteenth Report of the Transport, Local Government and the Regions Select Committee. Planning Green Paper*. House of Commons Paper HC476-I Session 2001-02. HMSO, London.

House of Commons (2003) *Affordable Housing. Third report for Session 2002–03 of the ODPM Housing, Planning Local Government and the Regions Select Committee*. House of Commons Paper 75-I. The Stationery Office, London.

House of Commons (2006) *Planning Gain Supplement: 5th Report of the Communities and Local Government Committee, Session 2005–06*, The Stationery Office, London.

House of Commons (2014) *Operation of the National Planning Policy Framework*. Fourth Report of the Communities and Local Government Committee, Session 2014–15. House of Commons Paper HC 190, The Stationery Office, London.

House of Commons Committee of Public Accounts (PAC) (2013) *The New Homes Bonus*. Twenty-ninth Report of Session 2013–14, House of Commons Paper HC 114. The Stationery Office, London.

House of Commons Hansard (2004) *Planning Obligations in England*. Written Statement 44WS, 17th June. Her Majesty's Stationery Office, London.

House of Commons Hansard (2008) *Public Bill Committee: Planning Bill House of Commons Debates*. 31st January. Her Majesty's Stationery Office, London.

House of Lords Hansard (2008) *Debate on Planning Bill: Cols 1237 to 1344*. 23rd October 2008, The Stationery Office, London.

Housing Corporation (2007) *The National Affordable Housing Programme: Pre Prospectus*, The Corporation, London.

Jackson, A., Monk, S., Royce, C., and Dunn, J. (1994) *The Relationship Between Land Supply and Housing Production*, Joseph Rowntree Foundation, York.

Johnston, B. (1996) Guidance double whammy hits affordable housing prospects. *Planning* **1167**, 8–9.

Joseph Rowntree Foundation (1994) *Inquiry into Planning for Housing*, Joseph Rowntree Foundation, York.

Jowell, J. (1977) Bargaining in development control. *Journal of Planning Law* 414–433.

Keogh, G. (1985) The economics of planning gain. In: Barrett, S. and Healey, P. (eds.) *Land Policy, Problems and Alternatives*, Gower, Aldershot.

Kirkwood, G. and Edwards, M. (1993) Affordable housing – desirable but unlawful? *Journal of Planning and Environment Law* 317–324.

Kochan, B. (2010) Growing by increments. *Planning* 5th November, p. 12.

Lee, B. (2008) Affordable housing safeguards sought. *Planning* **1792**, 1.

Lichfield, N. (1989) From planning gain to community benefit. *Journal of Planning and Environmental Law* 68–81.

Local Government Association (LGA) (2012) *Briefing Note on Planning Agreements*. LGA, London.

McAllister, P., Wyatt, P., and Coleman, C. (2013) Fit for policy? Some evidence on the application of development viability models in the United Kingdom planning system. *Town Planning Review* **84**(4), 517–543.

Merrick, N. (2006) All under one roof. *Inside Housing*, 24th November, pp. 34–35.

Mole, D. (1996) Planning gain after the Tesco case. *Journal of Planning and Environment Law* March, 183–193.

Monk, S., Crook, A.D.H., Lister, D., Rowley, S., and Whitehead, C.M.E. (2005) *Land and Finance for Affordable Housing: The Complementary Roles of Social Housing Grant and the Provision of Affordable Housing through the Planning System*, Joseph Rowntree Foundation, York.

Monk, S. and Whitehead, C.M.E. (2010) *Making Housing More Affordable: The Role of Intermediate Tenures*, Wiley Blackwell, Oxford.

Monk, S., Whitehead, C.M.E., Burgess, G., Crook, A.D.H., and Rowley, S. (2008) *Common Starting Points for S106 Affordable Housing Negotiations*, Communities and Local Government, London.

Monk, S., Whitehead, C.M.E., Crook, A.D.H., and Rowley, S. (2006) *Securing Affordable Housing Through the Planning System: Comments on Recent Reform Proposals: Evidence to Consultation of PGS*. University of Cambridge, Cambridge Centre for Housing and Planning Research, Cambridge.

Moore, V. and Purdue, M. (2012) *A Practical Approach to Planning Law*, Oxford University Press, Oxford.

National Audit Office (NAO) (2013) *The New Homes Bonus: Report by the Comptroller and Auditor General*. House of Commons Paper 1047, Session 2012-13, HMSO, London.

National Housing and Planning Advisory Unit (NHPAU) (2009) *The Role of the Highways Agency, the Environment Agencies and Private Utility Companies in Delivering New Housing Supply*, The Unit, Fareham.

Office of the Deputy Prime Minister (ODPM) (2003a) *Sustainable Communities, Delivering through Planning*, ODPM, London.

Office of the Deputy Prime Minister (ODPM) (2003b) *Contributing to Sustainable Communities – A New Approach to Planning Obligations*, ODPM, London.

Office of the Deputy Prime Minister (ODPM) (2004a) *A New Approach to Planning Obligations: Summary of Consultation Responses*, ODPM, London.

Office of the Deputy Prime Minister (ODPM) (2004b) *Draft Revised Circular on Planning Obligations: Consultation Document*, ODPM, London.

Office of the Deputy Prime Minister (ODPM) (2005a) *Consultation Paper on a New Planning Policy Statement 3 (PPS3)*, Housing, ODPM, London.

Office of the Deputy Prime Minister (ODPM) (2005b) *Planning for Mixed Communities, Consultation Paper*, ODPM, London.

Office of the Deputy Prime Minister (ODPM) (2005c) *Circular 05/2005 Planning Obligations*, ODPM, London.

Office of Fair Trading (2008) *Homebuilding in the UK: A Market Study*, The Office of Fair Trading, London.

Oxley, M. (2006) The gain from the Planning Gain Supplement: A consideration of the proposal for a new tax to boost housing supply in the UK. *European Journal of Housing Policy* **6**, 101–113.

Oxley, M. (2008) Implicit land taxation and affordable housing provision in England. *Housing Studies* **23**, 661–671.

Papas, C. (2007) Charged with delivery. *Planning* 19th October, 10.

Punter, L. (1999) *The Future Role of Planning Agreements in Facilitating Urban Regeneration: Independent Report for the Urban Task Force*, Department of the Environment Transport and the Regions, London.

Purdue, M., Healey, P., and Ennis, F. (1992) Planning gain and the grant of planning permission: is the US test of the 'rational nexus' the appropriate solution? *Journal of Planning and Environment Law* 1012–1024.

Robinson, N. (1996) Planning in ever decreasing circles. *Inside Housing* 18th October, 14–15.

Rogers, A. (1985) Local claims on rural housing. *Town Planning Review* **56**(3), 367–380.

Rose, D. (1998) Planning obligations and impact fees: an RTPI position? *Planning* 14th August, 21.

Rowley, S. and Crook, T. (2006) North fears southern siphon. *Planning* 28th July, 20.

Royal Town Planning Institute (RTPI) (1999) *Memorandum of Observations to DETR on Consultation Draft of Revised PPG3. Housing*, RTPI, London.

Royal Town Planning Institute and Halliwells LLP (2007) *Planning Gain Supplement. Response in Principle and Possible Options for Change*, RTPI and Halliwells, London.

Stephens, M., Whitehead, C.M.E., and Munro, M. (2005) *Evaluation of English Housing Policy 1975 to 2000*, Office of the Deputy Prime Minister, London.

Tilley, J. (2010) Levy looks set to live on. *Planning* 2nd July, 8.

Urban Task Force (chair Lord Rogers) (1999) *Towards an Urban Renaissance*, Department of the Environment Transport and the Regions, London.

Walker, D. (2010) Levy rules narrow council options on gain payments. *Planning* 7th May, 10.

Webb, S. (2013) Times to kiss goodbye to CIL? *The Planner* October, 40.

Webster, C.J. and Lai, L.W.C. (2003) *Property Rights, Planning and Markets: Managing Spontaneous Cities*, Edward Elgar, Cheltenham.

Whitehead, C.M.E., Monk, S., Burgess, G., and Crook, A.D.H. (2007) *Response to "Homes for the Future": More Affordable, More Sustainable*, University of Cambridge, Centre for Housing and Planning Research, Cambridge.

Whitehead, C.M.E., Monk, S., Lister, D., Short, C., Crook, A.D.H., Henneberry, J.M. and Rowley, S. (2005) *Value for Money in Delivering Affordable Housing Through S106*, Office of the Deputy Prime Minister, London.

Wilson, V. (2007) Budget hints at change. *Planning* 30th March, 10.

Winkley, R. (2004) Obligation alarm bells ringing. *Planning* 16th January, 15.

Young, G. (1991) *Proceedings of Standing Committee F: Planning and Compensation Bill.* House of Commons Hansard, 18th April, Col 116. HMSO, London.

5

Development Viability

John Henneberry
Department of Urban Studies and Planning, The University of Sheffield, UK

Introduction

Over the last 35 years, the key actors in the property market in the UK have been the subject of fundamental structural change. Private developers have become the dominant suppliers of accommodation. In the residential sector, this has long been so. But the decline in state provision and its shift from local authorities to housing associations, combined with the recent growth of the private rented sector, has reinforced that position. In the commercial property market, renting has overtaken owner-occupation as the main tenure. By the end of 2010, investors held 61% by value of the stock of retail, office and industrial property in the UK (Property Industry Alliance, 2011). At the same time, the economic, social and political salience of money and finance increased markedly. While this generally enhanced corporate and government access to debt and equity capital, '[f]inancial rationales and practices have re-shaped performance metrics […] across all sectors of the economy …' (Christopherson *et al.*, 2013, p. 353).

In parallel, the privatisation of public facilities and services – and, in the remaining state sector – the introduction of 'new public management' (Ferlie *et al.*, 1996), the outsourcing of activities to quangos and the private sector, and the rise of network governance (Jones *et al.*, 1997) have re-cast central and local government. A key element of this change was the shift to private utilities and the growth in private provision of and/or investment in public infrastructure (O'Neill, 2010). There has also been a move from general, direct taxation to indirect, hypothecated taxes and user charges.

Planning Gain: Providing Infrastructure and Affordable Housing, First Edition.
Edited by Tony Crook, John Henneberry and Christine Whitehead.
© 2016 John Wiley & Sons, Inc. Published 2016 by John Wiley & Sons, Inc.

Consequently, in the property development sector (as elsewhere), a greater proportion of the funding of facilities and services and the costs of the social and environmental impacts of development are being met by building producers and consumers rather than government (Bailey, 1994).

In the midst of this flux, the basic character of the planning system has proved to be largely immune to reform. The fundamentals of development plans and development control, the two main elements of planning, remained unchanged since their establishment. 'It is almost certainly the least changed feature ... introduced by the 1945 Attlee government' (Cheshire and Sheppard, 2004, p. 2). Local planning authorities' (LPAs) development strategies and decisions on individual planning applications were based on functional assessments of their land-use implications, not on their economic outcomes: '... it is for planners to plan and the economy to adjust to the plan' (Evans, 2003, p. 528). However, by the millennium, the maintenance of this position was becoming increasingly problematic.

Government began to examine the '... scope for improving the efficiency of the planning system through the use of economic instruments in planning policy' (DETR, 1998, p. 8). At the time, as the main example of such an instrument, planning obligations were a particular focus of attention. In order to make a proposal acceptable in planning terms, the cost of any works to mitigate its impact – defined in the associated planning obligation – had to be met by that proposal. The ability of a project to fund such works was, and is, related to its value and profitability. Consequently, this resulted in '... essentially financial matters being material to many planning decisions ...' (Campbell *et al.*, 2000, p. 773), although government guidance made no reference to this eventuality.

The first explicit mention of the significance of the relation between the profitability of a development and its ability to meet the cost of planning obligations was made in a government consultation over reform of the system. The fear was that '... authorities risk asking for too much, thereby threatening the viability of development' (DETR, 2001, p. 13). Subsequently, this concern was set out in more detail in a further consultation document. Planning obligations should support the delivery of sustainable development – including affordable housing, facilities and infrastructure – that benefits the community and contributes to economic growth. Obligations should also make allowance for the particular circumstances of individual proposals and should not be so onerous as to deter desirable development (ODPM, 2003, para 18). However, consideration of the impact of planning obligations on development viability was limited to two sentences in the 'Partial Regulatory Impact Assessment'. The '... issue of whether or not a development proposal is capable of bearing the burden of mitigating all its own costs ...' (ODPM, 2004a, p. 9) had effectively been ignored up to this date. However, the failure to address the effect of planning obligations – and other planning policies and requirements – on the financial structure of development could continue no longer.

The Government formalised its position on this fundamental point in the draft Circular (ODPM, 2004b, pp. 25–26, para 10) and in Circular 05/2005 *Planning Obligations* (ODPM, 2005).

> In some instances … it may not be feasible for the proposed development to meet all the requirements set out in … planning policies and still be economically viable … where the development is needed to meet the aims of the development plan, it is for the local authority and other public sector agencies to decide what is to be the balance of contributions made by developers and by the public sector infrastructure providers in its area supported, for example, by local or central taxation. (ODPM, 2005, pp. 10–11, para B10)

This statement captures the central dilemma for policymakers. How do they impose on developments a growing proportion of the costs of the provision of development infrastructure and of the mitigation of development impact without, at the same time, threatening the viability of the very schemes that they wish to encourage? In order to address this question, we need first to consider the nature of development viability.

Development viability

In the last 10 years, development viability and its assessment have become important aspects of the UK planning system (Coleman *et al.*, 2013; Crosby *et al.*, 2013; McAllister *et al.*, 2013). Development appraisals and viability models underpin negotiations between developers and LPAs over specific sites. Such analyses also inform policy concerning land allocations, affordable housing, planning obligations and the Community Infrastructure Levy (CIL). The first formal mention of the provision of 'financial information' was in Circular 05/2005 (ODPM, 2005) and related to the determination of levels of affordable housing (McAllister *et al.*, 2013, p. 496). Subsequently, Planning Policy Statement (PPS) 12: *Local Spatial Planning* (DCLG, 2008) required viability to be considered as part of the evidence base of core strategies and other development plan documents; and then PPS3: *Housing* (DCLG, 2010) stipulated that the economic viability of affordable housing targets must be assessed (Coleman *et al.*, 2013). The significance of financial considerations in planning was reinforced by the *National Planning Policy Framework* (DCLG, 2012).

> Pursuing sustainable development requires careful attention to viability and costs … [*developments*] should not be subject to such a scale of obligations and policy burdens that their ability to be developed viably is threatened. To ensure viability, the costs of any requirements likely to

be applied to development … should … provide competitive returns to a willing land owner and willing developer to enable the development to be deliverable. (DCLG, 2012, p. 41, para 173, square brackets added)

The tenor of the evolving treatment of development viability in government documents is consistent and is rooted in mainstream economics and the market paradigm. Unsurprisingly, the property industry's perspective on the matter is similar. The RICS (2012) issued guidance on financial viability for planning purposes that defined it as follows.

An objective financial viability test of the ability of a development project to meet its costs including the cost of planning obligations, while ensuring an appropriate Site Value for the landowner and a market risk adjusted return to the developer in delivering that project. (RICS, 2012, p. 4)

Furthermore

The fundamental issue in considering viability assessments in a town planning context is whether an otherwise viable development is made unviable by the extent of planning obligations or other requirements. (RICS, 2012, p. 10)

The effect of planning requirements on development viability is described in Figure 5.1, which echoes the representations of the RICS (2012, p. 9, Figure 1; p. 11, Figure 2) and Crosby *et al.* (2013, p. 8, Figure 1).

Where a scheme is not affected by planning obligations or CIL (Figure 5.1a), the market value of the land is the residual remaining after the development costs and the developer's return have been subtracted from the capital value of the scheme. In turn, the market value of the site is made up of

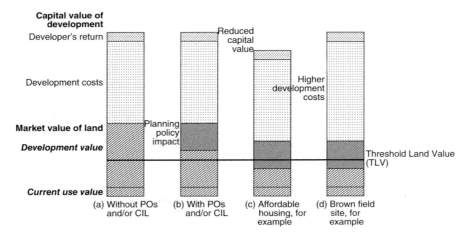

Figure 5.1   The financial structure of development.

the value of the land in its existing use (such as agriculture, in the case of green field development) and the uplift in value attributable to development (e.g. for housing). The development value of the land is retained by the landowner and provides the financial incentive for the land to be released. However, planning policies may impose additional costs on a development (Figure 5.1b) through planning obligations or CIL.[1] Interestingly, the RICS (2012, p. 9, Figure 1) also includes in this account other planning requirements that would often be covered by planning conditions, such as design standards and sustainability measures.

The impact of planning policy is to reduce the residual or market value of the land. If the uplift in land value is still sufficient to persuade the landowner to sell the site, then development will occur. In some circumstances this will not be the case. Planning requirements may reduce capital values; for example, through the allocation of part of a site for affordable housing rather than market housing (Figure 5.1c). Alternatively, the cost of developing some land – such as a brownfield site, especially if it is contaminated – may be higher than usual (Figure 5.1d). In both instances, the development value may be so reduced that it does not offer an adequate incentive for the landowner to sell the site. In the first two examples development is viable; in the second two it is not.

Consideration of the definition and treatment of viability and planning and its impact – and the way that these frame the above analysis – is instructive. First, there is the claim that such definitions are 'objective'. Then there is the characterisation of planning as a system that imposes 'obligations' and 'burdens' on the developer. It is therefore axiomatic that the key issue is whether planning requirements make 'otherwise viable' developments 'unviable'. Such logic ignores the political economy of land and property development, and the way this has changed.

As we have seen in earlier chapters, capital values are underpinned by the demand for accommodation of a growing economy and society. Development is enabled and further value is created by the provision of off-site infrastructure, facilities and services. Yet further value is created (e.g. by reducing negative externalities) and development is permitted by the planning system. The retention of the uplift in land value by the landowner is the price paid for a functioning land market. Until the onset of privatisation, the bulk of public infrastructure, facilities and services was directly supplied by the state and funded by a mix of direct taxation and user charges. Now such

---

[1] Planning and related policies, such as building regulations, impose other costs on development. For example, by requiring certain minimum standards for construction, the use of particular building materials, the provision of landscaping and so on. These also affect (increase) development value by enhancing the quality of development. In addition, there are the wider costs and benefits of planning. Restrictions on the supply of land for housing will raise its price, while the separation of incompatible uses will raise property values. Attention here focuses on the financial impact of planning obligations and CIL on development projects.

goods and services, whether supplied by public/arms-length bodies or private providers, are funded predominantly through charges on the consumers of them. The *quid pro quo* is lower levels of direct taxes on individuals and companies.

The 'objectivity' of the definition of viability is selective. In what sense is a development that cannot bear the cost of necessary off-site infrastructure, facilities and services 'otherwise viable'? Why are arrangements to fund the required facilities through planning obligations and/or CIL a 'burden' on development? The shift in the fiscal regime has increased the market nature of the land and property market. If landowners are not willing to bear a greater share of the costs of off-site infrastructure provision by accepting lower residual land values, then there will be less development. Alternatively, if development that is served by inadequate infrastructure goes ahead, it will function less effectively and have a lower capital value. In the latter case, the landowner and the developer are transferring (some of) the cost of infrastructure onto building owners and occupiers through lower standards relative to price. Clearly, the argument turns on the size of inducement necessary to persuade landowners to sell land: the threshold land value (TLV, see Figure 5.1).

Threshold land value

As McAllister *et al.* (2013, p. 504) point out, the commonly accepted test of viability is ' ... whether at a given level of planning obligations and/or CIL, the residual land value is higher than what has become increasingly known as Threshold Land Value (TLV)'. The Homes and Communities Agency (HCA) has defined TLV as ' ... the value required for the land to come forward for development ... ' (HCA, 2010, p. 8, cited in McAllister *et al.*, 2103, p. 504). But the identification or estimation of TLV, whether generally or for specific sites, is beset with empirical, theoretical or political problems. The use of market evidence of land transactions indicates the value at which land has been released for development. However, using such data to establish TLV involves circular logic because the effect of planning obligations is already incorporated in the land price (HCA, 2010; Crosby *et al.*, 2013; McAllister *et al.*, 2013).

Crosby *et al.* (2013) and McAllister *et al.* (2013) make the following argument on the issue. There is no robust empirical evidence of the size of the uplift required to bring land onto the market. The wide variation in the character of landowners, of sites and of market conditions makes impracticable the identification of a single point at which land would be released. In these circumstances, Government guidance on the broad principles that might be followed by policy may help. For example, landowners may be expected to receive a premium of a certain percentage of the existing use value of the land or of the uplift in land value. Perhaps not surprisingly, the RICS takes a different view.

> There must, however, be a 'boundary' placed on the effect on land, to reflect new policy or the burden of CIL charge, in terms of restricting any reduction so that it does not go below what land would willingly transact at in order to provide a competitive return to a willing landowner. (RICS, 2012, p. 16, para 3.3.6)

This would place a floor rather than a ceiling on the TLV but gives no indication of what a competitive return would be, other than by comparison with other land market transactions. This serves to entrench historic prices for land (McAllister *et al.*, 2013, p. 504). The matter remains unresolved.

Development appraisal

When decisions are made about whether or not to proceed with development, they are informed, *inter alia*, by development appraisals. These assessments of the financial structure and profitability of proposed development projects include estimates of development value and cost, the impact of planning obligations and CIL on both, and the implications for residual land value and viability. They therefore offer particular insights into the way that the issues raised by these economic instruments of planning are addressed in practice. To obtain these insights, we need first to consider the market context of development appraisal.

Property development within the wider property market

The property market consists of a set of inter-linked sub-markets (Keogh, 1994; DiPasquale and Wheaton, 1996; see Figure 5.2). The market for the use of space (the occupier market) is related to the asset (or investment) market for property ownership. Markets for owner-occupied space combine these two aspects of demand and internalise the tensions between them. In equilibrium, with a stock of space, S, and demand for space, D, rent, R, will be determined in the occupier market (Figure 5.2: 1). In the investment market (Figure 5.2: 2) asset prices (values), P, are derived by the application of the capitalisation rate (yield) to the rent. The yield is represented by the slope of Y (the rent-to-price ratio). Note that a steeper slope (a higher capitalisation rate) will reduce the price, that is, yields are inversely related to capital values. Investors are willing to accept a lower initial return on (i.e. pay a higher price for) property with high potential for rental and/or capital growth and a low risk of this potential not being fulfilled.

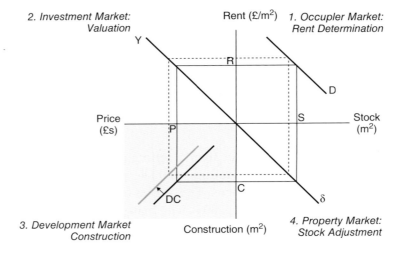

Figure 5.2　Property development within the wider property market.
Source: Dipasquale, Denise; Wheaton, William C., Urban Economics and Real Estate Markets, 1st Edition, @1996, p. 17. Reprinted by permission of Pearson Education, Inc.

In the development market, the relation between prices (capital values) and the development cost schedule, DC (Figure 5.2: 3), will determine the volume of new construction, C, that occurs in any period. Development costs have three main elements: construction costs, a return sufficient to compensate the developer for effort and risk, and land costs (with the minimum determined by the TLV). The slope of the DC curve implies that development costs increase with the level of development (e.g. because contractors raise tender prices in the face of higher demand for their services). For a given price, P, an amount of construction, C, will be viable because '... lower levels of construction would lead to excess profits, whereas higher levels would be unprofitable'[2] (Di Pasquale and Wheaton, 1996, p. 9). The impact that new construction, C, has upon the stock of buildings, S, will be affected by the depreciation rate, δ, in the property market (Figure 5.2: 4). As buildings become physically and functionally obsolescent they are removed from the stock. In equilibrium, new construction will match depreciation, maintaining a constant stock, S.

Change in any part of the property market will result in adjustments elsewhere that will (or may eventually) result in a new equilibrium. Consider the development market that is our focus. If the development cost schedule in a particular property market is higher – for example, because of higher construction costs related to a brownfield site, or higher charges or taxes on development, or more restrictive or demanding planning or building regulations – this will also result in a lower volume of viable development

---

[2] Assuming a competitive market.

and new construction, producing a smaller building stock (see grey/dashed lines) and higher rents or prices for accommodation. Beneficial shifts in these variables – for example, those arising from lower company taxation, or government grants for brown field development, or a reduction in TLV – would have the opposite effects.

The development market provides the link between the occupier and investment markets (or the owner-occupied market) and the building stock. It balances the demand for property with the cost of its production to determine the amount and type of accommodation that is supplied. This 'balancing act' is incorporated in the process of development appraisal, to which we now turn.

Development appraisal

A developer will assess the problems and potentials that are offered by a site. He or she will examine the technical feasibility of development, covering site constraints related to topography, geology and so on; its political and legal feasibility, allowing for planning constraints, ownership issues and so on; its design feasibility and the effectiveness with which a scheme may meet users' requirements; and its economic feasibility, whether the scheme offers a return that is a sufficient compensation for the risk and effort involved in its development.

The economic appraisal of a development proposal can be divided into two broad stages: market appraisal and financial appraisal. The purpose of the market appraisal is to establish the nature of the property market at a particular time, for a particular development, in a particular location. The developer needs to establish whether there is an unsatisfied demand for the proposed scheme. Assuming that such a demand exists, the developer will then undertake a financial appraisal of the scheme to assess its viability.

The basic method used to assess the financial viability of a proposed development is the residual valuation. This is based on the simple assumption that if the value of a finished scheme exceeds the cost of its development by a margin sufficient to leave the developer with an appropriate risk-adjusted return and the landowner with an uplift in land value sufficient to persuade her or him to sell the site, then development will occur. That is

Gross Development Value – Development Costs = Residual

Where the developer's minimum return can be estimated, the amount available to purchase the site may be calculated (the land value residual).

Gross Development Value – (Construction Costs + Developer's Profit)

= Maximum Price for Land

Where the purchase price of the site can be estimated, the amount of the developer's profit may be calculated (the profit residual).

Gross Development Value – (Construction Costs + Land Costs)

= Developer's Profit

The land value and profit residuals account for the vast majority of the applications of the residual method of valuation. Occasionally, the equation may be used in alternative forms to indicate the minimum value of the scheme that is needed to cover construction cost, land costs and developer's profit; or to establish a construction cost ceiling for a scheme, once its value, site cost and developer's profit have been estimated. Following the main formulation above, the two crucial stages in assessing the financial viability of a scheme are the calculations of its *value* and its *cost*. An example of a land value residual is presented below to illustrate the application of the method. It is based on a fictional scheme and uses generalised secondary data. The results should, therefore, be treated as broadly indicative of empirical circumstances.

Estimating the residual value of a residential development site

A house builder is considering the purchase of a greenfield site of 2 ha in an edge-of-town location in the outer South East of England. A scheme of 80 houses with 2–3 bedrooms (40 dwellings per hectare) would match both the character of local demand and the requirements of the LPA. The developer estimates that it would take 6 months from the date of site purchase to begin construction, 2 years to complete construction (the optimum sale rate in this locale is an estimated 10 units per quarter) and a further 9 months to complete all sales, giving a total development period of 3 years and 3 months. A profit of 15% of the value of the scheme would be considered a reasonable risk-adjusted return. The developer must estimate the maximum price he or she may offer for the site.

The starting point for this exercise is an assessment of the project's viability assuming (unrealistically) that there are no affordable housing requirements or other planning obligations or development contributions to be met or made in relation to the site. The developer expects the houses to sell for a total value of £16m (see Figure 5.3, lines 1–6). Construction costs – covering building costs, site works, professional fees and other costs – amount to £7.786m (lines 10–31). The developer must pay interest on the debt raised to cover these costs. In order to do so he or she assumes that construction costs are evenly spread through the building contract period so that half the borrowings are drawn down half way through the period. Consequently, finance costs (at 7%) are calculated on half the

1	**DEVELOPMENT VALUE**					
2		Number of	Area per	Selling price	Price per	Total
3	2/3 bed houses	units	unit (sq. m.)	per unit	sq. m.	proceeds
4	Private/market	80	80	£200 000	£2500	£16 000 000
5	Social/affordable	0	0	£0	£0	£0
6	**Total development value**					**£16 000 000**
7						
8	**DEVELOPMENT COSTS**					
9						
10	**Building Costs**					
11		Number of	Area per	Cost	Cost per	Total
12	2/3 bed houses	units	unit (sq. m.)	per unit	sq. m.	costs
13	Private/market	80	80	£68 000	£850	£5 440 000
14	Social/affordable	0	0	£0	£0	£0
15	Total building costs					£5 440 000
16						
17	**Site works**					
18	Site preparation, roads, parking, landscaping etc @ 25% of building costs					£1 360 000
19						
20	**Professional fees**					
21	Architect, QS, project manager etc @ 12.5% of building costs + site works					£850 000
22						
23	**Other costs**					
24	Planning fees, building regulations, etc @ 2% of building costs + site works					£136 000
25						
26	**Developer contributions**					
27		Number of	Area per	Total area		Total
28	£0 per unit	units	unit (sq. m.)	sq. m.		costs
29	£0 per sq. m.	80	80	6400		£0
30						
31	**Total construction costs**					**£7 786 000**
32						
33	**Finance costs**					
34	On half the total construction costs for building contract period @ 7% pa.					£564 096
35	On total construction costs + finance for post-contract period @ 7% pa.					£434 652
36	Total finance costs					£998 748
37						
38	**Marketing and sales**					
39	Agents fees, marketing costs, etc @ 2% of value of private/market units					£320 000
40						
41	**Total development costs**					**£9 104 748**
42						
43	**DEVELOPER'S PROFIT**					
44						
45	**Developer's profit on development value @ 15%**					**£2 400 000**
46						
47	**RESIDUAL LAND VALUE**					
48						
49	Residual (including finance on land + acquisition costs)					£4 495 252
50	Finance on land + acquisition costs for development period @ 7% 0.8026					£887 333
51	Residual (including acquisition costs)					£3 607 919
52	Acquisition costs @ 5.25% of acquisition price					£179 967
53	**Residual value of land**					**£3 427 952**

Figure 5.3   Example of simple land value residual.

construction costs for 2 years (line 34). To this must be added interest on the total construction costs and the accumulated finance costs at physical completion for the post-contract or disposal period of 9 months (line 35), giving overall finance costs of £0.999m (line 36). Marketing and sales costs of £0.320m (line 39) are payable at the end of the development period. The total development costs of the project are £9.105m (line 41).

The developer's profit of 15% of the project's value is £2.4m (line 45). When this and the development costs are subtracted from the development value, a residual of £4.495m remains (line 49). Allowance must then be made for financing the outlay on the site for the development period (£0.887m; line 50) and for site acquisition costs (£0.180m; line 52). The estimated residual value of the site is, therefore, £3.428m (line 53).

Current development appraisal and valuation texts (e.g. Havard, 2008; Syms, 2002; Wyatt, 2007) identify some problems with the simple residual method of valuation, of which the most important is its failure adequately to deal with time. This manifests itself in three main ways. Firstly it is the normal practice to use current costs and values to estimate the current residual. But costs and values will vary over the development period, so should no attempt be made to forecast their behaviour? Secondly, the impact of the temporal pattern of costs upon debt interest can only be crudely approximated through the use of the 'half rule of thumb' (line 34, above). In practice, construction costs follow an 'S' curve and the point of inflection is unlikely to occur half way through the building contract period. This leads to the under-estimation of finance costs where those costs are 'front-loaded', and to their over-estimation where they are 'back-loaded'. Thirdly, the simple residual assumes that all sales income is received at the end of the development period and that is when the developer's profit is realised. Consequently, the method cannot deal adequately with phased projects, where disposals occur part of the way through the development period. Housing developments typify such projects.

In order to address these problems, a cash-flow version of the residual valuation was developed. Figure 5.4 describes the application of the period-by-period variant of this method to the example project. It is assumed that costs and revenues are incurred and received quarterly in arrears (Wyatt, 2007). It will be evident that the approach allows the timing of development activities to be addressed more accurately. Some modest preliminary works occur in the pre-contract period (lines 10–12, Q2) and marketing begins as soon as the site is purchased (line 14, Q1). Building costs (line 8) increase from Q3 to Q5 and tail off between Q10 and Q12 – that is, into the post-contract or disposal period – to ensure that 10 units are completed in each of quarters Q6–Q13, when their sale occurs (line 4). The developer's profit is realised in Q13 (line 15). Interest is calculated on the capital outstanding in the previous quarter (lines 18–19) at 1.71%

	Pre-contract period		Building contract period								Post-contract/disposal period			All
ITEM	Q1	Q2	Q3	Q4	Q5	Q6	Q7	Q8	Q9	Q10	Q11	Q12	Q13	TOTALS
3 **Residential sales**														
4 Private/market	£0	£0	£0	£0	£0	£2 000 000	£2 000 000	£2 000 000	£2 000 000	£2 000 000	£2 000 000	£2 000 000	£2 000 000	£16 000 000
5 Social/affordable	£0	£0	£0	£0	£0	£0	£0	£0	£0	£0	£0	£0	£0	£0
6 **Total income**	£0	£0	£0	£0	£0	£2 000 000	£2 000 000	£2 000 000	£2 000 000	£2 000 000	£2 000 000	£2 000 000	£2 000 000	£16 000 000
7 **Building costs**														
8 Private/market	£0	£0	£226 848	£453 152	£680 000	£680 000	£680 000	£680 000	£680 000	£680 000	£453 152	£226 848	£0	£5 440 000
9 Social/affordable	£0	£0	£0	£0	£0	£0	£0	£0	£0	£0	£0	£0	£0	£0
10 Site works	£0	£136 000	£136 000	£136 000	£136 000	£136 000	£136 000	£136 000	£136 000	£136 000	£136 000	£0	£0	£1 360 000
11 Professional fees	£0	£85 000	£85 000	£85 000	£85 000	£85 000	£85 000	£85 000	£85 000	£85 000	£85 000	£0	£0	£850 000
12 Othercosts	£0	£13 600	£13 600	£13 600	£13 600	£13 600	£13 600	£13 600	£13 600	£13 600	£13 600	£0	£0	£136 000
13 Developer contributions	£0	£0	£0	£0	£0	£0	£0	£0	£0	£0	£0	£0	£0	£0
14 Marketing and sales	£16 000	£16 000	£16 000	£16 000	£32 000	£32 000	£32 000	£32 000	£32 000	£32 000	£32 000	£32 000	£0	£320 000
15 Developer's profit													£2 400 000	£2 400 000
16 **Total outgoings**	£16 000	£250 600	£477 448	£703 752	£946 600	£946 600	£946 600	£946 600	£946 600	£946 600	£719 752	£258 848	£2 400 000	£10 506 000
17 **NET CASHFLOW**	-£16 000	-£250 600	-£477 448	-£703 752	-£946 600	£1 053 400	£1 053 400	£1 053 400	£1 053 400	£1 053 400	£1 280 248	£1 741 152	-£400 000	£5 494 000
18 Cap. outstanding (Qn-1)	0	-£16 000	-£266 873	-£748 873	-£1 465 400	-£2 436 998	-£1 425 169	-£396 081	£650 563	£1 715 061	£2 797 717	£4 125 690	£5 937 220	
19 Quarterly interest on 18	0	-£273	-£4552	-£12 775	-£24 998	-£41 572	-£24 311	-£6757	£11 098	£29 256	£47 725	£70 378	£101 280	
20 Cap. outstanding (Qn)	-£16 000	-£266 873	-£748 873	-£1 465 400	-£2 436 998	-£1 425 169	-£396 081	£650 563	£1 715 061	£2 797 717	£4 125 690	£5 937 220	£5 638 500	

22 Finance rate (% p.a.)	7.00%
23 Quarterly equivalent (%)	1.71%

Residual on disposal (including finance on land+ acquisition costs)   £5 638 500

PV £1 for 13 quarters @   1.71%   0.8026

Residual on commencement (including acquisition costs)   £4 525 498

Acquisition costs @ 5.25% of acquisition price   £225 737

Residual value of land   £4 299 760

Figure 5.4   Example of basic cash-flow land value residual.

per quarter (equivalent to 7% per annum) to give the cumulative capital outstanding per quarter (line 20).

The phasing of the project has had a major impact on its financial performance – an impact that could not be captured by the simple residual. Sales income, resulting in a positive net quarterly cash-flow, is received from Q6 onwards. The capital outstanding becomes positive in Q8. Consequently, interest payments (Q2–Q8) become interest earnings (Q9–Q13), and the latter exceed the former by £0.145m. The difference in the estimated finance costs/earnings – related to the net cash-flow arising from construction costs and house sales – between the simple residual (−£0.999m) and the cash-flow residual (+£0.145m) is £1.143m. This difference accounts for the much higher residual produced by the cash-flow appraisal (£5.639m, line 22) than by the simple residual (£4.495m, Figure 5.3, line 49). However, the higher finance costs related to the purchase of the more valuable site should be noted (£1.11m, compared with £0.887m). The practical consequence is that, because of its shortcomings, the simple residual significantly underestimates the residual value of the project site (£3.428m, compared to £4.3m, line 26). This may result in the developer being outbid for the site by a competitor.

Both normatively (see, e.g. Syms, 2002, p. 157; Wyatt, 2007, p. 329) and in practice, appraisals often ignore interest earnings on positive periodic cash-flows. The effect is to increase finance costs and, therefore, to reduce the residual value of the site (to £4.102m for the example project). This is not the only instance where the application of the cash-flow version of development appraisal does not follow the tenets of investment evaluation and capital budgeting theory (see Brown and Matysiak, 2000 and the more recent and detailed critiques of Coleman et al., 2013 and Crosby et al., 2013). First, the developer's return is specified as a lump sum profit to be taken at the end of the project. This makes such profit time-invariant. Whatever the length of the development period, the profit remains a fixed proportion of development costs or value. An amount receivable in 2 years' time is more certain than the same amount (in present value terms) receivable in 3 years' time. The return on the latter project should be higher, to reflect the additional risk involved.

Second, the simple and cash-flow residuals assume that projects will be entirely funded by debt, ignoring the potential for leverage. Furthermore, the discount rate used is the cost of borrowing (the interest rate) rather than the return available on similar alternative investments (i.e. a risk-adjusted rate of return). 'There is little direct connection between the rate at which [a] company can borrow and the appropriate discount rate to be applied to a particular project' (Coleman et al., 2013, p. 150, square brackets added). For example, a large developer with a good track record and substantial assets with which to secure a loan will be able to borrow money at a significantly lower rate of interest than a small company with limited experience and few assets. The above residuals would indicate that the former would make a higher profit on the *same* project than the latter because of the difference in their costs of capital, not because of any difference in the character and riskiness of the project. The analysis of the project's performance should be separate from the assessment of how best to finance it (see below).

The theoretical shortcomings of simple and cash-flow residuals arise from the rigid format of the former and the practical application of the latter. There are other problems with development appraisal that arise from empirical and structural sources. The first relates to the complexity and heterogeneity of the subjects of appraisals. They incorporate a wide range of different inputs, each of which may vary significantly. For example, even on a greenfield site, unusual ground conditions may necessitate special – and more costly – foundations, leading to an increase in building costs. The second relates to the residual nature of the calculation, where the output, the developer's return or the land value, is the difference between two much larger inputs, the cost and the value of the project. In these circumstances, changes in either or both inputs – or important elements of them – will produce much larger relative changes in the output. To take a simple example, consider a project with a cost of 100 and a value of 120 that produces a profit on cost of 20 (20%). If the development cost increases by 5 (5%) and the value does not change, the profit will be reduced to 15 (15% of the original cost and 14.3% of the new, higher cost). In other words, the rate of profit has fallen by 25%, a reduction that is five times greater than the change in the cost. Such *gearing* indicates that the developer's return (or the residual land value) is sensitive to relatively modest changes in development costs and values. In the case of the example project, a 10% change in the sale price of the houses would result in a 25% change in the residual value of the land (a gearing of 2.5), while a 10% change in building costs would change the land value by 15% (a gearing of 1.5).

The impact of changes in each project variable upon the residual land value is crucial from the developer's point of view. Once the site has been purchased, the land value is fixed, so any subsequent departure from the esti-mated value of each variable will affect the return on the project. Developers assess the risk of the outcome being other than expected by undertaking sen-sitivity analysis (as above) and – because in the real world, changes in the variables do not take place in isolation but occur simultaneously – scenario and/or probability analysis to explore alternative out-turns (e.g. if prices fall and costs increase by 10% the residual land value falls by 40% or £2.47m).

This assessment of the potential level and volatility of returns underpins the calculation of the required, risk-adjusted rate of return (the discount rate) for the project. Brown and Matysiak (2000) argue for the use of CAPM for this purpose.[3] This approach has been criticised for the assumptions that it makes but is still widely used (Levy, 2010). However, its application in the poorly informed and highly heterogeneous development market is challenging. Allowing for this, once the discount rate for a development project is estimated, the decision about whether to proceed with the scheme turns on the cost of funding to the developer. If the latter is below the discount rate, then the development will be viable.

Assessing the impact of planning obligations and developer's contributions on the viability of development proposals

As the assessment of development viability has become a more important aspect of planning policy, so more guidance on appraisal has been provided to LPAs. This guidance is based upon simple residual or basic cash-flow methods of valuation. Consequently, '… the incorporation of flawed assumptions in development appraisal modelling is pervasive … in the UK planning system …' (Coleman *et al.*, 2013, pp. 161–162). Examples include the downloadable model of the Homes and Communities Agency (2010, cited in McAllister *et al.*, 2013), the Three Dragons Toolkit (Coleman *et al.*, 2013) and the Planning Advisory Service (2011) handbook on the assessment of viability. While these circumstances are not ideal, the high levels of input uncertainty that affect development proposals lead Coleman *et al.* (2013, p. 163) to observe that '… the use of poorly theorised, overly simplified development appraisal models may have limited implications for the robustness of appraisal outputs.' Therefore, this chapter explores the impact of planning obligations and developer's contributions on the viability of development through the application of the basic cash-flow residual (as described in Figure 5.4). In addition, the analysis adopts the standard practice of accounting only for finance costs and not for interest earnings (see earlier).

The effects of two requirements are examined (Figure 5.5). The first is an obligation to provide 35% of the units on the example site in the form of affordable housing. To simplify exposition, it is assumed that the physical form of the units is unchanged and that the developer builds the affordable units and transfers them to a housing association at the appropriate price. This has the effect of reducing the development value of the scheme by

---

[3]The capital asset pricing model (CAPM) takes the form $E(r_p) = r_f + \beta_p[E(r_m) - r_f]$, where: $E(r_p)$ = expected rate of return for project; r_f = risk free rate of return; $E(r_m)$ = expected market rate of return; β_p = market risk of project. The expected rate of return for the project is the combination of the expected rate of return on other similar investments in the subject market and an adjustment reflecting the degree to which the project return is expected to be more or less volatile than the market return.

Planning Obligation: Affordable Housing

2/3 bed houses	Number of units	Area per unit (sq. m.)	Selling price per unit	Price per sq. m.	Total proceeds
Private/market	52	80	£200 000	£2500	£10 400 000
Social/affordable	28	80	£126 000	£1575	£3 528 000
Total development value					**£13 928 000**

Developer contributions: CIL

	£0 per unit
	£125 per sq. m.

	Number of units	Area per unit (sq. m.)	Total area sq. m.
	80	80	6400

	Total costs
	£800 000

	Pre-contract period		Building contract period						Post-contract/disposal period					All
ITEM	Q1	Q2	Q3	Q4	Q5	Q6	Q7	Q8	Q9	Q10	Q11	Q12	Q13	TOTALS
Residential sales														
Private/market	£0	£0	£0	£0	£0	£1 300 000	£1 300 000	£1 300 000	£1 300 000	£1 300 000	£1 300 000	£1 300 000	£1 300 000	£10 400 000
Social/affordable	£0	£0	£0	£0	£0	£441 000	£441 000	£441 000	£441 000	£441 000	£441 000	£441 000	£441 000	£3 528 000
Total income	£0	£0	£0	£0	£0	£1 741 000	£1 741 000	£1 741 000	£1 741 000	£1 741 000	£1 741 000	£1 741 000	£1 741 000	£13 928 000
Building costs														
Private/market	£0	£0	£147 451	£294 549	£442 000	£442 000	£442 000	£442 000	£442 000	£442 000	£294 549	£147 451	£0	£3 536 000
Social/affordable	£0	£0	£79 397	£158 603	£238 000	£238 000	£238 000	£238 000	£238 000	£238 000	£158 603	£79 397	£0	£1 904 000
Site works	£0	£136 000	£136 000	£136 000	£136 000	£136 000	£136 000	£136 000	£136 000	£136 000	£136 000	£0	£0	£1 360 000
Professional fees	£0	£85 000	£85 000	£85 000	£85 000	£85 000	£85 000	£85 000	£85 000	£85 000	£85 000	£0	£0	£850 000
Other costs	£0	£13 600	£13 600	£13 600	£13 600	£13 600	£13 600	£13 600	£13 600	£13 600	£13 600	£0	£0	£136 000
Developer contributions	£0	£0	£33 360	£66 640	£100 000	£100 000	£100 000	£100 000	£100 000	£100 000	£66 640	£33 360	£0	£800 000
Marketing and sales	£10 400	£10 400	£10 400	£10 400	£20 800	£20 800	£20 800	£20 800	£20 800	£20 800	£20 800	£20 800	£0	£208 000
Developer's profit	£0	£0	£0	£0	£0	£0	£0	£0	£0	£0	£2 089 200	£2 089 200	£2 089 200	£2 089 200
Total outgoings	£10 400	£245 000	£505 208	£764 792	£1 035 400	£1 035 400	£1 035 400	£1 035 400	£1 035 400	£1 035 400	£775 192	£281 008	£2 089 200	£10 883 200
NET CASHFLOW	-£10 400	-£245 000	-£505 208	-£764 792	£1 035 400	£705 600	£705 600	£705 600	£705 600	£705 600	£965 808	£1 459 992	-£348 200	£3 044 800
Cap. outstanding (Qn-1)	0	-£10 400	-£255 577	-£765 145	-£1 542 989	-£2 604 711	-£1 943 543	-£1 271 097	-£587 180	£108 403	£814 003	£1 779 811	£3 239 803	
Quarterly interest on 18	0	-£177	-£4360	-£13 052	-£26 321	-£44 433	-£33 154	-£21 683	-£10 016	£0	£0	£0	£0	-£153 197
Cap. outstanding (Qn)	-£10 400	-£255 577	-£765 145	-£1 542 989	-£2 604 711	-£1 943 543	-£1 271 097	-£587 180	£108 403	£814 003	£1 779 811	£3 239 803	£2 891 603	

Finance rate (% p.a.)	7.00%
Quarterly equivalent (%)	1.71%

Residual on disposal (including finance on land + acquisition costs) £2 891 603
PV £1 for 13 quarters @ 1.71% 0.8026
Residual on commencement (including acquisition costs) £2 320 820
Acquisition costs @ 5.25% of acquisition price £115 765
Residual value of land £2 205 055

£570 783

Figure 5.5 The impact of planning requirements on residual land value.

12.95% to £13.93m (line 6), with no compensating reduction in construction costs (lines 8 and 9). However, marketing and sales costs, which relate only to the market units, are lower (line 14). The developer's profit (line 15) falls in absolute terms because of the reduction in the scheme's value. The second requirement is to pay CIL at the rate of £125 per m^2 of housing floor space to contribute to the cost of off-site infrastructure. Payments are made in line with housing construction. They increase construction costs by £0.8m (line 13) and finance costs by a proportionate amount, extending interest payments from Q8 to Q9 (line 19).

The outcomes of these changes are presented in Figure 5.6. We first consider the impact of the affordable housing requirement on the financial structure of the project. It reduces the development value by 12.95% but, because of gearing, the residual value of the site falls by 30.87% from £4.10 to £2.84m. The discrete effect of the CIL is more limited. It adds 6.57% to the development costs, reducing the residual site value by 15.21% to £3.48m. In combination, affordable housing and CIL reduce the development value and increase the development costs, lowering the residual site value by 46.24% to £2.21m. The impact of these requirements on the viability of the scheme depends upon the TLV. Clearly, the greater the reduction is in the residual land value, the more likely it is to be below the TLV.

The modelling has thus far assumed that the construction and sale of the market and the affordable housing will proceed in tandem and that the CIL will be drawn down in parallel with housing starts. This spreads the effect

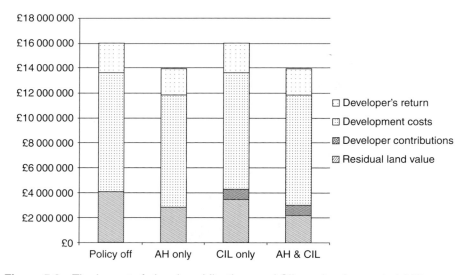

Figure 5.6   The impact of planning obligations and CIL on development viability.

of the planning obligations and CIL over the project. A change in the timing of these policy imposts will affect the financial structure of the project. Front-loading will increase finance costs and delay receipt of the higher sales prices, while back-loading will have the opposite effects. For example, if CIL is charged upon commencement of the project in Q1 and the affordable housing is built (sales during Q6–Q8) before the market housing (sales during Q8–Q13), then the residual land value will be reduced by a further 5.58% to £2.08m. In contrast, building the market housing (sales Q6–Q11) before the affordable housing (sales Q11–Q13) and delaying CIL until the completion of the project (Q13) will increase the residual land value by 1.93% to £2.25m.

Accounting for spatial and temporal variations in the development market

The inputs to and the outputs from appraisals are specific to individual projects. These development costs and values vary greatly across space and over time. Because of gearing, such variations have very significant impacts on development viability. Modelling gives some indication of the effects. New house prices range from an average of £331 176 in inner London to £148 061 in the North (Nationwide Building Society, 2014; see Table 5.1). The former are 67.64% higher than prices in the South East and the latter are 25.05% lower, giving a percentage range, around the South East base figure, of 92.69%. The regional variation in construction costs is smaller. Compared with the South East, tender prices are 19.64% higher in inner London and 14.29% lower in the East Midlands and the North West; a range of 33.93% (Langdon, 2010). If the development value and construction costs of the example scheme (located in the South East) are adjusted by the

Table 5.1 Regional variation in development values, costs and viability.

Region	New house prices		Tender prices		Reduction in residual land value	
	Q4 2013	% of SE	TPI 2010	% of SE	By region (%)	% of SE
Inner London	£331 176	167.64	536	119.64	27.90	60.33
Outer London	£272 559	137.97	492	109.82	32.05	69.31
South East	£197 552	100.00	448	100.00	46.24	100.00
East Anglia	£173 726	87.94	403	89.96	50.13	108.42
South West	£202 797	102.65	443	98.88	43.41	93.88
West Midlands	£166 934	84.50	394	87.95	52.38	113.29
East Midlands	£165 428	83.74	384	85.71	51.11	110.53
North West	£161 263	81.63	384	85.71	53.90	116.56
Yorkshire and Humber	£156 293	79.11	403	89.96	81.62	176.52
North	£148 061	74.95	408	91.07	77.25	167.05

Source: Nationwide Building Society and Davis Langdon.

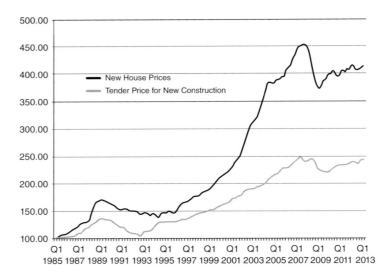

Source: Nationwide Building Society and Department of Business Innovation & Skills

Figure 5.7   Trends in new house prices and tender prices (in current prices; Q1 1985 = 100).
Source: Nationwide Building Society and Department of Business Innovation and Skills.

respective regional percentages, the resultant changes in regions' residual land values may be estimated.

Broadly, the stronger the housing market is and the higher the house prices, the smaller is the effect of planning policies on residual land values. Residual land values are reduced by 27.90% in inner London but by 81.62% in Yorkshire and Humber. Alternatively, such land values are reduced by 39.67% less in inner London than in the South East and by 76.52% more in Yorkshire and Humber than in the South East. In other words, the regional impact of planning obligations and developers' contributions is regressive. Furthermore, because the regional variation in commercial property values is greater than the variation in house prices, the range of regional impacts is greater in the industrial, office and retail sectors than in the housing market (Henneberry and Goodchild, 1996; Crosby *et al.*, 2013).

The impact of changes over time in development values and costs may be assessed in a similar way. Figure 5.7 describes trends in the nominal price of new houses (Nationwide Building Society, 2014) and the nominal tender price for new construction (Department for Business, Innovation and Skills, 2014) between 1985 and 2013. As with the regional analysis, the price varies more than the cost. New house prices peaked in Q4 2007 and troughed in Q2 2009 before recovering to their current levels. Compared with 2013, prices were 4.86% higher in 2007 and 13.87% lower in 2009, a range of 18.73%. For the same dates, tender prices were 0.55% lower in 2007 and 7.69% lower in

2009 than in 2013, a range of 7.14%. To provide an indication of the effect of these variations on the viability of the example development, its development value and construction costs were adjusted by the respective quarters' percentage changes. Planning policy reduced the residual land value at the market peak by 42.21% and by 54.82% at the market trough, compared with 46.24% during the recovery. Thus development viability is less affected by planning obligations and developers' contributions in periods when the market is strong than in times when it is weak; McAllister *et al.* (2014) report similar findings.

However, while the above analysis generally holds true, it is partial and understates both the risks of development and the potential impact of planning policy on development viability. This is because the modelling follows the practice of using development costs and values current at the time of the appraisal (see earlier). But costs and values are changing continually. If a developer commences a project at the peak of the market cycle, he or she will be faced with rapidly falling house prices that are not compensated by more modestly declining building costs (see Figure 5.7). We can model the effect of this scenario on the case study scheme. Using the development values and costs extant in Q4 2007 for the Outer South East, the cash-flow appraisal produces an estimated developer's profit of £2.52m and a residual land value of £4.63m (without any planning obligations or CIL). If (i) we assume that the developer buys the site for £4.63m and (ii) factor in the changes in house prices and tender prices for the development period (Q4 2007–Q4 2010), then the following occurs. First, the development value falls from £16.78 to £13.64m (–£3.14m). Second, the development costs fall from £9.63 to £8.82m (–£0.81m). This is a net reduction of –£2.33m. It must be met from the developer's profit. The profit therefore becomes £0.19m – a reduction of –92.5%. This would not represent a viable return to the developer.

If we now introduce the illustrative planning obligations and CIL into the scenario, the following outcomes occur. Their impact on the *estimated* viability of the project is to reduce the residual land value from £4.63 to £2.68m. If the site was purchased for that sum and the *actual* changes in house and tender prices are incorporated in the cash-flow appraisal, then development value will fall from £14.60 to £11.87m, development cost from £8.94 to £8.39m and the developer's profit £2.19 to £0.01m (–96%). In these circumstances, developers would be expected to cease development until housing demand and prices recovered and/or to attempt to renegotiate planning requirements to reduce their cost.

What is not often noted is that the reverse scenario applies for schemes that are started at the trough in the market cycle. If the above analysis is repeated for a project commencing in Q2 2009, the following are the outcomes. Where there are no planning policy requirements, the *estimated* developer's profit is £2.07m and the residual land value is £3.16m. If the site is purchased for that price, the use of *actual* house and tender price data suggests a developer's profit of £4.76m (an increase of £2.69m or 130%). If the illustrative planning obligations and CIL are included in the analysis, the *estimated* developer's profit and residual land value are £1.80 million and £1.43 million, respectively. The former increases to £3.90m if the site is bought for £1.43m and *actual* price data are used in the appraisal. In these circumstances, the scheme is much more profitable – and could bear significantly higher planning requirements than originally expected. This serves to emphasise the huge variations in property market conditions and development viability that exist and, consequently, the similar large variations in the scope for and impact of planning requirements on development projects.

Conclusion: addressing the viability dilemma?

The changing political economy of the UK has resulted in major changes in its fiscal strategies. The balance between direct taxes and indirect taxes/user charges has shifted significantly towards the latter. In the property sector, this means that a growing proportion of the costs of development infrastructure and of the mitigation of development impact must be met by the projects that give rise to these costs. The substantial growth in the use of planning obligations – and especially of affordable housing requirements – is the main means by which the state has sought to do this. Such an approach avoids the problems of earlier heroic attempts to deal with the 'land problem' (see Chapter 3). It is pragmatic, rooted in practice and sensitive to local empirical circumstances. However, it fails to acknowledge the structural issues at play. Such issues have been highlighted by the wider application of the concept of economic viability in UK planning policy, particularly in relation to CIL.

Development values and costs vary widely across space and over time. The financial structure of development projects and project viability are, therefore, site specific and volatile. There may be major differences in viability between adjacent sites, leave alone intra/inter-urban and regional differences. The use of planning obligations to meet the wider costs of development relies on case-by-case treatment. Relatively detailed assessments of individual schemes allow the latter's specific characteristics to be taken into account, even if the appraisals are not theoretically robust. However, because these are based on current rather than forecast costs and values, the developer remains exposed to the risk that market circumstances may change between the finalisation of the planning agreement and the completion of the development (Crosby *et al.*, 2013; McAllister *et al.*, 2013). This risk may be addressed by the renegotiation of the agreement.

The introduction of the CIL raises a new set of issues. It brings more development within the charging regime and so increases the potential revenue. It also avoids the need for negotiation over specified charges, speeding up the process. However, to do this, things must be simplified. Most LPAs use a limited number of hypothetical schemes to assess the impact of CIL and affordable housing requirements on their areas (McAllister *et al.*, 2013). This focuses on what are considered to be the main development types and sub-markets in the locale (Crosby *et al.*, 2013). Such an approach follows current government guidance (DCLG, 2013) that recognises the need to set ' ... differential rates [*of CIL*] as a way of dealing with different levels of economic viability within the same charging area ... ' (Ibid, p. 10, para 34, square brackets added) but simultaneously urges authorities ' ... to avoid undue complexity, and limit the permutations of different charges that they set ... ' (Ibid, p. 11, para 37).

The result is that a typical CIL charging regime consists of one or two levels of defined charge by type of development (and often not all types of development are covered), by one or two sub-areas (see Carpenter, 2013). These regimes will not reflect the heterogeneity of development conditions and viability that exist in any area. In addition, to avoid threatening the viability of various types of development in various locations, CIL income targets and associated charges tend to be conservative (McAllister *et al.*, 2013), depressing potential revenue. The relative fixity and uniformity of the charges results in major differences between the proportionate levies that are imposed on schemes, with the schemes with the highest value being affected the least (in a similar way to the inter-regional differences illustrated earlier).

These outcomes are inevitable when a cost-based charge is used to raise revenue, but its application is constrained by a viability test that does not allow for the changing political economy. The problems are reinforced by an approach that incorporates a structural tension between complex development circumstances and simple, clear CIL charging regimes. The unfolding UK experience in this regard offers important lessons for other jurisdictions.

References

Bailey, S. (1994) User charges for urban services. *Urban Studies* **31**, 745–765.

Brown, G. and Matysiak, G. (2000) *Real Estate Investment: A Capital Budgeting Approach*, Financial Times Prentice-Hall, Harlow.

Campbell, H., Ellis, H., Gladwell, C., and Henneberry, J. (2000) Planning obligations, planning practice and land-use outcomes. *Environment and Planning B: Planning and Design* **27**, 759–775.

Carpenter, J. (2013) *CIL Watch: Who's Charging What?* Planning Resource, London. Available at http://www.planningresource.co.uk/article/1121218/cil-watch-whos-charging-what, Accessed 13/03/2014.

Cheshire, P. and Sheppard, S. (2004) *The Introduction of Price Signals into Land Use Planning Decision-making: A Proposal*. Research Papers in Environmental and Spatial Analysis, 89, LSE, Department of Geography and Environment, London.

Christopherson, S., Martin, R., and Pollard, J. (2013) Financialisation: roots and repercussions. *Cambridge Journal of Regions, Economy and Society* **6**, 351–357.

Coleman, C., Crosby, N., McAllister, P., and Wyatt, P. (2013) Development appraisal in practice: some evidence from the planning system. *Journal of Property Research* **30**, 144–165.

Crosby, N., McAllister, P., and Wyatt, P. (2013) Fit for planning? An evaluation of the application of development viability appraisal models in the UK planning system. *Environment and Planning B: Planning and Design* **40**, 3–22.

Department for Business, Innovation and Skills (2014) *BIS Prices and Cost Indices, Tender Price Indices*. Available at https://www.gov.uk/government/publications/bis-prices-and-cost-indices, Accessed 06/03/2014.

Department for Communities and Local Government (DCLG) (2008) *Planning Policy Statement 12 (PPS12): Local Spatial Planning*, The Stationery Office, London.

Department for Communities and Local Government (DCLG) (2010) *Planning Policy Statement 3 (PPS3): Housing*, DCLG, London, June.

Department for Communities and Local Government (DCLG) (2012) *National Planning Policy Framework*, DCLG, London, March.

Department for Communities and Local Government (DCLG) (2013) *Community Infrastructure Levy: Guidance*, DCLG, London, April.

Department of the Environment, Transport and the Regions (DETR) (1998) *Research Newsletter 1998/99. Land Use Planning and Minerals, Land Instability and Waste Planning*, DETR, London.

Department of the Environment, Transport and the Regions (DETR) (2001) *Planning Obligations: Delivering a Fundamental Change*. Consultation Document, DETR, London.

DiPasquale, D. and Wheaton, W. (1996) *Urban Economics and Real Estate Markets*, Prentice-Hall, Englewood Cliffs, NJ.

Evans, A. (2003) The development of urban economics in the twentieth century. *Regional Studies* **37**, 521–529.

Ferlie, E., Ashburner, L., Fitzgerald, L., and Pettigrew, A. (1996) *New Public Management in Action*, Oxford University Press, Oxford.

Havard, T. (2008) *Contemporary Property Development*, 2nd edition, RIBA Publishing, London.

Henneberry, J. and Goodchild, B. (1996) Impact fees and the financial structure of development. *Journal of Property Finance* **7**, 7–27.

Homes and Communities Agency (2010) *The HCA Area Wide Viability Model: User Notes* (Consultation report version 2.1). Homes and Communities Agency, London. Available at http://www.homesandcommunities.co.uk/public/documents/AWVM-User-Notesv1-1.pdf, accessed 13/10/2014.

Jones, C., Hesterly, W., and Borgatti, S. (1997) A general theory of network governance: exchange conditions and social mechanisms. *Academy of Management Journal* **22**, 911–945.

Keogh, G. (1994) Use and investment markets in British real estate. *Journal of Property Valuation and Investment* **12**, 58–72.

Langdon, D. (eds.) (2010) *Spon's Architects' and Builders' Price Book* 2010, 135th edition, Spon Press, London.

Levy, H. (2010) The CAPM is alive and well: a review and synthesis. *European Financial Management* **16**, 43–71.

McAllister, P., Street, E., Wyatt, P., et al. (2014) *Section 106 Planning Obligations in England, 2011–2012*. Report of Study for Department of Communities and Local Government, HMSO, London.

McAllister, P., Wyatt, P., and Coleman, C. (2013) Fit for policy? Some evidence on the application of development viability models in the United Kingdom planning system. *Town Planning Review* **84**, 495–521.

Nationwide Building Society (2014) *Nationwide House Price Index*. Available at http://www.nationwide.co.uk/about/house-price-index/download-data, Accessed 06/03/2014.

Office of the Deputy Prime Minister (ODPM) (2003) *Contributing to Sustainable Communities – A New Approach to Planning Obligations*. Consultation Document, ODPM, London.

Office of the Deputy Prime Minister (ODPM) (2004a) Contributing To Sustainable Communities – A New Approach To Planning Obligations. Statement by the ODPM, House of Commons and House of Lords, 30 January 2004.

Office of the Deputy Prime Minister (ODPM) (2004b) *Draft Revised Circular on Planning Obligations*. Consultation Document, ODPM, London, November.

Office of the Deputy Prime Minister (ODPM) (2005) Circular 05/2005. *Planning Obligations*, The Stationary Office, London.

O'Neill, P. (2010) Infrastructure finance and operation in the contemporary city. *Geographical Review* **48**, 3–12.

Planning Advisory Service (2011) *Viability Handbook and Exercises*, Local Government Group, London.

Property Industry Alliance (2011) *Property Data Report*. Available at http://www.bco.org.uk/research/researchavailabletobuy/detail.cfm?rid=175&cid=0, Accessed on 24/07/2012.

RICS (2012) *Financial Viability in Planning*, RICS guidance note, 1st edition (GN94/2012), RICS, London, August.

Syms, P. (2002) *Land, Development and Design*, Blackwell, Oxford.

Wyatt, P. (2007) *Property Valuation in an Economic Context*, Blackwell, Oxford.

6

The Incidence and Value of Planning Obligations

Steven Rowley[1] and Tony Crook[2]

[1]Department of Economics and Property, Curtin University, Australia
[2]Department of Urban Studies and Planning, The University of Sheffield, UK

Introduction

There had been little systematically collected evidence about the use of planning obligations throughout England[1] until very recently when we conducted the first set of national studies covering incidence, value and delivery. There had, however, been a number of partial studies, particularly of the incidence of all obligations and some looking at the use of obligations to secure affordable housing. They showed how the use of obligations was limited until the late 1980s but then grew significantly. Before looking in detail at the most recent studies on the incidence and value of agreed obligations (Chapter 8 of this volume looks at delivery) we first review this earlier evidence.

The growth of obligations

One of the earliest studies was undertaken by a legal scholar who had noted the growing use of bargaining in development control and of planning by agreement from the 1960s onwards when the property boom of that era

[1]The abolition in 1968 of the requirement to seek Ministerial approval of agreements meant that there was no longer a central record of the number of agreements.

Planning Gain: Providing Infrastructure and Affordable Housing, First Edition.
Edited by Tony Crook, John Henneberry and Christine Whitehead.
© 2016 John Wiley & Sons, Inc. Published 2016 by John Wiley & Sons, Inc.

provided a financial context for local planning authorities (LPAs) to successfully bargain with developers using the (then) S52 powers of the planning legislation as well as various local acts. The numbers of agreements
were not large. Records of S52 submissions for Ministerial approval (which
was required before 1968) revealed that 542 agreements had been submitted for approval between 1964 and 1968, the vast majority being approved.
Those refused fell on technical legal, not policy grounds (Jowell, 1977; see
also: Moore and Purdue, 2012). Jowell (1977) additionally surveyed 28% of
English LPAs and found that whilst half had made agreements with commercial developers between April 1974 and September 1975, this was not done
routinely but for selected applications, for example, securing some residential accommodation as part of an office development, creating public access
or dedicating land for open space within new developments, extinguishing
existing 'non-conforming' uses, and securing community buildings (typically leisure), new infrastructure and commuted payments for off-site car
parking. A later study by Hawke (1981) of all English LPAs found them using
agreements to control aspects of the development process, to regulate occupancy and to secure infrastructure, but the study did not report on incidence.
Henry (1982) found the same pattern when examining the use of agreements
in Wokingham (a LPA in the county of Berkshire). Later Elson (1989) noted a
wider use for securing recreation, open space and other community facilities.

But it was not until a study of England as a whole in the early 1990s
(Grimley, 1992) that we gained insights into the overall incidence of the use
of agreements. This study was done to ascertain whether government advice
about the use of agreements was being followed and to assess the overall
incidence of agreements[2] entered into between April 1987 and March 1990
in a stratified sample of English LPAs, including minerals authorities. It
found that although all LPAs used agreements, the incidence was low with
only 0.5% of decisions[3] being accompanied by planning agreements, and
in no LPA did the percentage rise to more than 2% in any year between
1987 and 1990. The survey also showed that just over a quarter of all
agreements under negotiation were never concluded. The results confirmed
that the use of agreements had increased because of the increasing scale and
complexity of development in the 1980s together with more constrained
public sector budgets. But it was also due to new policy objectives on
the environment and affordable housing being pursued through planning
agreements. Agreements covered residential development more than others
and were largely to do with regulation and the control of development than
with wider social and economic objectives. No more than 5% addressed

---

[2]Excluding S278 highways agreements (see Chapter 4 on S278).
[3]We have assumed that 'decisions' in the study referred to permissions granted not to all
decisions on planning permissions, which of course include refusals for which a planning agreement would not be connected. If decisions include refusal then the proportion of permissions
with agreements would be higher given the refusal rate of applications.

the latter issues, a finding that was replicated in a study of Cambridgeshire a decade later (Bunnell, 1995). Infrastructure matters, especially related to highways, were also important. Significantly (given the general concerns about transparency and accountability discussed in Chapter 4) only one LPA kept a formal register of agreements and not all LPAs had formal policies on obligations (although the numbers who did were increasing).

Later evidence suggested a slow (but not universal) growth in the use of agreements to achieve wider social and economic objectives, with a greater range and increasing complexity of obligations being sought on each site (Healey *et al.*, 1993, 1995). Evidence from five case study LPAs over the period 1984–1991 showed that, after excluding permissions related to householder applications,[4] 1.07% of all major, minor and minerals permissions had agreements in the period 1984–1991. Although there was no systematic evidence about the extent to which obligations were subsequently delivered, in most cases evidence of non-delivery meant that the permission itself was not implemented because development was abandoned or stalled and/or new permissions (and agreements) sought. Whilst agreements for small-scale developments were not unusual (especially agricultural dwelling occupancy agreements) most related to 'large and complex schemes' (Ibid, 1993, p. 11). Nearly two-thirds of the agreements had negative obligations covering matters related to the construction period (such as lorry movements) or to post-completion arrangements such as occupancy or opening hours' restrictions. About 60% had positive obligations, especially covering residential permissions. These mainly covered highways, sewerage and drainage, parking and open space obligations and in only two LPAs were matters related to social policy significant. Given the later scale of the use of obligations to secure affordable housing (this chapter), it is noteworthy that there were only two obligations related to this in all five case study LPAs, with community facilities, recreation and public transport being more significant than housing obligations.

Healey *et al.* (1995) remarked how little was known about the use of obligations and the policy and practices involved, despite the increasing attention devoted to obligations within government policy and advice and in other reviews. Indeed they thought it would not be until the late 1990s that it would be possible to tell whether changes in government policy 'have produced a quantum change in the use of agreements or whether policy has merely consolidated existing practice' (Healey *et al.*, 1995, p. 113).

In the light of this, the study by Campbell and colleagues (Campbell *et al.*, 2000, 2001) provides the evidence about what did happen in the 1990s, based upon the results of a postal questionnaire sent to all LPAs and case studies examining the year ending June 1998. They found that 1.5% of permissions had an obligation associated with them, that the numbers

---

[4] These mainly cover minor extensions to existing dwellings.

appeared to have grown by 40% since 1993 and that there were about 4000 agreements made annually in England. The study showed, not surprisingly, that 17.7% of *all* major permissions had agreements, compared with only 1.7% of minor permissions, and that this rose to 25.8% of major *residential* permissions.[5] Overall, a larger proportion of permissions had agreements in southern than in northern England. As well as highlighting an increased use of obligations, Campbell and colleagues also noted a widening of the types of obligations. Restrictions of use and related matters involved 45% of obligations; 26% involved on-site capital works (19% by direct provision); 46% involved off-site capital works (19% by direct provision) and 32% involved the provision of facilities or services (10% by direct provision). With the exception of on-site capital works, developers made financial payments to perform the majority of their obligations. The findings showed how obligations were increasingly being used to secure general benefits for local communities and not just to address on- and off-site infrastructure and restrictions related to proposed developments. Campbell and colleagues also noted how many of the financial payments were paid into aggregate local authority funds, not restricted accounts for the obligations concerned. This was for two reasons. First, financial payments were more appropriate for minor permissions as they had to be aggregated with payments from other permissions to finance a facility or service. Second, because the payments were for services or facilities not directly connected to the permissions they took on some of the character of impact fees.

Campbell *et al.* (2000) also showed that LPAs were formalising obligations policy in their development plans, with 85% of LPAs having such formal policies in place and 45% also having supplementary planning guidance. Policy covered the use of obligations both to address impacts and to remove barriers to development and to secure wider economic and social contributions, including for affordable housing, public transport, and social and community facilities. These policies were supported by supplementary planning guidance in just under half the LPAs.

Following on from Campbell *et al.* were four studies commissioned by the Department for Communities and Local Government (DCLG) designed to collect detailed data on the incidence and value of planning obligations (Crook *et al.*, 2006a, 2008, 2010; University of Reading *et al.*, 2014). The evidence from the three studies of England in the 2000s (see below), together with the previous studies discussed above and the latest study of the period 2011–2012 (also see below) shows that the proportion of all non-householder permissions accompanied by a planning agreement peaked at just over 7% in 2007–2008 and then fell back after the global financial crisis (see Figure 6.1).

---

[5] Major permissions cover residential developments of 10 dwellings or more (or more than 0.5 hectares) and commercial floorspace of 1000 m^2 or more or a 1 ha site area.

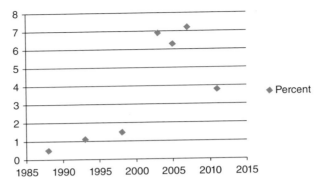

Figure 6.1   Percentage of all non-householder planning permissions that were accompanied by S106 planning agreements 1987–2011.
Note: 2011 percentage computed from data in a report by University of Reading *et al.* (2014) and DCLG Planning Applications statistics.
Source: Crook *et al.* (2006a, 2008, 2010).

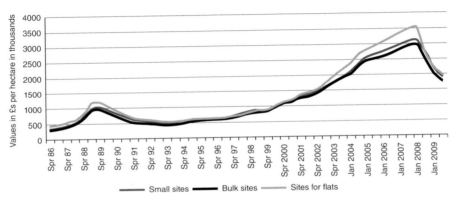

Figure 6.2   Value of residential land with planning permission in England and Wales outside London.
Source: Valuation Office Agency.

The increase in the 2000s was due to, in particular, the boom in house prices, residential development activity and development values during that period which allowed LPAs to negotiate contributions for affordable housing on a significant scale as well as associated infrastructure. The buoyancy of the property market, especially the housebuilding market, is illustrated in Figure 6.2, which shows the price of residential land with planning permission outside London, showing separately the per hectare price of 0.5 ha of suburban land, bulk residential land (2 ha) and for flats. It shows just how dramatic the increase was after the year 2000 but also the fall after the Global Financial Crisis after 2007. Published data is not available after 2009 but published indices have been made available and indicate that prices stabilised after January 2009 until 2011 after which

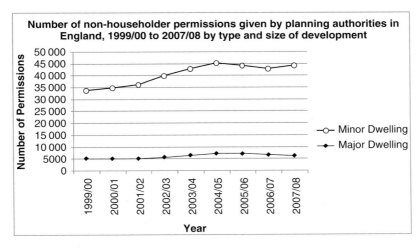

Figure 6.3 Numbers of planning permissions for housing.
Source: DCLG Planning Statistics.

no data at all is available. Figure 6.3 shows how the number of planning permissions for housing development also rose over this period including those for minor developments (less than 10 dwellings) rising from just under 35 000 to 45 000 over the years 1999–2000 to 2007–2008 at a time when permission for larger developments fell.

Methods for measuring the incidence and calculating the value of planning obligations in England

The four studies commissioned by DCLG delivered evidence gathered primarily from survey data collected from English LPAs. The first three studies were conducted by the authors and colleagues for the years 2003–2004, 2005–2006 and 2007–2008 and the fourth was undertaken by the University of Reading and the Three Dragons Consultancy for 2011–2012. Questions within the surveys evolved over the four studies and although new questions were added the methodologies for assessing the incidence and value of planning obligations, including affordable housing, allow a direct comparison of outcomes across the four study periods. The studies not only recorded the number of planning agreements but also placed a value on these agreements to calculate the total value of planning obligations in England for the first time.

Planning agreements are complex and often delivered over a number of years. This makes data collection problematic. The solution implemented was to collect information on the value of planning agreements agreed (signed) within the study year. Although not all planning agreements signed are actually delivered as, for example, developments granted planning permission are not always 'built out' (see Chapter 8), the agreed figure is more reliable than trying to estimate the value of contributions delivered over a number of years.

The original 2003–2004 survey was designed through extensive pilot work, including a review of hundreds of planning agreements. Although a single planning agreement attached to a planning permission may contain a single planning obligation, the vast majority contain multiple planning obligations covering a range of different contributions. From this initial work, a typology of planning obligations was developed and is shown in Table 6.1 consisting of six broad obligations split into various sub-headings.

The pilot research identified two broad types of obligation: direct payment obligations and in-kind obligations. Direct payment obligations are financial payments specified in a planning agreement and paid directly to the LPA, for example, a sum of money towards the provision of education facilities. In-kind obligations are specified works undertaken by the developer. The LPA receives no direct payment but there is a benefit derived from the works, for example, improvements to the local road network or a new school classroom.

Information about direct payments was relatively easy to collect with some LPAs recording details of agreed contributions (and payments made) within electronic databases or, if they did not, they were able to refer to the planning agreement where the sum was specified. The surveys were thus able to collect data on direct payment obligations for all planning agreements signed in a study year. Each payment under a specific typology heading was then summed to calculate the total direct payment per obligation within the LPA.

Given the survey did not achieve a 100% response rate[6] a method of calculating the total value of planning obligations in England for a given year was established. The typology of planning obligations formed the basis of data collection within the survey and also enabled the calculation of average values for each obligation type within the typology. This average was applied in two ways: first to calculate the value of in-kind obligations and second to 'gross up' the survey figure to calculate the total value of planning obligations in England for a given year. Rather than apply an average number of agreements and obligation value to each local authority throughout England, we adopted a typology for local authorities where it was assumed that LPAs within the typology would generate roughly similar obligation numbers and values, being within areas of similar demographic and social characteristics.

---

[6]The response to the survey improved over the course of the three studies (31%, 36% and 43%) for two reasons. First, LPAs understood the importance of the information and there was high-level support for the research and second, LPAs got better at recording planning agreement information within electronic databases making the retrieval of relevant information much easier. Response rates were not published for the 2011–2012 study.

Table 6.1   A typology of planning obligations.

Obligation type	Obligation details
Affordable housing	(a) On-site provision of various tenures: social rented, shared ownership, key worker, etc. Units developed and transferred to RSL: revenue from transfer depends upon agreement (b) Off-site provision: development and transfer of units on another site owned by the developer/landowner (c) On-site provision of land only: land transferred to a RSL or LA for free or at a rate below the market value (d) Off-site provision of land only (e) Commuted sum: payment of a sum in lieu of actual provision of units (f) Other affordable housing contributions
Open space and the environment	(a) Provision of open space either within a development or as a direct payment to the LA Landscaping. General environmental improvements (b) Ecology and nature conservation, countryside management and community forests (c) Allotments (d) Sport facilities: sport fields, clubhouses, etc.
Transport and travel schemes	(a) Traffic/highway works, temporary or permanent (b) Traffic management/calming (c) Parking: management or parking restrictions, car restrictions and car free areas, provision of parking areas (d) Green transport/travel plans (e) Public and local transport improvements (f) Pedestrian crossings, pedestrianisation and street lighting (g) Provision or improvement of footpaths or pathways etc. (h) Cycle routes, management, safety
Community works and leisure	(a) Community centres: construction, funding, improvement, etc. (b) Community/cultural/public art (c) Town centre improvement/management (d) Library, museum and theatre works/funding (e) Childcare/crèche facilities, provision and funding (f) Public toilets (g) Opening hours or noise restrictions (h) Health services: Community healthcare, construction of surgeries, etc, healthcare funding (i) CCTV and security measures (j) Waste and recycling facilities (k) Religious worship facilities (l) Employment and training (m) Local regeneration initiatives
Education	(a) Schools: development or funding for education at all levels: nursery, primary, secondary, higher, etc.
Other	(a) Legal Fees (b) Restrictions on use

Source: Crook *et al.* (2006a, 2008, 2010).

The degree of similarity between local authorities was established on the basis of an existing general purpose classification developed by Vickers for the Office of National Statistics (Vickers *et al.*, 2003). This typology created groups of local authorities similar in terms of the characteristics of their residents, reflecting the urban/rural character and socio-economic profile of the local authorities. The first three studies adopted an amended version of this typology consisting of six local authority families allowing for variability between authorities of different types in the analysis.

The six local authority families were as follows:

1. Established urban centres (30 LPAs) – former (mainly) northern and midlands manufacturing authorities, many undergoing significant regeneration and diversification.
2. Urban England (46 LPAs) – old mining and heavy manufacturing towns, regional centres and some young and vibrant cities.
3. Rural Towns (119 LPAs) – coastal towns and covering the main towns outside the above two families and also towns that are neither wholly urban nor rural.
4. Rural England (57 LPAs) – less densely populated but geographically extensive authorities.
5. Prosperous Britain (76 LPAs) – those areas in England that are in the commuter belts of the major cities and smaller historic cities. This was renamed Commuter Belt in the 2011–12 study.
6. Urban London (26 LPAs) – including many of the London Boroughs and some of their satellites.

The 'grossing up' method used the average value for each direct payment obligation to calculate the value of in-kind obligations making a necessary assumption that the extent of the work carried out by a developer was equivalent to the payment made to the LPA to carry out similar work. Therefore, if the average value of a direct payment provision of open space obligation derived from the survey within the Rural Towns family was £50 000 and there were 10 in-kind obligations within Rural Town LPAs then the value would be £500 000.

Second, to 'gross up' the direct payment and in-kind obligations from the survey to calculate a total value for England it was necessary to assume that survey respondents within one of the six families were representative of the whole family population. For example, if 50% of all local authorities categorised as Rural Towns responded to the survey then to calculate the total value of open space obligations within that family we took the total value of the subject obligation, say £1m, and multiplied the figure by 1/0.5. This method was repeated for all individual obligation types within all local authority families. As a check for accuracy, the method was repeated using Regions as the base for the grossing up exercise. The difference was 1.5%.

Estimating the value of affordable housing obligations agreed was dealt with separately because contributions are dominated by in-kind obligations, that is, the provision of dwellings by developers. A comparable method was used across the first three studies with a slightly different approach adopted for the 2011–2012 study. Data from the Department of Communities and Local Government's (DCLG) Housing Strategy Statistical Appendix (HSSA) were used to provide information on the number and tenure of affordable dwellings agreed by LPAs in each of the study years. An affordable dwelling's tenure and level of government subsidy have a direct impact on the financial contribution made by developers/landowners to deliver that affordable unit. The lower the subsidy available the higher the contribution required in terms of land or construction costs to make the affordable units viable for a registered social landlord.

The method used to value affordable housing outcomes combined the number of dwelling units agreed with the funding mechanism to calculate the developer subsidy required to deliver different unit tenures. The developer subsidy stems from the land contribution and any discount on the cost of constructing the units. Data on land values and house prices for each local authority were used to calculate the subsidy on an authority by authority basis. The contributions were then collated to generate an overall figure for the value of affordable housing in England with figures also presented by region and local authority family.

The 2005–2006 and 2007–2008 studies used additional data to slightly refine the original methodology adopted in 2003–2004 and utilised the following data:

- The number of affordable units agreed through the planning system (HSSA data Section N) for each LPA.
- The number of affordable units completed through the planning system (HSSA data Section N) for each LPA to generate subsidy patterns.
- Affordable units include social rented, intermediate rented, local authority, shared ownership and 'other' tenures.
- HSSA data on the number of units funded through the Housing Corporation's and (its successor body the Homes and Communities Agency) National Affordable Housing Program, developer contributions and a mixture of the two.
- Financial contributions (commuted sums) for delivered affordable housing and direct payment survey data for agreed affordable housing.
- Residential and industrial land prices for each local authority from the Valuation Office Agency (VOA).
- Median price of a three-bedroom house from Land Registry data.
- Cost of constructing a typical affordable unit.

The valuation methodology made a number of necessary assumptions. These assumptions were valid for the original study given the evidence gathered by the authors and colleagues from other work undertaken at the same time (e.g. Crook *et al.*, 2002; Whitehead *et al.*, 2005). Retaining these assumptions ensured that the results for the other two studies were directly comparable. One major assumption is the availability of public subsidy, at the time this was Social Housing Grant (SHG). If there is no public subsidy available then this increases the amount of developer subsidy required to enable the units to fall within the cost boundaries imposed on registered social landlords (these are mainly housing associations). Where subsidy is available to bring costs within limits then contributions are lower.

The HSSA provided data for each LPA on the number of units in each tenure. Social rented units with no public subsidy deliver the maximum contribution. First, the land contribution for rented units with no subsidy was calculated. This included the number of hectares of land necessary to deliver the agreed number of affordable units at the specified density, assumed to be 40–50 units per hectare, multiplied by the residential land value per hectare for each LPA area. For example, an authority negotiates 100 units with developers in S106 agreements. Assuming a density of 50 units per hectare this is 2 ha of land at, say, £3m/ha giving a land contribution of £6m. It was assumed for rented units with no public funding that 80% of the land is transferred for free making the actual contribution £4.8m (i.e. 80% of £6m). A contribution of 20% of the total cost of construction of each affordable unit was assumed for rented units with no subsidy. This is an assumption to balance out units transferred for free, units transferred at cost and units transferred at a discount on cost. For example 10 units with a 20% cost subsidy would be a contribution of £220 000.

For rented units with subsidy (i.e. SHG) it was assumed that the subsidy helped fund a proportion of land purchase; 25% of the total land contribution for rented units with a subsidy was transferred for free, therefore producing a much smaller contribution than for units receiving no subsidy. There was also calculated a 10% construction cost contribution from developers for these units. For shared ownership units with public funding it was assumed that the land was purchased from the developer and the units are transferred at cost so there is no direct developer contribution.

For shared ownership with no funding it is assumed that there was a 60% free land contribution (lower than the 80% for rented units). For every 1 ha of land transferred for shared ownership units not funded by subsidy, 60% was transferred for free. For other units where the tenure was unknown, contributions were based on a 20% discount on the median price of a three-bedroom house in the LPA area. There were only a small number of units falling into this category. This was used to ensure consistency with the significant discounted open market value tenure that was prevalent in the 2003–2004 study.

Actual direct financial contributions to an LPA in lieu of units were added to the total using the values recorded in the HSSA data. The HSSA data also provided information on the amount of free/discounted land transferred to the local authority again in lieu of units. This was valued using VOA data and added to the total. The method was consistent across all three initial studies permitting a direct comparison of the value of affordable housing agreed.

The 2011–2012 study (University of Reading and Three Dragons, 2014) adopted a different approach due to changes in the HSSA data and new affordable tenures being introduced. Instead cost and market value approaches were used to estimate value with data gathered relating to house prices; land values; constructions costs per square metre and assumptions were made in regard to residential densities; dwelling sizes and values paid for units by a registered provider assuming no subsidy.

The values reported in the remainder of this chapter are nominal values for the years in which the agreements and obligations were entered into.

The number of obligations in England

Table 6.2 describes the proportion of housing permissions with a planning agreement attached. As noted in the introduction the proportion grew rapidly in the 2000s largely as a result of increasing land values from 1.7% in 1998 to 7.2% in 2007–2008. The 2014 study did not publish comparable figures but from the data published on the number of agreements (Tables 6.3 and 6.4 below), we can infer that the percentage in 2011–12 would have dropped significantly from the peak of 7.2% in 2007–2008. In 2007–2008, over half of all major residential developments (those with 10 dwellings or more) had a planning agreement attached, double the rate of 1998. Although agreements cover only a small proportion of all permissions they cover the largest. In 2007–2008, for example, there were agreements on almost all the largest housing permissions: 96% of those with more than 1000 dwellings (a few of these very large sites were in LPA ownership and contributions were 'extracted' by sale agreements and not S106 agreements). They also covered 90% of those with 100 to 999 dwellings, as well as 80% of those with 16 to 99 dwellings. In all these size bands the proportions of permissions with agreements had increased since 2005–2006 (Crook *et al.*, 2010). The evidence showed that in the early 2000s LPAs tended to deal only with the largest sites, especially in southern England. In later years, this focus was maintained but LPAs increasingly struck agreements on smaller sites including using more standard charges and formulae, especially for infrastructure and education obligations. Indeed the growth in obligations of these 'non-housing' contributions is closely associated with the increased proportion of housing permissions covered by agreements.

Table 6.3 refers to the average number of planning agreements per local authority and shows that there are significant differences in frequency by

Table 6.2   Proportions of dwelling developments with planning agreements attached.

	2003/04	2005/06	2007/08
Dwellings – major developments	40.0	47.7	50.9
Dwellings – minor developments	9.2	7.2	9.4
All dwelling developments	13.9	13.5	14.4
Percentage of all permissions with agreements	6.9	6.4	7.2

Source: Crook *et al.* (2006a, 2008, 2010).

Table 6.3   Average number of planning agreements per local authority.

	2003/04	2005/06	2007/08	2011/12
Established urban centres	13.8	25.5	25	14.7
Prosperous Britain/Commuter Belt	33.9	28.3	27.6	25.6
Rural England	26.9	13.8	36.2	15.4
Rural Towns	15.1	17.1	12.9	18.3
Urban England	19.3	35.1	29.5	21.4
Urban London	25.9	41	47.5	34.6
England	22.5	26.8	29.8	21.7

Source: Crook *et al.* (2006a, 2008, 2010) and the University of Reading (2014).

Table 6.4   Average number of planning obligations per planning agreement by local authority family.

	2003/04	2005/06	2007/08	2011/12
Established urban centres	1.38	1.99	2.52	1.65
Prosperous Britain/Commuter Belt	1.57	2.8	3.24	2.16
Rural England	1	1.59	3.22	1.62
Rural Towns	1.68	2.28	4.51	2.08
Urban England	1.96	2.5	2.84	1.38
Urban London	1.84	2.26	1.62	3.99
England	1.45	2.44	2.96	2.06

Source: Crook *et al.* (2006a, 2008, 2010) and the University of Reading (2014).

local authority family. In 2007–2008 there were, on average, nearly 30 planning agreements per local authority with the highest numbers in London and Rural England. The 2007–2008 figure showed an increase of almost a third from 2003–2004 with the 2011–2012 figure demonstrating a fall after the global financial crisis back to 2003–2004 levels with Rural England and Established Urban Centres the hardest hit. There is a very strong regional pattern to the data with regions in the southern half of the country securing many more agreements than their northern counterparts (Crook *et al.*, 2010). The number of agreements is closely linked to development activity, proxied by the number of planning applications. Thus areas with more development activity, usually those where development is the most profitable, were the ones securing the most planning agreements.

A planning agreement may contain a single obligation but usually consists of a number covering a variety of contributions. Table 6.4 shows the average number of obligations per agreement by local authority family. This figure doubled for England over the period 2003–2004 to 2007–2008 (from 1.5 to 3) indicating that local authorities were managing to secure more contributions from individual planning agreements. Once again there was a big drop by 2011–2012 after the global financial crisis as LPAs were able to extract less from the lower development values. Interestingly London had the lowest number of obligations per agreement until 2011–2012 when there was a sharp rise. The number of planning obligations per agreement is linked to both the capacity of the development to deliver contributions and the policy and negotiation process. Although the number of obligations is important, it is more a reflection of the practices and processes employed by a LPA rather than the actual value of contributions secured from a development site.

Tables 6.5 and 6.6 highlight variations in process (see also Chapter 7) by examining changes to the number of LPAs using dedicated officers and also the use of standard charging when negotiation contributions. The table covers the last three studies as data were not collected in 2003–2004. In London there were big increases in the proportion of LPAs using a dedicated officer to negotiate agreements while all London LPAs had a monitoring officer in 2011–2012. In other families, the use of officers peaked during the 2007–2008 period where agreement activity was at its highest but even then only a minority of LPAs employed a dedicated officer to negotiate with landowners/developers who traditionally employed experienced consultants within the negotiation process.

The use of standard charging, usually a formula based on calculating a financial contribution per dwelling or square metre of floorspace, again peaked in 2007–2008. Standard charging ensured certainty for developers who knew exactly the contribution required as it was written into local planning documents. Payments in lieu of the on-site provision of affordable

Table 6.5 Use of an officer(s) dedicated to negotiating or monitoring agreements.

	2005/06		2007/08		2011/12	
	Negotiating (%)	Monitoring (%)	Negotiating (%)	Monitoring (%)	Negotiating (%)	Monitoring (%)
Established urban centres	8	50	10	70	5	57
Prosperous Britain	5	65	18	68	12	50
Rural England	20	50	26	76	26	56
Rural Towns	16	79	22	65	27	59
Urban England	29	71	24	81	12	71
Urban London	18	82	31	82	75	100

Source: Crook *et al.* (2006a, 2008, 2010) and the University of Reading (2014).

Table 6.6   The percentage of LPAs using standard charging to secure planning obligations.

	2005/06 (%)	2007/08 (%)	2011/12 (%)
Affordable housing	66	62	62
Open space	62	81	79
Community and leisure	21	45	46
Transport and travel	40	57	43
Education	52	75	53

Source: Crook *et al.* (2006a, 2008, 2010) and the University of Reading (2014).

housing were commonly derived through the use of a formula with the provision of open space (including ongoing maintenance, etc.) the most likely obligation to have a formula attached.

Table 6.7 shows the total number of planning obligations per LPA and the percentage of these that were in kind and not direct financial payments. The majority of planning obligations are in fact payments to the LPA and the figures show how the number of direct payment obligations grew rapidly across the first three study periods, falling back towards 2003–2004 levels in 2011–2012. Transport and travel and open space were the most common obligations with affordable housing most likely to be delivered in-kind usually through on-site dwellings. The number of obligations per authority doubled between 2003–2004 and 2007–2008: a reflection of policy and practice coupled with the ability of LPAs to extract value from a rising property market. The proportion of in-kind obligations generally fell with both developers and LPAs preferring the certainty of financial sums. In 2007–2008 many authorities were using planning obligations to impose restrictions on use, noise or parking for example, or to charge administrative fees which increased the number of other obligations quite significantly.

Table 6.7   Average number of total obligations per LPA by obligation type (proportion that were in-kind in brackets).

	2003/04	2005/06	2007/08	2011/12
Affordable housing	3.8 (82%)	6.5 (86%)	8.5 (89%)	4.3 (79%)
Open space	13.3 (17%)	14.3 (13%)	16.6 (15%)	14.1 (5%)
Transport and travel	11.4 (36%)	16.2 (26%)	17.3 (29%)	11.1 (19%)
Community and leisure	3.9 (23%)	6.9 (12%)	7.4 (19%)	10.2 (10%)
Education	2.6 (4%)	5.3 (2%)	4.6 (0%)	4.1 (0%)
Other*	2.7 (85%)	12 (22%)	20.2 (24%)	1.3 (0%)
All	37.8 (34%)	61 (25%)	74.7 (29%)	45.2 (16%)

*The vast majority of other obligations in 2005–2006 and 2007–2008 were small and used to cover administrative costs.
Source: Crook *et al.* (2006a, 2008, 2010) and the University of Reading (2014).

Affordable housing obligations in England

Due to the predominantly in-kind nature of affordable housing obligations the four studies dealt, as we saw above, with these obligations differently to the other obligation types. Before discussing the results from these studies in more detail we first review previous studies, including those by the authors of this volume, that looked specifically at how obligations secured affordable housing and, in particular, to ascertain the extent to which obligations secured both land and financial contributions for new affordable homes.

In the 1990s, evidence showed that housing associations secured the majority of the land they needed from the public sector, especially from local authorities (but this source of land was drying up), that much of it was brownfield, that very few, only 9%, of all the sites acquired between, for example, 1992–1993 and 1994–1995 involved planning obligations, and that housing associations found it difficult to acquire sites in high value areas (The Housing Corporation, 1996). This was confirmed by a 1993 study which found that LPAs did not expect planning obligations to be a major source of new affordable homes, except in areas of major land release, although in a more buoyant market LPAs might be in the position to negotiate more contributions (Jackson *et al.*, 1994). Likewise another study of the same period (Couttie, 1994) confirmed that LPA policies were poorly developed and that LPAs were often uncertain about the logic of using planning obligations with the result that developers did not know what was expected of them, the financial structures were very *ad hoc*; there were big gaps between what developers would provide and the public subsidy available, and there was poor coordination within LPAs between their housing and planning departments.

Another study, around the same time (Barlow and Chambers, 1992) came to similar conclusions showing that although by 1991 almost three quarters of LPAs had been involved in discussions, only a fifth had a planning policy on affordable housing or had schemes underway (with some implemented) and that only about 10 000 new affordable homes had been delivered via planning agreements in the whole of the 1980s, principally on large sites. The low output was partly because of the downturn in the property market at that time, continuing concerns about the legitimacy of the policy, problems of ensuring long-term affordability, and the late involvement of housing associations in the negotiations. At the time, it was not expected that more would be secured in the future. The study also found that developers much preferred to provide what was required through low-cost home ownership than through social rented housing. In general the land (on average the affordable elements constituted about a quarter of all dwellings on a site) was in most cases transferred at a discount on its market value or free. The researchers doubted that more than 2000 new affordable homes a year would be secured through planning obligations in the then property market climate.

A follow-up study carried out in 1993 by the same team (Barlow *et al.*, 1994) showed that by then seven in ten LPAs had relevant planning policies for affordable housing and of these three quarters had defined affordable and affordability, a big advance on the earlier 1991 study. Most left the proportion of housing on new developments that should be affordable to negotiation, not spelling it out in their policies, generally seeking a 20% contribution, primarily in the form of land and not through financial contributions. There was evidence that more was being successfully negotiated and delivered, that smaller sites were coming into the 'frame' and that LPAs were able to negotiate higher proportions of dwellings on sites as affordable, 28%, than their 20% targets. There was thus a new optimism that output could significantly improve with perhaps 15 000 new affordable homes being secured each year by the late 1990s if the private housebuilding market improved, a big advance on the position even a few years previously.

A later study, based on five case study LPAs, was more cautious (Kleinman *et al.*, 2000) finding that whilst using planning obligations had become 'much more common' (Ibid, p. 36) LPAs were achieving less than the maximum potential of 30% of new dwellings being affordable. The reasons included the way obligations made sites unviable, especially in northern and midlands regions, the competing requirements for obligations, and the need for public subsidy, especially in more expensive areas, to make what was provided through obligations genuinely affordable. Although perhaps 15 000 new affordable homes each year might be provided through planning obligations, this would still require considerable injection of public subsidy. Another study (Bishop, 2001) found that whilst most (85%) of LPAs had policies in their local plans by then, the needs assessments underpinning these were still not well developed and only a minority of LPAs had site specific policies, although most had policies on thresholds. Moreover, more than a third did not expect any private sector financial contribution to affordable homes on S106 sites and where LPAs did require this, there were a wide range of formulae for calculating what was required, including if any public subsidy was also to be made available, the latter often appearing to be very uncertain. Where subsidy was provided the evidence suggested it increased land prices and where it was not, developers favoured shared ownership (whilst LPAs wanted social rented housing). The researchers thought that in general LPA 'practice is still some way short of the best' (Ibid, p. 11). They also found varying definitions used for 'affordable' and some 'confusion' (Ibid, p. 13) about it, although most were seeking social rented or shared ownership housing but with a wide range of ways of ensuring availability in the long term (see also Driver, 1994). In view of the government's emphasis on securing on-site provision to help create mixed communities nearly half the LPAs in the study accepted commuted payments, often using the funds to improve the existing housing stock.

To sum up the position in the 1990s, up to 10 000 to 12 000 new affordable homes were being secured through S106 with an increase to 15 000 a year towards the end of the decade. Subsequent studies (Crook *et al.*, 2002, 2006b; Monk *et al.*, 2005, 2006; Crook and Whitehead, 2010) focused much more on outputs and outcomes. These showed a significant increase in the number of affordable homes being secured in the 2000s (Figure 6.4) and, as Chapter 8 shows, also being delivered. This reflected a 'booming' property market, the fact that policies and practices had become 'bedded down' more, and because housing associations were running out of traditional sources of land for development.

These all provided the context for LPAs to use planning agreements to extract some of the development value for both affordable housing and for other obligations. Obligations policies for affordable housing became more widespread, with 89% of LPAs having policies in place in their local development plans by 2001 (Crook *et al.*, 2002). Those that did not were in parts of England where the need for affordable housing was negligible. The fall in numbers agreed after 2007–2008 (see Figure 6.4) reflects the impact of the property crash after the global financial crisis.

In the 2000s housing associations' traditional sources of land for new homes were beginning to run out. Traditionally they had relied on public sector, generally inner city, land including that which had been acquired by local authorities under slum clearance programmes. This was no longer widely available and they had to look to other sources, especially in

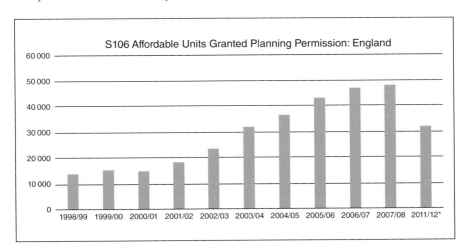

Figure 6.4 Number of affordable units granted planning permission in S106 agreements.
Source: Department of Communities and Local Government, HSSA data.
Note: * Figures for the year 2011–12 are estimates

the private sector and in new locations where they faced higher prices and competition from the private sector (Monk *et al.*, 2005). Planning obligations offered them the prospect of access to private market sites as well as the prospects of some private funding. The latter came from discounted or 'free' land, cash contributions, or a reduction in the price of dwellings sold to housing associations. The policy default (as we have seen in Chapter 4) was that the provision is made on the same site as the market homes so as to create mixed communities.

The number of new affordable homes agreed in England through S106 increased steadily throughout the early and mid-2000s. Much more was being approved as part of planning permissions in this period than in the 1990s but numbers started to tail off after 2006–2007 as a consequence of the downturn in the property market. There was also a strong regional pattern with most (70% or more, depending on the year) of the affordable homes agreed being in the southern regions. This is not only where need was (and still is) greatest but also where the property market was most buoyant and development values were adequate to support obligations. But the numbers agreed were greater than would have been expected on the basis of the southern regions' share of new housing permissions. Detailed evidence showed that S106 schemes were in the lower value parts of high status areas (in socio-economic classification terms) or in the higher priced areas of lower status areas (Crook *et al.*, 2006b). The majority of commuted payments made by developers and of land they transferred to LPAs for affordable housing was also in the South East, especially in London itself (Crook *et al.*, 2002, pp. 6–7).

A range of targets had been set by LPAs (reflecting variations in need) for affordable housing falling between 10% and 40%, with few having site-specific targets as well. These targets were higher in southern LPAs (30% and above) than in other regions (15–30%). On sites where agreements had been made between 1997 and 2000 an average of 17% of the total dwellings given permission were affordable, ranging from 22% in the South East to 11% in the North East. Although most new provision had been agreed in the regions with the greatest needs, there was no relationship between needs at the local level and the scale and type of obligations agreed. This was because there was insufficient land in adopted plans, with many LPAs having only brownfield sites above the (then) threshold, and because of the challenges, complexities and outcomes of negotiations (see Chapter 7, this volume). In larger LPAs in high demand areas planners and their colleagues became more adept at negotiations and thus became increasingly successful in achieving their targets. Getting housing associations involved early in negotiations and improved understanding of the impact of agreements on viability all helped getting successful agreements. Timing was also important to successfully getting agreement with the whole process from the start of pre-application discussions to finally concluding a S106 agreement taking up to 6 years (Crook *et al.*, 2002, pp. 22–23) during which time the economic and financial circumstances might well change.

In the latter part of the 2000s, this regional and sub-regional pattern did not change but the types of affordable homes agreed did (Crook *et al.*, 2006b; Crook and Whitehead, 2010; Crook and Monk, 2011). As the policy continued to 'bed down' a greater percentage of housing permissions had planning agreements attached to them. As we have already seen (this chapter) in 2007–2008 almost all sites with permission for 1000 dwellings or more and 90% of those with 100 to 999 had agreements, as did 80% of all sites with more than 15 dwellings. Hence almost all above threshold sites had agreements (Crook *et al.*, 2010). In the early years of the decade, LPAs tended to focus on larger sites when negotiating agreements but in later years more agreements were also reached on smaller sites. Agreements per LPA continued to be higher in southern than in midlands and northern LPAs but increased more between 2003–2004 and 2007–2008 in the latter two regions partly reflecting the later increase in development values in those regions compared with the southern ones and the later implementation of good practice (Crook *et al.*, 2010).

As LPAs managed to secure more affordable homes on more sites, there was also a change in the tenure of those that were agreed – and delivered (see also Chapter 8, this volume) with a greater proportion being shared ownership rather than social rented. There were seven reasons for this (Crook and Whitehead, 2010). First, as LPAs pushed for larger numbers on sites, developers resisted agreeing to more rented homes but acceded to providing the increase in the form of shared ownership dwellings because of the lower costs to them since housing associations paid more for these than for social rented dwellings. Second, developers much preferred shared ownership since they considered these had less impact on the value of their market homes being 'better' neighbours than social rented tenants, thus impacting less on viability. Third, much less (or no) public subsidy was required for shared ownership. Fourth, a range of housing was required to meet the needs for affordable homes, especially in relation to the needs of key workers excluded from home ownership in southern regions. Fifth, increased shared ownership made it possible for housing associations to make more surpluses as shared owners 'staircased' upwards and increased the share they owned, making it possible to cross-subsidise the rented provision. Sixth, the drive for increased densities on brownfield sites also led to more shared ownership as these were generally provided in the form of smaller units in flats. The seventh reason is that providing a broader range of affordable tenures contributes to the mixed communities agenda. For all these reasons the increase in affordable dwellings secured shown in Figure 6.4 has come much more in shared ownership and other intermediate dwellings than rented ones, although there was a reversal of this after the credit crunch when public subsidy was brought forward to keep the construction industry going, enabling housing associations to pay higher prices for social rented homes (and contribute to developers' cash flows).

The total value of planning obligations agreed in England

We now turn from the incidence of obligations in general and on the provision of affordable homes to estimate the total value agreed, starting with the value of affordable housing contributions agreed.

The total value of the affordable housing agreed is shown in Table 6.8. The value doubled between 2003–2004 and 2007–2008 when it peaked, falling around 10% by 2011–2012. The increase reflects both the growth in the number of new affordable homes agreed and in the value of the land and construction costs contributions made by developers. The different methodologies used to estimate value between 2007–2008 and 2011–2012 make direct comparisons problematic with the drop in the numbers agreed by one-third equating to only a 10% fall in value (although the values are all nominal). What can be concluded is that the value of affordable housing peaked during the strongest period of housing market activity.

Added to the total value of affordable housing obligations is the value of all other obligations. The average value by obligation type generated by the survey data was applied to in-kind obligations and 'grossed up' using the LPA typology described above to determine the total value of planning obligations in England. Table 6.9 shows the average value of direct planning obligations with the affordable housing figure being payments in lieu of dwellings delivered on or off site. Again the peak was 2007–2008 with the average value falling within all obligation types with the exception of transport and travel. These averages were then used to determine the value of in-kind obligations. The number of in-kind obligations was identified through the survey and the average direct payment obligation within each local authority family multiplied by the number of in-kind obligations.

Table 6.10 shows the total value of all planning obligations agreed at the national level. Added to the value of the direct payment, in-kind and

Table 6.8 The nominal value of all new affordable homes agreed.

2003/04	£1.2bn
2005/06	£1.9bn
2007/08	£2.6bn
2011/12	£2.3bn

Source: Crook *et al.* (2006a, 2008, 2010) and the University of Reading (2014).

Table 6.9   Average value of direct payment planning obligations per authority by type of obligation (thousands).

	2003/04	2005/06	2007/08	2011/12
Affordable housing	£249	£370	£592	£470
Open space	£25	£45	£33	£30
Transport and travel	£83	£76	£75	£132
Community and leisure	£59	£32	£68	£48
Education	£117	£84	£162	£154

Source: Crook *et al.* (2006a, 2008, 2010) and the University of Reading (2014).

Table 6.10   Total value of planning obligations agreed in England (£ billions).

	2003/04	2005/06	2007/08	2011/12
Direct and in-kind obligations	£0.70	£0.90	£1.30	£1.10
Land contributions	NA	£1.0	£0.90	£0.30
Affordable housing	£1.20	£1.90	£2.60	£2.30
Total	£1.9a	£3.70	£4.80	£3.70

Note: (a) Excludes land – data not collected in 2003/2004.
Source: Crook *et al.* (2006a, 2008, 2010) and the University of Reading (2014).

affordable housing planning obligations is the value of the land transferred to the LPA for contributions relating to education, transport, open space and community facilities. Data on direct land contributions was collected in the survey and the information gathered from responding authorities 'grossed up' using the family typology. Land contributions were valued using Valuation Office Data on the assumption that this land could otherwise have been used for residential development. Land contributions generated a considerable addition to the total value of planning obligations, especially in 2005–2006 and 2007–2008 where there were considerable land transfers in high-value London authorities. Land data were not collected for 2003–2004.

Table 6.10 provides the total value of planning obligations with contributions peaking at £4.8bn in 2007–2008. The year 2011–2012 saw a considerable drop with the market still recovering from the global financial crisis and development activity well below that of 2007–2008 and with the total value of obligations agreed being only three quarters of that agreed in 2007–2008. Considerable growth in value within the 2000s was caused by both an increase in development values driven by a buoyant property market coupled with evolving policy and practice within LPAs. The table shows that the value of affordable housing agreed was the largest proportion of the total value agreed, constituting over half in both 2005–2006 and 2007–2008 and over 60% in 2011–2012. The affordable housing contributions were worth £49 000 per dwelling agreed in 2003–2004 rising to £54 000 per dwelling in 2007–2008. Although only a minority of this comprised direct payments to LPAs these were still substantial rising from £178 000 per LPA in 2003–2004 to £579 000 in 2007–2008. Despite the significant amounts involved per dwelling agreed, these did not fully remove the need for public subsidy as well as we shall see below in this chapter. Of the value of the non-housing obligations in 2007–2008, £235m was agreed for open space provision, £462m for transport, £193m for community and leisure facilities, £271m for education facilities and £183m for other provision including fees for the agreements themselves (for which each LPA received an average of £25 000 for all agreements). The total sums agreed in each of the years also far exceeded the total value of development values captured annually through the various systems of national development value taxation described in Chapter 3. Because of this, we turn at the end of this chapter to look at whether the values shown in Table 6.10 were paid by landowners (and hence a *de facto* tax on development value) or by developers' in reduced profits and by purchasers of the market development completed on the S106 sites in the form of higher prices.

Planning obligations in Scotland and Wales

Evidence from Scotland and Wales suggested that policy and practice in the mid-2000s lagged significantly behind that in England. Although policy and practice in Scotland is similar to that in England, especially in relation to the policy tests of necessity, planning purpose and reasonableness (Scottish Government, 2012), the use of agreements in the mid-2000s appeared much more limited than in England. A specific study of affordable housing in rural areas found that, although Scotland lagged behind England, the needs for new affordable homes ranked as a lower priority than pursuing environmental objectives in both countries (Satsangi and Dunmore, 2003). However, a more recent study of the years 2004 to 2007 (McMaster *et al.*, 2008) showed that the use of obligations was on a rising curve and this was largely associated with major housing developments. Nonetheless, only 1.4% of all non-householder permissions had agreements over the study years[7] (although this rose to 3% for all major development and for minor housing developments). The value of the obligations secured was only £159m, significantly less than in England, even allowing for the much lower development activity, given the smaller size of Scotland compared with England.[8] The most common use of obligations was to secure recreation

---

[7] Proportion computed from data in McMaster *et al.* (2008).

[8] The mid-year estimate of the population of Scotland in 2007 was 5.1 million; it was 3.0 million for Wales and 51.1 million for England. *Source*: http://www.ons.gov.uk/ons/publications/re-reference-tables.html?edition=tcm%3A77-213833 (last accessed 8th October 2014).

facilities, although the upward trend was for affordable housing. The largest financial contributions were for transport and the largest in-kind contributions were for affordable housing, the latter principally being discounted land. The affordable housing contributions secured 241 new dwellings and the value of the in-kind and financial contributions accounted for only a fifth of the value of all obligations, a much lower proportion than in England, as we have seen. In Scotland a much smaller proportion, 17%, of major housing permissions had agreements than in England. The evidence in the report suggests that both policy and practice was less developed then than in England, explaining the lower level of obligations secured, but that policy and practice was evolving.

Although planning in Wales is now devolved to the Welsh Government, the Community Infrastructure Levy is not. The obligations policies set out by the former Welsh Office before devolution, including the policy tests that English LPAs were then required to follow (Welsh Office, 1997), have been maintained and, as in England, since made mandatory. The recent planning policy statement adopted by the Welsh Government includes those on affordable housing and the use of obligations to secure these (Welsh Government, 2014; see also Welsh Assembly Government, 2006). The picture on the use of obligations in the mid-2000s was similar to that in Scotland with only 3% of non-householder permissions in 2005–2006 having agreements attached to them. Although more major residential permissions had agreements (28%), this was less than in England at the same time (Rowley *et al.*, 2007). The value of obligations was between £26m and £31m, less than 1% of that estimated for England in the same year (£3.7bn), despite the fact that Wales has a population of 3.0m which, whilst small compared to England, is still the equivalent of 6% of England's total population. Whilst development values in Wales were on average much less than in England this was not the only factor behind the apparently poorer outcomes in Wales, because policy (e.g. high site thresholds for requiring affordable housing contributions) and practice (especially on negotiating agreements and the use of standard charging) were less well developed than in England.

Rural exceptions schemes

As we saw in Chapter 4, rural exceptions policies (RES) allow planning authorities to exceptionally give permission to new affordable homes on sites which would not normally be permitted for any new development but where permission is exceptionally granted as a means of securing development value (i.e. low-priced land) for the new homes. Williams *et al.* (1991) found that although policies were being put into place, the initial experience was of schemes involving lengthy and complex processes and that the depressed housing market at the time was creating difficulties in realising the new homes, especially those for low-cost home ownership. In a later study, Gallent (1997) reported slow progress in securing new affordable homes in rural areas. This was partly because of the very partial coverage of adopted and up-to-date development plans and the difficulties of securing private finance for rural exceptions schemes, although if the housing market picked up LPAs would be in a stronger position to secure more homes.

These studies also showed the significance of having a middle person between those seeking to secure provision and the LPA whose role was to secure the confidence of local communities in the process, such persons becoming known as 'rural housing enablers', particularly speeding up the processes in later years of projects. Finding acceptable sites and dealing with the complexities of 'signing off' agreements (especially related to mortgagee in possession clauses) were major stumbling blocks (Lavis, 1995). There were particular difficulties in securing RES in villages in greenbelts where the LPAs concerned did not want such provision, believing it inappropriate and, even where it was permitted, it took place outside rather than within villages (Elson *et al.*, 1994).

Who pays for the obligations?

In earlier chapters, we examined if planning obligations could be conceptually regarded as a *de facto* tax on development values, negotiated between LPAs and developers or landowners and hypothecated to help provide infrastructure and other local needs. Whatever the conceptual arguments, obligations can only be regarded as a development value tax if the cost of obligations is reflected in lower development values compared with the value had there been no obligations. In this section we look at the evidence about this.

There are at least three (not mutually exclusive) possibilities (Crook *et al.*, 2002; Crook and Whitehead, 2002): (i) landowners pay in lower land prices and as long as the same amount of land comes forward this is simply a financial redistribution from landowners to affordable housing and other obligations; (ii) developers pay through lower profit margins; if this comes from increases in land prices after developers have acquired the land, taking this increase in obligations will not impact on output, but if it comes from normal profits it could impact on both the market and the affordable housing provisions as well as the funding of other obligations; and (iii) purchasers of completed developments pay in higher prices. The cross-subsidy can also come from reducing costs, changing the dwelling mix or increasing densities, changes which all release more funding for cross-subsidy but which could impact negatively on new or subsequent occupiers. It is also possible that development values could fall if the prices for market houses drop as a consequence of the affordable housing obligation, if long running negotiations push up developers' cost, or if planning policies shift the locations of sites allocated for housing into higher cost or expensive to develop sites (such as brownfield sites). Finally, as far as ascertaining who pays for the affordable housing aspects of obligations, the availability of public subsidy complicates matters. Obligations can be a way of 'stretching' subsidy, of acting as an alternative or of changing the mix (type and size) of the affordable provision. As we have seen, the latter is now the principal way subsidy is used but this was not the case in the early 2000s.

There has in fact been much less research on these issues than there has been on measuring incidence and valuation, identifying good practice in negotiating obligations, including in assessing viability, and monitoring delivery. The evidence we have on 'who pays?' comes mainly from work to assess how much of the affordable housing secured is additional to what would have been provided in the absence of planning obligations. As well as the negotiating strength of developers in relation to landowners and LPAs, the type of developer appears to be critical to 'who pays'. Where agreements involve large 'current traders'[9], developers who operate nationally (sometimes through regional divisions as is the case with many of the volume house-builders), and LPAS have clear policies that they consistently implement, the costs of obligations are generally borne by landowners in lower prices (Crook *et al.*, 2002). All house-builders rely on networks, including strong personal contacts within the industry, agents and landowners to manage risk when acquiring land (Adams *et al.*, 2012). But compared with smaller developers large firms have the capacity to acquire large land banks including buying some land without planning permission (so-called strategic land) on option agreements where they agree to acquire land in the future, subject to a number of conditions such as achieving planning consent and then paying a discount on the market value with planning consent, a price which also takes account of the costs of agreed obligations. Large firms have the financial and organisational capacity and the skilled staff, including land agents, town planners and negotiators to do this, something which takes up a lot of time, with the elapsed time from acquiring an option to starting building on site being anything from between 10 and 20 years (Burgess *et al.*, 2014). And even where they buy land with existing consents (so-called short-term land), for example, from companies trading in land who will have obtained an outline and fully implementable consent with a S106 agreement in place (reflected in what they have paid for land), they will generally seek to amend the consent to maximise their margins and this may include renegotiating agreements.

---

[9] That is companies who buy land and build housing but who do not hold land or own properties after a site is built out and all properties sold.

In contrast, smaller developers and house builders operating locally often do not have the same financial and organisational capacity and although their local networks may lead them to acquire land that does not come to the attention of the larger developers they tend to acquire land with planning consent (or land which has been allocated for development in an adopted plan) which enables them to get on site quickly (Office of Fair Trading, 2008). In these circumstances they risk paying land prices which do not take adequate (or any) account of the cost of obligations tied up in a S106 agreement. Hence they may end up paying for obligations themselves in lower profit margins or in attempting to pass on the costs in higher prices, which may be difficult as all house-builders tend to be price takers not price setters, since most house prices are set in the much larger second-hand market. A review of competition in the housebuilding industry showed that firms competed for sales against each other and against existing homes so that, although some buyers might place a premium on a new home, generally the prices of existing homes constrain the prices of new ones (Office of Fair Trading, 2008). As Calcutt (2007) showed, an increasing share of new house-building output has been concentrated in the hands of a few large volume builders with the top 10 building 44% of new homes in 2006 (and the top 25 building 54%). They also focused more on larger sites (see also Europe Economics, 2014). This suggests that increasing proportions of negotiations and agreements are between LPAs and these large builders such that landowners are likely therefore, *ceteris paribus*, to increasingly be the parties paying for obligations.

The detailed evidence about who pays comes from our series of studies on planning obligations and affordable housing (Crook *et al.*, 2002; Monk *et al.*, 2005, 2006, 2008; Whitehead *et al.*, 2005). In this context costs were shared between developer and landowner, housing association debt funding and reserves contributions, and public subsidy. What exactly have been these proportions and what determines them has not been easy to discern. There are a range of factors at play including patterns of land values, what LPA policy requires in terms of number of units, their type, whether they are rented or a form of low-cost home ownership and their negotiations with developers, public subsidy policies, and competition between housing associations to secure land and housing on S106 sites.

It has been hard to collect a lot of information about specific sites in order to look at the financial impact of planning obligations on development, compared with what would have happened without the agreement. Partly this is a matter of participants in developments maintaining the confidentiality of commercially sensitive information and partly it is a matter of being unable to examine the 'counterfactual', that is, to look at other sites similar in all respects but where there are no agreements. Hence what follows is drawn from three sources of information. First, some analysis has been made of partial data on sites where affordable housing obligations have been part of the agreement. These have been identified from databases held by the Greater London Authority and the Homes and Communities Agency and provided to us on an anonymised basis. Second, we have modelled the residual value of a small sample of sites in London and elsewhere using both actual data in London and assumed data for sites elsewhere (i.e. we have used actual market prices and construction and all other costs, including financing costs and developers profits but where this is not available we have used relevant databases to derive the data needed). The analysis used discounted cash flow models of the kind described in Chapter 5 of this volume to compute the residual value, both with and without obligations (see Monk *et al.*, 2008, pp. 22–32 for model descriptions). The third type of information comes from the large amount of qualitative information gathered both about case study sites and from participants in focus groups held for a range of research projects.

The conclusion from all these evidences is that in over half the 92 cases we looked at (Crook *et al.*, 2002; Monk *et al.*, 2005, 2006, 2008; Whitehead *et al.*, 2005) developers were able to pass costs back to landowners, in a fifth the developer was also the landowner and in only 1 in 12 cases was the developer unable to pass all the costs back to landowners because insufficient information was available at the time of the transaction. The extent to which the landowner pays depended on (i) the type of developer and the timing of land acquisition; (ii) the clarity of LPA policy and the consistency of its implementation; (iii) levels of demand for completed developments; (iv) the negotiating skills of the parties involved; (v) the attitude of the LPA to the questions of 'who pays?'; and (vi) the availability of subsidy, the competition between housing associations for completed dwellings and the reserves they are willing to contribute to secure them.

Some of our modelling was designed to illustrate the impact of different obligations policies. In one example (using 2007 values and costs) we looked at the impact of these on brownfield developments and showed that policies which required developers to sell completed social rented affordable units (including the land) to housing associations at prices they could afford to pay from net rents alone (i.e. they received no grants) secured the maximum financial contributions from developers (Monk *et al.*, 2008). It also showed that the provision of social rented housing secured larger financial contributions than shared ownership units because housing associations were able to pay higher proportions of market values for these than for social rented dwellings. Providing only free land for affordable units (and also where the housing association received grant to build the units) made little impact on viability compared with a site with market units only, suggesting that bigger financial contributions could be achieved before viability was threatened. And when grant was factored into the modelling, residual land values were higher. In terms of viability, the high values of land in alternative uses in London meant that many affordable housing schemes made developments unviable. Outside London schemes were viable even with proportions of up to 40% of new homes being affordable and transferred for nil consideration (in terms of the residual value being at or above a benchmark price that made land saleable, even with obligations). The evidence also suggested that where housing associations are not involved in the negotiations leading to agreements, developers subsequently ask them to tender for the affordable units that the developers have agreed to provide. Unless the S106 agreement specifies the price at which the units can be sold, there is a risk that competition between associations to acquire additional stock increases the price paid with a positive impact on developer margins and possibly land prices (especially where there are overage arrangements within option agreements).

Some limited evidence from specific schemes of the actual division of total scheme costs between developers (and landowners), housing associations and public subsidy, comparing S106 sites with other sites (Whitehead *et al.*, 2005) shows how very complex the pattern is. Developer contributions ranged from 21% to 62% and while the highest contribution was for a scheme where all the affordable units were discounted market sales, there was no clear pattern with respect to other proportions with some shared ownership costs having low developer contributions and rented ones having high developer contributions. Housing association funding ranged from 19% to 79% of scheme costs, the lowest being for a scheme of social rented housing and the highest for one of shared ownership. The only schemes with no public subsidy were those with all dwellings being discounted market sales or shared ownership units. However, although there was no clear explanation of these variations in who paid the costs of these S106 schemes, the levels of public subsidy were much higher in new affordable homes secured on sites with no planning obligations. Examination of scheme files held by the Housing Corporation suggested that the costs of affordable dwellings built on S106 sites were related to cost indicators with, for example, subsidy covering 60% of social rented housing costs in London and 30% for shared ownership schemes in London.

Hence the evidence showed that whilst there had been some transfer from public to private funding, some of the affordable housing provision on S106 sites was still being funded by public subsidy. In the early years of the policy we found that nearly 80% of all dwellings completed between 2000–2001 and 2002–2003 had subsidy (Whitehead *et al.*, 2005). This is somewhat of a paradox given that the policy was designed to replace public subsidy with private funding. Our initial work on this (Crook *et al.*, 2002) showed that what S106 primarily did was to shift the geography of provision more than

the funding mix. Scheme costs incurred were related to the cost indicators used to provide public subsidy and because these did not vary greatly
with geography (except in London) public subsidy was necessary to help
housing associations acquire land in high value areas where, despite S106
agreements, developer contributions were not sufficient to avoid the need for
some subsidy. Evidence from the costs of land acquisition on S106 sites compared with others suggested this may be the case with higher land costs being
incurred on housing association schemes on S106 sites than on schemes not
on S106 sites in the South East and South West in 2002–2003 (Whitehead
et al., 2005). Hence what developer contributions were doing was to reduce
this high land value sufficiently to enable schemes costs to be contained
within the limits for public subsidy.

We thus concluded that planning obligations led to a substantial number
of new affordable homes being built on S106 sites and in areas where
associations had not built in the past, but that only small proportions
were genuinely additional given the public subsidy needed to bridge the
developer contribution in high value areas and the costs eligible for public
subsidy. Hence the main impact of S106 on affordable housing was to switch
the geography of new supply to high-value areas in the southern regions
with public subsidy and developer contributions opening up such areas to
provision for the first time whilst in northern regions it provided land for
small amounts of low-cost home ownership dwellings (see also Crook *et al.*,
2002). At the time (2005) we thought only about 2000 of the 12 799 new
dwellings completed on S106 sites in 2002–2003 were genuinely additional.
But that does not mean obligations were not crucial to opening up parts of
the country to affordable housing provision for the first time, areas where
land was generally too expensive for housing associations to acquire even
when public subsidy was available.

Our evidence (Whitehead *et al.*, 2005) also showed that the use of public
subsidy was unrelated to patterns of need, housing costs or development
values but rather to the clarity of LPA policies and the effectiveness of
negotiations (see also Chapter 7, this volume). But it did also show how
policy appeared to be 'bedding down' as the years went by with evidence
that the proportion of new affordable housing completions funded fully
or partially by developer contributions had increased from 30% to 48%
between 2000–2001 and 2002–2003, although the proportions that were
wholly funded by contributions, remained small, rising from only 7 to 9%
(Monk *et al.*, 2005). There was also a clear regional pattern to this, with
higher proportions wholly or partially funded by developer contributions in
the southern regions of England (where development values were higher).
For example, the proportions of completions with at least some developer
contributions rose from 25% to 49% in the southern regions but only from
22% to 33% in the three northern regions. As the supply of traditional sites

where there were no S106 agreements declined, public subsidy was being increasingly concentrated on S106 sites. However, the evidence also showed that the proportions of completions where there was no public subsidy at all were not highest in the southern regions but in some of the northern and midlands regions with evidence showing that this was a consequence of clarity about S106 policy on a zero- or low-grants regime, local practice to implement this by some offices of the Housing Corporation, and a focus on delivering affordable homes in the form of shared ownership, which required less or no grant. Paradoxically, the regions with the highest development values were also those with the lowest proportion of schemes with no public subsidy. Finally, case study evidence confirmed that developer contributions appeared to be highest on greenfield sites contributing between 39% and 46% of total schemes costs depending on the case study. It also showed that on some brownfield schemes developers simultaneously provided land and funding for both on-and off site contributions, together making up the total dwelling LPAs required from the relevant S106 sites (Monk *et al.*, 2005).

Our evidence also showed, in addition, that achieving numbers was not always the most important objective for LPAs and the mix (tenures, types and sizes) was also important especially as a mix emphasising large dwellings for social renting imposes higher costs on developers than smaller shared ownership dwellings (Burgess *et al.*, 2007; Monk *et al.*, 2008).

Moreover, we also found that LPAs were not always concerned about who pays for obligations. For example in terms of affordable housing contributions, many LPAs were simply concerned about securing the numbers required (and perhaps also tenure, type and size) but how this was financed was not, they believed, a matter for them, but a matter for landowners, developers and housing associations. Others, however, were concerned about it, including those who required affordable dwellings to be provided to housing association at a price which reflected what associations could pay out of the net rents without any grant input (Burgess *et al.*, 2007).

Finally, the impact of grants is hard to discern but there is some evidence that providing grant works through to higher land prices or that it enables developers to pay higher contributions for other obligations (Monk *et al.*, 2008; Whitehead *et al.*, 2005). Grant was the key to bridging gaps between what developers would provide and what housing associations could pay, especially the higher standards required for affordable compared with market sale dwellings. But there is also evidence of housing associations using their reserves where grant was not sufficient or unavailable and that some were using surpluses from market sales to do this, with a possible impact on increasing development values. In addition it is not always the case that shared ownership increases developer contributions, rather that associations' reserves contributions increase.

There is also evidence that, compared with a 'no obligations' regime, market units are more likely to be higher density and smaller (Crook *et al.*, 2002; Whitehead *et al.*, 2005). The question then arises if it is better to accept off-site provision because developers with a site full of market housing will make higher profits leaving a bigger development value which can be used to fund more provision off site than could be provided on site, provided of course that the costs of land and construction are similar for the site to be used for the affordable dwellings and can contribute to mixed communities (Whitehead *et al.*, 2005). That is not to say that requiring on-site provision of affordable homes is always negative in terms of development values since selling the latter to housing associations can have a positive impact on developers' cash flow in the early stages of a site, especially in an economic downturn, and also reduces overall marketing costs.

The evidence thus shows an incomplete and unclear picture. What we can say is that the clarity and consistency of LPA policy is critical to 'who pays' and so is the availability of public subsidy for affordable homes and the balance between shared ownership and social rented housing within the affordable 'mix', both grants and shared ownership potentially leaving landowners with higher prices. The stance a LPA takes on the issue is relevant too and those who believe that policy should influence funding outcomes especially by assuming zero grants for the sale of affordable dwellings are more likely to result in landowners paying. Where, however, LPAs' policies are unclear and inconsistently implemented developers can end up paying for at least some of the obligations themselves. This is especially the case where developers buy land in the expectation that they will need to provide a particular bundle of obligations but during negotiations more is asked for (and given to secure a consent) with the developer being unable to pass the extra costs back to landowners. Of course during a rising market, this might not matter if the extra obligations costs are covered by higher than anticipated sales prices, but in a downturn the costs may have to be absorbed by the developer. Nor are the costs of negotiating planning obligations trivial. They can be substantial contributing significantly to developers' costs whilst the delays caused by long-running negotiations may make it problematic for developers to open up new sites in time to meet demand (Burgess *et al.*, 2014).

Conclusions

There has been a very considerable growth in planning obligations in the last 20 years, especially in England, and substantial funding both in terms of finance and in-kind contributions has been secured, with over half having been agreed for new affordable homes. The growth has been possible because of a buoyant property market as well as the development of obligations policy and practice. The available evidence suggests that much of this has been provided by landowners as developers have mainly been able to pass the costs back to landowners. As far as affordable housing is concerned, the developer (and therefore landowner) contributions did not entirely negate the need for public subsidy but the policy has helped shift the geography of affordable homes into high-value areas thus contributing also to the mixed communities agenda. In the most recent years, the downturn in the property market has inevitably led to fewer obligations being agreed and less value being secured as a result, but the sums involved are still substantial.

References

Adams, D., Leishman, C., and Watkins, C. (2012) Housebuilder networks and residential land markets. *Urban Studies* **49**, 705–720.

Barlow J. and Chambers D. (1992) *Planning Agreements and Affordable Housing Provision*, University of Sussex Centre for Urban and Regional Research, Brighton.

Barlow, J., Cocks, R., and Parker, M. (1994) *Planning for Affordable Housing*, Department of the Environment, London.

Bishop, D. (2001) *Delivering Affordable Housing through the Planning System*, Royal Institution of Chartered Surveyors Policy Unit, London and The Housing Corporation, London.

Bunnell, G. (1995) Planning gain in theory and practice. *Progress in Planning* **44**, 1–113.

Burgess G., Crook, A.D.H., Jones, M., and Monk, S. (2014) The nature of planning constraints. *Written Evidence to the House of Commons Select Committee on Communities and Local Government Inquiry Into the Operation of the National Planning Policy Framework*. Available at http://www.parliament.uk/documents/commons-committees /communities-and-local-government/Report-on-nature-of-planning-constraints-v3-0.pdf, last accessed 30/10/2014.

Burgess, G., Monk, S., Whitehead, C.M.E., and Crook, A.D.H. (2007) *How Local Planning Authorities Are Delivering Policies for Affordable Housing*, Joseph Rowntree Foundation, York.

Calcutt, J. (2007) *The Calcutt Review of Housebuilding Delivery*, Department of Communities and Local Government, London.

Campbell, H., Ellis, H., Gladwell, C., and Henneberry, J. (2000) Planning obligations, planning practice and land use outcomes. *Environment and Planning B*, **27**, 759–775.

Campbell, H., Ellis, H., Henneberry, J., Poxon, J., Rowley, S., and Gladwell, C. (2001) Planning obligations and the mediation of development. *Royal Institution of Chartered Surveyors Foundation, Research Papers* **4**(3).

Couttie, D. (1994) Implementing affordable housing policies: the financial mechanisms. *Housing Research Findings*. Joseph Rowntree Foundation, York.

Crook, A.D.H., Currie, J., Jackson, A., Monk, S. et al. *Planning Gain and Affordable Housing: Making it Count*, Joseph Rowntree Foundation, York.

Crook, A.D.H., Dunning, R., Ferrari, E.T., Henneberry, J.M., Rowley S., Watkins C.A., Burgess G., Lyall-Grant F., Monk S., and Whitehead C.M.E. (2010) *The Incidence, Value and Delivery of Planning Obligations in England in 2007–08*. Department of Communities and Local Government, London.

Crook, A.D.H., Henneberry, J.M., Rowley, S., Smith, R.S., and Watkins, C.A. (2008) *Valuing Planning Obligations in England; Update Study for 2005–06*. Department of Communities and Local Government, London.

Crook, A.D.H., Henneberry, J.M., Rowley, S., and Watkins, C.A., with the Halcrow Group (2006a) *Valuing Planning Obligations in England*, Department of Communities and Local Government, London.

Crook, A.D.H. and Monk, S. (2011) Planning gains, providing homes. *Housing Studies* **26,** 997–1018.

Crook, A.D.H., Monk, S., Rowley, S., and Whitehead, C.M.E. (2006b) Planning gain and the supply of new affordable homes in England: understanding the numbers. *Town Planning Review* **77,** 353–373.

Crook, A.D.H. and Whitehead, C.M.E. (2002) Social housing and planning gain: is this an appropriate way of providing affordable housing? *Environment and Planning A* **34,** 1259–1279.

Crook, A.D.H. and Whitehead, C.M.E. (2010) Intermediate housing and the planning system. In: Monk, S. and Whitehead, C.M.E (eds.). *Making Housing More Affordable: The Role of Intermediate Tenures*, Wiley Blackwell, Oxford.

Driver, E. (1994) *Securing Low-cost Housing in Perpetuity*. Frere Cholmeley Bischoff (now Eversheds LLP), Nottingham.

Elson, M. (1989) *Recreation and Community Provision in Areas of New Private Sector Housing*, National House Building Council, Amersham.

Elson, M., Steenberg, C., and Mendham, N. (1994) *Green Belts and Affordable Housing: Can We Have Both?* The Policy Press, Bristol.

Europe Economics (2014) How to increase competition, diversity and resilience in the housebuilding market. Europe Economics, London.

Gallent, N. (1997) Planning for affordable rural housing in England and Wales. *Housing Studies* **12,** 145–155.

Grimley, J.R.E. (1992) *The Use of Planning Agreements*, Her Majesty's Stationery Office, London.

Hawke J.N. (1981) Planning agreements in practice. *Journal of Planning and Environment Law* **5,** 86–92.

Healey, P., Purdue, M., and Ennis, F. (1993) *Gains from Planning? Dealing with the Impacts of Development*, Joseph Rowntree Foundation, York.

Healey, P., Purdue, M., and Ennis, F. (1995) *Negotiating Development: Rationales for Development Obligations and Planning Gain*, E and FN Spon, London.

Henry, D. (1982) *Planning by Agreement in Berkshire*, Oxford School of Planning Working Paper 69. Oxford Polytechnic, Oxford.

Housing Corporation (1996) *Land, Planning and Housing Associations*, Housing Management and Research Division, Research Report 10, The Housing Corporation, London.

Jackson, A., Morrison, N., and Royce, C. (1994) *The Supply of Land for Housing: Changing Local Authority Mechanisms*, University of Cambridge Department of Land Economy, Property Research unit Occasional Paper, Cambridge.

Jowell, J. (1977) Bargaining in development control. *Journal of Planning Law* 414–433.

Kleinman, M., Aulakh, S., Holmans A., Morrison, N., Whitehead, C., and Woodrow, J. (2000) No Excuse not to Build. *Meeting Housing Need through Existing Stock and the Planning Framework*, Shelter, London.

Lavis, J. (1995) *Evaluating Rural Housing Enablers*. Housing Research Findings No 111. Joseph Rowntree Foundation, York.

McMaster, M., U'ren, G., and Wilson, D. (2008) *An Assessment of the Value of Planning Agreements in Scotland*, Scottish Government Social Research, Edinburgh.

Moore, V. and Purdue, M. (2012) *A Practical Approach to Planning Law*, Oxford University Press, Oxford.

Monk, S., Burgess, G., Whitehead, C.M.E., Crook, A.D.H., and Rowley, S. (2008) *Common Starting Points for Section 106 Affordable Housing Negotiations*, Department of Communities and Local Government, London.

Monk, S., Crook, A.D.H., Lister, D., Lovatt R., Ni Luanaigh A.N., Rowley S., and Whitehead C.M.E.. (2006) *Delivering Affordable Housing through Section 106. Outputs and Outcomes*, Joseph Rowntree Foundation, York.

Monk, S., Lister, D., Short, C., Whitehead, C.M.E., Crook, A.D.H., and Rowley, S. (2005) *Land and Finance for Affordable Housing: The Complementary Roles of Social Housing Grant and the Provision of Affordable Housing through the Planning System*, The Housing Corporation, London, and The Joseph Rowntree Foundation, York.

Office of Fair Trading (2008) *Homebuilding in the UK. A market study*, The Office of Fair Trading, London.

Rowley, S., Crook, A.D.H., Henneberry, J., and Watkins, C.A. (2007) *The Use and Value of Planning Agreements in Wales*, Welsh Assembly Government, Cardiff.

Satsangi, M. and Dunmore, K. (2003) The planning system and the provision of affordable housing in rural Britain: a comparison of the Scottish and English experience. *Housing Studies* **18**, 201–217.

Scottish Government (2012) *Planning Obligations and Good Neighbour Agreements*. Circular 3/2012, The Scottish Government, Edinburgh.

University of Reading and Three Dragons (2014) *Section 106 Planning Obligations in England 2011–2012*, Department of Communities and Local Government, London.

Vickers, D., Rees, B., and Birkin, M. (2003) *A New Classification of UK Local Authorities using 2001 Census Data*, Working Paper 03-03. School of Geography, University of Leeds, Leeds.

Welsh Assembly Government (2006) *Technical Advice Note 2. Planning and Affordable Housing*, Welsh Assembly Government, Cardiff.

Welsh Government (2014) *Planning Policy Wales*, Welsh Government, Cardiff.

Welsh Office (1997) *Planning Obligations*, Circular 13/97, Welsh Office, Cardiff.

Whitehead, C.M.E., Monk S., Lister, D., Short, C., Crook, A.D.H., Henneberry, J.M., and Rowley, S. (2005) *Value for Money in Delivering Affordable Housing through S106*, Office of the Deputy Prime Minister, London.

Williams, G., Bell, P., and Russell, L. (1991) *Evaluating the Low Cost Rural Housing Initiative.* HMSO, London.

7

Spatial Variation in the Incidence and Value of Planning Obligations

Richard Dunning, Ed Ferrari, and Craig Watkins
Department of Urban Studies and Planning, The University of Sheffield, UK

Introduction

As Chapter 6 has already demonstrated, the incidence and value of planning obligations in England has varied greatly across space and over time. The purpose of this chapter is to explore that variation in the incidence and value of obligations in different parts of the country and to offer an explanation for these patterns. This chapter thus seeks to develop an understanding of the relative importance of the various influences that might theoretically be expected to impact on both the ability of local planners to secure planning agreements and the value that might be attached to these.

As the policy framework emerged, as Chapter 4 explained earlier in this volume, it was widely predicted that there would be a close relationship between development activity, the buoyancy of local real-estate markets, including the level and rate of inflation of real-estate prices, and the planning system's capacity to capture development value (Bill, 2004; ODPM, 2004). There was also good reason to believe, based on numerous academic studies that the skill sets within local planning authorities (LPAs) might be important (Claydon and Smith, 1997; Campbell *et al.*, 2000). The discretionary and flexible nature of obligations allow for considerable

Planning Gain: Providing Infrastructure and Affordable Housing, First Edition.
Edited by Tony Crook, John Henneberry and Christine Whitehead.
© 2016 John Wiley & Sons, Inc. Published 2016 by John Wiley & Sons, Inc.

variation in implementation and local practice. The negotiated nature of contributions means that the emphasis for developing the effectiveness of policy and practice has been placed on good practice and the enhancement and dissemination of policy advice (see Chapter 4, this volume; DCLG, 2006a; Audit Commission, 2006a,b; LGA, 2012). Planners are faced with the tricky task of securing obligations, whilst ensuring that development remains viable. The wide variation in local market and institutional contexts means that a 'one size fits all' approach would be inappropriate and ineffective. Consequently, establishing best practice throughout the country has been a rather drawn-out process of culture change.

The analysis and discussion that follows in this chapter draws primarily on the quantitative and qualitative evidence collected in national studies undertaken in 2003–2004, 2005–2006 and 2007–2008 (Crook *et al.*, 2006, 2008, 2010). By tracking trends over time, the research findings serve to highlight the importance of local systems, processes and practice. The chapter also refers in places to work by McMaster *et al.* (2008) that focuses on planning agreements in Scotland, evidence from Wales compiled by Rowley *et al.* (2007), a study for HCA and TSA on affordable housing delivery (Crook *et al.*, 2011) and recent research undertaken by Oxford Brookes University for the Joseph Rowntree Foundation that explores the effectiveness of planning obligations in England (Brownhill *et al.*, 2014). Taken together, this research base presents a compelling picture of the importance of local practice and of the need to share good practice to ensure effective policy implementation. This is an issue picked up again in Chapter 8 of this volume on the delivery of planning obligations.

The chapter has five sections. In the next section, we review the literature about the relationship between obligations as policy and the practice of implementation, and its impact on the variation in the number and value of obligations. We also summarise the evidence about the spatial variation in the number and value of obligations secured. The section 'Regional variations in the value of planning obligations' uses regression analysis to explore the relationship between the number and value of obligations secured by local authorities and a range of authority-level variables including social and economic indicators, historic and current land and property market trends and government best practice performance measures. The fourth section 'Qualitative explanations for spatial variations in planning obligations' seeks to explain what the models cannot by drawing on qualitative evidence from policy makers and practitioners. In the last section, we offer some brief conclusions derived from the research findings and offer some thoughts on the challenges ahead.

Defining and disseminating good practice in planning obligations

Review of earlier evidence

Adopting obligations policies is a necessary but not sufficient condition for LPAs to get good outcomes. Many agents are involved and market conditions vary, so that negotiating outcomes becomes a central part of implementing obligations policies (Ennis, 1997). If all LPAs adopted the same or similar approaches to negotiating planning obligations (framing policy, conducting negotiations, addressing viability considerations and drawing up legal agreements), spatial variations in the incidence and value of obligations would be largely related to market factors and not to policy or practice differences between LPAs. But in fact, as this chapter shows, there are variations in practice as well as in market factors and both these factors are needed to explain the quite large differences in the incidence and value of obligations that exist (see Bunnell, 1995; Campbell *et al.*, 2000; Claydon and Smith, 1997; Farthing and Ashley, 2002; Healey *et al.*, 1993 for earlier studies on the relative impact of market, policies and practices, especially negotiating practices).

Healey *et al.* (1993), for example, looked at practice in five LPAs noting that 'practice was largely *ad hoc* and variable between local authorities' and noted that 'in part the difficulty stems from the absence of government advice' (p. 29). They identified six sets of challenges covering (i) little coordination between the many agencies involved; (ii) few attempts to prioritise the types of contribution sought through obligations; (iii) a wide variety of approaches to drafting legal agreements; (iv) different resources for conducting negotiations (noting that LPAs with adopted policy and in strong markets had advantages in negotiating with developers); (v) arrangements for monitoring; and (vi) being accountable to all the parties involved. Campbell *et al.* also found that 'practice … and the reasons underlying their use vary considerably from authority to authority and in some cases from site to site within a specific authority' (2000, p. 766). Others found how government guidance was not always followed but argued that the strength of the property market meant that developers were often prepared to enter into and conclude negotiations on matters that were outside guidance on what was appropriate in order to get planning consent (see, e.g. the evidence in Grimley JR Eve, 1992). A recent international comparison examining England, the Netherlands and Spain also found positive relationships between having clarity about policy and required obligations and the amounts secured (Gielen and Tasan-Kok, 2010).

Of course, determining planning applications is not costless to LPAs, although many of these costs are now offset by fees paid by applicants for planning permission and, as we saw in Chapter 6 of this volume, the specific administrative costs LPAs incur when negotiating and monitoring planning obligations are to an extent funded by developers as part of their planning obligations. Moreover, as well as exhorting LPAs to make more use of planning obligations and institute better practice, governments have also incentivised them to get policies in place and to agree more planning permissions for new housing. This was done through a special grant called the Housing and Planning Delivery Grant and allocated to LPAs by a formula based upon their adoption of up-to-date plans and of the number of permissions for new housing (DCLG, 2007). This grant has now been incorporated into the New Homes Bonus (see Chapter 4, this volume). Nonetheless, LPAs' professional staff capacity is not limitless and large numbers of LPAs, especially smaller authorities, will not have many (if any) professional staff with significant experience of negotiating planning obligations. It is not surprising then, as Chapter 6 of this volume has shown, that LPAs tended to focus their efforts on negotiating obligations on larger developments.

These spatial variations and inconsistent and ill-developed practices led to the government and related bodies trying to identify and then disseminate good practice so as to maximise outcomes. Indeed, one government minister, upon the publication of some of our own research reported in this volume, remarked that far more could be achieved if all LPAs took steps to match the well-performing ones (DCLG, 2006). The government's desire to ensure that LPAs secured more obligations was the background to several attempts to identify and disseminate good practice, principally from the mid-2000s onwards when systematic evidence showed that performance was patchy across LPAs. Four key areas became the focus of good practice attention: obligations policy, negotiating practices and skills, understanding viability and monitoring delivery. It is noteworthy that all these matters had been studied a decade previously and acknowledged then as key to securing affordable housing (e.g. see Barlow *et al.*, 1994; Driver, 1994). This suggests that good practice takes time for innovators to develop and then for adopters to take it on and embed it as normal practice.

Good practice research and advice

The National Audit Office (2005) specifically examined practice in securing affordable housing in high-demand areas, finding that planning obligations were the most complex part of the overall supply chain. It found that LPAs were implementing government guidance inconsistently (e.g. about thresholds) and staff often lacked financial and negotiating skills. Planning obligations were the cause of most delays in the delivery chain, taking between 6 and 67 weeks to reach agreements (see also Grimley JR Eve, 1992). Because the preference of the Housing Corporation (then the government body providing funding for housing associations) was not to pay grant on S106 schemes,[1] this added to delays because of its impact on sites' financial viability. To overcome these and other barriers, the NAO recommended that LPAs had 'concordats' with housing associations and better integrated their planning and housing departments.

The Audit Commission's later studies (2006a) also showed wide variations in obligations outcomes and found that three groups of variables explained these: (i) market factors, (ii) incomplete or absent formal policies and (iii) spare capacity in infrastructure making it unnecessary to use obligations to secure more. It argued that variations were 'a valid reflection of local or site circumstances but in others it is due to factors within councils' control' (Ibid, para 21). This explained why, on a hypothetical site and using their existing policies, some LPAs would have achieved as little as £500 but others as much as £30 000 per dwelling in obligations. Whilst the LPAs that achieved the most were in the higher property value areas, there was still wide variety in outcomes amongst LPAs with similar local property values.

In its advice, the Commission urged LPAs to address the practices that were under their control: the policy base, the reliability of procedures and the skills of their staff. LPAs without clear policies left too much to negotiation and were open to successful challenge from developers. Those with formal policies achieved better than average outcomes. So too did those where there was clear council leadership and where policy and delivery were fully integrated into wider council policy. Specific good practices made a difference: (i) testing viability, (ii) embedding processes, (iii) involving local communities, (iv) transparency about agreements and delivery, (v) ensuring money received in obligations payments was spent on the infrastructure identified in agreements and (vi) keeping abreast of good practice in other LPAs. Its obligations 'roadmap' showed how LPAs could move from circumstances where there was no clarity about (or unreasonable expectations of) developer contributions, inconsistency between sites, long processes and uncertain outcomes to a position where it was 'easy' to work out what contributions were required, and policy was applied consistently and swiftly and with good audit trails (Audit Commission, 2006b). Contributions need not be uniform across a whole LPA area. Instead, policy might state what would be required for most developments (such as greenfield sites in high value areas) but have lower requirements in those areas where costs and/or requirements might justify this and a few areas or locations where case-by-case determination

---

[1]Zero grant is now the formal policy of the successor body, the Homes and Communities Agency – see Chapter 4, this volume.

would be needed, but in the latter cases also setting out the process that would be involved – to promote certainty (Ibid, p. 13).

The variations identified by the Audit Commission had persisted despite the earlier dissemination of good practice by the government (DTLR, 2002). The research underpinning this advice found few examples of good practice and the recommendations were interestingly labelled 'towards better practice' (Ibid, pp. 105–114) covering a very wide range of matters including: (i) more consistent definitions of affordable housing, including low-cost home ownership as well as social rented housing; (ii) better housing needs assessments, linked to the types of affordable housing required; (iii) justification of thresholds and targets adopted; (iv) using supplementary planning guidance to update adopted plans; (v) corporate approaches, especially the priority given to affordable housing, compared with other obligations required (e.g. schools, open space, playing fields, etc.); (vi) more involvement of planning committees in approving key matters and greater use of model legal agreements; (vii) better understanding of development economics; (viii) more clarity in requests for, and use of, commuted sums as alternatives to on-site provision; (ix) ensuring good liaison with housing associations and making them parties to S106 agreements; and (x) better monitoring. Interestingly, other research at the same time noted that not all planners were convinced of the merits of having the clarity provided by policy in development plans as this could impair their ability to negotiate contributions successfully (Campbell *et al.*, 2001).

In later advice (DCLG, 2006), the government reiterated the matters that it and others had already recommended, including: (i) making obligations 'plan led' by setting out policy in a development plan or supplementary planning documents; (ii) ensuring agreements met the government's five policy tests; (iii) stating where in-kind or financial contributions were appropriate (and setting out standards for the former), specifying any phasing and ongoing maintenance payments required; and any proposed pooling arrangements; (iv) having protocols about LPAs' processes for negotiations and making agreements available for public inspection; (v) having skilled and dedicated staff, especially for negotiations; (vi) using published and evidence-based formulae and standard charges where appropriate; (vii) having standard legal agreements; (viii) using independent third parties as mediators; (ix) monitoring implementation and securing performance bonds from developers to provide funding in cases of default. Much of this advice provided more details about the then government's policy on obligations set out in a 2005 circular (see Chapter 4, this volume) (ODPM, 2005).

This reiterated much of the earlier advice specifically relating to improving the delivery of affordable housing which found that more could be delivered if LPAs worked better corporately both internally and externally, including better links with their legal services, improved their skills and had much greater clarity about obligations policy in their development plans, including looking at viability issues and ensuring that appropriate detail was available in supplementary planning guidance (ERM Planning *et al.*, 2003). In the same vein, advice from the Royal Town Planning Institute and the Housing Corporation urged planners, private developers and housing providers (including housing associations) to work better together to resolve the tensions between them. It suggested that they should do this by adopting a streamlined approach to implementation, a more inclusive planning and decision-making process, with much more integration (but also realistic practice) nurturing more certainty and transparency in the process and having positive and proactive approaches to development. In particular, it commended a shared appreciation of development economics and social costs (Carmona *et al.*, 2001).

But despite this regular reiteration of good practice advice, evidence continued to show that it was far from universally adopted. For example, studies commissioned by Inspire East, the Royal Institution of Chartered Surveyors and the Joseph Rowntree Foundation (Burgess *et al.*, 2007a,b; Monk *et al.*, 2008a,b) showed that whilst there had been a steady increase in obligations being secured, policy was far clearer and more robust in some LPAs than in others. Where policy was clear and formally adopted (and hence evidently backed by elected members), developers knew what to expect and LPAs had a stronger basis for negotiations. There were also variations in practice with few LPAs having model agreements and dedicated teams leading structured negotiations. In particular, the shopping lists for different obligations were rarely prioritised, undermining both the clarity developers needed and negotiations with them. It appeared that this resulted in affordable housing being squeezed when developers attempted to limit their contributions during negotiations (Burgess *et al.*, 2007b). It was thus evident that good practice was far from universal and that many LPAs continued to have difficulties addressing viability issues in negotiations and also in justifying needs assessments. Viability issues were becoming an increasing issue when LPAs sought to increase the proportions of new homes that were affordable and developers sought to replace the affordable rented homes required with low-cost home ownership ones instead.

Similarly, a study for the South West office of the Housing Corporation (Three Dragons *et al.*, 2007) concluded that 'policies need to be clearer, planners need better negotiating skills and a better understanding of development economics' (Ibid, para 8). The latter was important because of the Corporation's zero grant policy for S106 sites (grant being paid only where it would increase the rented provision for affordable housing compared with low-cost home ownership units and/or change the mix and size of affordable dwellings). The consultants for this study found big variations in the amounts of affordable housing expected (as would be likely, given variations in needs) but few policies dealt with the funding of provision because planners lacked an understanding of development economics. As a result, LPAs in high-value areas were not securing the scale of affordable housing that development values justified and were also agreeing grant-funded schemes in such areas.

Thus, despite all the advice that has been disseminated, many LPAs continued to lack an understanding of development economics, making negotiations with developers one sided, an increasingly important barrier to good outcomes when site viability issues became more and more central to negotiations. This led to the development and use of several 'tool kits' to help LPAs assess site viability (e.g. GLA, 2001; GVA Grimley, 2006; Chapter 5, this volume). These toolkits became even more important when affordable housing grants became no longer available to housing associations and of even greater importance during the downturn in development after 2007 (HCA, 2009) when matters of viability came very much more to the fore and when clear evidence was needed to defend appeals against refusals of planning permission which also involved unsuccessfully resolved S106 agreements (PINS, 2009). In addition, evidence on the value for money achieved by using planning obligations to secure affordable housing also fostered the importance of understanding viability issues. This was because of the risks that grants were unnecessarily being paid for affordable housing on S106 sites where a zero grant approach would have still left sites viable. In such cases, grants seeped into funding other obligations and into higher land values because of their impact on raising development values compared with a zero grant position (Monk *et al.*, 2005a,b).

Subsequent evidence confirmed that these risks still existed four years later showing, for example, that affordable housing grants were still being paid out on S106 sites that had high development values. Calculations suggested that £319m of public funds could be saved each year (in 2008–2009) if there were better practices within LPAs and in other agencies when assessing site viability and the need for grants on S106 sites, along with consistent application of policy and well-structured negotiations. This evidence showed the very large number of approaches to setting targets for specific sites, ranging from simply setting total numbers at one extreme, through to specifying particular types, as well as numbers of affordable homes, to stating what developers were expected to provide (such as free or discounted land or discounts on prices to be paid for the new homes by housing associations) and finally to explicitly requiring developers to sell the new homes at prices housing associations could fund from net rents (Tribal Group, 2007).

Partly, this range reflected policy and market differences, but it also reflected differences in professional cultures amongst planners, some of whom did not accept that the role of planning was to help secure the funding as well as the land for new affordable homes. This matches other findings about professional cultures in planning for obligations practice; for example, ethical concerns that seeking obligations might undermine adopted policies as LPAs sought to maximise contributions. Whilst planners generally welcomed planning obligations as a means of securing funding for the vital infrastructure needed to support new development, they did not see their role as negotiating the funding, rather seeing their role as securing the funding required and not entering negotiations based on viability and what could be afforded. If the infrastructure was needed, it should be paid for. The growth of planning obligations, introducing new ways of funding what had once been funded from the public purse, had brought a new financial calculus and market logic into the judgements of planning professionals with planners having divergent perspectives on this, partly because of the way planning obligations policy and practice has evolved in an *ad hoc* way (Campbell and Henneberry, 2005; see also Campbell *et al.*, 2000).

It was to address these variations in the targets and baselines, to enhance certainty for developers as to what was required and to help LPAs negotiate contributions, especially for affordable housing, that the government looked at how far a national common starting point for negotiations on each site could help. Research (Monk *et al.*, 2008b) suggested, however, that this could only have a limited impact because of variations in viability and that LPAs already successfully used a variety of starting points. These included specifying the number of affordable dwellings units needed (leaving the funding arrangements to be negotiated between developers and housing associations), requiring serviced land to be transferred for nil consideration and requiring developers to sell completed units at prices reflecting the discounted net rents housing associations would receive. The latter secured the biggest financial contributions but also at the risk of making sites unviable. And LPAs did not only want to secure large numbers of affordable homes as there were trade-offs to be made between absolute numbers and specific tenures and the size and types of dwellings with, in particular, large family dwellings for social rented housing imposing higher costs on developers than other mixes. Although LPAs did not have the same objectives for all sites (also making common starting points unfeasible), having clear policies in adopted development plans, supported by all departments and elected councillors, and having staff with a good understanding of development economics and good negotiating skills were better keys to successful outcomes than one common starting point (Ibid, p. 18). Not least was the importance of ensuring clarity for developers many of whom had to deal with multiple LPAs (Ibid, p. 19). This was much more important than having common starting points (Ibid, p. 20).

The economic downturn further reinforced the importance of LPAs having clear evidence on housing needs and on-site viability so that LPAs could arrive at levels of contribution that could reasonably be expected, especially on sites that were stalled where the possibility of deferring obligations was being considered (HCA, 2009; Chapter 8 this volume). But regardless of the stage in the economic cycle, the importance of having evidence on need and on viability has also been reflected in court decisions. For example, in 2008 the Court of Appeal made it clear in the *Blyth* case[2] that LPAs had to have policies based on clear evidence on housing need and on economic viability if their core strategies were to be sound.

Implications of evidence and good practice guides

As we shall see below, there is evidence that practice has improved and led to the extraction of more development value through setting out clear policies and adopting good practice. Indeed, some research has pointed to the policy 'bedding down' as LPAs began to implement it better and as developers came to accept it more (Monk *et al.*, 2005b).

   We can conceive of each LPA being in one of the four categories (as shown in Figure 7.1), but their positions changing over time. The ideal position is in box (b) where LPAs have effective policies and good practice in place. The worst position is in box (c). Few are likely ever to have been in box (d) where despite effective policy, LPAs have poor practice. As we show later in the chapter, over time, many LPAs have, in effect, migrated from box (c) towards box (b). They did this by moving either directly to (b) after upgrading both policy and practice or by moving via box (a) after initially upgrading practice and then finally putting stronger policy into place.

		Policy	
		Weak	Strong
Practice	Strong	(a) Tactically strong; strategically weak	(b) Tactically strong; strategically strong
	Weak	(c) Tactically weak strategically weak	(d) Tactically weak; strategically strong

Figure 7.1   Transitions in policy and practice.

---

[2] [2008] EWCA Civ 861; [2009] JPL 335.

A note on Scotland and Wales

Studies of the planning obligations systems in Scotland and in Wales revealed a very similar picture with considerable variations in incidence, related to variations in good practice in Scotland (McMaster *et al.*, 2008). This was also the case in Wales (Rowley *et al.*, 2007), despite earlier efforts to improve practice such as better working relationships between housing and planning officials and organisations (see, e.g. Tewdwr-Jones *et al.*, 1998).

Regional variations in the value of planning obligations

Table 7.1 shows the regional variation in the total value of obligations secured. The need to explore these variations is underscored when we look at the value of obligations secured with affordable housing and land contributions stripped out (see Table 7.2). This shows Greater London performing far less well than might be expected in 2003–2004. It also shows the South East performing relatively poorly (compared with the previous period) in 2005–2006, while over the same period development value capture in Yorkshire and Humber improves dramatically. It seems unlikely that the volatility in these values can be explained by changes in the economy or real estate market activity and/or shifts in property values. Rather there would appear to be quite significant differences between LPAs that are unrelated to these contextual factors.

Figures 7.2 and 7.3 shed some further light on the extent and nature of the spatial variations in the use of obligations in England. These figures break

Table 7.1   Total Value of planning obligations (including affordable housing and land contributions).

Region	2003–2004	2005–2006	2007–2008
North East	£22m	£38m	£42m
North West	£71m	£77m	£340m
Yorkshire and Humber	£54m	£137m	£216m
West Midlands	£80m	£84m	£166m
East Midlands	£87m	£173m	£158m
East of England	£179m	£422m	£459m
South East	£440m	£444m	£587m
South West	£217m	£240m	£358m
Greater London	£725m	£1230m	£1630m
Total	£1875m	£2845m	£3955m
Land contribution	NA	£960m	£900m
Total value		£3805	£4855

Source: Chapter 6 this volume.

Table 7.2   Total value of planning obligations (excluding affordable housing and land contributions).

Region	2003–2004	2005–2006	2007–2008
North East	£13m	£23m	£15m
North West	£40m	£28m	£210m
Yorkshire and the Humber	£4m	£58m	£100m
East Midlands	£48m	£33m	£67m
West Midlands	£32m	£85m	£37m
East of England	£61m	£234m	£161m
South East	£261m	£159m	£275m
South West	£120m	£86m	£170m
Greater London	£97m	£231m	£306m
Total	£675m	£937m	£1341m

Source: Chapter 6 this volume.

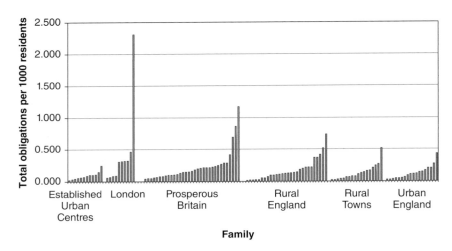

Figure 7.2   Variability in the number of obligations per 1000 residents by local authority type 2005–2006.

down the 2005–2006 and 2007–2008 survey data and show the distribution of obligations secured for each LPA on a per head of population basis. The LPAs are broken down into different LPA types (based on the Vickers *et al.* (2003) classification for ONS). There are clearly very wide discrepancies in obligations secured within each family of similar LPAs in both time periods. Within London, for instance, it is possible to discern three (high, medium and low) subgroups from the 2005–2006 data. Again this begs the question – how do we explain the variation in outcomes? The remainder of this chapter seeks to understand and explain these striking variations.

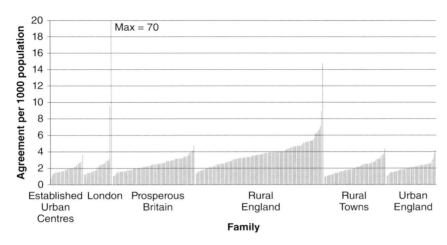

Figure 7.3 Variability in the number of obligations per 1000 residents by local authority type 2007–2008.

Quantitative analysis of the drivers of the incidence and value of planning obligations

Although there have been no previous attempts to systematically model the number or value of planning obligations, there are a number of factors that we might reasonably expect to have a causal relationship with the nature and monetary value of agreements secured in different parts of the country. Specifically, there are three categories of variables that are likely to be influential: size and buoyancy of land and property market; local social and economic conditions; and local policy stance and planning practices.

This section of the chapter presents the results of our attempts to model the relationship between these drivers and the outcomes observed in England. The primary purpose of the analysis is to understand why there are different outcomes in different LPAs. This is explored by using the survey returns from a cross-section of LPAs (see Chapter 6, this volume, for a discussion of the sample), to estimate regression equations for three time periods: 2003–2004, 2005–2006 and 2007–2008. Although the composition of the sample changes between periods, this approach allows us to control for heterogeneity and allows us to comment on the way in which the drivers of obligations levels have changed over time.

The basic cross-sectional equations take the general form:

$$\text{OB-NO} = f\,(\text{PMKT, LV, SIZE, SOC, ECO, PLAN}), \quad \text{and}$$

$$\text{OB-VAL} = f\,(\text{PMKT, LV, SIZE, SOC, ECO, PLAN}),$$

where OB-NO is the number of planning obligations secured in each year; OB-VAL is the annual monetary value of planning obligations; PMKT is a suite of property market indicators including the level of transactions, current and lagged nominal and real office rents, current and lagged nominal and real house price levels, and price inflation rates (derived from Land Registry, Investment Property Databank and HBOS); LV are the nominal and real land values and the year-on-year changes in land values (from the Valuation Office Agency); SIZE is the size (and change in size) of the LPA as measured by the past and future number of (and change in) households and the size of the local population (derived from Census of Population data and Official Household Projections); SOC is a vector of variables that reflect the socio-economic characteristics of the LPA including Deprivation Index scores, the proportion of households in various socio-economic groups including retired households (from ONS and the Census); ECO is a vector of economic performance indicators including levels of economically active households, and the unemployment rate (from the Census of Population); and PLAN is a series of indicators of the performance of the LPA including the levels of planning application (major and minor), the level of permissions granted, the ratio between permissions and application, and best value measures of the speed (within 8 weeks; or within 13 weeks) of planning decisions (from PS2 and Best Value data supplied by the Department of Communities and Local Government).

The equations are estimated using a general-to-specific procedure. In other words, we start with the large number of possible explanatory variables described above and then, on a step-by-step basis, remove those that have the lowest statistical impact on the model before re-estimating the relationships. This stepwise strategy ultimately leads to a parsimonious model that has the best fit (strongest explanatory power) to the data and, as far as possible, provides coefficient estimates for statistically significant variables (that is, those that are shown to influence the number or value of obligations) that are theoretically plausible in terms of the signs (positive or negative relationships) and magnitudes.

The modelling procedure assumed a linear relationship between the explanatory variables and the number and value of obligations. We made no attempt to experiment with non-linear (e.g. exponential, multiplicative, logarithmic or semi-log) forms. Nor did we seek to model the interactions between explanatory variables. Inevitably, as tends to be the case with models of this sort, the equations are subject to standard statistical problems including multicollinearity (caused by the inter-relationship between variables) as well as autocorrelation and heteroscedasticity (which may indicate that the error terms are not independent and, as a result, might render the coefficient estimates biased and unreliable). We addressed these issues by excluding variables that are highly correlated with each other or the dependent variable. We also used number of households as a denominator for many variables (e.g. the number of economically active households) to

Table 7.3 The key variables in the average number of planning obligations by LPA across 2003–2004, 2005–2006 and 2007–2008.

				Model of number of planning obligations by LPA			
	Adjusted R^2	Household growth	House price change	Pct quick responses	Average land value	Total major decision	No. of households
03–04	0.159	2.409	−2.641	−1.717	–	–	–
05–06	0.225	1.797	–	–	1.837	3.721	–
07–08	0.408	2.297	–	–	–	–	7.746

ensure a degree of standardisation in variable distributions. These steps are generally thought to be adequate as a means of determining the existence (or otherwise) of statistical relationships and the overall explanatory power of these relationships (Leishman, 2003). We would, however, advise caution in interpreting and using the individual coefficient estimates from the models.

Table 7.3 provides a summary of the models of the number of planning obligations for each of the three time periods. It is interesting to note that, although we applied the same approach and tested the influence of the same variable for each time period, the factors that proved to be significant changed over time. While we acknowledge that this might be a result of changes in the composition of the sample, as we explain below, these results appear to offer a plausible account of the major influences on obligations secured. Importantly, the quantitative evidence resonates strongly with more qualitative accounts (see the next section for a full discussion).

So what do the models tell us? In the first study period, the number of obligations secured by LPAs was explained mainly by the year-on-year change in house prices and by the speed of planning decisions (specifically the number of decisions processed within 13 weeks). Surprisingly, these statistical relationships were both negatively signed. The former would seem to indicate that the highest levels of obligations were not being secured where house price inflation was greatest. Rather, where prices were rising quickly the number of obligations were low, perhaps for reasons associated with capacity.

Similarly, the inverse relationship between the number of obligations and speed of planning decisions also seemed to point to capacity issues. It implies that decisions were being taken more quickly where the number of obligations were low. This seems to suggest that obligations added to complexity, an issue borne out by qualitative evidence (see Crook *et al.*, 2007 for some reflections on this in the context of the introduction of the Community Infrastructure Levy). In short, there was little evidence of the expected link between the number of obligations secured and the size of the market and/or the performance of the local economy. The number of obligations appear to be have been largely driven by local practice and capacity issues. While it is worth noting that the quantitative model for this period had only limited explanatory power, it does offer a picture that was slightly at odds with the prior expectations of several commentators but proved to be consistent with qualitative research undertaken at the time (Crook *et al.*, 2006).

Interestingly, neither of these variables remained significant in the second study period. In this period, the number of obligations secured was most strongly related to average land values and to the total number of major planning decisions. In other words, it seems that as the implementation of local obligations policies and practices were bedding in and best practice began to be shared nationally (see DCLG, 2006), the size and profitability of the market became more important in explaining the variation in the number of obligations secured. The number of obligations tended to be higher where large, profitable development schemes were most prevalent.

By the third period, the most dominant factor in the model was the growth in size of the LPA as measured by the change in numbers of households. The variability around practice and market conditions appeared to have evened out and LPAs seem to have been able to secure similar numbers of obligations where growth rates were similar, even though market and economic conditions might have varied. Interestingly, the explanatory power of the model increased in the third period. This suggests a 'bedding down' of practice across the UK and a more stable set of relationships between the economy, markets and practice and number of obligations. This is almost certainly attributable to the considerable activity in sharing best practice nationally (see, e.g. DCLG, 2010, 2012; LGA, 2012).

Table 7.4 summarises the parsimonious models of the value of planning obligations for each time period. These results offer a subtly different but complementary picture to the findings discussed above.

In the first time period, where the number of obligations secured appeared to be related to capacity constraints in practice, values were driven by very similar factors. The speed of planning decisions had a positive impact on the value of obligations. This chimes with qualitative evidence that LPAs who had well-developed systems and processes to support S106 negotiations tended to negotiate higher-value obligations (see below, and

Table 7.4 The key variables in the average value of planning obligations by LPA across 2003–2004, 2005–2006 and 2007–2008.

	Model of value of planning obligations by LPA						
	Adjusted R^2	Pct quick responses	Pct unemployed 1991 census	Pct grant	Average land value	No. of household	Total major decisions
03–04	0.164	1.754	−2.212	2.105	4.530	–	–
05–06	0.291	–	–	–	6.412	−2.270	2.142
07–08	0.014	–	–	–	1.662	–	–

Crook *et al.*, 2006). The results seem to suggest that higher values were secured where greater numbers of applications were granted. When taken together with the evidence about the factors underpinning the number of obligations and findings from in-depth interviews, it becomes evident that these higher obligations values were not achieved in the largest, most active, highest market value LPAs. The most buoyant markets seemed to be held back (in terms of the number and value of obligations secured) by planning capacity constraints (see above). The economy did still play a part in shaping the spatial variation in value capture. There was evidence of a negative relationship between the value of obligations and unemployment rates. This implies that stronger local economies were in large part unlikely to be able to negotiate higher values.

By 2005–2006, the influence of practice-related variables had diminished. As with the analysis of the drivers of the number of obligations, values were statistically related to average land values, and to the number of major planning applications approved. Thus, as might be expected, as the policy regime matured, the prevalence of high value, major schemes was reflected in the value of obligations. Even at this point, however, the modelling work highlights a negative relationship between obligation values and change in the number of households. This suggests that the fastest growing LPAs were likely to negotiate lower value obligations than those operating in what might be viewed as less favourable context.

The equation for this period had the highest explanatory power of the three periods. In contrast, the equation for 2007–2008 was unable to offer much explanatory power. Average land values were the single biggest influence on values. There was no evidence of a systematic relationship between spatial patterns of obligations values and of the other social, economic or policy factors that might have been expected to underpin them.

The overall conclusion from our quantitative analysis is that the factors that influence the number and value of obligations are complex and ever changing. It is clear that, even where there were similarities in the socio-economic and market context, the incidence and value of the obligations secured have been highly variable. Our attempts to explain this variation by modelling the relationship between policy outcomes and socio-economic and real estate market indicators were largely unsuccessful – in that more was left unexplained than could be explained statistically by the regression equations. Nonetheless, we would argue that the analytical exercise was instructive. The models suggested that much of the variation, particularly in 2003–2004, was attributable to local variations in practice and in the capacity to negotiate and secure obligations. Although this influence became less important statistically as best practice changed nationally and LPAs developed their internal systems and processes and adopted more consistent approaches to securing obligations. This broad picture resonates with the qualitative evidence developed over this period, that the significance of local variations in practice remain paramount in shaping the effectiveness of planning obligations mechanisms.

Interestingly, the broad picture of culture change is very similar to that reported in Scotland (see McMaster *et al.*, 2008) and Wales (Rowley *et al.*, 2007). The significance of best practice and the need to develop skills and capacity remains a key concern to date (Brownhill *et al.*, 2014).

Qualitative explanations for spatial variations in planning obligations

This section draws on in-depth interviews conducted between 2003 and 2011 as part of a series of research projects (see Crook *et al.*, 2006, 2008, 2010, 2011; Rowley *et al.*, 2008). These interviews offer a more qualitative explanation for trends in the quantum of planning obligations secured, and the spatial variation. The interviews were conducted with policymakers and practitioners involved in the negotiation of planning obligations, and in the monitoring of their delivery, within sample local authority areas. In each of the projects, the local authorities were purposively sampled to represent a range of contexts, including both 'rural' and 'urban' areas, including major metropolitan authorities, as well as those working in the north, south and midlands of England. They provide comprehensive evidence of the way in which practice has changed locally and nationally.

The changing practice context

Practitioners generally supported the basic premise that changing patterns of planning permissions and land values were important 'background contextual drivers' for the patterns of change observed in the use of planning obligations. Basic market conditions, both at a national level and at other levels, could be used to explain broad-brush 'macro' trends in the ability of authorities to enter into, negotiate and secure the benefits from obligations with developers. But there was also near universal agreement with the picture of local variation in all aspects of the use of obligations (outlined earlier in this chapter) and the suggestion that these variations could not be wholly explained by market differentials.

Consistent with studies that emphasise the importance of discretion and flexibility (e.g. Claydon and Smith, 1997; Campbell *et al.*, 2001), practitioners generally agreed with the view that there was unevenness in levels of professionalism, the adoption of specific practices (including the implementation of local policies and systems) and the development of specific local planning policy in relation to planning obligations as exemplified by the approach to using S106. Despite such variations between different places and market contexts, improvements in professionalism and practice were considered by a broad base of participants to be very important attributes in explaining the success, or otherwise, of planning obligations as a mechanism for extracting development value and supporting a range of broader social and infrastructural objectives. Tellingly, there was a sense that the impact of officers could 'work both ways'. For instance, as Crook *et al.* (2010) note, in those localities affected worst by the effects of the economic downturn (as transmitted through local land markets), the role of professionalism and proactivity among officers in setting policy and negotiating agreements was emphasised in helping to mitigate the worst effects. Conversely, in those localities where economic fundamentals remained strongest during and following the downturn, it was considered that poor practice or a less tenacious approach to the negotiation or enforcement of planning obligations could be highly deleterious to outcomes despite benign economic conditions.

Despite agreement on the importance of local agency in securing outcomes and explaining local variation in obligations use, some participants suggested that there was an important set of exogenous political factors that served to shape local practice over time. Local land and property market conditions often had the effect of reinforcing these. Several practitioners working within the context of economically restructuring northern metropolitan areas cited cases where the impetus to secure obligations was dampened for reasons linked, both directly and indirectly, to the imperative to accelerate the redevelopment of specific major regeneration sites. Such reasons included:

- The use of land sale agreements as specific mechanisms to subsidise or 'de-risk' marginal developments. By way of example, such agreements may seek specific contributions from developers as a condition of land transfer (e.g. as part of the sale of public land), in so doing extracting social value from the development in a way that is outside the scope of S106 legislation.
- 'Political waivers' granted by elected members keen to ensure that specific projects did not stall, even when adopted policy might otherwise presuppose the agreement of a higher level of S106 contribution from developers.
- Long time lags between the granting of outline to full planning permission and change in local conditions, market context or sentiment in the intervening period leading to representations by the developer to reduce the level of contribution sought as a condition of the full permission.

Notwithstanding the contextual differences, the extent of culture change across England since 2003 is considerable. Crook *et al.* (2006, 2008) demonstrate clearly that one reason why many authorities were slow to secure

Table 7.5   Use of an officer(s) dedicated to negotiating or monitoring agreements.

	Negotiating		Monitoring	
	2005–2006 (%)	2007–2008 (%)	2005–2006 (%)	2007–2008 (%)
North West	8	11	50	67
Yorkshire	17	13	83	50
West Midlands	7	17	60	83
East Midlands	19	19	69	69
East of England	8	28	75	84
South West	14	27	57	73
South East	19	21	64	67
Greater London	24	33	76	100

Source: Crook *et al.* 2008, 2010.

contributions from developers was a lack of expertise in the negotiation process. Developers would use complex feasibility analyses to explain why they could not afford to make contributions and in many instances planning officers did not have the skills to challenge such analyses, meaning that the LPA could do little but accept the developer's arguments. As skills and experience with LPAs grew, officers got better at negotiating and identifying the level of contributions developers could afford on a given site (Crook *et al.*, 2008). Table 7.5 shows that there was an increase in most regions of LPAs with a dedicated officer for negotiating and monitoring. (Interestingly, Yorkshire saw a decline in the percentage for both negotiating and monitoring, all others remained the same or increased.) The latest study indicates that outside London there has been a reduction in dedicated staff since 2008 (University of Reading and Three Dragons, 2014).

Of course, there is a limit to the resources an LPA can put into negotiations, and these resources were often pale by comparison with large development firms using planning consultants, but there is no doubt that practice within LPAs improved over time and this was partly due to the employment of dedicated officers to negotiate. As more and more obligations were agreed, LPAs also employed staff to monitor delivery, particularly the payment of financial contributions and, to a lesser extent, the in-kind works.

Our studies shed some light on the resourcing decisions within LPAs. They illustrate clearly a shift towards better resourcing of negotiations. In the 2005–2006 and 2007–2008 surveys, local authorities were asked to rank the main reasons behind a change in the use and value of planning agreements between the two periods. Table 7.6 outlines the results presenting a rank detailing the importance of each factor in 2005–2006 and then 2007–2008 and also an assessment of whether the factor had a positive impact on the number and value of agreements in 2007–2008. The results show significant changes in the key drivers between the two study periods. For example, in 2005–2006 land and property prices were only the fifth

Table 7.6 Ranking of the main reasons for any changes between 2005–2006 and 2007–2008 in the number and value of planning agreements.

	Rank 2005–2006	Rank 2007–2008	Positive effect (2007–2008)
Changes to land values and property prices	5	1	41
Employment of a local authority S106 Officer	8	2	64
Introduction of standard charges and formulae as set out in Circular 05/05 'Planning Obligations'	4	3	54
Introduction of new policy or supplementary guidance within your authority	2	4	66
Changes in the skill and experience of developers, landowners and their agents	7	5	38
Changes in the skill and experience of LA staff	1	6	50
Other Government guidance such as the Planning Obligations Practice Guide and model agreements	6	7	63
Changing developer/Landowner attitudes towards S106 contributions	3	8	50

Source: Crook *et al.* (2008, 2010).

most important factor in explaining changes in the number and value of planning agreement but in contrast it was the most important factor in 2007–2008, although less than half reported a positive effect, confirming the impact of a decline in market conditions in the beginning of 2008. The skill and experience of staff and changes to local policy were the key drivers of change in 2005–2006 indicating that S106 policy was still being embedded within the planning framework and LPAs were still developing processes but getting much better at it. By 2007–2008, the market was the major driver; however, policies and processes were still evolving and changes in local policy and practice still ranked very highly, most notably the employment of an S106 officer and the standardisation of charges referred to above. At this point, although it seemed to have become more important, respondents reported that having government guidance outside standard charging seemed to have little impact on the number and value of agreements with the LPAs own initiatives being much more important.

Stretching the 'rational nexus'

As discussed earlier in this volume (specifically in Chapter 4; see also Crook, 1996), there is a tacitly understood 'rational nexus' argument that may be seen to limit the application of planning obligations in theory to the provision of social goods necessarily arising as a result of the proposed development. Variations in local policy, practice, context and resources inevitably shape the extent to which this nexus remains sacrosanct but at the same time make the collection and analysis of consistent data on the uses to which S106 contributions are put very difficult.

The qualitative insights generated by Crook *et al.* (2010) shed some light on this. Several participants to that study stated that they had detected increased pressures from within local authorities, including from elected members, to use S106 agreements to fund a large, and broadening, array of different types of development. This had occurred in some cases to the extent that concerns were being expressed that S106 was *de facto* being used to underpin the delivery of a range of basic public services in the face of austerity pressures on local government finance.

These pressures included requests from several 'internal' agencies seeking access to what was regarded at the time as – in the context of diminishing mainstream 'pots' – an 'expanding pie'. Some participants agreed that, on occasion, the 'rational nexus' between development and the external costs imposed by that development had been stretched and that some applications of S106 were difficult to justify in terms of a direct, causal connection between the granting of planning permission and the resultant externalities.

Participants suggested that in a number of cases there was a need for better training on what planning obligations could be used legitimately for – including the view that extended or tailoring such training to the needs of elected members could be particularly beneficial.

Delivery

The qualitative research findings highlight the important and often overlooked gap between negotiation of agreement and their delivery (Crook *et al.*, 2008, 2010). Following pre-application talks with developers and the formal negotiation of S106 agreements, the delivery of legally agreed obligations provides a further opportunity for variations in policy and practice to determine the quantum and spatial pattern of planning obligations outcomes. Despite trends towards the increased use of standard charging, and the expansion of the average number of obligations (e.g. of different types, purposes and scopes) that were associated with agreements, the picture on the eventual delivery of agreements and the fulfilment of obligations was mixed. As the next chapter, Chapter 8, shows the general view amongst those charged with monitoring S106 agreements was that, while most obligations were met by developers 'in the end', the monitoring of delivery was generally 'problematic'. Several reasons were provided in explanation. Many of these related to process mechanisms, and the resources underpinning them, within planning authorities. Despite the routinisation of S106 negotiations and the deep level of embeddedness in practice of legislative powers, many practitioners cited a lack of a formalised infrastructure for monitoring contract delivery. Practice varied, as did the adoption of consistent systems for specifying and monitoring contract 'trigger points' or milestones. Some officers complained about the lack of resources to undertake site visits and inspections on the ground (see Table 7.6 for some evidence of the shift of resources). This type of local intelligence was considered to be paramount in a local authority's ability to track developments and the progress of agreements, and the delivery of contracted deliverables.

Equally significant was the stalling of development sites associated with the economic downturn. While this was acknowledged to have had an impact on the delivery of agreed obligations, the general view was that such delays affected the timing, but not the eventuality, of obligations being met because there was widespread evidence that local authorities were adopting a more flexible approach to the delivery of agreements. Typical example practices cited by planners included the renegotiation of agreements, conversion to commuted sums in lieu of the original agreement, and allowing the payment of cash obligations on a phased basis or by instalments. It was also noted that widening access to (and skills in the use of) administrative and secondary data sources, particularly through Open Data Initiatives, was beginning to permit more effective monitoring of delivery – such as through the joining up of address-based datasets (e.g. via local land and property gazetteers) or the use of proprietary or open-access aerial imagery (e.g. Cities Revealed or Google Maps) and other geospatial datasets.

Conclusions

This chapter explored the spatial variations in the number and value of planning obligations secured across England. Based on the available evidence, it argues that the variation is not merely a product of macro and microeconomic forces, although of course they do play a role. Nor is the variation simply a product of differences in the levels of activity in the development sector or prevailing land markets. Rather much of the variation can be attributed to local variations in the approach to implementing policy, and to local institutional structures and processes. The findings from research in England resonate with those from Scotland and Wales.

In-depth interviews with practitioners provide a qualitative insight that suggests that the internal working of local authorities played a significant role in 'capturing' S106 receipts during the last decade. The gaps between LPAs who did well in terms of the number and value of obligations secured only began to close as information about best practice was shared nationally. The widespread improvement in planning practice in this area helped underpin the increases at national level in the number and value of planning obligations delivered and this is discussed more fully in the next chapter. This change reiterates the literature findings and discussion at the start of this chapter. Using the conceptual model of LPAs as weak or strong in policy and practice outlined earlier, the evidence suggests that whilst spatial variation in the value and number of planning obligations is in part a result of economic and wider land market variables, LPAs have moved from weak to strong in terms of local policy and practice as evidence of best practice has been disseminated. The analysis of the spatial patterns of the incidence and value of planning obligations reinforces the widely held view that, to ensure policy effectiveness, there needs to be ongoing investment in sharing best practice and in skills development and training. Specifically, as Brownhill *et al.* (2014) and Crosby *et al.* (2010) highlight, much more needs to be done to enhance competence in development viability.

References

Audit Commission (2006a) *Securing Community Benefits through the Planning Process: Improving Performance on Section 106 Agreements*, Audit Commission, London.

Audit Commission (2006b) *Route Map to Improved Planning Obligations*, The Commission, London.

Barlow, J., Cocks, R. and Parker, M. (1994) *Planning for Affordable Housing*, Department of the Environment, London.

Bill, P. (ed.) (2004), *Building Sustainable Communities: Land Development Value for the Public Realm*, The Smith Institute, London.

Brownhill, S., Cho, Y., Keivani, Y., Nase, I., Downing, L., Valler, D., Whitehouse, N. and Bernstock, P. (2014) *Are Planning Obligations Delivering Enough Affordable Housing and What Alternatives Are There?* Joseph Rowntree Foundation, York.

Bunnell, G. (1995) Planning gain in theory and practice. *Progress in Planning* **44**, 1–113.

Burgess, G., Monk, S. and Whitehead, C.M.E. (2007a) *The Provision of Affordable Housing Through S106: The Situation in 2007*. Royal Institution of Chartered Surveyors Research Paper Series, Vol. 7. Royal Institution of Chartered Surveyors, London.

Burgess, G., Monk, S., Whitehead, C.M.E. and Crook, A.D.H. (2007b) *How Local Planning Authorities are Delivering Policies for Affordable Housing*, Joseph Rowntree Foundation, York.

Campbell, H., Ellis, H., Glaswell, C. and Henneberry, J. (2000) Planning obligations, planning practice and land-use outcomes. *Environment and Planning B* **27**, 759–775.

Campbell, H., Ellis, H., Henneberry, J., Poxon, J., Rowley, S. and Gladwell, C. (2001) *Planning Obligations and the Mediation of Development RICS Research Papers*, Vol. 4, Royal Institution of Chartered Surveyors Foundation, London.

Campbell, H. and Henneberry, J. (2005) Planning obligations, the market orientation of planning and planning professionals. *Journal of Property Research* **22**, 37–59.

Carmona, M., Carmona, S. and Gallent, N. (2001) *Working Together: A Guide for Planners and Housing Providers*, Thomas Telford Publications for the Royal Town Planning Institute and the Housing Corporation, Paddock Wood.

Claydon, J. and Smith, B. (1997) Negotiating planning gains through the British development control system. *Urban Studies* **34**, 2003–2022.

Crook, A.D.H. (1996) Affordable housing and planning gain, linkage fees and the rational nexus: using the land use planning system in England and the USA to deliver housing subsidies. *International Planning Studies* **1**, 49–71.

Crook, A., Burgess, G., Dunning, R., Ferrari, E., Henneberry, J., Lyall Grant, F., Monk, S., Rowley, S., Watkins, C. and Whitehead, C. (2010) *The Incidence, Value and Delivery of Planning Obligations in England in 2007–08*. Department of Communities and Local Government, London.

Crook, A.D.H., Henneberry, J.M., Rowley, S. and Watkins, C.A. (2007) Levy raises complexity fear. *Planning*, 19th January, p. 16.

Crook, A., Henneberry, J., Rowley, S., Watkins, C. and the Halcrow Group (2006) *Valuing Planning Obligations in England*, Department of Communities and Local Government, London.

Crook, A., Rowley, S., Henneberry, J., Smith, R. and Watkins, C. (2008) *Valuing Planning Obligations in England: Update Study for 2005–06*, Department of Communities and Local Government, London.

Crook, A., Whitehead, C.M.E., Jones, M., Monk, S., Tang, C., Tunstall, R., Bibby, P., Brindley, P. and Ferrari, E. (2011) *New Affordable Homes: What, for whom and where have Registered Providers been building between 1989–2009?* Tenant Services Authority and Homes and Communities Agency, London.

Crosby, N., McAllister, P. and Wyatt, P. (2010) *Fit for planning? An Evaluation of the Application of Development Appraisal Models in the UK Planning System*, Working Papers in Real Estate and Planning 10/10, Henley Business School, University of Reading, Reading.

Department of Communities and Local Government (DCLG) (2006a) *Planning Obligations: Practice Guidance*, Department of Communities and Local Government, London.

Department for Communities and Local Government (DCLG) (2006b) *Statement by Minister of Housing*. Press release. Department of Communities and Local Government, London.

Department for Communities and Local Government (DCLG) (2007) *Housing and Planning Delivery Grant: Consultation on Allocation Mechanism*, Department of Communities and Local Government, London.

Department of Communities and Local Government DCLG (2010) *New Policy Document for Planning Obligations: Consultation*, Department of Communities and Local Government, London.

Department for Communities and Local Government (DCLG) (2012) *Renegotiation of Section 106 Planning Obligations*: Consultation, Department of Communities and Local Government, London.

Department for Transport Local Government and the Regions (DTLR) (2002) *Delivering Affordable Housing Through Planning Policy*, Department for Transport Local Government and the Regions, London.

Driver, E. (1994) *Securing Low-Cost Housing in Perpetuity*. Frere Cholmeley Bischoff (now Eversheds LLP), Nottingham.

Ennis, F. (1997) Infrastructure provision, the negotiating process and the planner's role. *Urban Studies* **34**, 1035–1954.

ERM Planning, CgMS and London Residential Research (2003) *Improving the Delivery of Affordable Housing in London and the South East*, Office of the Deputy Prime Minister, London.

Farthing, S. and Ashley, K. (2002) Negotiations and the delivery of affordable housing through the English planning system. *Planning Practice and Research* **17**, 45–58.

Gielen, D.M. and Tasan-Kok, T. (2010) Flexibility in planning and the consequences for public value capturing in UK, Spain and the Netherlands. *European Planning Studies*, **18**, 1097–1131.

Greater London Authority (GLA) (2006) *Affordable Housing Development Control Toolkit*. Greater London Authority, London.

Grimley GVA (2006) *Housing Corporation Economic Appraisal Tool*, The Housing Corporation, London.

Grimley JR Eve (1992) *The Use of Planning Agreements*, Her Majesty's Stationery Office, London.

Healey, P., Purdue, M. and Ennis, F. (1993) *Gains from Planning? Dealing with the Impacts of Development*, Joseph Rowntree Foundation, York.

Homes and Communities Agency (HCA) (2009) *Investment and Planning Obligations: Responding to the Downturn*, Homes and Communities Agency, London.

Leishman, C. (2003) *Real Estate Market Research and Analysis*, Palgrave, London.

Local Government Association (LGA) (2012) *Briefing Note on Planning Agreements*, Local Government Association, London.

McMaster, R., U'ren, G., Carnie, J., Strang, G. and Cooper, S. (2008) *An Assessment of the Value of Planning Agreements in Scotland*, The Scottish Government, Edinburgh.

Monk, S., Burgess, G., Cousins, L. and Dunmore, K. (2008a) *Good Practice Guide to Delivering New Affordable Housing on Section 106 Sites*, Inspire East, Thetford.

Monk, S., Burgess, G., Whitehead, C.M.E., Crook, A.D.H. and Rowley, S. (2008b) *Common Starting Points for Section 106 Affordable Housing Negotiations*, Department of Communities and Local Government, London.

Monk, S., Lister, D., Short, C., Whitehead, C.M.E., Crook, A.D.H., Henneberry, J.M. and Rowley, S. (2005a) *Value for Money in Delivering Affordable Housing Through S106*, Office of the Deputy Prime Minister, London.

Monk, S., Lister, D., Short, C., Whitehead, C.M.E., Crook, A.D.H. and Rowley, S. (2005b) *Land and Finance for Affordable Housing: The Complementary Roles of Social Housing Grant and the Provision of Affordable Housing Through the Planning System*. The Housing Corporation, London and Joseph Rowntree Foundation, York.

National Audit Office (2005) *Building More Affordable Homes: Improving the Delivery of Affordable Housing in Areas of High Demand. House of Commons Paper 459, Session 2005–06*, The Stationery Office, London.

Office of the Deputy Prime Minister (ODPM) (2004) *A new approach to planning obligations: summary of consultation responses*. ODPM, London.

Office of the Deputy Prime Minister (ODPM) (2005) *Circular 05/2005: Planning Obligations*, Office of the Deputy Prime Minister, London.

Rowley, S., Crook, A.D.H., Henneberry, J. and Watkins, C. (2007) *The Use and Value of Planning Obligation in Wales*, Welsh Assembly Government, Cardiff.

The Planning Inspectorate (PINS) (2009) *Checklist for Planning Obligations*, The Planning Inspectorate, Bristol.

Three Dragons, Roger Tym and Partners and Cambridge Centre for Housing and Planning Research (2007) *Forecasting and Managing Planning Obligations for Developer Contributions to Affordable Housing. A Feasibility Study*. The Housing Corporation, Bristol.

Tribal Group (2007) *Affordable Housing Investment and Section 106: How Can We Extract More Value Through Communities England*, Tribal Group, Manchester.

Tewdwr-Jones, M., Gallent, N., Fisk, M.J. and Essex, S. (1998) Developing corporate approaches for the provision of affordable housing in Wales. *Regional Studies* **32**, 85–91.

University of Reading and Three Dragons (2014) *Section 106 Planning Obligations in England 2011–12*, Department for Communities and Local Government, London.

Vickers, D., Rees, B. and Birkin, M. (2003) *A New Classification of UK Local Authorities using 2001 Census Data*, Working Paper 03–03, School of Geography, University of Leeds, Leeds.

8

Delivering Planning Obligations – Are Agreements Successfully Delivered?

Gemma Burgess and Sarah Monk
Department of Land Economy, Cambridge University, UK

Introduction

The objective of development control is both to enable and structure new development that is beneficial to the economy and the locality, and to create sustainable development. However, such development will at the same time often generate negative impacts both on the immediate locality and on services and infrastructure more widely. This in turn can result in local opposition to development. An important aspect of the land-use planning system has therefore been to mitigate these negative impacts and to provide benefits, especially to the local community.

Chapter 4 (this volume) explained how local planning authorities (LPAs) have long had powers to require contributions from developers both in the form of infrastructure and affordable housing and through financial contributions. These agreements, most of which are made under S106 of the Town and Country Planning Act 1990, are 'struck' alongside the process of securing planning permission. Planning obligations may include affordable housing and contributions to local infrastructure such as education, transport, open space, children's play areas and community facilities.

This chapter looks at how successful this process has been in actually delivering the agreed contributions. It discusses why delivery of planning obligations should be considered an important issue and the types of contributions that are secured from developers. The evidence for successful

Planning Gain: Providing Infrastructure and Affordable Housing, First Edition.
Edited by Tony Crook, John Henneberry and Christine Whitehead.
© 2016 John Wiley & Sons, Inc. Published 2016 by John Wiley & Sons, Inc.

delivery is explored and issues that arise in monitoring the collection of agreed contributions are discussed. The chapter then turns to the impact of the economic downturn on the delivery of planning obligations and the impact of the transition to a new system for capturing development value through the Community Infrastructure Levy (CIL).

The research shows that the planning obligations specified in S106 agreements with developers are normally successfully delivered. However, as the impact of the economic downturn and the slowdown in the market and build rates have been felt since 2007, the delivery of planning obligations has been affected. As sites have slowed or stalled completely, agreed contributions have not been delivered. Local authorities and developers have a range of strategies to deal with the downturn, including in some cases the renegotiation of planning agreements to reduce contributions on the grounds of viability. The chapter also shows that the impact of the new CIL on the delivery of planning obligations is still very uncertain.

Why consider delivery of planning obligations?

Chapter 6 showed that a considerable value of planning obligations has been secured through the system of negotiated S106 planning agreements between local authorities and developers. Obligations may be delivered as a financial contribution to a local authority, but are often delivered in kind, in the form of roads, open space, education facilities and affordable housing for example, provided on site by the developer.

If the S106 approach is to work effectively, LPAs need to have the commitment and capacity both to negotiate the agreements and to ensure that they are implemented. There is considerable evidence on negotiations and particularly on how the results vary between authorities in ways that cannot be explained by local market variables (Chapter 7, this volume; Crook *et al.*, 2006, 2008, 2010). However, little is known about whether and how these obligations eventually get delivered in practice and how many agreements are later subject to renegotiation. The issue of delivery has become more significant in recent years because of two concerns: first, that not all obligations are delivered either because developers evade them or because LPAs themselves do not monitor and enforce effectively; and second, many agreements may currently be the subject of renegotiation because the recession has made them unviable (Chapter 5, this volume).

Although contributions that will be made by the developer are specified in S106 agreements, previous work has shown that planning obligations may not be delivered for a number of reasons (Crook *et al.*, 2006, 2008, 2010). For example:

1. Agreed obligations may be altered through changes in the scheme and also in the obligations – some may be agreed with the LPA very formally, others informally and yet others not at all.
2. Projects may be phased and obligations or parts of them may be triggered at various stages of a development. This means that obligations may be delivered over a number of years.
3. There are an increasing number of planning agreements on large schemes in which the value of the planning obligation/level of affordable housing is made dependent on external factors or on sale values. This approach has been increasing as a response to Government pressure to ensure that development is viable.

This chapter draws on several pieces of research which analysed the delivery of planning obligations (Burgess *et al.*, 2007b; Crook and Whitehead, 2010; Crook and Monk, 2011; Monk *et al.*, 2005a, 2006, 2008). In particular, Crook *et al.* (2006, 2008, 2010) analysed the value of the planning obligations delivered through the S106 system in England in three national studies in 2003–2004, 2005–2006 and 2007–2008. In the most recent study, not only the value of agreed planning obligations was analysed, but also specifically the delivery of agreed obligations. Questionnaires were sent to 354 LPAs across England, with a response rate of 43% (Crook *et al.*, 2010). Primary data were also gathered on the delivery of planning obligations in 24 case study LPAs and on four sites in each of those LPAs. In 2011, further research built on these findings by exploring the impact of the downturn on delivery of planning obligations through S106 and the impact of the transition to the CIL (Burgess and Monk, 2012).

Types of planning obligations

Planning obligations secured in S106 agreements may be delivered by developers as financial contributions to the local authority, or as in-kind contributions such as roads, open space and, in particular, affordable housing.

Looking at the evidence of the value of planning obligations over several years (Crook *et al.*, 2006, 2008, 2010), research conducted in 2010 found that the number of obligations secured within each individual agreement had increased, and planning authorities had negotiated a much wider range of contributions than in previous years, with significant increases in the North and Midlands between 2005–2006 and 2007–2008 (Chapter 6, this volume; Crook *et al.*, 2010). This is likely to be a result of both the spread of good practice and experience on the part of local authorities and as a result of a buoyant housing market with rising house prices and land values.

As part of the research published in 2010, 24 local authorities were sampled to explore the delivery of planning obligations (Crook *et al.*, 2010). In each local authority, the four S106 agreements sampled included a commercial, a mixed use, a large residential and a small residential development. As well as analysing the agreements, interviews were conducted with LPA officers and others involved in delivery such as staff of housing associations (HAs) and other developers and all the sites were visited to check on the ground whether the agreed planning obligations had actually been delivered.

The evidence from the 96 case study sites confirmed that agreements attached to commercial sites contained fewer obligations than those for residential and mixed-use sites. All of the major residential sites with 50 or more units had an affordable housing requirement. This varied widely between one developer contributing free land only for 10% affordable housing, to another site where 81% of all the dwellings were affordable housing. Most major residential sites with 50 units or more had a requirement for between 20% and 30% affordable housing. For all types of sites, there were more direct financial contributions than in-kind contributions.

Table 8.1 shows the wide range of different obligations that were secured by the case study local authorities through S106. On the 96 sites, the number of different obligations per site ranged from 1 to 20 (on a large mixed-use site) for financial contributions and from 0 to 10 for in-kind contributions (other than affordable housing). Only 46 of the 96 sites included an affordable housing contribution, whether in kind or financial. Affordable housing, open space, highways, education and transport were the most commonly secured contributions.

Figure 8.1 clarifies how these contributions were expected to be delivered according to the S106 agreements. It shows that most planning obligations other than affordable housing were in the form of financial contributions to the local authority. Even so, affordable housing is so dominant that on-site contributions generate the majority of benefits. Indeed, the 2010 study showed that affordable housing accounted for £2.6bn of the £4.9bn total value of all obligations agreed in 2007–2008 in England (Chapter 6, this volume; Crook *et al.*, 2010).

Case-study evidence of successful delivery of planning obligations

As part of the analysis of our case studies, a delivery typology was created to categorise the outcomes (Crook *et al.*, 2010). The categories range from all the contributions being delivered in line with the S106 agreement to a clear breach where the obligations specified in the agreement had not been fulfilled.

Table 8.2 shows that in the majority of the case study agreements, 51%, the contributions agreed were delivered in line with the S106 agreement and

Table 8.1 Types of contributions secured on case study schemes.

	Type of contribution	In kind	Financial	Total
1.	Affordable housing	35	11	46
2.	Open space	12	33	45
3.	Highways/Street layout	11	21	33
4.	Education		31	31
5.	Transport/Bus	1	27	28
6.	S106 monitoring fee		23	23
7.	Children's/Youth play area/Facilities	3	20	23
8.	Community facilities including buildings	9	13	22
9.	Sport leisure recreational facilities	1	15	16
10.	Public art	9	7	16
11.	Libraries		15	15
12.	Pedestrian footpaths	4	11	15
13.	Traffic calming/Management	1	13	14
14.	Employment/Training	3	10	13
15.	Car parking/Cycle parking	5	5	10
16.	Health/Social services		10	10
17.	Landscaping/Environmental improvements	2	6	8
18.	Legal fees		7	7
19.	Cycle routes		6	6
20.	CCTV/Public safety	2	4	6
21.	Land	6		6
22.	Woodlands/Community forests		4	4
23.	Remediation		4	4
24.	Dog/Litter bins		4	4
25.	Pollution/Waste management		2	2
26.	On-site facilities (window cleaning, mini bus, etc.)	1	1	2
27.	Transport strategy contribution		2	2
28.	Childcare facilities	1	1	2
29.	Bus shelter		2	2
30.	Air quality monitoring		2	2
31.	Travel plans		2	2
32.	Archaeological report	1		1
33.	Civic amenity		2	2
34.	Town centre improvements		1	1
	Total number of contributions by type	107	314	422

Source: Case-study authorities, in Burgess *et al.* (2011), adapted from Crook *et al.* (2010), and reproduced with the permission of the editors of *People Place & Policy Online*.

to expectations and LPAs expected another 20% to be delivered in full when contributions were due. A further 10% of cases were delivered, but with agreed changes. In only 13% of cases were the obligations not delivered as agreed. In another 6% of cases the outcome was unknown.

In some cases, successful delivery required considerable effort on the part of LPAs. Discussions with local authority officers and visits to the sites also showed that there were subtleties in what was delivered on the ground. For example, as part of the mixed communities agenda, most local authorities require the affordable housing to be pepper-potted amongst the market housing and often stipulate that it should be of the same design as

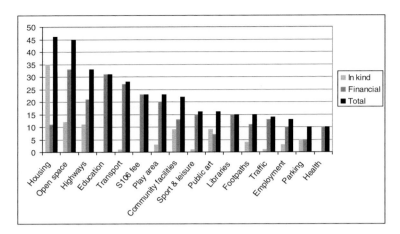

Figure 8.1   Method of delivery for most common planning obligations for case study schemes.
Source: Case-study authorities, in Burgess *et al.* (2011), adapted from Crook *et al.* (2010) and reproduced with the permission of the editors of *People Place & Policy Online*.

Table 8.2   Typology of delivery of planning obligations 2007–2008.

Outcome	Number of sites	Proportion of sites (%)
Delivered in line with S106 and to expectations	48	51
Expected to be delivered in full in due course	19	20
Delivered but with agreed changes	9	10
Not delivered as agreed	12	13
Outcome unknown	6	6

Source: Case-study authorities, in Burgess *et al.* (2011), adapted from Crook *et al.* (2010) and reproduced with the permission of the editors of *People Place & Policy Online*.

the market housing so as to blend in, and whilst the standards required of any grant-funded affordable housing are high, on most sites it was relatively easy to spot the affordable housing. It was often located in the least desirable part of the site, or in one case of an apartment development with luxury facilities and high service charges, as a separate smaller block fronting the busy road.

There were internal issues in LPAs about spending the money from direct payments on what was agreed in the S106. LPA officers were sometimes put under pressure from other departments to spend the money on something other than what was agreed. They resisted, particularly with an increase in Freedom of Information requests on behalf of developers looking to get money back from local authorities if it had not been spent in time or on the agreed infrastructure.

These case studies found that the earlier anecdotal evidence which suggested that some obligations were not being delivered was not confirmed by the evidence, but they also identified reasons why there were valid concerns about delivery. The case studies showed that in many cases delivery took a long time. After an agreement is signed, it may be up to two years before the developer begins work on site and even longer before staged payments are triggered. On some sites, particularly large developments taking place over a number of years, direct payments and the provision of in-kind contributions are linked to agreed trigger points, such as the occupation or sale of a proportion of the market units. This is preferred to collecting all financial contributions on commencement, as it allows developers to manage their cash flows and increases viability. It can take years on large and complex schemes for all contributions to be triggered and delivered. For example, highways and landscaping may not be completed until a scheme is almost finished, which can be several years after the agreement was signed and development commenced. Equally, some contributions may take a long time to be delivered if contributions are being pooled across a number of sites, such as payments towards community facilities.

Another reason why it had previously been difficult to say for certain if agreed planning obligations were delivered were the difficulties of monitoring them. The research showed that if S106 contributions are monitored, they are generally delivered. Monitoring, of itself, appears to have an independent impact on outcomes as monitored schemes are more likely to deliver obligations in full. However, whilst in some LPAs monitoring was very well developed, with comprehensive databases that record all information, provide automatic prompts on triggers and track spending at all stages, the research found that in other LPAs it was not as advanced. Monitoring spending in most LPAs was an emerging practice and some staff said that relationships with other departments did not make this an easy process. One flaw in the monitoring process is that, in practice, LPAs rarely know when work on a development has started. This can be a particular problem both in rural LPAs where sites are far apart and in LPAs where there are large numbers of S106 agreements. Other triggers for payment are often at different stages of completion or occupation of an agreed proportion of homes. The only way to monitor this is by visiting the sites. As one LPA officer said, they 'go out checking for curtains', often visiting sites and counting properties to assess whether triggers have been reached. Monitoring is time and resource intensive and most LPAs felt that they were doing what they could within resource constraints.

Quantitative evidence on the delivery of obligations

In an earlier examination of the delivery of obligations, Monk *et al.* (2006) noted that many of those engaged in planning obligations considered that delivery was a significant problem. They also noted that LPAs (particularly smaller ones) were not adequately monitoring delivery, especially 'in-kind' contributions, such as affordable homes, with the result that perception rather than hard information tended to dominate discussions about delivery. As we discuss below, issues of delivery have become increasingly important, given the reliance many LPAs place on obligations to deliver infrastructure with some commentary suggesting that financial payments were accumulating in LPAs 'coffers', but not being spent (Tarver, 2014). After the Global Financial Crisis, there were additional concerns that renegotiations would lead to a loss in capacity to deliver the necessary infrastructure to support new development. But whilst delivery became increasingly important, there was also a knowledge vacuum about it.

In our study of obligations that were agreed in 2007–2008 (Crook *et al.*, 2010) we also asked the large sample of LPAs about delivery of previously agreed obligations. We found that over a fifth estimated that by 2007–2008 they had received over 90% of the direct payment obligations originally agreed in 2005–2006 and over a third had received three quarters or more. Only a quarter had received less than half. They were also asked to estimate the extent to which, since 2003–2004, developers had failed to pay in full by the end of 2007–2008 the direct payment obligations that had been agreed and that had been triggered by the development taking place since then. One in eight (12%) said this had never occurred and just over one in four (27%) said that this happened only occasionally, but just over half (52%) said it happened frequently (and 9% were unable to estimate). Despite this, LPAs were receiving significant sums with £560m in payments being received in 2007–2008 (from whenever the agreement had been signed). This amounted to an average of £1.6m per LPA, but with significant variations between authorities with those in the urban London 'family' of local authorities receiving £7.6m on average in 2007–2008 in direct payments and those in rural England receiving £93k on average that year. Just under £1.3bn worth of affordable housing was delivered in 2007–2008 (both as financial and in-kind obligations) compared with £1.9bn worth of affordable housing that had been agreed two years earlier in 2005–2006. This suggests that a significant proportion of affordable housing obligations were being delivered, if it is assumed that 20% of permissions do not proceed at all (so that only £1.5bn was tied up in obligations in those where development commenced) and that there is a minimum delay of two years from an agreement being signed and the new affordable homes being completed.

LPAs were also asked about the extent to which agreements were ever renegotiated once signed. About one in twelve were, with no evidence of an increase between 2003–2004 and 2007–2008. Many of the renegotiations related to the timing of payments, to the substitution of an existing agreement from an old to a new planning permission (where the latter had superseded the original permission), 'switching' from direct to in-kind payments for the same obligation (and vice versa) and changes in the details of the affordable housing to be provided on a site, often with an increase in rented units in place of units in intermediate tenures (or vice versa) and (but more rarely) agreements by LPAs to receive commuted payments instead of on-site provision of affordable homes.

But by 2007–2008, LPAs were anticipating that they would have greater difficulties in getting agreements implemented, given the changes in the economic cycle. This was confirmed by later quantitative evidence (University of Reading *et al.*, 2014) which examined the year 2011–2012 and looked explicitly at the extent to which planning obligations impacted on viability and led to 'stalled' developments. There was a particular concern that, given the large proportion of obligations that were for affordable housing, the subsequent fall in house prices could have impacted significantly on the viability of S106 sites so that it was no longer possible for developers to meet the costs of obligations that were entered into in 2007–2008 or earlier.

Over a third (36%) of LPAs had one or more agreements the subject of renegotiations in 2011–2012 and in almost all cases these were agreed. Developers argued that they had been affected by the economic cycle and a lack of demand and finance but also by matters that were not directly related to the changed market conditions such as changes in ownership or finding unforeseen abnormal costs. The outcomes of renegotiations were mainly related to the affordable housing element and included reducing contributions overall, introducing staged implementation (and staged payment for other obligations), sometimes with clawback provisions if the market improved, and changing the tenure of the affordable homes from social to affordable rented (where new homes could be rented for up to 80% of local market rents). Half LPAs had agreed in 2011–2012 to permit reduced affordable housing contributions on viability grounds, the majority being LPAs in rural areas. There were similar variations in the types of LPAs where agreements were still under renegotiation in April 2012, most being in rural LPAs and few in London or other urban areas (University of Reading *et al.*, 2014).

This evidence also showed that there were stalled sites right across England but they were especially concentrated in high-density brownfield sites and most stalled housing sites were in areas of lower land values. Although large greenfield urban extension sites were less likely to be stalled, their size meant they represented a large proportion of the stock of new dwellings given planning permissions, especially in growth areas and growth points. The reason for this is largely due to the downward turn in the housing market but additional reasons include difficulties in securing development finance and disagreements amongst consortia of land owners. The evidence also showed significant regional variations in the impact of the changes in house prices and development costs that had occurred since 2007–2008, with London recovering more strongly than elsewhere but in low- and medium-value areas recent cost increases had not been matched by increases in house prices since 2007–2008.

The factors affecting the delivery of affordable housing obligations

In our earlier analysis of a series of case study sites where agreements with affordable housing obligations had been signed between 1998 and 2005 (Monk *et al.*, 2006), we showed that there was an inevitable gap between the time when new affordable homes were secured in an agreement and the time when they were completed, depending on many factors including the resolution of any conditions on the planning consent, the opening up of the site (including putting in the on-site infrastructure of roads, sewers and other utility connections) as well as the progress being made on the 'market' parts of sites, especially where the pace of completing the affordable element was linked to the completion and sale of the market element.

Thus, while it might take two years or more between agreements being signed and new affordable homes being completed, in most of the cases we studied the number of homes agreed was delivered. Where they were not, it was not due to obligations on affordable homes holding back or preventing development, but either to permissions not being implemented at all or to the way developers tended to re-plan and then renegotiate planning consents and conditions on large sites after the initial consent has been granted and planning obligations agreed. This often involved the original applicant selling off part of the consented site to other developers who would then re-apply for consent and agreed a new set of obligations. When development is finally completed, site evidence showed that most agreed obligations were delivered as originally agreed and that renegotiation occurred only in a minority of cases and usually in relation to changing the phasing of delivery (often in accordance with cascade clauses in agreements that permitted modifications either of the numbers or the tenure of the affordable homes in relation to defined changes in the market).

Renegotiations thus occurred because the market had changed or because sites had been broken up and parts sold on to other developers. Mainly, these changes to agreements involved formal deeds of variation but less often they were agreed informally. The obligations related to affordable housing tended not to be changed unless there were changes to tenure or to the types and sizes of dwellings, and to overall site densities (sometimes meaning more affordable homes were delivered). In a few cases, what was delivered was not what was expected and was usually the result of poor drafting of agreements which did not specify requirements in sufficient detail. At the time this study was undertaken (2006), the housing market was buoyant, enabling private developers to agree obligations and deliver them. We predicted that in a downturn there would be more attempts to renegotiate existing agreements and a greater reluctance to enter into new ones.

Trends in the delivery of affordable housing

Monk *et al.* (2005a) showed how sites with S106 agreements had risen as a proportion of the total number of sites that HAs were working on, rising from an average of 2.4 sites per association in 1989–1990 to 3.4 in 2003–2004, with the number of other sites falling from 4.4 to 3.2 over the same period, with each type of site producing on average of between 12 and 20 dwellings depending on the year and the type of site. The provision secured through S106 sites was in higher value areas compared with previous HA provision, which tended to be on brownfield and inner city sites formerly in public ownership. The supply of the latter sites was both diminishing in number and increasingly also had high remediation costs. The evidence confirmed the way planning obligations were leading HAs to acquire and/or build new affordable dwellings in high-value areas.

Figure 8.2 shows the number of new affordable homes secured in new planning agreements increasing steadily between 1998–1999 and 2007–2008. Monk and Crook (2011) showed how planning obligations policy has been extremely successful as a mechanism for agreeing contributions of new affordable homes in mixed tenure schemes on S106 sites. Inevitably, it is more successful during a housing boom as it is entirely dependent on the provision of market housing, and Figure 8.2 also shows how the economic situation in the credit crunch years has had an impact with fewer new homes being secured in agreements than in earlier years.

Figure 8.3 shows the proportion of new affordable homes completed on S106 sites as a proportion of all new affordable housing completions and acquisitions between 1999–2000 and 2008–2009, however funded, and illustrates not just how much the use of S106 increased, but also how dependent HAs became on planning obligations to secure new affordable homes, with more than 60% of all affordable completions delivered this way in the last three years of this period (Crook and Monk, 2011). In terms of absolute numbers, in 2008–2009 a total of 51 525 affordable completions and acquisitions were delivered, of which 32 286 were delivered through the S106 system.

Table 8.3 shows the tenure of affordable completions by region on S106 sites for the years 2001–2002, 2005–2006, 2007–2008 and 2008–2009. The proportion of social rented units fell nationally from 77% in 2001–2002 to

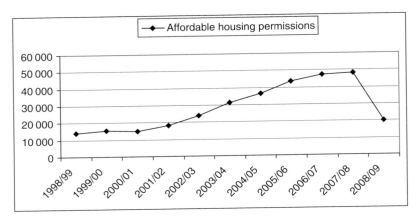

Figure 8.2 New affordable homes secured on S106 sites in England.
Source: DCLG HSSA statistics.

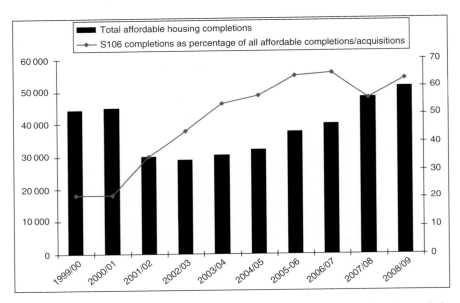

Figure 8.3 Completions of all new affordable homes in England and S106 completions as a percentage of the total.
Source: DCLG HSSA statistics.

57% in 2007–2008, with a slight revival in 2008–2009. Meanwhile, the proportion that was intermediate housing (mainly shared ownership) rose, with a slight drop in 2008–2009. This small change in the most recent figures in the table reflects difficulties in the housing market following the 'credit crunch' (including selling low-cost home ownership homes), so the government brought forward subsidy for HAs from funds allocated for 2010 and 2011 to keep the construction of new social rented houses going.

Table 8.3 Tenures of affordable completions on S106 sites by region.

Tenure	Rent				Shared ownership				Other tenures*			
Year	2001/02	2005/06	2007/08	2008/09	2001/02	2005/06	2007/08	2008/09	2001/02	2005/06	2007/08	2008/09
North East	83	73	80	73	13	24	17	24	4	3	3	3
North West	63	46	29	57	11	37	49	37	26	17	22	6
Yorks/Humber	88	63	54	66	9	24	39	26	3	13	7	7
East Mids	59	54	50	64	13	40	43	32	28	6	7	4
West Mids	69	50	49	62	6	34	41	31	25	16	10	7
East	90	65	64	67	5	27	33	28	5	8	3	5
London	75	68	63	49	20	29	37	41	5	3	<1	10
South East	78	57	57	55	20	35	41	38	2	8	2	7
South West	82	60	55	65	9	35	34	31	9	5	11	4
England	**77**	**60**	**57**	**59**	**13**	**33**	**38**	**35**	**10**	**7**	**5**	**7**

*Other tenures include discounted market sale units (up to 2007–2008), local authority units and units of unknown tenure.
Source: DCLG HSSA statistics.

This otherwise downward trend in S106 social rented housing and the upward trend in intermediate, especially low-cost home ownership housing was associated with rising house prices between 2001 and 2007. The associated increase in development values allowed LPAs to secure increases in the proportions of affordable housing on S106 sites, especially for those priced out of market housing but ineligible for social rented housing. The trend was also influenced by policy decisions to limit grants on S106 schemes especially in the more expensive southern regions. Because developers became more willing, in terms of increased financial contributions, to provide more shared ownership units than to increase social rented units it also enabled more affordable housing to be delivered with much less subsidy than social rented, sometimes without any public funding at all. It also allowed specific needs such as key workers to be met (Monk *et al.*, 2005b; Crook and Whitehead, 2010). The pricing of shared ownership has also allowed HAs to 'cross-subsidise' social rented housing from the surplus they make when selling additional equity shares to shared owners when they 'staircase' upwards, therefore enabling more social units to be built for the same funding.

However, the increasing focus on intermediate housing has not been without controversy. Developers like it because they think that purchasers are better neighbours for those buying their market housing; HAs favour it because it enables cross-subsidy; government favours it because it requires less public subsidy; but, although LPAs see it as a way of increasing the overall output of affordable homes, they often oppose it because it is still too expensive for many households in need (Crook and Whitehead, 2010). Many would prefer public subsidy to go to social renting, especially as waiting lists are at a record level. But although LPAs much prefer to see social rented homes, they have also wanted to increase overall output and have thus been willing to accept the increase coming from low-cost homeownership on S106 schemes.

As we saw in Chapter 4 (this volume), Government policy also sees the mix of new affordable housing as meeting other policy goals, such as mixed communities. There has long been a view among governments and their advisors that large-scale, monotenure, social housing estates concentrate the poorest households, causing stigmatisation and segregation because of perceived high crime rates and anti-social behaviour. Mixed tenure is seen as avoiding this, and using planning obligations to mix market and affordable housing on the same sites meets this goal. Planning obligations and mixed communities policies have thus encouraged intermediate tenures. Developers welcome them on market sites, claiming that social rented homes hinder sales and reduce prices, hence harming profitability and site viability. Although S106 has been successful as a means of delivering affordable housing in mixed tenure schemes, it is inevitably more successful in a housing boom as it is highly dependent on a buoyant private housing market, and Figure 8.2 suggests that the credit crunch had an impact, with a fall in the number of new affordable homes agreed on S106 sites.

But notwithstanding the overall increase in completions, affordable housing has not always been LPAs' priority for S106 sites. Monk *et al.* (2008) showed, in particular, that affordable housing would not always be a high priority on difficult brownfield sites which had site contamination and clearances to address and where there are other priorities for planning obligations such as highways or open space. Delivering affordable housing through obligations is expensive and where other matters have to be achieved through obligations on sites like this, it is often the affordable housing that has to 'give to make the site viable for development' (Monk *et al.*, 2008, p. 18). And in addition, achieving numbers was not always the most important objective as the mix (tenures, types and sizes) is also important especially as a mix emphasising dwellings for social renting imposes higher costs on developers than smaller shared ownership dwellings (Monk *et al.*, 2008). Burgess *et al.* (2007) also showed that when developers attempted to squeeze contributions they also sought to swap shared ownership for social rented housing as this required a lower financial contribution and allegedly impacted less on the house prices of the market homes on S106 sites.

Brownhill *et al.* (2014) looked specifically at how far planning obligations were delivering new affordable homes to those in poverty. They argued that whilst the numbers delivered through S106 were important they were not enough to meet the total need for affordable homes and vary greatly, due to market variation and volatility, as we have seen from other research reviewed in Chapter 7 (this volume), over time and space. They noted that in 2011–2012 when markets were weaker S106 delivered only 16 936 or 32% of all new affordable homes in contrast to the larger numbers in earlier years (although the picture improved to 42% in 2012–2013). In their defined case study areas, the proportions ranged from 2% (Birmingham) to 87% (Oxfordshire). This range was due to the varying strength and volatility of local housing markets, LPAs negotiating capacity, local and sub-regional planning frameworks, the strength of the political commitment to affordable housing and competing calls on planning obligations funding from other infrastructure needs. They showed that only in London was S106 delivering significant numbers in areas with high levels of poverty and also that not all housing provided through S106 was accessible to those on lowest incomes. Delivery to those on the lowest incomes was also affected by the balance between home ownership and rented properties, allocation policies and the size of properties. The introduction of the affordable rent model (see Chapter 4, this volume) was a factor in areas with high market rents, not helped by changes in the definition of affordable housing in the National Planning Policy Framework (NPPF) which makes it harder for LPAs to specify the need for social rented housing in their policies (Chapter 4, this volume).

The impact of the economic downturn on delivery

As we have seen, previous research showed that the majority of agreed planning obligations are delivered as agreed. However, the case study S106 agreements had all been negotiated before the housing market downturn. During the research for the 2007–2008 study (Crook *et al.*, 2010), the first effects of the downturn were being felt, and this was followed up in later research (University of Reading *et al.*, 2014). A fundamental concern with respect to the S106 approach has been the extent to which contributions depend on levels of market activity and on the economic environment. The recession has negatively affected both these factors, and therefore hampered effective delivery of affordable housing (Burgess *et al.*, 2011). As Chapter 5 in this volume explains with detailed examples, financial viability is affected by a range of factors. It is a major reason why developers have sought to reduce their S106 contributions since the downturn.

Since the downturn, all case study LPAs in the 2007–08 study reported a considerable fall in the proportion of planning permissions with agreements that were actually going ahead. The most common reason why planning permissions with agreements did not proceed was because the agreement was superseded by a new agreement for the same site, usually when the plans for the site changed and a new permission and/or agreement was required. LPA officers reported that sites often changed hands and the new developers generally wanted to alter the developments.

As a result of the property market and economic downturn since 2007, the case study LPAs had more instances in which they had to threaten developers with legal proceedings because they were increasingly failing to pay their contributions on time. LPA staff were spending more time chasing payments and there were more breached agreements than ever before. A number of LPAs said that they were pursuing late payments through legal channels, often for the first time. Some were also putting notes on the local land charges register if there was an outstanding contribution on a site, to try to ensure that the obligation could be pursued if the site was sold on so that payment would rest with new owners in the future. However, more recent research (Morrison and Burgess, 2014) suggest that the years 2009–2011 were the worst years for breaches of agreements and that these were mainly amongst smaller developers.

Local authorities and developers have made a range of responses to the downturn (Morrison and Burgess, 2014). Developers may halt developments or not take sites forward at all and wait until the market recovers. They may approach LPAs to renegotiate the planning obligations agreed in the S106 on the grounds that it is no longer viable to deliver the agreed contributions as values have fallen. The case study local authorities in the 2007–2008 study (Crook *et al.*, 2010) had some examples of sites that were underway where developers had breached the agreed schedule for delivering planning obligations, but also others where the developer had renegotiated the payment schedule to ease cash flow.

In fact, many of the case study LPAs had renegotiated payment schedules for financial contributions both formally and informally since the downturn, often moving triggers from early stages such as on commencement to later stages in the development. More recent research (Morrison and Burgess, 2014) suggests that proactive LPAs wanting to see development takes place are flexible in allowing such alterations to payment schedules.

In the 2007–2008 study, in only one case had the LPA accepted a lower contribution and most said that they were 'taking a hard line' and refusing to reduce contributions (Crook *et al.*, 2010). Any renegotiation would require developers to submit viability studies at their own cost and also to pay for the LPAs' due diligence on their submitted study. However, more recently the continued market downturn has led to renegotiation on the grounds of viability. More recent evidence suggests that LPAs are realistic about current market conditions and prefer to see development go ahead rather than stall because of viability (Morrison and Burgess, 2014). Those interviewed said that they would renegotiate agreements where the developer goes 'open book' and demonstrates that the scheme is no longer viable. This may result in a reduced affordable housing contribution and/or change in tenure. One LPA said that most renegotiations on the grounds of viability had been on agreements signed in 2005–2006 before the downturn when land values had been higher. It is possible to renegotiate lower affordable housing contributions but to also include a claw back clause that would enable the LPA to increase the affordable housing contribution if the market and therefore viability subsequently improves. However, this is only useful on large developments that come forward over long time periods, rather than on small sites that will be built out more quickly.

Whilst the recession and market downturn since 2007 have reduced the amount of development value that can be extracted from schemes, and there have been renegotiations to reduce the proportion of affordable housing on some developments, delivery of affordable housing through S106 still continues. Some LPAs saw increased amounts of affordable housing delivered as developers sold whole developments to HAs (Crook *et al.*, 2010). Some schemes that had a proportion, for example, 30%, of the housing agreed to be affordable in the S106 agreement were selling the whole scheme to HAs. Some developers were building the affordable housing first to help their cash flow. There were a few instances in the 2007–08 study of reducing the amount of shared ownership units as these had become more difficult to sell and instead increasing the amount of social rent, or exploring 'Rent to Buy', a new initiative to enable those renting affordable homes to save up to buy their homes.

Recent Government legislation, introduced in 2013, enables developers to request renegotiation on the grounds of viability (see Chapter 4, this volume). It has been argued that some planning obligations negotiated in different economic conditions now make sites economically unfeasible – resulting in no development, no regeneration and no community benefits (DCLG, 2012a). The Growth and Infrastructure Act 2013 inserts new sections (106BA, BB and BC) into the Town and Country Planning Act 1990 to introduce a new application and appeal procedure to review affordable housing obligations on the grounds of viability of S106 agreements agreed prior to April 2010. The measure aims to bring stalled sites forward by reducing affordable housing contributions.

The new application and appeal procedures do not replace existing powers to renegotiate S106 agreements on a voluntary basis (DCLG, 2013). The application and appeal procedure will assess the viability of affordable housing requirements only. It will not reopen any other planning policy considerations or review the merits of the permitted scheme. An application may be made to the LPA for a revised affordable housing obligation. This application should contain a revised affordable housing proposal, based on prevailing viability, and should be supported by relevant viability evidence. Operation of the clause will cease on 30 April 2016, as the ability to renegotiate is seen by government as a reflection of the current difficult market conditions, and not as a permanent change. The review and appeal guidance also introduces a test of viability. It is strongly encouraged that existing methodologies for testing viability are used, and whilst no particular method is prescribed, Annex A identifies variables which could be relevant in the reassessment of viability (DCLG, 2013). Recent interviews with LPAs found that some use consultants to conduct site-specific viability assessments as part of renegotiations but others do it in-house, although all appear to use external consultants for their CIL viability modelling (Morrison and Burgess, 2014).

It remains to be seen what the impact will be on the delivery of affordable housing of this new time-limited application and appeal procedure. Many local authorities are already renegotiating S106 agreements based on current market conditions. Where developers use the new appeal process to renegotiate the amount of agreed affordable housing, it has to be proved that reducing the affordable housing will improve viability. But it is possible that in many cases this would not be sufficient for developers to bring stalled developments forward, given the many other costs and market constraints.

Prior to the legislation coming into force, the Coalition Government funded a mediation service based in the Homes and Communities Agency so that LPAs and developers who disagreed after sitting down together to review agreements on stalled sites could call in mediators. It was reported that of the 127 stalled sites looked at by the ATLAS (Advisory Team for Large Applications) team in the HCA only 16 were stalled because S106 agreements made them no longer viable. In many other cases the lack of development finance was the main reason (Matheson, 2012; Rogers, 2012). But it is the affordable housing contributions that tend to get renegotiated, not infrastructure contributions which planners see as more essential requirements (Mathers, 2013) because it is vital that renegotiations do not produce viable schemes which are no longer acceptable in planning terms (Carpenter and Marrs, 2012). Early reports suggested that up to 16 000 affordable dwellings were at risk (Bury, 2011), a trend confirmed by later reports showing that the CIL levies (see below) being sought by LPAs meant they were also reducing affordable housing targets to retain site viability (Bury, 2012). Others argued (e.g. Ashworth, 2012) that other obligations should be reviewed, not just those requiring on-site affordable housing contributions, while yet others showed how S106 agreements for affordable homes in fact acted as catalysts to private house building as they helped developers' cash flow problems in periods of economic downturn. Thus, S106, far from rendering the provision of private homes unviable, secured more of them (Duxbury, 2013). At one time the government discussed (and consulted on) the idea that CIL might fund affordable housing, but its later moves to enhance viability of stalled development sites through renegotiations of contributions nullified this option.

The most recent research evidence on stalled sites (University of Reading *et al.*, 2014) shows that, despite public policy concerns, viability modelling across a representative range of sites and locations undertaken by the research team showed that scheme viability had not deteriorated between 2007 and 2010, because building costs fell more than house prices, although subsequent cost increases and some falls in house prices since 2010 had reduced viability by 2012 in some locations. Factors such as the increased costs of development finance and having to extend sales periods can affect viability, although the latter also means developers can defer construction costs except on multi-storey developments. Urban extensions posed significant additional costs to developers because of the bigger upfront costs of opening up sites and putting in on-site infrastructure, but removing affordable housing obligations would not always make viable what had become non-viable because of the wide variations in the circumstances of each site.

The same research team (University of Reading *et al.*, 2014) also looked at stalled sites (ones with a detailed consent which had not been implemented at least a year later) to see whether planning obligations, especially for affordable housing, were themselves the cause of this delay. They found that over 8 in 10 stalled sites were residential, that two thirds of these were for flats and that the majority brownfield were in low land value urban areas. In their analysis of a small indicative sample of 18 case studies (which included those where permission had been granted but S106 negotiations had not been completed) they concluded that whilst changed market conditions (falling prices and sales rates) were an important reason why most sites had 'stalled', there were also many other factors including ownership changes, failures to agree with third parties and high abnormal costs. Whilst planning obligations were not seen as the key factor in sites becoming stalled, they did become a key issue in subsequent renegotiations, with the evidence confirming that LPAs are usually prepared to renegotiate where viability was an issue. Most of the negotiations focused on affordable housing requirements where requirements varied from 20% to 30% (with the lower value sites at the bottom end of this range). In line with other evidence, the number of new affordable homes agreed were not always the key issue as the specific tenures required also affect viability. In a few of these case studies, completing the affordable homes agreed and selling them to HAs helped the developers' cash flow. Other obligations were also critical to the viability of stalled sites, especially formula charges for education and highways and their impact on funding new infrastructure in the initial phases of large developments. Whilst it appeared that most renegotiations had gone smoothly, there remained major challenges in developers demonstrating the impact of changes on viability.

Implementing the community infrastructure levy

In addition to the impact of the downturn and new legislation dealing with viability issues, there have recently been significant changes to the way in which capturing development value will be undertaken in the future. The main change is the introduction of the CIL, as discussed in Chapter 4 of this volume. CIL is a new planning charge that came into force on 6 April 2010 through the Community Infrastructure Levy Regulations 2010 (now amended by the Community Infrastructure Levy (Amendment) Regulations 2011 (DCLG, 2011)). It allows local authorities in England and Wales to raise funds from developers undertaking new building development in their area (DCLG, 2011). The money can be used to fund a wide range of infrastructure that is needed as a result of development. This includes new or safer road schemes, flood defences, schools, hospitals and other health and social care facilities, park improvements, green spaces and leisure centres.

CIL is intended to be fairer, faster and more certain and transparent than the current system of planning obligations which has been accused of causing delays as a result of lengthy negotiations (DCLG, 2011). Levy rates are intended to be set in consultation with local communities and developers and it is anticipated that CIL will provide developers with much more certainty 'up front' about how much money they will be expected to contribute.

It is still difficult to predict the impact that the combined introduction of CIL and scaled back S106 obligations will have on the ability of planning obligations to secure contributions. But the initial evidence is not encouraging. A large proportion of English LPAs have no up-to-date local development framework (House of Commons, 2014). This makes it difficult to ensure that CIL and S106 policy fits within this framework, a particularly important problem, given the way the NPPF emphasises the importance of LPAs testing the viability of their core strategies as a whole, making it sensible to adopt CIL charging schedules simultaneously (Allison, 2012). Hence, a parliamentary select committee reviewing the NPPF recommended that all LPAs should have adopted local plans in place within three years (House of Commons, 2014). Only a very small proportion of LPAs were charging CIL by September 2013. By then only 48% had adopted plans and only 4.9% were charging CIL levies (Carpenter, 2013c). Moreover, as many as 58% had not published CIL plans at all, especially outside London, the South East, South West, East and the Midlands region. A year later in its recent, 2014, review of the NPPF, a parliamentary select committee heard evidence that only a small number of LPAs had chosen to use CIL and that 68% of councils would not have CIL in place by April 2015 (House of Commons, 2014). Charging schedules show that CIL rates tend to be higher in London and the South East (National Planning Practice Guidance, 2013) with few LPAs charging for commercial and industrial development, but mainly for residential and for out of town (and not town centre) retail developments.

In London, only two boroughs had their own charging schedules in place at the beginning of 2013 (Redbridge and Wandsworth) but the Mayoral CIL charge is applicable to all boroughs having come into operation in April 2012 intended to raise £300m towards the £14.5bn costs of Crossrail (a new cross London railway line) but by February 2013 less than half the anticipated CIL receipts for 2012–2013 had been collected (Carpenter, 2013a). As we saw in Chapter 4 of this volume, in late 2013 DCLG announced that LPAs will have a further year (i.e. until 2015) to get their CIL schedules in place after which date they will no longer be permitted to pool S106 receipts from more than five sites with tariff payments under S106 agreements for infrastructure not funded by CIL. Given the slow pace of CIL income being achieved by LPAs one (the London Borough of Wandsworth) is using Tax Increment Financing (introduced in 2010) to borrow against future CIL receipts to help fund the extension of an underground line to Battersea but doubts have been expressed about the risks involved as future CIL receipts could not be guaranteed (Marrs, 2011).

In the early days of CIL, reports indicated the very different approaches to deciding on charging schedules that the early adopters were taking (Webb, 2011). But despite this initial activity and although many LPAs welcomed CIL in the hope that, because it would apply to all sites, it would bring in more receipts than did S106 on fewer sites, there have been long delays in getting CIL schedules set up. A long and complex process is involved, starting with estimating the infrastructure requirements to support new development, estimating funding likely to be received from other sources, and considering how far CIL can be used to fund the balance and then making a judgement about what is required and a charging schedule's impact on site viability (all in the light of what might be needed for residual S106). The draft schedule then has to be subject to consultation and an inquiry led by a planning inspector. This is very demanding of LPA staff at times of tight revenue budgets for all local authorities, even where LPA departments secure much of their funding by application fees paid by developers. In many cases, inspectors are requiring LPAs to think again about CIL charging schedules to ensure that they are consistent with their S106 affordable housing targets in their adopted core strategies (even if Supplementary Planning Documents have lower targets), making it clear that CIL charges must be compliant with core strategies in adopted plans (Carpenter, 2013b).

This slow take up of CIL can be seen as a paradox given that CIL was introduced to improve the transparency, speed and certainty with which planning obligations were extracting development value. As we have seen in Chapter 4 of this volume, S106 was seen as lacking in transparency and site-by-site negotiations often dragged on and were only agreed very close to the award of planning permission. S106 negotiations also placed burdens on hard-pressed LPA staff. Although there was surprise when the Coalition did not abolish CIL (Watson, 2011), the expectation was that CIL schedules would quickly emerge as local authorities followed the advice and experience gained by early adopters. However, this early optimism has been followed by concerns that what was once conceived as a simple fixed tariff (with some limited variations in types of development and in specific zones of a LPA area) has now become very complex with the occasional observation that it may now involve almost as much 'haggling' as did negotiated S106 obligations. The regulations were originally poorly drafted in 2010 and there have been four amendments since then (Chapter 4, this volume). What was designed to simplify the collection of funds for infrastructure has now become very complex indeed although the main principle that CIL charges are not negotiable has remained (Editorial, 2013; Webb, 2013). As well as deferring for a year (to 2015) the date when pooling of more than five S106 contributions for infrastructure will no longer be possible, the most recent changes included provision for allowing developers to claim exceptional relief, to phase CIL payments and make in-kind contributions to discharge CIL liabilities, to make more developments exempt from CIL and requiring LPAs to further demonstrate that their CIL charges do not make development unviable (whilst also raising the funding for the infrastructure needed to support developments; DCLG, 2013).

The Parliamentary select committee reviewing the NPPF argued that the growth in the number of these exemptions, the limits placed on S106 pooling when CIL is introduced and the requirements that LPAs share their CIL proceeds with local communities (see Chapter 4) may well be a reason why

> so many LPAs are now reluctant to adopt CIL because they do not consider it to be as effective a means of funding infrastructure as planning obligations.... it is clear that some councils consider section 106 agreements a more effective means of securing infrastructure contributions from developers. We consider that, if councils wish to continue using section 106 they should be able to do so, without the Government placing unnecessary restrictions upon them. (House of Commons, 2014, paras 19 and 20)

In the meantime, commuted payments for affordable housing for S106 are increasing, creating concerns that these risk not achieving the mixed communities objectives and also mean that less land will be provided for affordable homes because the costs of land acquired using commuted payments are expensive (Brown, 2012). The increase in commuted payments arises partly because more small development sites are involved as there was (until very recently – see Chapter 4) no longer any threshold for negotiating affordable housing contributions and on-site provision for these is problematic. To improve flexibility, one LPA in London is allowing landowners to sell land below market value to an affordable housing provider, in exchange for an affordable housing credit which the landowner can then use for other schemes (Lloyd, 2012).

Also putting affordable housing contributions at risk was the proposal that enables private rented housing to count towards the proportion of affordable homes made in the Montague review on how to attract institutional investment into the private rented housing (DCLG, 2012b). In addition, concerns have been reported that CIL proceeds may not be spent on the infrastructure required for the developments on which it is charged, as CIL does not have the same contractual relationship between the payment of the contributions and the obligation on the LPA to undertake the work for which the funds are provided (Ashworth, 2013).

By late 2013, housing market confidence was returning with share values of house builders rising. Planning permissions have also risen, reflecting this confidence and the approvals regime created by the NPPF, with approvals in England up by 35% in the year ended September 2013 compared with the year before (DCLG statistics). Nevertheless, given that development values have fallen so substantially since the credit crunch, it may well take a significant recovery in the market before CIL and scaled back S106 can deliver the infrastructure and affordable homes secured by S106 in the past. The evidence of this volume also shows that, when securing obligations, how important it is to have effective policy and practice in place as well as to have high development values. Local policy and practice will be as crucial in the future as in the past.

Conclusions

There was successful delivery of an increasing number and value of planning obligations through S106 during the period of a buoyant rising market. It became a valuable way of securing financial and in-kind infrastructure to mitigate against the negative impacts of development.

However, the impact of the downturn has been stalled sites and a lack of development. Developers in some cases have argued that agreed contributions are no longer viable. Renegotiation downwards has been permitted to try and ensure development goes ahead. But the time-limited nature of the new government legislation allowing renegotiation suggests that improvement in the market in the future is expected and that developers will return to delivering higher levels of planning obligations than through the recession.

The impact of the CIL on capturing development value is uncertain. But the views of the early implementers of the levy suggest that, as long as rates are realistic and based on viability not policy, then the CIL will not hinder development, and it is the current market conditions that are keeping development at low levels, rather than the extraction of development value, whether through S106 or CIL. However, this does require LPAs to be realistic about what is viable and can therefore be extracted under current local market conditions.

The future of affordable housing delivered through planning obligations depends not so much on CIL as on the wider interaction of house prices and local policy and practice. The overall economic context and its impact on the housing market more broadly is critical. For affordable housing through the planning system, this has always been the case and the introduction of CIL does not change this. LPAs thus have to be aware of variations in local viability and the complex interplay of factors that shape the extraction of development value and viability.

References

Allison, D. (2012) Viability: five key tests. *Planning* 7th September, pp. 17–19.

Ashworth, S. (2012) Affordable homes plans need work. *Planning* 2nd November, p. 23.

Ashworth, S. (2013) Point of principle in levy proposals. *Planning* 17th May, p. 23.

Brownhill, S., Cho, Y., Keivani, Y., Nase, I., Downing, L., Valler, D., Whitehouse, N. and Bernstock, P. (2014) *Are Planning Obligations Delivering Enough Affordable Housing and What Alternatives Are There?* Joseph Rowntree Foundation, York.

Brown, C. (2012) Cashing in commuted sums. *Inside Housing* 22 June, pp. 12–13.

Burgess, G. and Monk, S. (2012) *Capturing Planning Gain – The Transition from Section 106 to the Community Infrastructure Levy*, Royal Institution of Chartered Surveyors, London.

Burgess, G., Monk, S. and Whitehead, C.M.E (2011) Delivering local infrastructure and affordable housing through the planning system: the future of planning obligations through Section 106. *People, Place and Policy Online:* **5**, 1–11.

Burgess, G., Monk, S., Whitehead, C.M.E. and Crook, A.D.H. (2007) *How Local Planning Authorities are Delivering Policies for Affordable Housing*, Joseph Rowntree Foundation, York.

Bury, R. (2011) Planning blow risks 16,000 affordable homes. *Planning* 25th November, p. 2.

Bury, R. (2012) Councils cut housing targets due to infrastructure levy. *Planning*, 10th August, p. 4.

Carpenter, J. (2013a) London levy set to fall short of Crossrail target. *Planning* 22nd February, pp. 4–5.

Carpenter, J. (2013b) Examiner vetoes council homes policy. *Planning* 8th March, pp. 6–7.

Carpenter, J. (2013c) CIL Watch. *Planning* September.

Carpenter, J. and Marrs, C. (2012) S106 mediators to help stalled sites. *Planning*, 24 August, pp. 6–7.

Crook, A., Burgess, G., Dunning, R., Ferrari, E., Henneberry, J., Lyall Grant, F., Monk, S., Rowley, S., Watkins, C., and Whitehead, C. (2010) *The Incidence, Value and Delivery of Planning Obligations in England in 2007–08*, Department of Communities and Local Government, London.

Crook, A., Henneberry, J., Rowley, S., Watkins, C.M.E., and the Halcrow Group (2006) *Valuing Planning Obligations in England*, Department of Communities and Local Government, London.

Crook, A.D.H. and Monk, S. (2011) Planning gains, providing homes. *Housing Studies* **26**, 997–1018.

Crook, A., Rowley, S., Henneberry, J., Smith, R. and Watkins, C. (2008) *Valuing Planning Obligations in England: Update Study for 2005–06*, Department of Communities and Local Government, London.

Crook, A.D.H. and Whitehead, C.M.E. (2010) Intermediate housing and the planning system. In: S. Monk and C.M.E. Whitehead (eds), *Making Housing More Affordable: The Role of Intermediate Tenures*, Wiley Blackwell, Oxford.

Department of Communities and Local Government (DCLG) (2011) *Community Infrastructure Levy: An Overview*, Department of Communities and Local Government, London.

Department of Communities and Local Government (DCLG) (2012a) *Renegotiation of Section 106 Planning Obligations: Consultation*, Department of Communities and Local Government, London.

Department for Communities and Local Government (DCLG) (2012b) *Review of the Barriers to Institutional Investment in Private Rented Homes, Report of the 'Montague' review*, Department of Communities and Local Government, London.

Department of Communities and Local Government (2013) *Section 106 Affordable Housing Requirements: Review and Appeal*, Department of Communities and Local Government, London.

Duxbury, N. (2013) CLG found to undervalue affordable housing. *Planning*, 1st March, p. 3.

Editorial (2013) Levy proposals may bring back haggling. *Planning*, 19th April, p. 3.

House of Commons (2014) *Operation of the National Planning Policy Framework: Fourth Report of the Communities and Local Government Committee, Session 2014–2015*, House of Commons Paper HC 190. The Stationery Office, London.

Lloyd, T. (2012) Westminster's discount drive. *Planning*, 1st June, p. 5.

Marrs, C. (2011) Northern line extension could win levy borrowing boost. *Planning*, 5th December, pp. 6–7.

Mathers, V. (2013) The Planning Negotiator. *Planning*, 22nd February, pp. 12–13.

Matheson, A. (2012) Stalled housing developments and reworking planning obligations. *Planning*, 2nd November, p. 21.

Monk, S., Burgess, G., Whitehead, C.M.E., Crook, A.D.H. and Rowley, S. (2008) *Common Starting Points for Section 106 Affordable Housing Negotiations*, Department of Communities and Local Government. London.

Monk, S., Crook, A.D.H., Lister, D., Lovatt, R., Ni Luanaigh, A.N., Rowley, S. and Whitehead, C.M.E. (2006) *Delivering Affordable Housing Through Section 106: Outputs and Outcomes*, Joseph Rowntree Foundation, York.

Monk, S., Lister, D., Short, C., Whitehead, C.M.E., Crook, A.D.H. and Rowley, S. (2005a) *Land and Finance for Affordable Housing: The Complementary Roles of Social Housing Grant and the Provision of Affordable Housing Through the Planning System*, The Housing Corporation, London and Joseph Rowntree Foundation, York.

Monk, S., Lister, D., Short, C., Whitehead, C.M.E., Crook, A.D.H., Henneberry, J.M. and Rowley, S. (2005b) *Value for Money in Delivering Affordable Housing Through S106*, Office of the Deputy Prime Minister, London.

Morrison, N. and Burgess, G. (2014) Inclusionary housing policy in England: the impact of the downturn on the delivery of affordable housing through Section 106. *Journal of Housing and the Built Environment*, **29** (3), 423–438.

National Planning Practice Guidance (2013) *How Should Viability be Assessed in Plan-Making?* Department of Communities and Local Government, London. Available: http://planningguidance.planningportal.gov.uk/blog/guidance/viability-guidance/how-should-viability-be-assessed-in-plan-making, accessed 30/10/2014.

Rogers, R. (2012) Finance, not the Green Belt, is the best path to development. *Financial Times*, 11th September, p. 13.

Tarver, N. (2014) £1.5bn 'community cash' unspent by English councils. *BBC News*, 7 January 2014. Available: http://www.bbc.co.uk/news/uk-england-25094100, accessed 7/1/2014

University of Reading, Three Dragons, Hives Planning, David Lock Associates and DLA Piper LLP (2014) *Section 106 Planning Obligations in England 2011–12*, Department for Communities and Local Government, London.

Watson, S. (2011) Planning gain goes local. *Planning*, 26th January, pp. 18–19.

Webb, F. (2011) Variable rates. *Planning*, 12th August, p. 20.

Webb, S. (2013) Times to kiss goodbye to CIL? *The Planner*, October, p. 40.

9

International Experience

Sarah Monk[1] and Tony Crook[2]

[1]*Department of Land Economy, Cambridge University, UK*
[2]*Department of Urban Studies and Planning, The University of Sheffield, UK*

Introduction: making comparisons and transferring experience

This chapter looks at the experiences of four other countries in capturing development value for infrastructure and affordable housing. We also compare these with the experiences of England. This enables us to define what is distinctive about the English experience and explore the limits of transferring policy and practice between jurisdictions. The four countries are Australia, Germany, the Netherlands and the USA. They have been chosen to illustrate different approaches which arise from their different market economies, different planning systems and different approaches to property rights and public ownership of land. In two planning systems (Australia and the USA), the costs of providing infrastructure and affordable housing are mainly directly placed on developers while in the other two (Germany and the Netherlands) these have been mainly secured through land adjustment processes and sales of publicly owned land, although this is now changing.

While there are considerable hurdles in making comparisons, a key benefit of looking at other countries, as Booth (1993) emphasised, is that they help to test hypotheses about the nature of policy and in so doing force analysts to enquire more about the nature and purpose of their own policies and systems. As Henneberry and Goodchild (1993) remarked, when examining impact fees in the USA, the interest in looking at other countries is in 'identifying the distinctive features of national practice and of testing commonly held assumptions' (p. 11). Hence, whilst careful comparative research

Planning Gain: Providing Infrastructure and Affordable Housing, First Edition.
Edited by Tony Crook, John Henneberry and Christine Whitehead.

can disentangle complex evidence about comparisons and point to general lessons, it can also help distill and re-examine assumptions about theory and practice made within researchers' own countries (Heidenheimer *et al.*, 1990).

Comparative studies are, of course, fraught with difficulties. They study the 'how', 'why' and 'to what effect' of the actions of different levels of government. They have to address the problems of defining terms and measures to get comparability, of coping with a large number of variables, of understanding the dynamics of causes and policy responses and of uniqueness (Heidenheimer *et al.*, 1990). The methodological problems of doing comparative planning research have been stressed in a number of previous studies. Masser (1986), for example, argued that a major problem is the way phenomena and context are closely intertwined and showed that, by setting up research teams in the countries being compared and identifying the equivalence of the issues being examined, some of these issues can be addressed. Others have stressed the problems of culture, as well as those of language, which inhibit comparisons. Thus, Booth (1993) argued trenchantly that the relationships between policies, plans and their implementation are not technical processes and thus constants in planning processes everywhere that can be understood by anyone involved in land-use planning in any country. Instead, they are concepts which are deeply embedded in the culture of countries and thus have many different meanings, a problem going beyond the issue of translation. The latter problem that land-use planning is rooted in the political and administrative culture of each country and in legal frameworks affecting property rights and the conduct of administration has been recognised in many comparative studies of planning, including long-standing studies (e.g. Davies *et al.*, 1989; Wakeford, 1990) as well as more recent ones (e.g. Norton and Bieri, 2014). As a result, and as Newman and Thornley (1996) also observed, differences between planning systems in Europe (for example) are deep seated and there has been no convergence around a standard European model, notwithstanding the emergence of European wide spatial planning initiatives.

In approaching these challenges, we wanted not only to choose countries which varied quite explicitly in the way they handled infrastructure and affordable housing within their planning systems (i.e. comparing those involving the fixing of charges and negotiating contributions with those involving public land ownership approaches), but also countries with different market economies, social and welfare policy approaches (the latter being related to countries' approaches to affordable housing), constitutional arrangements and different legal traditions.

In relation to market economies, we distinguished between liberal market (LME) and coordinated market economies (CME), following Hall and Soskice (2001). In the former, competitive market arrangements dominate the economy while in the latter there is more reliance on non-market relationships. Australia and the USA are examples of LMEs (as well as

Britain), and Germany and the Netherlands are examples of CMEs. With respect to welfare regimes, we followed the categories of Esping-Anderson (1990) who distinguished between liberal welfare states and conservative or corporatist systems. In the first category means tested assistance and modest universal transfers dominate with the state encouraging market provision by restricting public provision and subsidising private provision. Australia, the USA (and Britain) are examples. Germany and the Netherlands are examples of conservative/corporatist welfare regimes where status differentials are preserved for the sake of social integration and family and non-state provision of welfare is emphasised (we have not chosen to examine in this chapter a country with a social democratic welfare regime such as those found principally in the Nordic countries).

In so far as our four countries' planning systems (like Britain's) are used to support affordable (including rental) housing provision, they are also examples of Kemeny's (1995) binary classification of rental markets into unitary and dualist. In the former (of which Germany and the Netherlands are examples), private and non-market provision is integrated. Social rented housing is often provided by hybrid organisations crossing the private and public divide and these organisations often house a wide range of households, not just those in need. In dualist rental markets (of which Australia, USA – and Britain – are examples), not-for-profit provision is restricted to a residual social rented sector of low-income households where tenants often pay rents covering more than the historic costs of provision (encouraging better-off tenants to leave) and landlords sell-off properties, also for surpluses. Countries with dualist rental markets often have high levels of homeownership. This binary classification is not unproblematic and some (e.g. de Kam *et al.*, 2013) have argued that account also needs to be taken of the large amount of self-building in a number of countries, such as Germany (as is also the case in Australia).

Our four countries are examples of both federal (Australia, Germany and the USA) and unitary (the Netherlands – and Britain too) systems of government. They are also examples of different legal traditions, factors which are important in understanding their planning systems. As far as Europe is concerned (and looking at England[1] as well as at Germany and the Netherlands), Newman and Thornley (1996) distinguished the planning systems of European countries in terms of administrative and legal 'families'. Many European countries, including the Netherlands, are part of the Napoleonic 'family'. In this family, the law is based on complete systems of rules or codes which are derived from abstract principles. Those countries which had been invaded during the Napoleonic era, including the Netherlands, retained this legal approach when they regained their freedoms. In this family, the basic building block of local administration is very small but under this system

---

[1] We discuss England alone because Scotland has a separate legal system and there are devolved governments in both Scotland and Wales.

the unit of government has a much greater degree of independence from central government than in England, albeit with some oversight from central government. Germany which did not become a unified country until the nineteenth century is arguably a branch of the Napoleonic family and shares the approach of systematisation and codification initially developed from its history of Roman law. The written constitution means that the responsibilities of each level of government cannot be altered except by a change in the constitution.

England is distinct as Britain's unwritten constitution provides no 'protection' to local governments because Parliament's sovereignty enables it to determine what local governments may and may not do and has moved local government to more of an agency mode away from an independent policy mode (Stoker, 1991). Newman and Thornley (1996) also point out that, unlike many other countries, the political spheres of central and local government in England are generally different with little interchange of politicians whilst the leadership (despite more recent changes) and local government tend to be collegial rather than led by a strong Mayor (there are of course recent exceptions since their analysis). England's legal style is also different from other European countries being based on a common law approach in which law develops on a decision-by-decision basis on a cautious evolutionary approach. The unwritten constitution, as others have argued (e.g. Loughlin, 2013) not only allows some ambiguity in arrangements but also facilitates pragmatism in the workings of the constitution (something critical, we shall argue, to the way planning obligations have evolved in England). Finally Newman and Thornley point out that local government units in England are generally much larger in population than those in Europe and often provide a much wider range of services.

In the USA, the written constitution and the federal system of government shapes the planning system and its ability to extract development value. The constitution safeguards private property rights against abuse by government and amendments to the constitution provide rights of due process. The constitution also prescribes the relationship between the federal and state governments, and the federal system is one of checks and balances rather than (as in many European federal systems) a means of coordinating the different roles of the levels of government. In the US system, the States cede some authority to the federal government whilst local governments are creatures of the States and subject to their control. Government interference in property rights is restrained and the courts play an important role in safeguarding the protection. As Norton and Bieri (2014) assert, this explains why, as we shall see, there is a more 'minimalist' approach to planning than in many other countries, especially European ones, and there is thus a 'strong preference for allowing and promoting individuals to productively use their land through market development and exchange' (Ibid, p. 386). This leads to the paradox that the judicial role is crucial, involving 'the legal resolution of policy choices after the fact [and] litigating local zoning decisions piece-meal' rather than collectively made planning and policy choices before (Ibid, p. 386). A final comparison within federal systems is that local governments in the USA depend much more on local taxes especially property taxes to fund services than do their counterparts in, for example, Germany.

Australia, like the USA, has a written constitution which amongst other things protects property rights and provides for rights to just compensation when property is taken. The Commonwealth is the federal government and the six states and two territories form the second tier. Each of the latter has their own separate system of planning operating largely independently from each other. Like the USA, Australia follows the common law tradition of case law evolving through precedent.

This chapter relies for its evidence on secondary sources, principally litera-ture, and research conducted by the authors, including reporting and updat-ing some of our own work (especially Monk *et al.*, 2013; but also Crook, 1986) and that of our collaborators in this project (e.g. Henneberry and Good-child, 1993, 1996; Gurran and Whitehead, 2011) and of other colleagues, including, for example, work commissioned by the former National Hous-ing and Planning Advisory Unit (Oxley *et al.*, 2009). The very recent study by Monk *et al.* (2013) of the planning systems in a range of countries (includ-ing the four examined in this chapter) drew not only on relevant litera-ture, including policy documents as well as academic analyses and com-mentaries, but also on advice from country experts. In the case of all four countries described in this chapter, we have examined the most recent lit-erature, including policy documents, in order to update earlier findings.

Australia

Planning policy, planning legislation and its administration

Australia's five major cities (Adelaide, Brisbane, Melbourne, Perth and Syd-ney) are all highly suburban, with low densities by world standards, and high levels of home and car ownership (Monk *et al.*, 2013). In 1991, about 75% of the housing stock consisted of detached houses, with very little high density housing except in Sydney. Around 70% of households owned or were buying their dwellings, 5% rented from a public housing authority and 20%–25% rented from a private landlord. This pattern had changed only lit-tle in the previous 30 years (Forster, 2006). Federal government policies have encouraged home ownership, provided limited funding for public housing systems in each State, and neglected the private rental sector (PRS). How-ever, since the early 1990s, rates of home ownership have fallen (particularly for young people), housing densities and the PRS have increased, coinciding with increasing house prices and affordability problems, particularly in the most desirable and pressured areas.

The planning system is largely governed by each of the six state and the two territory governments, with the Commonwealth (i.e. federal) government having very little formal involvement, aside from matters of 'national environmental significance'. Each state and territory has its own (often different) planning legislation governing land allocation and development control. Increasingly, the states have adopted overarching strategic policies (including metropolitan and regional planning) with varying levels of local involvement. More detailed decisions about local planning objectives, land allocation (zoning), density and design controls and the majority of development control/management, are undertaken by local government which is relatively weak and with limited powers and responsibilities (Austin *et al.*, 2014; Gurran, 2011). Local plans must be consistent with the relevant state or territory legislation, as well as with any other relevant plans or policies and require approval by the relevant State Planning Minister. They specify broad objectives for development within the designated locality; categorise land according to permissible or desired uses (often through formal land-use zones); articulate certain development standards (ranging in detail from basic density controls through to specific aesthetic considerations, depending on jurisdiction); and outline other considerations relating to issues such as cultural heritage. Permission for most developments is not assumed or granted as of right for developments that comply with the plan. Most development proposals are subject to discretionary development control, including code-based assessment processes and negotiations, the latter particularly for projects that do not conform precisely to criteria specified in the plan. The Australian system thus has the dual features of USA zoning and British discretionary plans and this is likely to remain a defining feature of Australian planning (Gurran *et al.*, 2008). In many jurisdictions, different planning procedures apply for very large (in scale or value) projects on new greenfield or urban renewal sites, typically managed by a state government agency rather than a local authority. In some cases, special purpose vehicles have been established to facilitate planning processes in designated metropolitan growth areas.

Thus, the basic planning system is a discretionary planning regime where the right to develop requires planning permission in the context of zoning arrangements setting out permissible land uses and standards. Zoning effectively allocates development value at the time of the zoning. The states control the direction and timing of development, the designation of greenfield areas for urban development and their inclusion inside metropolitan areas by extending growth boundaries. They also zone land for different uses and make use of other regulatory tools that are available to enable urban development in planned urban corridors. Metropolitan councils and state governments have generally acted in a reactive manner when approving applications for greenfield development (Goodman *et al.*, 2010), aside from the limited actions of state land organisations, established in each state and territory during the early 1970s by the Commonwealth (then Labour) government. These government land authorities were intended to facilitate the release of new land for suburban residential development, and help stabilise the land market in response to demand (Milligan, 2003). However, during the 1980s most of these became government enterprises, required to deliver commercial returns and therefore limited in their potential for proactive land or housing outcomes. Interest in government land authorities playing more proactive roles in strategic land delivery for housing supply and affordability has increased recently (Milligan *et al.*, 2009) with the five major cities' strategic plans having to make provision for significant numbers of extra dwellings over the next 20–25 years. Since the post-war years, each has undertaken various approaches to metropolitan planning (Hamnett and Freestone, 2000). Current plans reflect the promotion of more intense, mixed uses around transportation hubs, a greater mix of housing types and greater housing affordability, alongside objectives for environmental protection and economic growth. More fundamentally, the Australian planning system reflects the country's heritage and primacy of the market and limits planning to improving efficiency and dealing with externalities and not to promoting equity and redistribution.

Planning policy is based on three principles: containment, consolidation and 'centres' (Bunker and Searle, 2009; Forster, 2006). Consolidation aims to reduce the rate of urban expansion by encouraging new development, usually at higher densities, within the existing built-up area. All states have adopted containment policies, including the use of urban growth boundaries, which have been extended over time, increasing the supply of urban land on the metropolitan fringe. Since 1991, urban consolidation policy has been responsible for a significant rise in medium density housing in the inner and middle rings of all five major cities (Forster, 2006). Yates (2001, cited by Goodman *et al.*, 2010) argued that this might improve housing affordability because of the savings in land and infrastructure costs associated with dwellings on smaller plots and in more compact settlement patterns, also enabling older householders to downsize from family homes, thus helping younger, growing households to enter the property market.

Developer contributions to infrastructure

Funding for the infrastructure needed to support new development became a particular problem in Australia as governments shifted away from funding urban infrastructure through taxation or borrowing towards a 'user pays' model. While local governments still use rate revenue to support infrastructure, local rates are increasingly required to fund a number of other services and activities as well. In this context, development contributions, long collected for basic utilities and roads within new subdivisions, have assumed greater importance. All Australian planning jurisdictions have introduced arrangements to collect financial or in-kind contributions to meet all or part of site-based, neighbourhood or local-level infrastructure.

Infrastructure contributions first emerged after the Second World War when private developers wanted to share the costs of the infrastructure needed to support the boom in housing construction (Gurran *et al.*, 2008). The ability to levy contributions as a condition for planning permission has since been incorporated into State and Territory planning legislation, although the approaches vary (Gurran *et al.*, 2008, 2009; Gurran, 2011). New South Wales (NSW), Queensland and Victoria have the most extensive provisions for collecting contributions and permit the widest range of community applications for their use. In NSW, the range of contributions is widest, from site-based costs to regional transport (in Sydney's growth centres). In Queensland, contributions to urban water supply, drainage, water quality, transport infrastructure and infrastructure for local community purposes, such as public recreation predominantly serving a local area, may be levied by local councils if they have a priority infrastructure plan or, where there is no such plan, through state charges. Victoria permits contributions to be collected via a Development Contributions Plan, as a condition of a planning permit, or as voluntary agreements. Contribution Plans form part of the local council planning scheme, and therefore require state ministerial endorsement as they are seen as amendments to the statutory planning scheme. Contributions may cover 'development infrastructure' where contributions are not capped (for instance, local roads, parks, maternal and child health centres, kindergartens and public transport infrastructure), and 'community infrastructure' – all other community facilities – which are capped.

In contrast, contributions in South Australia are limited to open space, access roads and water supply, plus car parking where on-site provision is not viable, although there are other 'service rates' and 'service charges' which could be seen as *de facto* contributions. In Tasmania, if contributions are sought, both the amount of the contribution and its use are negotiated locally and form a planning agreement between the local authority and developer. In Western Australia, the State regulates contributions through policies, conditions imposed through planning and conditions of approval for the subdivision of land. Social infrastructure is not generally funded, except for land for schools. In Canberra (Australian Capital Territory Planning and Land Authority, ACTPLA), there are no provisions for infrastructure contributions, but the costs of infrastructure can be offset by land sales or by a levy on permitted uses associated with redevelopment. Where land is owned by the ACTPLA, the government may discount the price of land in return for developers providing infrastructure for the new development or it may levy a charge for change of use when permission to change an existing land use is granted, effectively capturing part of the value uplift associated with the change (Bourassa *et al.*, 1997; Gurran *et al.*, 2008).

There are differences in terms of the magnitude of contributions and the formula for their determination, especially between formulae that impose a flat fee per dwelling, site or area, and formulae that require a percentage levy based on construction costs. When fees are imposed per dwelling, more expensive development is favoured because the fee is the same irrespective of the overall value, so the fee becomes a smaller proportion of the whole. This raises both sustainability and equity concerns. Similarly, if the fee is set per residential lot rather than per hectare, it disadvantages smaller lots and favours larger ones. This is particularly problematic in medium density housing where flats face similar contributions to houses yet may have less impact on the need for infrastructure or services within the locality. Considerable differences in approaches to contribution setting exist, not only between the states and territories, but also at local government level. Not all financial obligations associated with the planning and development are levied under planning legislation, with a number of other agencies responsible for roads or utilities potentially levying their special purpose charges in relation to their own formula for determination. Arrangements for the timing of contribution payments differ between and within jurisdictions, and in relation to particular projects.

Jurisdictions generally rely on three key principles to support their contribution requirements. First, the principle of 'nexus' is important because it establishes a link between the development, the need for the service being charged, the location of that service and the time by which the service is provided. Second, the principle of 'fair apportionment' is also important as it means that only the share attributable to the development should be charged. Third, the principle of 'reasonableness' applies to the amount of contribution required relative to the overall development. These principles are less relevant in relation to voluntary agreements between authorities and developers, or when a system of flat levies is used. Most jurisdictions have also established systems to ensure that the calculation and application of development contributions are transparent, although again processes differ at the local level. Developers are usually able to go to appeal over the amount of contribution required as a condition of consent.

Recent evidence (Gurran *et al.*, 2009) showed divergence between the states and territories in relation to the overall range of development contributions collected and the scale of these charges. There was significant variation in the contributions typically required in each state or development context, even between two projects within the same local government area. In NSW and Victoria, growth areas contributions per lot were likely to reach around $100 000 or more, while in Queensland, contribution amounts were expected to reach around $45 000 per lot. Although development contributions clearly represent a significant cost item, developers generally support them whilst also being concerned about the lack of certainty and inconsistency about what obligations would be incurred for a particular project, and the timing, location and quality of the infrastructure ultimately provided. Local government respondents to the survey by Gurran *et al.* (2009) worried about shortfalls between planned infrastructure provision and the contributions actually collected. Reforms being considered relate to affordability, introducing standard charging and enabling more negotiations (to reduce appeals). Finally, the timing of the contribution requirement is important in terms of who is likely to bear the cost – the landholder, the developer or the final home purchaser. If the fee is required at the time of rezoning or land sale, it is easier to pass it back to the landowner. If imposed during the construction phase or prior to occupation, the fees are more likely to be passed on to the purchasers – or result in lower profits for developers. Arrangements for the timing of contribution payments differ between and within jurisdictions, and in relation to particular projects.

Developer contributions to affordable housing

There is a diversity of policies and practices between state and territory governments. The key policy 'driver' is the failure of new dwelling construction to keep pace with rising demand in the 2000s (National Housing Supply Council, 2011). This is generally attributed to planning and other regulations (Gurran and Phibbs, 2013), although there is little evidence that these increased during this period (Yates, 2011) and it is not clear if changes to the planning system would increase housing supply, because increased urban growth puts pressure on land prices. While there is no overall shortage of land in Australia, there are physical and planning constraints on urban land supply. If urban land scarcity is the problem, then any increase in demand raises house prices (Yates, 2011, p. 276). Demand for housing is projected to continue rising over the next 20 years (National Housing Supply Council, 2011) with the gap between supply and requirements widening so that housing output will need to be raised well above past trends to reduce rising house prices and improve affordability (Gurran and Phibbs, 2013). An annual supply gap of 24 000 homes has been identified (National Housing Supply Council, 2011). Historically, most provision has been made by the private house building industry with a very small public and not-for-profit sector so that the institutional infrastructure for linking private with affordable provision has until recently been limited.

Most state governments do not require affordable housing under Australian planning legislation. Exceptions include South Australia and pilot schemes in NSW. The Australian Capital Territory system can also be characterised as a way of capturing land value for affordable housing as a charge is made when lease conditions specifying land use are changed to permit higher densities. More generally, the zoning system, with its underlying assumed development rights resting with the landowner, affects the supply of land for development and effectively sets land values long before development (Gurran and Whitehead, 2011). This means that the potential to capture development value and to negotiate community benefits such as affordable housing is lost as development potential has been established in advance of planning proposals. It also means that if local authorities want to acquire land that has not yet been zoned for public purposes they must pay the market price.

Because of this, housing for low- and middle-income groups was seen as the remit of the federal government who provided funding for affordable housing. Public housing has become a marginal and highly targeted housing tenure, falling from around 18% of the stock in 1981 to less than 5% in 2009, largely through Right to Buy and reduced public funding (Gurran and Whitehead, 2011). The growing residualisation of this limited amount of public housing, the shortage of publicly owned land and the growing problems of affordability led some states to look at ways the planning system could secure more affordable homes and provide them in mixed communities (Austin *et al.*, 2014). All state governments are in the process of moving from the former government build-and-manage model of affordable housing towards a model where non-governmental actors fill this role – with or without additional government subsidy. Under this new model, the planning system plays a key role in securing affordable housing provision, both through not-for-profit housing development and private sector developer contributions and with an emphasis on attempting to reduce the constraints on supply arising from the planning system (Davison *et al.*, 2012). The reasons for introducing a new model include the tightening supply of traditional forms of public or social housing and declining commitment of public resources for housing (Milligan *et al.*, 2007); the declining access to home ownership for those on the margins of affording this tenure, and a loss of low-cost private rental housing, particularly in high-value well-located areas (Yates *et al.*, 2004); concerns about the macroeconomic and labour market impacts of a shortage of affordable housing (Berry, 2006a, b); and increased evidence of socio-spatial polarisation in Australia's major cities, with low- and moderate-income earners effectively 'priced out' of the housing market in many formerly affordable suburban areas (Yates *et al.*, 2004).

Initiatives to use the planning system to address these issues by securing more affordable homes do not include many state wide schemes but fall into several categories (Davison *et al.*, 2012; Gurran and Whitehead, 2011).

These are measures to retain or offset the loss of affordable homes in new projects (NSW since the 1990s), to overcome local planning barriers to mixed communities (also NSW since the 1990s), to allow planning bonuses for voluntary affordable contributions (some local government areas in NSW since mid-1990s and all of South Australia since 2006) and to introduce mandatory requirements for the same (some inner city areas of NSW and all new residential areas of South Australia).

Most of these initiatives are on redevelopment sites and few are on new greenfield sites. Although the majority require some public subsidy, the links between the funding and planning sectors have been tenuous, limiting what can be achieved. Examples include a pilot inclusionary zoning scheme in Sydney in the early 1990s. In 2001, Brisbane set up its own affordable housing provider with a compulsory development contribution scheme although that did not last after a change in the political control of the council. More recently, in South Australia a 2006 amendment to its Development Act allowed local plans to include provisions for affordable housing which put into practice a State affordable housing target of 15% in new development areas, including 5% high-needs housing. This initially applied to the redevelopment of public land, but is increasingly being extended to private land when major new residential areas are established or rezoned for higher density development. By introducing the planning obligation at the time of a residential rezoning, the costs to the developer are able to be absorbed by the value uplift thus enabling the capture of increased development values for affordable housing (Gurran *et al.*, 2008; Gurran and Whitehead, 2011).

Initiatives in Queensland and NSW are quite different and have not produced the scale of new affordable homes required. In Queensland, a state Urban Land Development Authority was set up in 2007 with a target to provide 15% of all dwellings on its projects as affordable homes funded by inclusionary planning requirements and incentives as well as surpluses arising from the wider redevelopment projects. In NSW, new floorspace bonuses are permitted if affordable rental housing is provided in projects. New affordable housing is allowed on commercial sites where housing would not otherwise be permitted (Gurran and Whitehead, 2011). All states apart from Victoria and Tasmania now permit affordable housing to be a planning matter to be considered under limited circumstances (Austin *et al.*, 2014).

Recently, the government of West Australia consulted on four options to secure more affordable homes through its planning system (Government of Western Australia, 2013). The options were as follows: (i) securing diversity in housing types such as smaller (implicitly lower cost) dwellings; (ii) providing incentives such as density bonuses to encourage provision of affordable homes within schemes; (iii) negotiating affordable homes when land was rezoned; and (iv) making it mandatory for developers to provide affordable homes within new schemes. The consultation paper specifically noted that mandatory provisions worked best when land was rezoned and significant value uplift occurred, ensuring that any cost associated with the affordable homes is offset by the value uplift achieved through rezoning. If mandatory provisions are introduced afterwards, the extra costs of providing the affordable homes would have to absorbed by the developer (which may make any development unprofitable) or passed on to the purchasers of other homes on the site. Following the consultation, the state government agreed that local government should explore the use of voluntary agreements using incentives outlined in local planning documents (Western Australia Planning Commission, 2014).

All these different approaches have generally not achieved affordable housing on the same site as market housing. This has limited the opportunities for mixed communities and made it more difficult for affordable housing providers, primarily community-based providers, to compete in the land market, even when there are opportunities to match their own investment with government funding schemes (Gurran and Whitehead, 2011). Thus, capturing development value to secure affordable housing has been relatively unsuccessful and where it has succeeded has required density bonuses and similar arrangements to ensure that developers make the provision, often in the face of limited political support for securing the provision and in the face of developer resistance, even where the local market provides opportunities for making the provision. This presents a paradox just at a time when community-based associations have grown in scale and asset base making it possible to match this with policies that lever contributions from developers through planning agreements, based on the South Australia model (Austin *et al.*, 2014).

Germany

Planning authorities and the planning system

Local authorities in Germany play important roles in assembling land for development and ensuring a supply of serviced land for development. Planning is carried out within a decentralised system characterised by hierarchical planning powers among the different levels of government and a strong legal framework (Pütz *et al.*, 2011; Sieverts, 2008; Van den Berg, 2008). The government levels involved are the federal government, the 16 state governments, the 114 planning regions and approximately 14000 municipalities. The states, regions and municipalities are the planning authorities while the federal government sets the overall framework and policy to ensure consistency between state, regional and local planning (Schmidt and Buehler, 2007). Under the Federal Spatial Planning Act, the federal government provides the framework for the 16 state governments to exercise spatial planning at the state level. Planning takes different forms in each state, and the weight given to spatial planning differs from state to state (Kunzmann, 2001). The state governments administer federal government financial incentives for development, supplementing them with their own resources. They set quantitative housing targets which the municipalities then translate into land-use plans indicating where housing may be built (Needham, 2012). The principles of 'subsidiarity', 'municipal planning autonomy' and 'mutual influence' are the bases on which the government acts more as 'enabler' than 'provider' in development.

Germany has a strong ethos of environmental management and mechanisms for integrating environmental concerns into decision making such as the long-standing 'landscape plans' which provide, in effect, strategic environmental assessment of other plans and programmes, and regional resource management. Federal spatial planning in Germany is limited essentially to the development of guiding principles which provide the legal basis for state spatial planning and specifications for sectoral planning. The task of federal spatial planning is to focus on sectoral planning and public investment from the point of view of regional and national structural policy. The key decisions are usually taken at the lowest political level, and a higher political level intervenes only if the subject cannot be handled or organised by the lower one. The position of local municipalities, where the main spatial planning authority is located, is strong and municipal autonomy is constitutionally guaranteed. However, there is a collaborative mechanism in the German planning system. On the one hand, the planning strategies from a lower planning tier have to be taken into account when devising plans and principles at a higher level, especially in planning infrastructure. On the other hand, each lower level is obliged to consider the guidelines and principles of the higher level.

Municipal land-use planning is regulated by the Federal Building Code which includes regulations on the content and procedures related to the preparation of local land-use plans and rules for assessing development proposals outside areas covered by these plans. They are the main bodies in the planning process and follow the principles and guidelines from higher planning tiers, in combination with implementing other policies (e.g. housing policies) of the federal and state governments. The municipal administration produces preparatory land-use plans and binding urban land-use plans. Taken together, these are the most influential instruments in German land-use planning. This lowest planning level is responsible for a large number of site-specific recommendations and measures, and adds greater detail to the provisions of the higher planning levels. Preparatory land-use plans set out the municipalities' objectives for future land use and preliminary zone designations for settlement development and for other types of land use.

The urban land-use plans contain very precise and binding designations for all urban development at municipal level, and hence there is little discretion in the German land-use planning system (Pütz *et al.*, 2011). Municipalities are also responsible for providing the infrastructure to support development.

Recently, Germany has placed increased emphasis on regions, as opposed to individual cities or the national economy, as the appropriate scale through which to encourage development (Schmidt and Buehler, 2007). The main task of regional planning is to establish regional plans which are usually part mandatory on local governments and part advisory. Further regional planning tasks include participating in the setting of planning objectives at the local level and establishing sectoral plans and programmes (Pütz *et al.*, 2011). While the German constitution guarantees municipalities the right to independent self-government, in reality municipalities operate within a planning system that requires the cooperation of all levels of government. As such, decisions concerning land use, taxation and economic development usually have to be consistent with the wider regional, state and federal government frameworks (Schmidt and Buehler, 2007).

Germany's economic development has recently been characterised by growing regional disparities, with stronger growth in the west and southwest, especially along the Rhine, Main and Neckar rivers and in Bavaria, than in the north (with the exception of the city of Hamburg) and east. Germany has a large private rented sector which has remained fairly stable over the past three decades. Some 49% of the total housing stock was private rented in 2005 (Kemp and Kofner, 2014), while subsidised dwellings (and dwellings subject to rent regulation and administrative tenant allocation) comprised 14% of the total stock. While home ownership has increased in the former East Germany, the impact of this on Germany as a whole is limited by the relatively small proportion of the total population living in this region. The response to demand for housing is linked to regional policy, that is the commitment for 'balanced development' across regions. Accordingly, significant efforts are made to strengthen economies and reduce outmigration from 'lagging regions' (Beckman *et al.*, 2000). A combination of strong competences, financial incentives and in some cases powers to subsidise housing and/or provide infrastructure has encouraged local authorities to allocate land for housing.

Special mechanisms for controlling growth

The German spatial planning and development control system does not contain any regulations or policies for the containment of urban growth, although the German Federal Building Code, the core document of the statutory planning legislation, states that land shall be used sparingly and with due consideration (Baing, 2010). The legislation also has an emphasis on reusing land and infill development. Many of these regulations are linked to supporting the policy objective of protecting land with good soil from development. The focus is thus less on wider spatial planning objectives but more on avoiding specific loss of good agricultural land. A unique element of the German planning system is the Federal Building Code which contains a regulation to compensate for intrusions into nature and landscape. This compensation either takes place in the same spatial and functional context as the site itself or is pooled to allow landscape improvements on a larger scale (Baing, 2010).

However, these environmental constraints did not prevent extensive urban sprawl during the 1990s. The 2002 National Strategy for Sustainable Development aimed to reduce the rate of urban expansion from 100 to 30 hectares a day by 2020 (Baing, 2010). The policy framework was updated with measures favouring development inside existing urban areas. To encourage redevelopment inside urban areas, a new simplified process intended to make it quicker and more economically viable for investors to develop there has been introduced (Baing, 2010).

Land readjustment

Where the ownership of land is very fragmented within or on the edge of the built-up area, the government can initiate a process of land readjustment (Hayashi, 2000). Land readjustment or 'pooling' has been used for many decades to enable the costs of infrastructure to be shared by all the landowners and the municipality in regeneration schemes. It initially involved rural land for development but was later extended to built-up land. In the 1960s, the Federal Building Act was used to provide large-scale urban development land for residential areas. In the 1970s, its purpose changed to the redevelopment of inner city areas and in the 1990s it changed again in order to address housing shortages as well as to provide land for industries and office buildings (Hayashi, 2000). Land readjustment can be carried out either by voluntary arrangements or through compulsory measures. It can be a total reallocation of land to provide owners with plots suitable for building on and to provide the municipality with land for local infrastructure. It can also be a more limited adjustment of adjacent plot boundaries (Konursay, 2004). This allows the municipality to influence the form of development, recoup the costs of servicing and infrastructure, and possibly to receive some of the uplift in land value, as well as to remove delays caused by a lack of infrastructure.

The municipality decides the boundary of the scheme, the rights and claims of all plots within the area are established and added together, and then land for public uses such as streets and public space is appropriated from the total land area. The remaining private property will be returned to all owners according to their share of the original value or land area. If it is divided according to value, the landowner has to pay the uplift in value to the municipality, which enables the latter to recoup the costs of infrastructure. If it is returned to the original owners, the municipality retains the increase in value up to 30% on greenfield land and up to 10% on inner city land. However, there can be difficulties in bringing land forward because of regional or local governments' reluctance to allocate land of any kind in their plans. This occurs for example in high demand areas where there are planning constraints on suburban expansion in more urbanised regions because of regional planning policy preferences to protect green space (Ball, 2012).

'Circular land-use management' was introduced in 2002 to reduce land utilisation (that is, to reduce the land 'take' for housing by increasing the density of development). It builds on the concept of a use cycle from the allocation of building land through its development, use, eventual abandonment and reuse. It allows the zoning of new land for development on a small scale under certain conditions. The aim is to reduce new development on greenfield sites and to reuse brownfield land (Preuß and Ferber, 2006). Research by Preuß and Ferber (2008) suggested that economic instruments for circular land-use management needed a mix of policies to (i) influence property prices (e.g. by reforming the property tax system or land-transfer tax reform) to roll back/decrease the incentives to build on previously undeveloped sites for public and private parties who want to build; (ii) introduce price mechanisms for zoning new land for development (such as establishing tradeable land-use certificates or apportioning building land for zoning in combination with cost-benefit analysis) to further motivate municipalities to encourage development in previously developed land; and (iii) create financing options and tailor funding measures to suit circular land-use management (e.g. by reforming the fiscal equalization scheme at municipal level, low-interest loans, real estate funds, demolition liability insurance and subsidising re-naturalisation) to greatly strengthen development on previously developed land. They also found that a circular land-use management policy requires cooperation between the German federal government and other important groups of stakeholders – the states, public stakeholders at the municipal and regional levels, private enterprise, institutions which own land, the real estate industry and private households and small-scale property owners – in order to establish appropriate framework conditions for circular land-use management.

Provision of housing and related infrastructure

In Germany, the provision of local infrastructure is the sole responsibility of the local authority that can use grants from the state, and/or charges on landowners to recover the costs (Oxley *et al.*, 2009). Because plans tend to involve extensive negotiation between a wide variety of local agencies and require subsidy commitments by some levels of government in order to achieve desired planning outcomes, Ball (2012) argued that Germany had a slow response to sudden increases in housing demand. Additionally, some municipalities refuse to sanction land release for housing construction because they are concerned that they will have to bear the full infrastructure costs associated with suburban expansion. This is a consequence of the lengthy and uncertain time before revenue receipts from property taxes and state subventions become available as a consequence of those investments. It is now government policy to stimulate housing building within existing built-up areas, especially through regeneration projects in the east and north of the country. Municipalities have a high degree of government involvement in the housing development process (Schmidt and Buehler, 2007). They often acquire or own property and can supply housing land actively by offering it from their own land banks and by releasing their land holdings in the built-up area. Also, they can designate urban redevelopment zones where development is desired but is not taking place (such as large derelict sites and greenfield sites) by purchasing all the land at existing use value (Baing, 2010).

While a developer acquires the building site, it is the responsibility of the municipality to service the land and provide the infrastructure (streets, parking areas, technical services, green space and also 'social infrastructure' such as playgrounds). This puts municipalities in a strong position to influence common facilities and to recoup the related costs. The applicant for a building permit on such a site is required to contribute to those costs, to a maximum of 90%, with the remaining costs (at least 10%) paid by the municipality (Needham, 2012). Special local laws are used by municipalities to vary the level of charges for landowners (Oxley *et al.*, 2009). The actual provision of the infrastructure is commissioned by the municipality. In addition, the owner has to pay the costs of measures to compensate for any destruction of nature and landscape caused by the development (Baing, 2010). However, if the municipality demands too much, land will not be brought onto the market. There are also a range of loans, subsidies and cheap building land available for constructing both owner-occupied and rented housing, which are targeted at households with a limited income (Needham, 2012).

The Netherlands

Planning institutions and planning policies

The Netherlands is a decentralised unitary state with a planning system which places great emphasis on environmental protection, land conservation, preventing development in rural areas and preserving open spaces

(Needham, 2007; Oxley *et al.*, 2009). It has mechanisms that create vertical and horizontal integration between levels of government and between sectors (Newman and Thornley, 1996). Tensions have been growing between sectors, especially environment, land-use planning and economic development and especially between spatial and infrastructure planning (Wolsink, 2003). The dominance of the public sector in determining spatial development has also weakened in favour of more market-oriented approaches. Until recently, land-use planning had a 'top down' and highly prescriptive approach with central government setting policy that was then implemented by each municipality's adopted land-use plan. Building permits are only granted if proposed developments conform to such plans.

Dutch planning has also had a strong master planning and engineering heritage, a reflection of the Netherlands need, going back over many centuries, to work collectively to reclaim land, create flood defences and build drainage systems (Faludi and van der Valk, 1994). Planning has thus been about creating plans, raising the investment to realise them and giving approvals for projects (Oxley *et al.*, 2009). Local authorities play important roles in this, either assembling land for development or promoting schemes that support the supply of serviced land for residential development. Although property rights continue to rest with the landowner, municipalities have, for many years, purchased land, serviced it and parcelled it into smaller plots and sold them on to developers at a price covering the infrastructure costs.

In the past, the Netherlands had a three-tiered hierarchy of plans involving central government, provinces and municipalities (the latter include water boards). Central government set overall aims and the key spatial strategy and each province had its own regional plan. These were implemented through detailed and binding land-use zoning plans adopted by municipalities and framed within their own structure plans, but approved by their province. In the early post-war years, central government played major roles in making (and implementing) development plans but latterly there has been more emphasis on local decision making and public–private partnerships (Busck *et al.*, 2009), reflecting changes in the socio-economic environment and greater roles for private development and investment.

Dutch provinces and municipalities all have the same statutory powers for purchasing undeveloped land, installing the necessary services and parcelling it up for sale to private developers at a price that covers the costs. However, in recent years there has been a move away from public sector-led development to more market-oriented approaches. Under the New Spatial Planning Act 2008, the hierarchy of plans has been removed so that strategic level goals have no binding power, only legal ordinances have that power. Each tier now generally has the same planning powers so that national government can now create a structure plan at the local level to deliver its own strategy (covering matters of national significance), provinces can do the same (e.g. on urbanisation policy), whilst municipalities can adopt their own local plans without seeking provincial approval. Central government, province and municipality each have to set out their own spatial policy in a new instrument, the 'structure vision'. Municipal land-use plans have been retained as the most important planning instrument. They are legally binding, over the whole of each municipality, must be prepared and also must be revised every 10 years. If proposed developments conform to the plan, they must be granted permission. If not they must be refused, although it is possible to subsequently amend the plan to allow development to proceed. Hence, while there is no discretion, in practice plans can be amended to enable acceptable development to proceed. Municipal plans can also specify the different types of housing that can be built: social renting (with definitions about maximum rents), social owner-occupied housing (with definitions about maximum prices and stipulations, who owns and for how long) and privately commissioned housing. Hence, a form of inclusionary zoning is possible with the Dutch planning system, although its potential has not been fully realised because municipalities have been slow to recognise the benefits (de Kam, 2014).

Dutch cities have strong initiatives to control urban sprawl, protect green spaces and prevent ribbon development (Zonneveld, 2007; Halleux *et al.*, 2012). Current planning for urban development has concentrated development in the Randstad, a poly-nuclear pattern of urban centres in the western part of the Netherlands (including the major cities of Amsterdam, The Hague, Rotterdam and Utrecht). In the 1970s and 1980s, spatial planning channelled development into designated 'growth centres' (Dieleman *et al.*, 1999) and in the mid-1980s, national policy aimed for even stricter control through a 'compact city' policy (Geurs and van Wee, 2006).

The compact city policy is now a key element of Dutch urban planning (Korthals Altes and Tambach, 2008). It was originally a local initiative facilitated by central government through the provision of urban development grants and policy designed to create high urban densities, so that open space outside of cities could be preserved. Now building on previously developed land is a top priority (Korthals Altes, 2007). In the major cities of Amsterdam, Rotterdam and The Hague, a period of decline during the 1970s was followed by substantial growth in the 1980s, 1990s and early 2000s. In 2004, the Dutch Government set a target of 25%–40% (depending on the region) of all houses to be built within existing built-up areas (Halleux *et al.*, 2012). Nearly all provinces succeeded in achieving this target (Buitelaar, 2012). Housing growth is now concentrated in 26 urban regions. The first priority is to build on locations within built-up areas, second on greenfield land directly adjoining the central city, preferably within cycling distance and third in areas adjoining other towns and villages in the urban region, including former growth centres (Korthals Altes, 2007). This policy has succeeded in producing a large increase in housing within cities in relatively compact form during the 1980s, when major state funding was made available for urban renewal (Dieleman *et al.*, 1999).

Changing housing policies

After the Second World War, the government's strong spatial planning strategy was supported and reinforced by a comprehensive housing policy with one ministry responsible for both housing and planning (Priemus, 1998). About 95% of all housing production was subsidised in the 1950s (van der Schaar, 1987) and by subsidising most housing projects, the Dutch central government exerted a strong influence over the location as well as the production of new dwellings (Faludi and van der Valk, 1994).

Until the 1990s, there was not a market-led approach to the provision of housing and infrastructure. The supply of land and housing was funded and regulated by central government and driven by municipalities and, increasingly from the 1970s, also by large and well-resourced not-for-profit housing associations. This produced a distinctive housing tenure in the Netherlands, with a large and diversified social housing sector, peaking at 42% in the 1980s (Milligan, 2003). However, since the 1990s, profound political, economic, demographic and social changes in the Netherlands have contributed to fundamental shifts in housing (and related planning and regulatory policies) and in the structure and operation of the Dutch housing market.

Owner occupation in the Netherlands rose from 45% to 57% between 1990 and 2010 and social renting declined from more than 40% to 35% (Andrews *et al.*, 2011). Private renting fell from 17% to 8% between 1980 and 2010 (Van der Heijden and Boelhouwer, 1996; Andrews *et al.*, 2011; Haffner, 2014). Housing output was also falling behind demand, declining to around 20 000 units a year in the 1990s, compared with 60 000 in the 1980s. The reason was a lack of effective demand, although limited land supply was also a factor in periods of higher demand.

In this move to more market-led housing provision, there has been an increasing emphasis on promoting owner occupation, although Dutch housing associations remain significant producers of new housing. National urban renewal policy (from 1995) has focused on promoting a greater mix of tenure in those areas with high concentrations of social housing, by building for homeowners and demolishing or selling social rented housing. Most direct government subsidies for the provision of social housing and for urban renewal were withdrawn in the 1990s. Since then housing associations have had to rely mainly on their own resources to undertake housing development or renewal projects (Gurran *et al.*, 2007). However, the Dutch government continues to provide location subsidies for infrastructure development and site remediation, as well as block grants to cities and municipalities for stimulating urban renewal processes. Regional provinces also use location subsidies in particular to influence the distribution of where new social housing is supplied in the region.

Providing land and related infrastructure

The supply of residential land is controlled by municipal governments (Vermeulen and Rouwendal, 2007). In the past this was mainly achieved through an 'active land policy' (Buitelaar, 2010; De Kam, 2013; Van der Krabben and Needham, 2008) whereby most designated development land was bought and sold by municipal land companies (van der Valk, 2002). In a country where much of the land is below sea level, the state inevitably takes a major role in planning and providing expensive site infrastructure. Municipalities thus bought land, subdivided it, provided the infrastructure and the utilities, and sold off the subdivided plots to property developers, housing associations or owner occupiers (the latter building for their own occupation). Municipalities could use a municipal pre-emption right of compulsory purchase to facilitate land assembly by designating an area within which a landowner who wanted to sell their property was obliged to first offer it to the municipality (Buitelaar, 2010). Initially, this only applied to urban renewal areas but when land assembly for urban extension areas was inhibited by private land acquisition and speculation in the 1990s and led to rising land prices, its application was extended to greenfield locations. Between 2000 and 2006, the use of pre-emption rights doubled from 33% of all municipalities in 2000 to 68% in 2006, or from a total of 22 700 hectares to 40 800 hectares (Buitelaar, 2010). Under this system, the costs of construction were subtracted from the potential sales revenues to give a residual land value that is used to finance the acquisition and conversion of land, and the provision of local public goods. This system thus levies an (implicit) tax on the development value of residential development land (Vermeulen and Rouwendal, 2007). Two thirds of dwellings were built in the year 2000 with this land development model (Groetelaers and Korthals Altes, 2004), but this proportion has since decreased. The model whilst heavily used with respect to the development of newly developed land was much less used with respect to redevelopment (Van der Krabben and Needham, 2008).

Where active land policy is not pursued, a 'facilitatory policy' enables developers to build on their own land provided they get planning consent and pay a fee to cover the infrastructure costs. Initially, these payments were negotiated under agreements, but in 2008 they were made mandatory. This requires local authorities to have land development and servicing plans as part of their land-use plans which set out formulae for calculating the cost to the public sector and their recovery from developers, including options to charge lower fees to those building new social housing – and recovering

losses arising from such concessions from private developers. Getting planning consent is conditional on developers paying the infrastructure charges.
Charges are based on recovering the costs of public facilities. In calculating
these costs, the initial value of the plot (e.g. the standardised costs of land
acquisition) and the future value (based on the possible use of the serviced
building plot) are taken into account. Where there is no land development
and servicing plan, developer contributions to infrastructure costs are subject to negotiation. In practice, the latter approach dominates with most
municipalities preferring to negotiate an agreement than to draw up a land
development and servicing plan because of the latter's complexity and risks
of legal challenge (de Kam, 2014).

The use of trade-offs in both active and facilitatory approaches whereby
more profitable land uses cross-subsidisation for less profitable uses means
that the implicit taxation of development value at one location is explicitly
linked to the funding of development at another location (de Jong and Spaans,
2009). In this way, cross-subsidisation enables high infrastructure costs to
be part funded from other profitable developments. A combination of high
agricultural land prices and high infrastructure costs also suggests that the
development values gained by developers are quite low, with profits coming
from sales of new homes and not from land trading (De Kam, 2013; Korthals
Altes, 2009; Oxley *et al.*, 2009).

As we have seen, housing associations were the main providers of social
rented housing in the Netherlands. As well as being directly subsidised by
central government, they also relied on municipalities, especially for land. In
the early 1990s, subsidies for housing construction were removed and housing associations were liberalised. The proportion of low-cost social housing
in the housing programme fell from 73% to 18% between 1991 and 2001
(Korthals Altes, 2007). As land values increased, municipalities became less
willing to buy land explicitly for social housing and housing associations
instead acquired land directly from property developers or landowners, with
the percentage acquired from municipalities falling from 60% to less than
15% between 1995 and 2008 (Buitelaar, 2010). As housing associations currently receive no subsidies (with the exception of housing for special needs),
every new unit constructed makes a loss (capitalised net rental income being
less than the costs of construction), even when land is purchased relatively
cheaply. Housing associations can raise cheap loans on the security of their
existing stock and because of government guarantees, and cover losses from
reserves, selling existing housing (market values exceeding historic costs) or
by building expensive housing for sale. The inclusionary housing policy has
not had as much impact as intended despite the formal inclusion of policies in municipal plans, partly because other ways of securing land for social
housing available before the inclusionary policy was introduced to enable

housing associations to secure the land they need, including through their construction of mixed tenure housing schemes (de Kam, 2013).

The Dutch planning system has thus exercised strong controls over the location of development and supported development in desired locations. Thus, it is the availability of land at particular locations rather than the total supply of land that has been restrained. To ensure that land is suitable for development, large infrastructure costs have to be incurred. Korthals Altes (2007, p. 235) claims that 'the Netherlands has long been considered a text-book example of the combination of strong urban planning controls and an ample supply of developable land'. Its highly regulated planning system has been able to provide fully serviced plots because a balance has been struck between restriction and the encouragement of development on sites that were in line with planning policies and serviced with infrastructure.

However, this has now changed and fully serviced housing plots are no longer easily available for a cost-related price. Developers expect to pay current market prices and there is more uncertainty about market sales and greater complexity in terms of production (Korthals Altes and Groetelaers, 2007). There are now strong arguments that the availability of development land has not kept up with demand and this has had adverse consequences for housebuilding levels. As Oxley *et al.* (2009) reported, the previous arrangements kept house prices stable, but more recently house prices have risen steeply and local governments are now competing with developers to buy agricultural land. As a result, rising prices go hand in hand with stagnating housing production in a highly regulated system of land-use planning (Korthals Altes and Groetelaers, 2007). Falls in production between 2000 and 2004 have been blamed on attempts by the central government to combine market-oriented housing production with strong environmental constraints and to concentrate house building in urban areas (Boelhouwer *et al.*, 2006).

United States

The constitution, planning and its administration

The USA has a LME and a liberal welfare state and a decentralised political system. It has a great variety of separate land-use planning systems. Land-use planning is a matter for each local government (which are creatures of the states) and not the federal government. Some states have enabling legislation on planning regulations while others largely delegate this to all or some of their local governments. As a result, the courts are often the only way local government actions can be challenged. The federal government has of course played an indirect role through its other responsibilities, such as highways, and specifically in terms of supporting affordable housing through a range of subsidies and tax credits (Herbert *et al.*, 2012; Schwartz, 2006). The latter can be combined with local planning powers, especially inclusionary zoning (see below) to secure new provision. Property rights are protected in the constitution and thus the removal of rights is limited by the constitution unless compensation is paid. This not only applies to the compulsory purchase of land but any regulation that may diminish land value can be considered as a regulatory 'taking', and this places limits on capturing development value, for example by impact fees (Cullingworth, 1993; Hagman and Misczynski, 1978; Nelson *et al.*, 2008; Wakeford, 1990).

The ideological primacy of the market, the protection afforded to property and the very local basis of planning all limit what planning can achieve and also lead to a wide variety of local approaches to zoning and to its underlying policy objectives. Land-use planning is thus primarily limited to addressing efficiency objectives by dealing with market failures, specifically externalities, and not (in general) promoting equity and the pursuit of social justice through spatial planning.

The importance attached to decisions being made at the very local level includes matters related to property and sales taxes thus limiting the sharing of expenditure and revenues across metropolitan areas with several jurisdictions (e.g. the state of Pennsylvania has over a thousand local governments). It places limits on what can be achieved through spatial planning at the strategic level. It also limits shared services so that each local jurisdiction has to raise much of the capital and revenue itself to provide essential facilities including key infrastructure to service new development. Because property taxes are crucial to a local government's income, zoning is used to maintain the tax base and to limit the development of land uses that require expensive public provision or which may lower the tax base.

Land-use planning is undertaken at the local level within each state (counties and districts). Local police power for the health, safety and welfare of people is the legal basis for zoning maps which define permitted land uses, including the specification of relevant standards (Pendall *et al.*, 2006). The landmark Euclid case in the federal Supreme Court held zoning to be a valid exercise of police power in the interests of general welfare but that the conception of welfare was a purely local one (Cullingworth, 1993). Zoning can be permissive in the sense of permitting a range of possible uses on a given site or it can be very restrictive by limiting what is allowed to one specific use. While compliance with the zoning plan is mandatory, it is possible to obtain departures from zoning plans by seeking consent from the relevant authority. The courts have held that zoning is not in itself a taking, provided the regulation is in pursuit of public purposes and the owner is not deprived of an economically viable use of the land. The 14th amendment guaranteeing equal treatment before the law limits the use of discretion that local government can use in the pursuit of their zoning plans. There has been very little debate about explicitly capturing land value increments to fund infrastructure and affordable housing (Hagman and Misczynski, 1978; Mallach and Calavita, 2010).

Limits are placed on urban development specifically through the use of urban growth and urban service boundaries and areas (Anthony, 2004, 2006; Gale, 1992; Monk *et al.*, 2013; Pendall *et al.*, 2002; Pollakowski and Wachter, 1990; Schmidt and Buehler, 2007). The latter two are designed to secure the most economic provision of infrastructure for supporting new development, especially water and sewerage, by limiting where they can be constructed and ensuring new provision is sensibly sequenced, backed up by zoning or other ordinances which prevent development until it can be hooked up to new infrastructure and finance is in place to build the infrastructure. They deal mainly with water, sewerage, transportation and open spaces and less with other facilities such as schools. Urban growth boundaries are found in many metropolitan areas (e.g. Portland in Oregon State) and are used to limit urban growth by preventing growth outside the boundaries. They appear to have impacts on prices in property markets as well as increasing the density of development within the boundaries. This is particularly true if local zoning is not used to increase the supply of land zoned for housing nor as a means of securing more affordable homes. Boundaries are set out in local and county plans and are only rarely coordinated at the metropolitan level, although a handful of states require them. Their use has grown in recent years, especially in Western and Mid-Atlantic states, and generally their aim is to shape rather than constrain growth. State growth management policies shape the pattern of development by requiring counties and local districts to integrate zoning plans and ordinances, taxation and development impact fees policies, and growth and service boundaries. That this does not always happen, despite mandated policies and regulations, is testament to the power of local government to make its own decisions.

Developer contributions to infrastructure: impact fees

As far as infrastructure provision is concerned, many local governments charge developers impact fees to pay for off-site capital provision (and exactions pay for on-site infrastructure). These fees are a regulatory matter and not a financing device, and the authority to charge comes from state statute or from 'home rule' powers. They are a pervasive part of the US system of planning, having evolved from subdivision controls (Nelson, 1988; Nelson *et al.*, 2008). They are used in almost all states and have become increasingly important as local government finances have become more and more constrained, with local politicians loathe to ask voters to pay more in taxes, especially property taxes, and with little funding for infrastructure coming from federal and state governments, despite increased mandates requiring local government to upgrade facilities and at higher standards (e.g. to reduce water pollution). This was exacerbated by the emergence of a 'benefit' principle rather than an 'ability to pay' principle underpinning taxation. Fees thus emerged as the key alternative in the 1970s, especially in areas of rapid development such as Florida. Fees evolved at the local level and were neither federal nor state government initiatives. They were designed both to slow down development by facing developers with the costs of their infrastructure or at least to ensure that existing residents did not have to pay to provide it for newcomers (Wakeford, 1990).

Fees are charged under the aegis of local police powers as these allow local governments to protect their citizens' health, safety and general welfare from the detrimental aspects of urban growth and also enable them to reconcile the demands for growth and services with the demands for lower taxes. Fees and land development dedications are also regarded as more appropriate than negotiated 'exactions' as they provide certainty and speed. They are also seen as more equitable because the fees are based on the costs required to support new development, typically being schedules of charges related to the size of proposed developments (e.g. $x per dwelling). Evidence in the 1980s suggested that negotiations were more likely to occur in areas where the property markets were buoyant and presented more opportunities to maximise charges (Bunnell, 1995). As developers are paying for the new infrastructure through fees, this not only generates significant local revenue but also reduces local opposition to new development. Fees have increased ahead of both general and construction cost inflation rising from an average of $5781 in 1988 to $11 012 for single-detached family houses in 2004, partly reflecting the rising costs of provision but also the increasing number of utilities whose funding is based upon fees (Nelson *et al.*, 2008).

Fees are designed to fund system improvements benefiting many development projects or even the entire local government area whereas project-level improvements, benefiting a single development, are dealt with by project-level agreements. Impact fees are calculated by analysing the numbers of people in each specific development and multiplying this by the infrastructure required by each person and the costs of provision. Care is taken to eliminate double charging, particularly the future stream of property tax income levied on the new developments. The calculations are made for each geographically defined service area. Fee schedules and any exemptions (e.g. for affordable housing) are required to be published in a comprehensive local plan in some states (and desirable practice in any case). If fees are not used, they have to be repaid, either to the current owner, if the fee runs with the land, or the original payer. Steps also have to be taken to ensure those who pay benefit from the facilities provided. The most common use of fees is water supply and waste water sewerage, followed by transport, including highways and bridges. As fees are only paid when development proceeds, or is completed, this creates a problem funding the upfront costs of the major works needed for these developments, a problem addressed by local governments borrowing against the security of future fees income. Fees have high administrative costs for local governments in terms of devising schedules and levying fees. Despite this, fees are usually a small proportion of development costs and the income received is also a small proportion of overall local government capital expenditure.

Some states have statutes authorising fees but not necessarily for all local governments, so for example Arkansas has given municipalities, but not counties, authorisation to collect fees for water and waste water facilities (Nelson *et al.*, 2008). Fees are closely scrutinised by the courts since the use of the police power has to be exercised in accordance with the taking clause in the 5th amendment to the constitution which permits the taking of property rights for public use only with payment of just compensation whilst the 14th amendment ensures due process and equal protection before the law. Critics of fees argue that they are neither constitutional nor authorised by state statute and hence *ultra vires* or, if there is statutory authority, a fee ordinance is a disguised tax which violates state strictures on taxation. Critics also argue that fees are discriminatory as different developers may pay different amounts, prior developers may have paid nothing and fees violate property rights since they are a 'taking' without compensation.

In the light of the US Supreme Court decisions in the Nollan and Dolan cases, and provided local governments follow the dual rational nexus and rough proportionality rules, the courts have generally held that fees are a valid exercise of police powers by showing that the development causes a need for the facilities in question, and that the contribution required is proportionate to that need and will be used to provide the facility (Nolan *et al.*, 2008; Purdue *et al.*, 1992). This requires demonstrating a rational nexus between the charge exacted and the need generated by the development upon which it is based. Local authorities also need to show that what is provided from the fee provides some benefit to the payer of the fee (and hence is not a 'taking' without compensation since value would have been returned) and that the charge is roughly proportionate to the need for the facility provided (which permits average fees for all dwellings and hence they need not be differentiated by size of dwellings) and is spent on, and only on, the facilities which the development generated. Demonstrating exclusiveness of benefit is also important and by charging fees only to those that create the need for the new facility allows those that are not using the service to be excluded from paying fees. Fees cannot be charged on new development to resolve deficiencies in the existing system, only to upgrade them in relation to the demand generated by new development. If these tests are not proven, courts may dismiss the fee as an unauthorised tax or a non-permissible exercise of local government police power. But over the years, despite continuing litigation by developers, the courts have generally upheld fees as proper regulatory measures and not unconstitutional taxation.

The impact of fees on prices and land values

There has been much debate and discussion about the impact of fees on house prices and land values (Been, 2005; Ihlandfeldt and Shaughnessy, 2004; Lefcoe, 1993; Nelson *et al.*, 2008) and also about the impact of urban growth management (e.g. see Brueckner, 2000). Much recent work assumes that impact fees work in a normally competitive market with a normal price elasticity of demand. Most are implemented in growth areas where every local government area faces competition in the housing market from another. Earlier work assumed that fees impacted on price and developers' profits and reduced supply in the short run, and that the share of the fee between land owners, builders and house buyers depended on the relative elasticities of supply and demand for land and houses. Such work assumed that fees would impact on the price of existing as well as new homes in so far as they were close substitutes. Because developers were assumed to have choice about where to build and could operate across several local government areas, it was assumed that fees were either priced into what consumers paid for new dwellings or backwards into what developers paid for the land. But others (Been, 2005; Yinger, 2008) have argued that consumers are prepared to pay for the higher prices because they value the new facilities provided and are capitalising the lower property taxes they would otherwise have to pay for these in what they are willing to pay for new homes. Recent work also countenances the former view that landowners pay by arguing that fees increase the overall supply of developable land and it is this that results in lower land prices, not the impact fees.

The empirical evidence suggests that fees lead to higher prices because fees reduce uncertainties for developers, reduce potential property taxes for those who buy the new homes and that owners are prepared to pay for new community facilities (and buyers of existing homes for improvements to existing facilities e.g. because school overcrowding falls). The impact on lower priced, compared to higher priced homes, is proportionate to their value. There is no evidence from any research on the impact of fees on the prices of undeveloped land. Evidence on the impact on new construction, especially on affordable housing, is ambiguous and fewer good studies exist than those that look at price effects. What evidence there is suggests that fees increase output in suburban areas (demand side effect and improving the speed at getting other permits) and do not reduce it in inner city areas. The positive impact for affordable units is limited to inner city area, with exclusionary zoning restricting their development elsewhere.

Developer contributions to affordable housing: inclusionary zoning and linkage fees

As far as housing and zoning plans are concerned, zoning can be exclusionary because by defining minimum lot sizes, densities and house sizes in particular areas it does not permit the construction, say, of low-cost housing (Downs, 1973) or can be inclusionary by permitting, say, higher densities or more floor space than normally allowed if some affordable housing is also provided in specific locations or areas. The use of the latter measures came to the fore after local communities in the 1970s onwards perceived that existing federal measures including public housing programmes (withdrawn in the 1980s) and low-income housing tax credits were not providing adequate levels of affordable housing. Nor was this being addressed by the filtering down of once newly built housing which had become too expensive. Inclusionary zoning (IZ hereinafter) requires or encourages (through incentives) developers to include housing for low- and medium-income households in their developments, for example to make 20 of 100 new dwellings available to low- or medium-income households. It also makes it possible for those occupying this affordable housing to live in areas normally inaccessible to them by virtue of the high rents or prices prevailing. The first such approaches were enacted in the early 1970s in Virginia, Maryland and California but since the 1990s has spread to other states and specifically a number of big cities, including New York and Chicago (Brunick, 2004; Mallach and Calavita, 2010; Schwartz, 2006).

IZ is normally implemented through zoning ordinances but it can also be produced in other ways, including building permit approvals and negotiations. Local authorities differ in what percentage of new homes they want to be affordable (but most are in the range of 10%–20%), how affordability is defined (mainly in relation to area wide median incomes) and for how long the homes have to remain affordable (usually between 10 and 30 years), and to whom. In return, developers get increases in densities or floor space on the rest of a development (or other waivers including on fees and standards) to help fund the affordable housing element, although some arrangements allow developers to buy themselves out of the obligation by a one-off fee payment to a housing trust fund or agreement to make provision elsewhere themselves. A few local governments in very high demand housing market areas have imposed IZ without the need for bonuses. Generally, the ordinances apply throughout a local government area but may not apply to some zones, for example small lots and high-rise buildings. The first IZ policy to take effect was in Montgomery County, Maryland in 1974 where 13 000 IZ homes have since been constructed. Although over 600 local authorities have adopted IZ policies and some 130 000 to 150 000 homes (depending on the source of estimates) have been built in the last four decades, most (until the 1990s) were in affluent suburban communities and in three states (California, Massachusetts and New Jersey which require almost all local authorities to implement IZ) plus Washington DC. Most are located in lower-income neighbourhoods than other programmes that fund new affordable homes and in recent years more cities are using this approach. Some local governments have topped up the developer funding with their own contributions, especially if they require provision for very low-income households. Other states (including Connecticut, Rhodes Island, Oregon and Florida) encourage IZ through zoning plans but have not made this mandatory, so cannot insist on compliance.

The courts have generally held that IZ is a lawful pursuit of land-use regulation. In the landmark Mount Laurel decision, the New Jersey Supreme Court ruled that every municipality in the state had to offer housing for all income groups and each had to take its fair share of the region's housing needs. Most localities require up to 20% of units to be for low-income households in exchange for density bonuses but in 2004 the state of New Jersey required authorities to require one affordable dwelling to be provided for every eight market homes built and for every 25 jobs created. At the end of 2003, 315 of New Jersey's 566 municipalities had IZ ordinances in place. The state's affordable housing act also allows municipalities to transfer half of their fair share allocation to other municipalities. All told nearly 70 000 new affordable homes have been built or converted following the Mount Laurel decision.

California has policies in places that require local governments to provide for a fair share of regional needs for affordable housing in their local general plans (and has produced a model ordinance) but is unable to ensure their compliance with these policies. Although there was much opposition to these policies, especially in the 1980s and 1990s, with only one in five localities having housing plans in place and submitting them for state approval, recent years have seen more adopting them as concern grew about the lack of affordable homes in the state and by 2002 seven in ten had adopted housing policies as part of their general plans. Those with IZ are mostly in the expensive housing areas along the Pacific coast.

In general, however, IZ has fallen far short of its alleged potential. This is because it depends on the strength of the local housing markets and its volatility over time and on the types of development taking place (less is produced when developers shift to smaller units) and without targeted additional subsidy IZ cannot help those with less than 60% to 80% of area median income. Policies that mandate local governments to include housing policies to meet the needs of low-income households typically do not have precedence over environmental protection policies with few plans addressing how zoning (including density and IZ approaches) might improve the supply of new affordable homes. However, there is evidence that the requirement to include such policies does improve understanding of the issues even if it has not yet led to the incorporation of policies (Aurand, 2014). And in Massachusetts, a combination of central state and local government action secured 32 500 affordable dwellings for those with less than 80% of the median income and opened up the suburbs to mainly moderate-income groups which local communities and house builders find more acceptable than low-income households (Hananel, 2013).

Linkage fees

Because of concerns that impact fees worsen the affordability of housing for low- and medium-income residents (by increasing the price of dwellings), some local governments have begun to explore using fees to fund what have been called 'soft' facilities including child care, public art and affordable housing. Such fees are called 'linkage fees' to distinguish them from impact fees and are charged to developers of new commercial floor space whose developments require extra child care facilities and affordable dwellings for the workers employed in the new offices, shops and the like. The courts have held that such fees do not represent unconstitutional takings but a charge to cover the costs of new provision which rationally relate to the new commercial development. Linkages fees have thus been justified by the same rational nexus and proportionality arguments that justify impact fees in general. But they are also seen as more akin to a betterment type levy (hence a taking) than impact fees.

Summary and conclusions: comparing the English and international experience

Our four case-study countries exhibit different approaches to securing a share of the development values that arise when planning consent is granted and to using it to fund infrastructure and other community needs, including affordable housing. However, in none of them is there any formal taxation of development value.

Municipalities in Germany and the Netherlands, both operating within a hierarchical system of planning strategies and adopted local plans, secure contributions to infrastructure and affordable homes by a variety of means, but both rely on a system of prescriptive zoning plans to enable them to do so. These plans (and associated documents such as those related to infrastructure costs), authorised under national legislation, permit municipalities to collect infrastructure costs from developers, either through a charging system or through the prior acquisition of development land which is then serviced by the municipalities and sold on to developers at market prices taking account of the work done. Where neither of these approaches operates, municipalities negotiate costs with developers. These methods secured the serviced development land needed to build the large numbers of new homes required after the Second World War and also provided a framework for the allocation of housing funds. Zoning plans in the Netherlands also distinguish the land needed for different housing tenures, including affordable housing. In more recent years, these systems have changed as a more plural and market-oriented approach to development emerged. As a result, land banking or land re-adjustment is now less central than in the past with a greater reliance on a private market in land in parallel with more negotiations to secure infrastructure contributions. In some ways, the planning systems in both the Netherlands and Germany match the nature of CMEs. They also reflect the needs of both countries after the last war to plan for substantial reconstruction and to build many new homes, whilst also protecting valuable agricultural and other rural land. In the Netherlands, the systematic approach matched the planning heritage of a country that has long worked collectively to win and to protect its land from the sea.

In both Australia and the USA, development rights lie with landowners and there is also no formal tax on development value. Unlike Germany and the Netherlands, the systems to secure contributions from developers for infrastructure and affordable housing are not in general *de facto* levies. Nor is there in either country a national planning system with a hierarchy of plans from national strategic to local land-use plans conforming to and implementing higher level strategies. In the USA, contributions to infrastructure are very much a matter for local councils. There is no national planning legislation, and prescriptive land-use zoning plans are legitimised in terms of the use of police powers to secure the health and safety of local citizens. The practice of charging impact fees to help pay for infrastructure arose from the problems local authorities experienced in raising infrastructure funding through property and other local taxes. The sanctity of property rights is embedded in the federal constitution so that any 'taking' of these rights (such as charging impact fees) must be constitutional. As a result, a highly codified set of legal principles has developed, subject to judgements both in the federal and state supreme courts, to enable impact fees to be levied by demonstrating a rational nexus and proportionality to the developments for which fees are charged. Likewise, the practice of using IZ to secure more affordable housing arose from local initiatives partly to break the hold of exclusionary zoning and partly also to provide a land-use framework for federal and state funding for new affordable homes. To cover developers' costs in providing such housing, they are often incentivised by density and other zoning bonuses. Over time, some states have legitimised this practice in legislation, but it is mainly in the form of facilitating rather than mandating the practice.

There are similarities to the USA in the approaches taken in Australia where there is also no nationwide policy or practice, but varying approaches in each state. As with the USA, planning aims to address market failures rather than pursue broader social and economic objectives. Australian states have discretion when deciding on planning applications, although zoning plans set out permissible uses. Every state and territory has legislation permitting the levying of infrastructure charges, but the details vary about what may be funded and how. The practice of charging arose (as in the USA) following restrictions on local councils' finances. Councils' discretion is limited as they must demonstrate a rational nexus and proportionality in their charging policies and schedules. Securing affordable housing through the planning system is much more limited in Australian states and territories than in the other three countries examined in this chapter and although practice is developing, little has been secured to date and the legal authority to secure affordable housing varies. The need to develop policy has grown out of the increasing restrictions on the limited stock of social housing at a time when housing output lags behind need and demand. In some states, developers are provided with bonuses to help fund the provision of affordable homes on development sites. Practice initially developed for regeneration sites, but is now emerging on greenfield sites as well.

The English experience (see Chapters 3 and 4 and 6–8 of this volume) has both similarities and differences, compared with the four case-study countries. In England, development rights were nationalised but most land was left in private ownership. Unlike the other four countries, there were attempts to use national legislation to tax development value, but these failed because the tax kept development land off the market and public spending was inadequate to create public land banks to compensate for land withholding (and to secure development value). In contrast, in both Germany and the Netherlands short-term land banking has been an important means both of ensuring that land needed for development was available and of funding the infrastructure needed.

The use of planning obligations in England to fund infrastructure and affordable housing was initially the outcome of a series of local initiatives rather than of national policy development and based much more on negotiations than mandated tariffs or charges. Obligations grew in use and scale because the shortage of public funding to finance development infrastructure and new affordable homes led local planning authorities in England to use existing legislation to raise funding and land from developers. The use of obligations in England has many similarities to the emergence of impact fees and infrastructure charges in both Australia and the USA where local initiatives in the face of inadequate local government finance led to the use of fees and charges to finance infrastructure and in all countries has been most successful in buoyant property markets.

The successful use of planning obligations in England has however also depended on the subsequent national endorsement of local initiatives and on the inclusion of policies in adopted local development plans, thus helping to shape developers expectations and enabling them to pass costs back to landowners. At the same time, the recognition of the costs and delays of negotiations has led to more use of standardised tariffs and charges. Meantime, in the USA there has been a trend towards more negotiations and a move away from fixed charges, especially in the most buoyant property markets.

The English experience thus falls somewhat between, on the one hand, those in Germany and the Netherlands where there has generally been a greater 'top-down' cascade of relevant policies and of enabling statutes allowing municipalities to acquire development land and to secure development values and, on the other hand, those in Australia and the USA where there is much less policy and guidance emanating from federal and state governments and very little exercise of a public sector role in land banking. There is also substantially less social rented housing in Australia and the USA than in both Germany and the Netherlands. The two CME countries (Germany and the Netherlands) have historically exhibited more coordination between the various sectors involved in development, whilst in the three LME countries (Australia, England and the USA) there has been more reliance on the private market, both in land and in development, hence constraining the role of development value taxation and of land banking in securing infrastructure and new affordable homes, although in England this has involved a more 'plan-led' approach. That said, the evidence shows that the different systems in each country are increasingly exhibiting common elements with more reliance on developer contributions to infrastructure and affordable housing and with attempts to secure this through the planning system. This trend arises partly as a result of the growing role of the private sector in development and partly because of increasing fiscal austerity in all countries. It is also apparent that the use of infrastructure charges has become a means of systematically pricing the externalities of development (i.e. the infrastructure needed) into developers' costs.

Calavita and Mallach (2010) when reviewing planning policies to promote inclusionary housing saw many commonalities between countries which had prompted the exploration and instigation of policy, including the changing balance between public and private responsibilities for social welfare and its funding, the changing roles of central and local governments and global concerns to address social segregation in housing markets. But in discerning differences as well as similarities, de Kam *et al.* (2014) distinguished between countries' desires to secure more affordable homes and the possibilities of doing so. They thought that the desire for policy was greater in countries with dualist rental housing markets (e.g. through saving public spending). They also thought that the possibilities of doing so were greater in those where there are large private development surpluses (often greater in countries with significant planning constraints), the means of extracting this, and planning systems that can restrict development rights and require that specific types of housing (including affordable) are built. The distinction between planning systems with discretion and those without was also critical because this affects both the certainty available to landowners and developers and the ability of planning agencies to negotiate, both of which are fundamental to securing affordable homes through planning systems.

In reviewing our four case-study countries (and also having looked back at English policy and practice), in all countries where zoning plans determine land use (subject to any discretion to make changes), the certainty provided by zoning plans determines land value well in advance of any development taking place. Unless requirements for infrastructure and community needs are also explicitly made part of rezoning plans or the zoning of new development areas, this limits the possibility of securing significant development values to help fund infrastructure and affordable housing (hence, the need to offer density and other bonuses to secure affordable homes, including through IZ). In England, the greater discretion in the planning system (notwithstanding the existence, although far from universal, of adopted plans) creates more uncertainty about where development may take place and hence about development values until permission is granted. This enables local councils in England to use their ability to negotiate during their consideration of planning applications to collect significant development value to fund both infrastructure and affordable housing. It also enables these costs to be passed back to landowners, hence becoming a *de facto* tax on development values. However, whereas in both Germany and the Netherlands it has been possible to pursue public sector land banking as a means of delivering infrastructure and affordable housing at a cost to developers and landowners, such practice has had only limited success in England. In a recent review of the international experience of flexibility in planning systems, Gielen and Tasan-Kok (2010) argued that when adopted plans provide substantial certainty about what new development will be permitted, less development value is captured than in those systems where the plans provide less certainty about the outcomes of applications, unless these plans also provide certainty about the contributions to infrastructure that will be required. The next and final chapter reflects further on these differences and the lessons that may be learned.

References

Andrews, D., Sánchez, A. and Johansson, Å. (2011) *Housing Markets and Structural Policies in OECD Countries*, OECD Economics Department Working Paper No. 836. OECD Publishing, Paris.

Anthony, J. (2004) Do state growth management regulations reduce sprawl? *Urban Affairs Review* **39** (3), 376–397.

Anthony, J. (2006) State growth management and housing prices. *Social Science Quarterly*, **87** (1), 122–141.

Aurand, A. (2014) Florida's planning requirements and affordability for low income households. *Housing Studies*, **29** (5), 677–700.

Austin, P.M., Gurran, N. and Whitehead, C.M.E. (2014) Planning and affordable housing in Australia, New Zealand and England: common culture; different mechanisms. *Journal of Housing and the Built Environment*, **29** (3), 455–479.

Australian Government (2010) Australia's Future Tax System: A Review (Henry Review). Available: http://taxreview.treasury.gov.au/content/Content.aspx?doc=html/pubs_reports.htm

Baing, A. (2010) Containing urban sprawl? Comparing brownfield reuse policies in England and Germany. *International Planning Studies* **15** (1), 25–35.

Ball, M. (2012) *European Housing Review 2012*, RICS Research Report, Royal Institution of Chartered Surveyors, London.

Barlow, J., Bartlett, K., Hooper, A. and Whitehead, C.M.E. (2002) *Land for Housing: Current Practice and Future Options*, Joseph Rowntree Foundation, York.

Beckman, G., Breuer, B., Crome, B., Fuhrich, M., Gatzweiler, H.-P., Goeddecke-Stellman, J., Guttler, H., Metzmacher, M., Muller, A., Renner, M., Schmitz, S., Thul, B., Walther U.-J., Weigandt, C.-C. and Zarth, M. (2000) *Urban Development and Urban Policy in Germany*, Federal Office for Building and Regional Planning, Bonn.

Been, V. (2005) Impact fees and housing affordability: cityscape. *A Journal of Policy Development and Research* **8** (1), 139–185.

Berry, M. (2006a). *Housing Affordability and the Economy: A Review of Macroeconomic Impacts and Policy Issues*, Australian Housing and Urban Research Institute, National Research Venture 3, and Housing Affordability for Lower Income Australians, Research Paper 4. AHURI, Melbourne.

Berry, M. (2006b) *Housing Affordability and the Economy: A Review of Labour Market Impacts and Policy Issues*, Australian Housing and Urban Research Institute, National Research Venture 3 and Housing Affordability for Lower Income Australians, Research Paper 5. AHURI, Melbourne.

Boelhouwer, P.J., Boumeester, H. and van der Heijden, H.M.H. (2006) Stagnation in Dutch housing production and suggestions for a way forward. *Journal of Housing and the Built Environment* **21** (3), 299–314.

Booth, P.A. (1993) The cultural dimension in comparative research: Making sense of development control in France. *European Planning Studies* **1** (2), 217–229.

Bourassa, S.C., Neutze, M. and Strong, A.L. (1997) Assessing betterment under a public premium leasehold system: principles and practice in Canberra. *Journal of Property Research* **14**, 49–68.

Brueckner, J.K. (2000) Urban sprawl: diagnosis and remedies. *International Regional Science Review* **23** (2), 160–170.

Brunick, N.J. (2004) The inclusionary housing debate: the effectiveness of mandatory programs over voluntary programs. *Zoning Practice* **9**, 2–7.

Buitelaar, E. (2010) Crack in the myth: challenges to land policy in the Netherlands. *Tijdscrhift voor Economische en Sociale Geografie* **101** (3), 349–356.

Buitelaar, E. (2012) Transparency of land markets: not only a matter of market outcomes. Experiences from the Netherlands. *Études Foncières* n. 159.

Bunker, R. and Searle, G. (2009) Theory and practice in metropolitan strategy: situating recent Australian planning. *Urban Policy and Research* **27** (2), 101–116.

Busck, A.G., Hidding, M.C., Kristensen, S.B.P., Persson, C. and Præstholm, S. (2009) Planning approaches for urban areas: case studies from Denmark, Sweden and the Netherlands. *Danish Journal of Geography* **109** (1), 15–32.

Calavita, N. and Mallach, A. (2010) National differences and commonalities: comparative analysis and future prospects. In: N. Calavita and A. Mallach (eds), *Inclusionary Housing in International Perspective: Affordable Housing, Social Inclusion and Land Value Recapture.* Lincoln Institute of Land Policy, Cambridge, MA.

Crook, A.D.H. (1986) Affordable housing and planning gain, linkage fees and the rational nexus: using the land use planning system in England and the USA to deliver housing subsidies. *International Planning Studies* **1** (1), 49–71.

Cullingworth, J.B. (1993) *The Political Culture of Planning: American Land Use Planning in Comparative Perspective*, Routledge, London.

Davies, H.W.E., Edwards, D., Hooper, A.J. and Punter, J. (1989) *Planning Control in Western Europe*, HMSO, London.

Davison, G., Gurran, N., van den Nouwelant, R., Pinnegar, S., Randolph, B. and Bramley, G. (2012) *Affordable Housing, Urban Renewal and Planning: Emerging Practice in Queensland, South Australia and New South Wales*, Australian Housing and Urban Research Institute Final Report No 195. AHURI, Melbourne.

De Jong, J. and Spaans, M. (2009) Trade-offs at a regional level in spatial planning: two case studies as a source of inspiration. *Land Use Policy* **26** (2), 368–379.

De Kam, G. (2014) Inclusionary zoning in the Netherlands: breaking the institutional path? *Journal of Housing and the Built Environment* **29** (3), 439–454.

De Kam, G., Needham, B. and Buitelar, E. (2014) The embeddedness of inclusionary housing in planning and housing systems: insights from an international comparison. *Journal of Housings and the Built Environment* **29** (3), 389–402.

Dieleman, F. M., Dijst, M. J. and Spit, T. (1999) Planning the compact city: the Randstad Holland experience. *European Planning Studies* **7** (5), 605–621.

Downs, A. (1973) *Opening Up the Suburbs: An Urban Strategy for America*, Yale University Press, New Haven.

Esping-Anderson, G. (1990) *The Three Worlds of Welfare Capitalism*, Polity Press, Cambridge.

Faludi, A. and van der Valk, A.J. (1994) *Rule and Order: Dutch Planning Doctrine in the Twentieth Century*, Kluwer Academic, Dordrecht.

Forster, C. (2006) The challenge of change: Australian cities and urban planning in the new millennium. *Geographical Research* **44** (2), 173–182.

Gale, D.E. (1992) Eight state-sponsored growth management programs: a comparative analysis. *Journal of the American Planning Association* **58** (4), 425–439.

Geurs, K. T. and van Wee, B. (2006) Ex-post evaluation of thirty years of compact urban development in the Netherlands. *Urban Studies* **43** (1), 139–160.

Gielen, D.M. and Tasan-Kok, T. (2010) Flexibility in planning and the consequences for public-value capturing in UK, Spain and the Netherlands. *European Planning Studies* **18** (7), 1097–1131.

Goodman, R., Buxton, M., Chhetri, P., Schuerer, J., Taylor, E. and Wood, G. (2010) *Planning Reform, Land Release and the Supply of Housing*, Australian Housing and Urban Research

Institute Positioning Paper No. 126. AHURI, Melbourne.

Government of Western Australia (2013) *Planning Provisions for Affordable Housing: Discussion Paper*, Government of Western Australia Department of Planning, Perth.

Groetelaers, D.A. and Korthals Altes, W.K. (2004) Policy instruments in the changing context of Dutch land development. In: Deakin, M., Dixon-Gough, R. and Mansberger, R. (eds), *Methodologies, Models and Instruments for Rural and Urban Land Management*. Ashgate Publishing Company, Aldershot.

Gurran, N. (2011) *Australian Urban Land Uses: Principles, Systems and Practice*, Sydney University Press, Sydney.

Gurran, N., Milligan, V., Baker, D. and Bugg, L.B. (2007) *International Practice in Planning for Affordable Housing: Lessons for Australia*, Australian Housing and Urban Research Institute Positioning Paper No 99. AHURI, Melbourne.

Gurran, N., Milligan, V., Baker D., Bugg, L.B. and Christensen, S. (2008a) *New Directions in Planning for Affordable Housing: Australian and International Evidence and Implication*, Australian Housing and Urban Research Institute Final Report No 120. AHURI, Melbourne.

Gurran, N. and Phibbs P. (2013) Housing supply and urban planning reform: the recent Australian experience. *International Journal of Housing Policy* **13** (4), 381–407.

Gurran, N., Ruming, K. and Randolph, B. (2009) *Counting the Costs: Planning Requirements, Infrastructure Costs and Residential Development in Australia*, Australian Housing and Urban Research Institute Final Report Series 140. AHURI, Melbourne.

Gurran, N., Ruming, K., Randolph, B. and Quintal, D. (2008b) *Planning, Government Charges, and the Costs of Land and Housing*, Australian Housing and Urban Research Institute Positioning Paper No 99. AHURI, Melbourne.

Gurran, N. and Whitehead, C.M.E. (2011) Planning and affordable housing in Australia and the United Kingdom: a comparative perspective. *Housing Studies* **26** (7–8), 1193–1214.

Haffner, M. E. (2014) The Netherlands. In: A.D.H. Crook and P.A. Kemp (eds), *Private Rental Housing: Comparative Perspectives*, Edward Elgar, Cheltenham.

Hagman, D.G. and Misczynski, D.J. (eds) (1978) *Windfalls for Wipeouts: Land Value Recapture and Compensation*, American Society of Planning Officials, Chicago.

Hall, P. (2014) *Good Cites: Better Lives*, Routledge, London.

Hall, P.A. and Soskice, D. (2001) *Varieties of Capitalism, The Institutional Foundations of Comparative Advantage*, Oxford University Press, Oxford.

Halleux, J.-M., Marcinczak, S. and van der Krabben, E. (2012) The adaptive efficiency of land use planning measured by the control of urban sprawl. The cases of the Netherlands, Belgium and Poland. *Land Use Policy* **29** (4), 887–898.

Hamnett, S. and Freestone, R. (eds) (2000) *The Australian Metropolis: A Planning History*, Allen and Unwin, Sydney.

Hananel, R. (2013) Can centralisation, decentralisation and welfare go together? The case of Massachusetts Affordable Housing Policy (Ch. 40B). *Urban Studies* **51** (12), 2487–2502.

Hayashi, K. (2000) Land Readjustment in International Perspectives: Applicability and Constraints of Technology Transfer in Urban Restructure. Available: www.earoph.info/pdf/2000papers/31.pdf

Heidenheimer, A.J., Heclo, H. and Adams, C.T. (1990) *Comparative Public Policy*, St Martin's Press, New York.

Henneberry, J. and Goodchild, B. (1993) *Impact Fees for Planning*, Department of the Environment, London.

Henneberry, J. and Goodchild, B. (1996) Impact fees and the financial structure of development. *Journal of Property Finance* **7** (2), 7–27.

Herbert, C.E., Belsky, E.S. and Apgar, W.C. (2012) Critical Housing Finance Challenges for Policymakers: Defining a Research Agenda, Working Paper 12-2, Joint Center for Housing Studies of Harvard University, Cambridge, MA.

Ihlanfeldt, K.R. and Shaughnessy, T.M. (2004) An empirical investigation of the effects of impact fees on housing and land markets. *Regional Science and Urban Economics* **34**, 639–661.

Kemeny, J. (1995) *From Public Housing to the Social Market: Rental Policy Strategy in Comparative Perspective*, Routledge, London.

Kemp, P. and Kofner, S. (2014) Germany. In: A.D.H. Crook and P.A. Kemp (eds), *Private Rental Housing: Comparative Perspectives*. Edward Elgar, Cheltenham.

Konursay, S.Y. (2004) *Land Readjustment Process in Urban Design: Project Management Approach*, İzmir Institute of Technology, İzmir.

Korthals Altes, W. K. (2007) The impact of abolishing social-housing grants on the compact-city policy of Dutch municipalities. *Environment and Planning A* **39** (6), 1497–1512.

Korthals Altes, W.K. and Groetelaers, D.A. (2007) Planning and stagnation of housing production: a changing context for Dutch provinces. In: F.D. Moccia, L. Lieto, L. de Leo and G.C.E Coppola (eds), *Planning for the Risk Society: Dealing with Uncertainty, Challenging the Future*, Association of European Schools of Planning, Naples.

Korthals Altes, W. K. and Tambach, M. (2008) Municipal strategies for introducing housing on industrial estates as part of compact-city policies in the Netherlands. *Cities* **25** (4), 218–229.

Kunzmann, K.R. (2001) State planning: a German success story? *International Planning Studies* **6** (2), 153–166.

Lefcoe, G. (1993) *Planning Controls and Affordable Housing: The US Experience*, Joseph Rowntree Foundation, York.

Loughlin, M. (2013) *The British Constitution*, Oxford University Press, Oxford.

Mallach, A. and Calavita, N. (2010) United States: from radical innovation to mainstream housing policy. In: N. Calavita and A. Mallach (eds), *Inclusionary Housing in International Perspective: Affordable Housing, Social Inclusion and Land Value Recapture*, Lincoln Institute of Land Policy, Cambridge, MA.

Masser, F.I. (1986) Some methodological considerations. In: F.I. Masser and R. Williams (eds) *Learning from Other Countries*, Geo Books, Norwich.

Milligan, V. (2003) How different? Comparing housing policies and housing affordability consequences for low income households in Australia and the Netherlands, *Netherlands Geographical Studies*, Vol. 318, Royal Dutch Geographical Society, Utrecht.

Milligan, V., Gurran, N., Lawson, J., Phibbs, P. and Phillips, R. (2009) *Innovation in Affordable Housing in Australia: Bringing Policy and Practice for Not-for-Profit Housing Organisations Together*, Australian Housing and Urban Research Institute Final Report Series 134. AHURI, Melbourne.

Milligan, V., Phibbs, P., Gurran, N. and Fagan, K. (2007) *Evaluation of Affordable Housing Initiatives in Australia*, Australian Housing and Urban Research Institute National Research Venture 3 and Housing Affordability for Lower Income Australians. AHURI, Melbourne.

Monk S., Whitehead, C.M.E., Burgess, G. and Tang, C. (2013) *International Review of Land Supply and Planning Systems*, Joseph Rowntree Foundation, York.

National Housing Supply Council (2011) State of Supply Report 2011. Australian Government. Available: www.nhsc.org.au/content/state_of_supply/2011_ssr_rpt/docs/nhsc-keyfindings-2011.pdf

Needham, B. (1997) Land policy in the Netherlands. *Tijdschrift voor Economische en Sociale Geografie* **88**, 291–296.

Needham, B. (2007) *Dutch Land Use Planning: Planning and Managing Land Use in the Netherlands, The Principles and Practice*, Sdu Uitgevers, Den Haag.

Needham, B. (2012) Institutions for housing supply. In: S. J. Smith (ed), *International Encyclopaedia of Housing and Home* Vol. **4**. 99–108.

Nelson, A.C. (ed) (1988) *Development Impact Fees: Policy Rationale, Practice, Theory and Issues*, American Planning Association, Chicago.

Nelson, A.C., Bowles, L.K., Juergensmeyer, J.C. and Nicholas, J.C. (2008) *A Guide to Impact Fees and Housing Affordability*, Island Press, Washington.

Newman, P. and Thornley, A. (1996) *Urban Planning in Europe: International Competition, National Systems and Planning Projects*, London, Routledge.

Norton, R.K. and Bieri, D.S. (2014) Planning, law and property rights: a US-European cross national contemplation. *International Planning Studies* **19** (3–4), 379–397.

Oxley, M., Brown, T., Nadin, V., Qu, L. and Tummers, L. (2009) *Review of European Planning Systems*, National Housing and Planning Advice Unit, Fareham.

Pendall, R., Martin, J. and Fulton, W. (2002) *Holding the Line: Urban Containment in the United States*, Brookings Institution, Washington.

Pendall, R., Puentes, R. and Martin, J. (2006) *From Traditional to Reformed: A Review of the Land Use Regulations in the Nation's 50 Largest Metropolitan Areas*, Brookings Institution, Washington.

Pollakowski, H. and Wachter, S. (1990) The effects of constraints on housing prices. *LandEconomics* **66** (3), 315–324.

Preuß, T. and Ferber, U. (2008) *Circular Land Use Management in Cities and Urban Regions – A Policy Mix Utilizing Existing and Newly Conceived Instruments to Implement an Innovative Strategic and Policy Approach*, Deutsches Institut für Urbanistik, Berlin.

Priemus, H. (1998) Contradictions between Dutch housing policy and spatial planning.*Tijdscrhiftvoor Economische en Sociale Geografie* **89** (1), 31–43.

Purdue, M., Healey, P. and Ennis, F. (1992) Planning gain and the grant of planning permission: is the US test of the 'rational nexus' the appropriate solution? *Journal of Environment and Planning Law* 1012–1024.

Pütz, M., Kruse, S., Casanova, E. and Butterling, M. (2011) CLISP – Climate Change Adaptation by Spatial Planning in the Alpine Space: Climate Change Fitness of Spatial Planning. WP 5 Synthesis Report. ETC Alpine Space Project CLISP, Zurich.

Schwartz, A. (2006) *Housing Policy in the United States: An Introduction*, Routledge, Abingdon.

Schmidt, S. and Buehler, R. (2007) The planning process in the US and Germany: a comparative analysis. *International Planning Studies* **12** (1), 55–75.

Sieverts, T. (2008) New tasks for spatial planning in Germany. In: B. Scholl (ed.) *Spatial Planning and Development in Switzerland: Observations and Suggestions from the International Group of Experts*, Swiss Federal Office for Spatial Development, Zurich.

Stoker, G. (1991) *The Politics of Local Government*, Macmillan, London.

Van den Berg, M. (2008) Perspective on strategic planning in the Netherlands. In: B. Scholl (ed.), *Spatial Planning and Development in Switzerland: Observations and Suggestions from the International Group of Experts*, Swiss Federal Office for Spatial Development, Zurich.

Van der Heijden, H. and Boelhouwer, P. (1996) The private rental sector in Western Europe:developments since the Second World War and prospects for the future. *Housing Studies* **11** (1), 13–33.

Van der Krabben, E. and Needham, B. (2008) Land readjustment for value capturing: a new planning tool for urban development. *Town Planning Review* **79** (6), 651–672.

van der Schaar, J. (1987) *Growth and the Flowering of the Dutch Housing Policy*. Delft University Press, Delft.

Van der Valk, A. (2002) The Dutch planning experience. *Landscape and Urban Planning* **58** (2–4), 201–210.

Vermeulen, W. and Rouwendal, J. (2007) Housing supply and land use regulation in the Netherlands. *Tinbergen Institute Discussion Paper Ti 2007-058/3.*

Wakeford, R. (1990) *American Development Control*, HMSO, London.

Western Australia Planning Commission (2014) *Planning Provisions to Encourage Affordable Housing*, The Commission, Perth.

White, M. and Allmendinger, P. (2003) Land use planning and the housing market: a comparative review of the UK and the USA. *Urban Studies* **40** (5–6), 953–972.

Wolsink, M. (2003) Reshaping the Dutch planning system: a learning process. *Environment and Planning A* **35**, 705–723.

Yates, J. (2011) *Housing in Australia in the 2000s: On the Agenda Too Late?* Paper presented at the Reserve Bank of Australia's decadal review of the Australian economy, Sydney.

Yates, J., Wulff, M. and Reynolds, M. (2004) *Changes in the Supply of and Need for Low Rent Dwellings in the Private Rental Market*, Australian Housing and Urban Research Institute Final Report. AHURI, Melbourne.

Yinger, J. (2008) The incidence of impact fees and special assessments. *National Tax Journal* **51** (1), 23–41.

Zonneveld, W. (2007) A sea of houses: preserving open space in an urbanised country. *Journal of Environmental Planning and Management* **50** (5), 657–675.

10

Summary and Conclusions

Tony Crook[1], John Henneberry[1], and Christine Whitehead[2]

[1]*Department of Urban Studies & Planning, The University of Sheffield, UK*

[2]*LSE London, the London School of Economics, UK*

Introduction

Governments across the world are interested in the issue of land value capture as a major source of revenue as the economy grows, urban infrastructure is provided and in market economies land prices rise. Some countries do this by nationalising land; others by annual local taxation of regularly updated property values; and still others by specific betterment levies (e.g. see the reviews and reflections in Ingram and Hong, 2012 and de Kam *et al.*, 2014; as well as the overviews of four countries in Chapter 9, this volume). As we have seen, increases in land values are significantly the result of many public decisions as well as economic growth more generally. But in the absence of general land and wealth taxes, measuring and capturing these increases for the public good is difficult. The UK and especially England has taken a particular approach to capturing land values that arise when land changes to a higher valued use. This approach has been seen as relatively successful, especially in achieving funding for local infrastructure and both land and finance for affordable housing, which is why it is often seen as an example to be admired if not copied. This is why it is important for its origins and its place within a specific planning practice to be understood.

This chapter summarises the evidence in the book about the experience in England under three headings: the policy, the economic and the financial

Planning Gain: Providing Infrastructure and Affordable Housing, First Edition.
Edited by Tony Crook, John Henneberry and Christine Whitehead.
© 2016 John Wiley & Sons, Inc. Published 2016 by John Wiley & Sons, Inc.

aspects of planning obligations. It assesses why planning obligations have proved a means of achieving some, although by no means complete, success. Finally, we look at implications for future policy and practice in England and lessons for other countries.

Policies for capturing development value

The starting point is that in the UK, the act of granting permission allocates development rights to the relevant parcel of land and crystallises the value of the land in its new use. This provides the basis for measuring and capturing all or some of the increased value that arises from granting that permission as well as the fact that that permission unlocks opportunities better to utilise infrastructure and to respond to demand. A core element of the book has been to clarify how policies of value capture have developed in the UK, concentrating particularly on England where the policy has been most productive.

National approaches

Policy on capturing development value when permission is granted has changed quite fundamentally in England in the post-war years. Initially central government attempted formally to tax development value through national legislation and nationally set taxes. Chapter 3 showed that these national taxes proved unsuccessful in capturing much development value, partly because their complexity led to many delays in assessing and collecting tax liabilities and partly because developers responded by restructuring their land holdings and their development proposals to minimise liabilities. The taxes also kept development land off the market because landowners anticipated that a change of government would lead to the repeal of the legislation and because so little benefit remained with the private decision maker.

The key lessons are that national taxation of development value is difficult to achieve unless developers are left with some incentives, achieved by fixing the tax at considerably less than 100%, and unless adequate provision is made to combat any residual land withholding through a publicly led land banking approach. But an additional lesson is that public sector land banking can be beneficial in its own right. Land identified for development in local planning authorities' (LPAs) plans may not come forward at the times and in the places required for a variety of reasons, including the fragmented nature of land ownership, the variety of motives for owning land (financial and otherwise) and the oligopolistic nature of developers who are also land traders. Land banking can overcome these and other barriers. And where the agency that undertakes land banking can acquire allocated land at or near its existing use value and sell on serviced land at the value in its proposed use, the agency is in a position to capture all or most of the expected betterment directly.

Locally based approaches

In contrast to the failure of national tax measures to capture development value, local negotiations in the form of planning obligations in England have proved far more successful. As we saw in Chapter 4, they evolved from a long-standing aspect of planning legislation designed to enable LPAs to regulate site-specific aspects of development in ways that could not be achieved through conditions on planning permission. Instead, LPAs negotiated desired outcomes with applicants for planning permission and then agreed them in enforceable contracts running alongside planning permissions. Beginning in the 1970s, a number of LPAs began to negotiate obligations to secure contributions to the off-site infrastructure for new development which would otherwise have had to be refused permission because of a lack of public sector resources. Subsequently, these and other innovative LPAs started to negotiate obligations for the provision of other community needs for which public funds were scarce, especially affordable housing.

As Chapters 6 and 8 showed, these negotiations have succeeded in delivering substantial contributions in both cash and in kind. There are two main reasons for this success. First, the approach arose from 'bottom-up' innovation by LPAs based on well-entrenched powers. Central government's role was not to prevent their use, but to shape practice and ensure it was embedded as policy in adopted development plans. Moreover, the courts played an important role in legitimating the use of obligations as being lawful.

The second reason for the success of planning obligations is that they were (and are) attractive to developers as well as to LPAs given the economic and fiscal climate each faces. At times of market buoyancy, developers are anxious to secure planning permissions so that profitable schemes can be got underway before market conditions change. If an impediment to getting permission is the lack of adequate infrastructure it makes sense for developers to help supply or fund it, provided this does not undermine scheme viability. And the ability to negotiate contributions enabled developers to safeguard viability – in contrast to spatially invariant national taxes or levies. From the perspective of LPAs, who faced increasing funding restrictions from the 1980s onwards, planning obligations offered an alternative route to securing key infrastructure including schools and affordable housing. In effect, they were collecting a hypothecated charge. Further, to the extent that central government was committed to the provision of affordable homes but was also facing periods of fiscal austerity, it made good sense to endorse the emerging use of obligations that required developers to provide land and some funding for affordable homes.

Thus the success of obligations arose from the ways LPAs successfully adapted national legislation to help them negotiate contributions. In contrast to invariant national taxes, these can be conceptualised as locally negotiated levies that take account of local market and site circumstances and which are hypothecated to meet locally determined needs.

As Chapters 6 and 8 also confirmed, a particular achievement has been to secure significant contributions of new affordable homes, with up to two-thirds of all new affordable homes being provided through planning obligations in 2007–2008 in the areas where need was greatest, helping also to build mixed communities. This success is due to two factors. First, the endorsement by central government in 1991 of using planning obligations to secure affordable homes, making this a material consideration and consistently stating this in all subsequent planning policy. Second, the buoyancy of the development market up to 2007–2008 allowed developers to defray the costs of provision from the development values created by the market. This buoyancy also allowed LPAs to press for more provision, which developers were then willing to accept, specifically as shared ownership dwellings. This made sense financially to developers and to housing associations even though LPAs would have preferred more rented homes. It also stretched government grant further, not the least given the zero grant policy on S106 sites.

Since 2007–2008 the amounts secured have fallen in the overall slow-down of private markets. As S106 site viability issues also came to the fore, governments enabled developers to re-negotiate the affordable housing element of their agreed obligations. The intention was to unlock 'stalled sites' whose viability was allegedly affected by the agreements for affordable homes struck in an earlier more buoyant period. But many other factors were also holding up development including the difficulty of getting development finance and selling market houses. Moreover, selling affordable homes to housing associations made positive contributions to private developers' cash flow during the market 'downturn'. As the market has picked up, there has been a slight increase in new affordable homes being agreed, suggesting that the output of affordable homes from planning obligations will also increase.

Adopting planning obligations is a matter of choice by each LPA. We saw in Chapter 7 how significant the variations are in the extent to which obligations and their value are secured even amongst LPAs with similar socio-economic circumstances. Rather it is the variation in local policy and practices which lie behind these variations, including how good LPAs are at conducting negotiations. These differences cause problems for developers related to the length of time taken to negotiate and agree obligations and the uncertainties about what might be charged. Although there is evidence of more good practice being adopted, especially as policy became 'bedded down', the variations have persisted, despite much effort from a wide range of bodies, including central government, to identify and disseminate good practice. As central government has pointed out, if all LPAs operated as well as the best performing ones much more benefit could be secured overall. In particular, obligations could cover many more sites. In addition, the 'free rider' issue, where the lead developer on a larger site might end up paying for most of the required infrastructure, had to be tackled.

As a consequence, there were a series of consultations about the introduction of tariffs. Government consultations built on LPA initiatives with respect to standard charging especially related to open space, education and transport. Although affordable homes contributions were almost always the outcome of site-specific negotiations a few authorities, notably Milton Keynes, also introduced a standard charge for all contributions across all sites within a new development area, effectively introducing average cost charges for all developers.

As we showed in Chapter 4, the tariff proposal and its variant (the optional planning charge) were not, in the end, introduced. There were objections to the principle with many arguing that it was in effect a tax on development value. This criticism arose because, although tariffs would have been based on infrastructure costs and not explicitly on percentages of development value, it was suggested that development value also had to be taken into account. Others argued that tariffs would be inconsistent with a rational nexus approach, and that it would also risk undermining the mixed communities agenda. There were also practical objections. Local circumstances differ, so a standard tariff might be set too high and development would be lost or it might be set too low and revenue would be lost at both site and authority levels.

The later debates around Planning Gain Supplement (PGS) and Community Infrastructure Levy (CIL) looked for other ways of providing more certain and speedier outcomes but they also re-opened the question of whether a levy should explicitly tax some of the development value created by planning permission. This is what PGS would have achieved. However, it would need to have been set low enough to avoid deterring development and most of the proceeds would have gone to the relevant LPA. The levy would also have been charged on all but the smallest of sites thus ensuring that all development made a contribution. However, PGS attracted widespread criticism especially on the practicalities of assessing and distributing it.

In some ways, these discussions exposed the ambiguity that has characterised the use of obligations. Were they 'simply' a charge to cover the infrastructure costs generated by new developments and to make a reasonable contribution to community needs or were they a *de facto* tax on development value hypothecated for local investment? Charging developers for off-site infrastructure is now accepted as entirely legitimate but doubts have continued to be raised about its use for new affordable homes. As we have suggested in Chapters 2 and 4, planning obligations are in fact a hybrid, combining elements of a charge based on the costs of remedying developers' negative externalities with elements of an equitable tax on development value, partly hypothecated to meet the need for affordable housing.

As we saw in Chapter 4, CIL is not an explicit levy on development value and was introduced after PGS was abandoned. Whether it is charged at all is a matter for discretionary judgement by LPAs (although those not set-ting up a charge lose some of their powers to pool obligations' contributions from several sites). It exacts a locally determined charge placed on all but the most minor development to fund 'gaps' in overall infrastructure fund-ing after taking account of total estimated spending on infrastructure in a LPA area and what is expected from other sources. It also abandons the rational nexus as a justification for charging for infrastructure and intro-duces average cost principles. Planning obligations have been retained for addressing site-specific matters and affordable housing but what is available to pay for these is what is left over after the CIL payment has been made. An important potential advantage of CIL compared with planning obliga-tions is that infrastructure contributions come from most developments, potentially increasing what can be 'extracted'. CIL is, however, still in its infancy and its introduction in the small number of LPAs that have adopted it has been more challenging and complex than initially anticipated, creat-ing some uncertainty for developers. Moreover, as we saw in Chapter 4, the most recent changes to the rules for both CIL and planning obligations have exempted more developments, including small ones, from being charged CIL and from contributing to affordable housing through planning obligations. At the same time other changes to CIL require LPAs to pass up to a quarter of their CIL proceeds over to parish councils and neighbourhood groups to spend on new local facilities. These changes are cumulatively reducing what can be collected and requiring some of them to be used for matters other than infrastructure.

International experience

Our review of international experience showed that policy and practice in England is different from that in other countries. Planning obligations in England operate in the context of a system where development rights have been nationalised and are allocated to development sites only when plan-ning permission is granted. Relevant policy has to be taken into account by LPAs when deciding whether or not to grant permission but so too must other material considerations. However, this framework is also affected by the very considerable discretion inherent in the English planning system. This creates uncertainty and transactions and other costs for developers and LPAs alike.

In contrast, zoning arrangements of planning systems in many other jurisdictions foster more certainty, including about the price of land for developments that conform to the zoning scheme. As we saw in Chapter 9, countries with zoning arrangements still require developers to contribute to infrastructure and to affordable housing. This means that unless the zoning schemes or other legally enforceable prescriptions identify what will be required of developers by way of contributions, it is much more difficult to secure these, including negotiating them with developers. Thus planning authorities in asking for contributions (and this is especially the case for affordable housing in many, but not all, states in Australia and the USA) have to make concessions to developers to enable them to defray these costs through, for example, allowing higher densities to enhance income or reducing their costs in some ways.

In some other jurisdictions, public sector led land banking has offered significant opportunities both to assemble development land in accordance with published development plans and to secure infrastructure and affordable housing. In both Germany and the Netherlands, this enabled acquisition of land at or near its existing use value, followed by investment in infrastructure and then sales to developers at the market value for its future use. In principle, this ensures that developers pay the market value of the infrastructure in the price they pay for the land net of any costs that they are expected to incur, for example, in the form of affordable homes.

Overview

The success of planning obligations in England owes much to its origins in local discretion. Its success in the late 1990s and early 2000s also owes much to the buoyant development market in which substantial contributions were agreed – and subsequently delivered. It also owes much to the growing acceptance of the policy by developers and to the way good practice has become more prevalent, albeit not universally adopted. But the downturn in the market has raised major questions about the viability of both obligations and the related CIL, whilst the legitimate demands to improve transparency and certainty and reduce transaction costs has created more standardisation in the approaches used, thus limiting LPA opportunities for innovation. What has been achieved in the last two decades is the now widespread acceptance of the use of obligations to fund infrastructure and also to tax development value by means other than national levies. Whether a different approach is now needed is something we turn to in the last section of this chapter.

The economics of planning obligations

The rationale for planning obligations comes mainly from the specifics of the UK planning system. However, it is strongly supported by economic theory and by economic conditions in the land market, particularly in England. Economic theory makes it clear that there will be surplus values over and above those necessary to ensure the efficient use of land where land is heterogeneous as is inherently the case in urbanised economies. Land in England is relatively heavily used as compared to countries with lower densities of population and activities. Economic growth and the provision of scarce infrastructure provide the environment for large increases in land prices when the regulatory system allows change in use. This provides a base line for the creation of large-scale planning gains and therefore the incentive to capture at least some of this gain for public purposes. Moreover, it is highly desirable because, if operated effectively, it does not interfere with the efficient allocation of land to its highest and best use but reallocates resources from landowners to local communities and the national good and provides finance for necessary investment in infrastructure.

The sources and measurement of value

The economics of planning obligations depends fundamentally on the economics of planning gain. Only if land prices rise as a consequence of planning permission (or rezoning) to an extent greater than the cost of undertaking the development is there any surplus which can be designated as planning gain and potentially captured for the public good through planning obligations.

As is made clear in Chapter 2, the extent of planning gain depends on two main factors:

1. The value of the land in the projected use, which in principle should be the highest valued use, although this will depend on the options allowed by the regulatory framework. The value is determined by the discounted value of the stream of expected net revenues less the costs of the development necessary to achieve these revenues.
2. The value of the land in its best alternative use, which in a planning constrained system is likely to be its current use but could be a potential alternative use which would be allowable under the planning rules.

At its simplest there are two options – existing use and the new highest valued use. The difference between the two is the maximum amount available for capture when permission is given to transfer to this new use. Efficiency is achieved by allowing the change in use. However, the landowner is the main beneficiary – so there is an equity case for land value capture.

The complexities in assessing development gain

In practice the system is not simple – there are a large number of complications that impact on whether the system can generate the best land use outcomes and whether particular capture policies, including planning obligations in cash or kind, work effectively. Most importantly, the system is one where the gains arise from moving from one regulated position to another based on the market only to the extent that the developer puts forward the most appropriate option but determined by a whole range of different objectives.

First how is this difference to be measured? The actual price is hidden in option values and other complexities while the existing use value is a composite of land buildings and other elements, for example, contamination. So this difference is either obtained by administrative valuation or is based on evidence of preparedness to sell – or, if the ownership remains the same, to develop. Importantly, pre-planning permission land values themselves often reflect the hope and expectation of obtaining that permission so price increases arising at the time of permission may significantly underestimate the actual uplift.

Second, prices may not reflect underlying values so capturing apparent gains may adversely affect decisions. For instance, the value with planning permission may be distorted upwards by differential hope values between competitors, notably with respect to their expectation that they can modify a planning ruling. If the resultant market price is too high then trying to capture the full amount would actually make the development non-viable. Unexpected cost increases would have a similar effect as can uncertainties in the amount to be captured. The evidence presented in Chapters 5, 7 and 8 on how planning obligations are limited by uncertainties about future value, how they are renegotiated in the light of economic change and how difficult the negotiations are exemplifies these difficulties.

Another difficult issue is that there may be more than one possible change of use. For instance, the land might be used for commercial purposes where the value is less than for residential but higher than in existing use. These additional possibilities need to be taken into account when estimating the amount available for capture. Only if the value of the land in its best use remains above that of the next best alternative once the capture costs are taken into account will the transfer to highest value, and by assumption most efficient, use actually occur. A related uncertainty may be around future options making developers wait to see whether there are better possibilities. This is one reason why the amounts of planning gain available in the areas of high demand may not be as large as most people expect – especially where mixed use is an option. This problem is made more apparent when the system 'taxes' particular uses more highly than others. Thus, for instance, the fact that affordable housing is only a material consideration for residential development should in principle result in more land going to other uses in urban areas. This is also one of the distortions that CIL aimed to remove because it is applied to all development (Chapter 4). Greenfield sites where the only option is residential are a far simpler environment for determining planning obligations in a way that does not distort outcomes (and as Chapter 6 showed the majority of obligations have been on larger residential sites).

Further, political risks can be a really important factor affecting whether development goes ahead, especially if there is little agreement about value capture policies. More generally continuous legislative and regulatory changes in how the system operates make it impossible to estimate future costs and, therefore, to transfer all the cost to the landowner. One of the reasons why the S106 system has worked so well can be attributed to policy and practice stability. As a result, all stakeholders have to a greater or lesser degree signed up to the system. However, CIL and new financial viability rules have to some extent undermined that sense of certainty. This is a prerequisite for achieving the economic benefits with respect to both efficiency and equity as well as the necessary funding to support future infrastructure investment (Chapters 4 and 5).

A more positive issue relates to whether the takings from capture are to be used to improve infrastructure and the economic environment. If additional infrastructure is enabled, this may further increase land values and therefore potential capture. But if the possibilities are not realised, it may also add to the uncertainties of whether the infrastructure investment will be made.

These are among the reasons why it has proved so difficult to determine the amount that can be captured. Chapter 3, in particular, reflects on the immediate post-war national taxation approach. This initially attempted to capture high proportions of the estimated increase and was a signal failure putting off development and raising very little revenue. But the chapter also shows that just cutting the tax rate on increased value may not be enough to generate the development required because of uncertainties with respect to future changes in the rate of tax and the range of possibilities for development.

Planning obligations avoid some of these problems notably because the amount taken is a result of negotiation and the developer may argue that high requirements make the development non-viable. In other words, no one tries to assess the difference in value as a result of planning permission; they simply agree a set of obligations in cash and kind that fall within that total. If the requirements are reasonably clear the developer should also be able to negotiate down the price of the land to reflect the costs of meeting these obligations. So the landowner pays and the land price is reduced by the amount of the obligation.

There are, however, two related factors which have impacted on the capacity to realise the economic benefits of planning obligations. First, on the positive side, the long period of economic and housing market growth that we saw for a decade from the mid-1990s was beneficial in enabling all parties to come to grips with the policy. All parties could gain after planning permission was granted from the continued uplift in prices. It did mean that LPAs did not maximise the long-term value of their planning obligations (although there were increasing opportunities to build in some adjustments) but equally it oiled the negotiation process (see Chapters 6 and 7).

On the other hand there were issues about relative information and power – developers had the capacity to learn from one another how best to make the most of the opportunities while local planners found it difficult to spread good practice and to come to grips with the complexities of negotiations. There was, therefore, often not a flat playing field for the negotiations although national planning guidance provided some support as Chapter 7 showed.

Planning constraints

A particularly important issue with respect to planning gain is that its existence may generate perverse incentives for planners. The gain can, and does, arise not just from increased efficiency but also from the effects of constraint which cannot be justified by the need to offset external costs of development. These constraints benefit existing owners at the expense of new entrants to the housing market and may also help inefficient productive activities to stay in business. But they also add to land values and therefore planning gain.

A planning authority can increase the amount of potential gain by imposing stronger planning controls – so that much of the increased value comes from the fact that inadequate quantities of land with permission are being provided so the permitted use of land is inefficient. The greater the constraint, the greater the potential for the authority to benefit from increased planning gain. Moreover, this financial incentive is strongest where the benefits from the capture go to the local area. In this context the possibility of imposing higher levels of obligation may modify both the general policy but more importantly the specifics of individual planning permissions.

Approaches to capturing gains

Economists are inclined to argue that the different instruments by which capture can be achieved are in principle the same. In practice there are very considerable differences in potential outcomes from different approaches. This is reflected both in the English experience over time (Chapters 4 and 7) and in international examples (Chapter 9).

We have noted earlier that the UK system of taxing increased land values has been built around the granting of planning permission. However, the gains that occur are the result not only of the specific change of use but also the better use of infrastructure and other external factors which affect the costs and revenues related to the new use and to more general economic growth.

By concentrating on planning permission, the capture regime only addresses the benefits relating to changed development and it does nothing to capture the betterment from infrastructure and other public investments where no change of use is involved; nor to tax increasing land values arising from increased economic activity. As such, the emphasis on planning gain rather than a more general property tax with regularly updated valuations can really only be seen as second best. Yet the UK has increasingly moved away from property taxation, which effectively keeps pace with increasing values, making it difficult to capture most increased land values that arise from public investment and thus denying ourselves a reasonable source of funding for infrastructure provision. It is perhaps in this context that the potential benefits of hypothecation which comes with the use of planning obligations should be viewed.

The empirical chapters in this book have pointed to the potential benefits of public land banking of undeveloped land with on-sale into development once infrastructure has been put in place. This allows direct capture of the benefits except to the extent that the purchase price reflects hope values. The English experience of development corporations and new towns has shown it to be an effective way of enabling very large, very long-term investments. As such it is a particularly useful instrument addressing the type of urban investment which is complementary to the planning obligations approach. Its potential mainly in the form of joint ventures for both regeneration and new greenfield sites provides an important option where complexity and uncertainty rules out the effective use of planning obligations.

Finally, the evidence of the last two decades suggests that the economics of planning obligations makes sense and can generate at least some of the potential benefits. It has worked more easily in growing markets, which was the experience from the early 1990s to the financial crisis in 2008. We now have to learn how to make it work effectively in less buoyant markets – both across regions and over time. But it should always be remembered that even in downturns economics would expect there to be significant planning gain available – because regulations have been relaxed to enable new opportunities to be realised. This is not the time to give up on a well-established approach to allocating the benefits of economic growth and development.

The financial aspects of planning obligations

As we have seen, the means by which public infrastructure, facilities and services are planned, developed, managed, delivered and funded have been subject to fundamental re-structuring over the last 40 years in the UK. In particular, in the mixed funding economy for infrastructure, general taxation plays a lesser role while the contribution of indirect and hypothecated taxes and user charges has grown significantly. In the property sector, building producers and consumers now meet a larger proportion of the costs of development-related infrastructure than was previously the case.

Consequently, in order for the necessary infrastructure, facilities and services to be provided, the development that gives rise to their need has to be sufficiently valuable and profitable to meet an increasing proportion of their costs. These circumstances give rise to a fundamental tension between the need to secure adequate funding for the required infrastructure, on the one hand, and the need to maintain development viability in order for the desired projects to proceed, on the other. As we saw in Chapter 5, this dilemma was first explicitly acknowledged by the UK government in 2001. At that time, government suggested that any shortfall between the cost of necessary infrastructure and the ability of a development project to pay for it without threatening its viability might be met by public sector infrastructure providers and/or local and central taxation. Since then – and following the Global Financial Crisis (GFC) – recourse to the latter sources of finance has become more difficult. This has further increased the onus on developments to fund infrastructure and, consequently, has exacerbated the tension between development contributions and development viability.

It is no surprise that development viability has become a significant aspect of UK planning policy and practice. Development and wider property market appraisals inform negotiations between developers and planners over specific sites, land allocations in development plan documents, affordable housing policy, planning obligations policy and the introduction of the CIL and its charging regimes.

Ultimately, viability will turn on whether – after development costs, including any costs arising from planning policy (mainly related to planning obligations, CIL and affordable housing requirements) – the residual value of the land (its market value in these circumstances) has increased sufficiently above the value in its previous use to persuade the owner to sell the site. However, the threshold at which this occurs is an empirical matter. Threshold land value (TLV) will vary widely with differences in the character of the landowner, her/his expectations, the state of the land and property market, the nature of the subject site and so on. In addition, the land value is a geared residual. This means that variations and changes in its determining variables – development costs and values – exaggerate the variability and volatility of residual land values (i.e. of development viability). Development costs and values differ over time, across space and between different types of site. Each has an influence on the operation and impact of planning obligations. That influence is underpinned by one main factor. It is that, all other things being equal, the greater is the demand for development, the greater will be the value and viability of development and, therefore, its ability to meet infrastructure costs.

Since 2000, the increase in house prices and in the associated value of housing land has produced more scope for extracting development value. In the period before the GFC, there was a rapid growth in the number of planning obligations, the number of affordable housing units included in them and the extent of other developer contributions (see Chapter 6). The opposite occurred after the GFC. The effect of market booms and slumps on the state's ability to extract development value was clear. There is also a strong regional pattern to the implementation and the outcomes of planning obligation policy. More planning obligations are secured in the most profitable markets in London and the South of England than elsewhere. In addition, those obligations contain greater developer contributions. For example, the proportion of affordable units included in housing developments is higher in the South than in the North of England and CIL rates are higher in the South (see Chapter 8). Planning obligations are more likely to make development unviable in the North and Midlands of England than in the South (see Chapter 5). Allowing for variations in value, different types of site will give rise to varying development costs. These affect viability and, therefore, the scope for planning gain. The greatest developer contributions are obtained in planning obligations related to large, greenfield sites because, *inter alia*, these are likely to have the lowest development costs (see Chapter 6). The opposite is the case with high-density brownfield sites where developers are often faced with considerable additional costs relating to land decontamination, the demolition of structures and so on.

The variability and volatility of the development value captured through planning obligations raises issues about its suitability as a basis for policy – in relation to the provision of infrastructure, the supply of affordable housing and the distribution of development more generally. Planning obligations are a market-based economic instrument. They produce more 'planning gain' in areas of high development values. This is good, in the sense that contributions to the funding of development infrastructure will follow effective demand and support development in strong markets. However, it is also regressive and may not address need. This is because development values vary more than costs (both spatially and temporally, see Chapter 5). For example, the difference between the highest and lowest regional house prices in England (between Inner London and the North) is 124% while the difference between those regions' tender prices for construction is 31%. Planning obligations are based on the *cost* of providing necessary infrastructure, not on the *value* of the subject scheme (apart from the need for that value to be sufficient to meet the cost of the obligation). Thus planning obligations for a given type of contribution impose a greater proportionate burden on low- than on high-value locations. And this is within the context where there is in any case less scope for obtaining 'planning gain' in the former than the latter because fewer schemes are able to meet the costs of obligations while remaining viable. For similar reasons, 'planning gain' is also regressive temporally. Planning obligations impose higher proportionate costs on development during market downturns than in periods of market growth.

Redistribution of the burdens and benefits of planning obligations and CIL is determined by their organisational and administrative structures. A national system would allow inter-regional redistribution and transfers between time periods. A regional system would allow intra-regional redistribution and temporal transfers conditioned by each region's market context. However, planning obligations are site-specific while CIL only allows sub-regional pooling of income. While this particularity is one of their strengths, it severely limits the potential for redistribution.

One of the major benefits of government spending is that it acts as an economic stabiliser. Through spatial and temporal redistribution it mitigates the effects of regional inequalities and economic cycles. The gain in market sensitivity achieved by the use of planning gain to contribute to the funding of development infrastructure is at the cost of increasing the variation and volatility of development, thus diminishing the effect of the 'government stabiliser' in the property sector. The substantial increases and then decreases in the supply of both market and affordable housing that have occurred since 2000, before and after the GFC, have not provided a consistent base for housing policy. There have also been some not entirely expected financial and market-driven outcomes of the increasing importance of 'planning gain' and development viability. Perhaps the most significant is the impact of planning obligations on the geography of the supply of affordable housing. This has been altered by the pattern of development viability. The balance has moved from provision on publicly owned, brownfield sites in the more deprived areas of all regions to sites, including greenfield sites in

high-value areas in the South of England (see Chapter 6). This is not necessarily an undesirable outcome, given the emphasis on mixed, sustainable
communities in government policy.

The ease with which the costs of planning obligations or impact fees may
be passed on to landowners varies with the time when such obligations
are identified. If this occurs at the time of re-zoning (e.g. in Australia and
the USA, see Chapter 9) and prior to land sale, then such costs should be
incorporated into land values in the form of lower actual or expected prices
achieved by landowners. If it occurs later, then the landowner is unlikely
to bear the cost: the developer and/or the future occupier must do so (see
Chapter 9).

The developer, even when purchasing a site via an option, must ultimately
commit to the development and accept the risk that changes in market
circumstances during the development period will result in a financial outcome different from that expected. Development periods in the UK vary from
around 12 months for small projects to several years or a decade or more for
larger schemes – ample time for changes to occur (see Chapter 5). This may
place developers and planners in a difficult position in a downturn such as
that experienced after the GFC. The developer cannot pass on the cost of any
consequent effects to the landowner because he or she is the landowner. If
the land was bought in competition with other developers there may be no
excess profit to absorb the reduction in value and profitability. The only flexibility that remains is that relating to the cost of planning obligations and
CIL. Hence the recent pressure to reduce the scale or scope of obligations.
The alternative is that the development will stall.

The opposite circumstances pertain in an upturn, when there are opportunities to increase the amount of development value captured as prices rise.
This has sometimes been addressed by phased obligations and, in practice,
by changed permissions and therefore changed obligations. However, there
has been rather less debate about this side of the equation – in part because
it has oiled the wheels until the mid-2000s.

Further detailed changes to practice have been developed to try to maintain viability in the recent market downturn. In the cases of some large
residential schemes, the scope of the planning obligation – for example, the
proportion of units that must be affordable – has been made dependent on
external factors such as sales values to ensure viability. Developers may also
try to manage the design of schemes to minimise the impact of affordable
housing requirements on project value and viability. Planners prefer affordable units to be indistinguishable physically from market units and to be
distributed throughout a scheme. Developers prefer to locate all the affordable units in a separate and least desirable part of a site, for example, fronting
a busy road and acting as a screen for the market housing (see Chapter 8).

Many of these problems are avoided in countries where the local state takes a more active role in managing the planning and development of housing, such as Germany or the Netherlands (see Chapter 9). The use of land readjustment or pooling, either by agreement or compulsorily, gives municipalities the land required for infrastructure and a share of the land value uplift to cover the costs of that infrastructure. This allows municipalities much more influence over development in their areas. It avoids the capture of land value uplift by landowners and removes their ability to withhold land from the market. TLV is not relevant. This is at a cost to the local state. It must commit capital upfront to construct infrastructure and take the risk that sufficient land development value will be created to cover the cost of that capital. Arguably, the state is in a better position to do this than private developers. Compulsory powers applicable to a potential extensive area of land subject to planned development provide a greater chance of marriage value being created and realised. And the cost of capital to a municipality is normally lower than it is to a developer. What is lost is a degree of market sensitivity.

This refers to one of the central lessons of the English experience of capturing land value uplift for public benefit: that of the need for and effectiveness of local flexibility, sensitivity and particularity. The financial structure of individual developments – their value, cost and viability – varies very greatly. Site and project characteristics and market contexts differ within and between urban areas and regions – often over relatively small distances and short periods of time. Planning obligations are the result of individual, project-based negotiations that allow for development heterogeneity. Consequently, they have the flexibility to address specific circumstances and changes in those circumstances. In this way, the potential for obligations to undermine development viability is avoided in a way that is not possible in more rigid zoning systems. It is these clear, practical advantages that have garnered for obligations the broad support of both developers and planners in England.

Conclusions

Finally, we now turn to the question of whether our findings suggest ways forward for policy in England and whether there are implications from the English experience for other jurisdictions. The core finding from our evaluation of 'planning gain' is that planning obligations have proved a practical way of capturing some development value. They are not part of national taxation arrangements but are now well embedded in local policies and practices. Contributions are negotiated, thus taking account of viability, and are hypothecated for local need, thus benefiting local communities. They are significantly less controversial than in the past and the clarity and stability in policy and practice provides a measure of certainty for developers. Although CIL is still in its infancy, it has the key advantage of securing contributions from more development sites than S106 has done in the past and could prove equally acceptable over time as practice develops and it becomes part of the 'normal', working alongside S106.

Looking forward: England

With respect to England, the short- and medium-term futures are likely to involve periods of continuing fiscal austerity. There will be a need to provide the infrastructure required to support local economic growth and to increase the output of new homes across a range of tenures, including affordable ones. In combination, these circumstances are likely to place an imperative on securing private funding to help with the provision of both infrastructure and affordable housing and, consequently, the capture of development value is likely to be of continuing importance.

Among the lessons from our findings are that negotiated planning obligations work better in England than national taxes but work best under specific circumstances. These include the existence of a buoyant development market, clarity about required contributions in development plans, good negotiating skills in LPAs and a policy and process that ensures sites remain viable so that they will be brought forward for development. Policy stability is a major key to success because it shapes owners' and developers' expectations. However, there will be spatial variations to how well this works arising from differences in financial fundamentals and in the priorities, practices and competence of LPAs.

Looking ahead to where development is needed, the locations of new housing and related development will include new settlements, urban extensions, brownfield sites in existing settlements, especially London, and small-scale windfall sites within many settlements, both towns and villages. The greatest development pressure will be in southern England where new settlements and urban extensions will be important methods of securing the land required both for housing and for new industrial and commercial development.

What role can capturing development value play in ensuring that this development land is serviced and can accommodate new commercial development and new affordable housing? The evidence presented here suggests that a twin-pronged approach is required.

First, there is a clear case for using public land banking to secure the development land needed for new settlements and major urban extensions. Although public sector land banking has had mixed success in England, it worked well for New Towns (and in Comprehensive Development Areas within existing towns) – and has been central to effective policy in both Germany and the Netherlands. In England, land was bought at prices that took no direct account of the development value created by the designation of a New Town. This allowed the New Town Development Corporations to capture much of the development value through subsequent sales of development land and also to keep rents affordable on the houses built on the land that they acquired. Setting up joint venture companies involving local authorities, public and private landowners, and developers is the most obvious way forward. Each local authority area planning new settlements or major extensions would have its own joint venture company. Often this will mean several local authorities working together. New legislation is not required. The members of the joint venture would take shares based on the proportions of the total value of the land attributable to their individual ownerships. The venture would pay for land at its existing use value (which would inevitably include some hope value from any anticipated development), service it and then either develop the land itself or sell it on to others. In this way the development value generated by their efforts, other investments and the granting of planning permission would be captured by the venture with the returns shared by all members and their populations.

A clear separation of interests and powers between the joint venture and the LPA would be needed so that that the latter is not compromised in the exercise of its planning policies by its interests as the local authority shareholder. Mindful of the problems that beset previous attempts at land banking (such as the Community Land Scheme) the joint venture would inevitably require long-term funding. Under current arrangements it should be feasible to arrange this via private bond issues and investment by local authority pension funds as well as through borrowing, secured on both future income streams and shareholders' existing assets. Tax Increment Financing and revolving infrastructure funds, including those for Housing Zones (see Chapter 4, this volume) are other possible sources of funding. In this context, the operation of planning obligations and CIL on the land owned by the joint venture company would be suspended and the company would agree a programme of funding with its LPA members to help finance the infrastructure and the land for commercial development and for affordable housing required within the relevant new settlement or urban extension.

Second, outside the areas of new settlements and major urban extensions the current system for capturing development value still seems to be the most appropriate way forward, not least because this would avoid a period of policy instability at a time when there is an urgent need for new development. Planning obligations are a well-understood and accepted mechanism. To make the system work better in terms of both increasing contributions and speeding up decisions requires much better coverage of local plans with guidance on CIL charges and contributions policies linked to these. Some changes are desirable, such as limiting the exemptions to CIL and planning obligations. Inevitably, the economic cycle will affect what can be secured by planning agreements and LPAs should build in clauses which enable payments to be deferred during downturns until markets pick up again as well as to ensure that unexpected future gains can be captured, at least in part. Because, in general, less planning gain can be secured outside the South East there may be a case in equity for focusing grant resources for carefully evaluated strategic investment in these areas to compensate for the lower planning obligations element that can be secured.

Looking forward: international experience

What can be learned from the experience in England that might be of relevance for other countries? There are two key points to stress. The first is that the approach would be difficult to transfer because of the high degree of discretion built into the English planning system and because development rights remain nationalised. This makes it possible to lever substantial contributions from development value because the land value in a new development does not crystallise finally until a planning consent is granted and the associated planning obligations have been agreed, making it possible to pass the costs back to landowners. However, the system bears little direct relationship to the systems found in most other countries.

The second is that in many other countries that have zoning systems which determine how land may be developed and used, the opportunities to capture development value through the planning system may be limited. It can, however, work well where zoning plans and associated ordinances or regulations spell out clearly what is required of developers by way of contributions to infrastructure and affordable housing so that land prices reflect these costs. It can also work where planning concessions (such as density bonuses) create the extra value that enables developers to fund these requirements. This has been the case with impact and linkage fees in parts of the USA where practice is well developed. The same is true in Australia although policies are less developed. The international evidence also suggests that various forms of public land banking offer good prospects for capturing development value and can work well in planning systems that allow such acquisitions by public bodies and can fund them.

These two points suggest that there are no easy direct transfers. Even so there are some more fundamental issues exemplified in the English experience that are relevant for all countries looking to capture some of the benefit of development for the public good. First, it almost certainly has to be only *some* of that development gain that is captured. Incentives for efficient

investment must remain in place and be adequate to ensure that development which will help economic growth occurs in all types of area. Second,
the role of local authorities is central to ensuring a nuanced policy that takes
account of the circumstances surrounding individual sites. Third, a strong
link between revenue raising and ensuring that those funds are invested in
community infrastructure helps make the imposition of taxes more acceptable to developers and to local decision makers. Finally, policies need many
years to bed down – policy stability is a prerequisite for both good planning
and effective value capture.

One last point: both in England and elsewhere methods for capturing
development value have evolved in response to the specifics of each legal
and regulatory system and particularly in response to areas of limited public
funding. We doubt if the latter will change. But even it did, there remains
a strong case for requiring developers to contribute to the infrastructure
costs they impose on local communities as well as a more general equity
case for 'taxing' gains that arise from public decisions. In sum, capturing
development value by the variety of instruments we have described and
analysed makes sense in terms of both efficiency and equity. The system
in England has worked reasonably well in its specific context and will
undoubtedly continue to evolve as the economic and political environment
changes. We need to ensure that it continues to help provide infrastructure
and affordable housing from the enhancement of value that follows from
planning permission.

References

De Kam, G., Needham, B.,and Buitelar, E. (2014) The embeddedness of inclusionary housing in
  planning and housing systems: insights from an international comparison. *Journal of Housings and the Built Environment* **29** (3), 389–402.
Ingram, G.K. and Hong, Y.-H. (2012) *Value Capture and Land Policies*, Lincoln Institute of Land
  Policy, Cambridge, MA.

Index

Figures and tables are indicated by *italic page numbers*, footnotes by suffix 'n'

Planning Gain: Providing Infrastructure and Affordable Housing, First Edition.
Edited by Tony Crook, John Henneberry and Christine Whitehead.
© 2016 John Wiley & Sons, Inc. Published 2016 by John Wiley & Sons, Inc.